Economics

Thirty-fourth Edition

EDITOR

Don Cole

Drew University

Don Cole, Professor of Economics at Drew University, received his Ph.D. from Ohio State University. He has served as a consultant to a variety of public and private organizations and is co-founder of the Drew University Semester on the European Union in Brussels, Belgium. An innovator in the use of computer-assisted instruction in economics, Dr. Cole is the author of articles on various subjects, including economic policy, monetary theory, and economic education. He is also the editor of over thirty McGraw-Hill Contemporary Learning Series publications, including *The Encyclopedic Dictionary of Economics* and two other *Annual Editions* anthologies, *Microeconomics* and *Macroeconomics*.

2460 Kerper Blvd., Dubuque, IA 52001

Visit us on the Internet
http://www.mhcls.com

Credits

1. **Introduction**
   Unit photo—Don Farall/Getty Images
2. **Microeconomics**
   Unit photo—Creatas Images/Jupiter Images
3. **The Economics of Work and Income**
   Unit photo—PhotoDisc/Getty Images
4. **Macroeconomics**
   Unit photo—Ryan McVay/Getty Images
5. **The Changing Global Economy**
   Unit photo—C. Borland/PhotoLink/Getty Images

Copyright

Cataloging in Publication Data
Main entry under title: Annual Editions: Economics. 34th Edition.
1. Economics—Periodicals. I. Cole, Don, *comp*. II. Title: Economics.
ISBN-13: 978–0–07–352843–4   ISBN-10: 0–07–352843–9   658'.05   ISSN 1092–776X

Thirty-fourth Edition

Cover image © Royalty Free/CORBIS and PhotoDisc Collection/Getty Images
Printed in the United States of America   1234567890QPDQPD987654   Printed on Recycled Paper

Preface

In publishing ANNUAL EDITIONS we recognize the enormous role played by the magazines, newspapers, and journals of the public press in providing current, first-rate educational information in a broad spectrum of interest areas. Many of these articles are appropriate for students, researchers, and professionals seeking accurate, current material to help bridge the gap between principles and theories and the real world. These articles, however, become more useful for study when those of lasting value are carefully collected, organized, and reproduced in a low-cost format, which provides easy and permanent access when the material is needed. That is the role played by ANNUAL EDITIONS.

This thirty-fourth edition of *Annual Editions: Economics* has been largely revised since previous editions and continues the tradition of providing the most up-to-date readings on contemporary economic issues. In view of the recent explosion of interest in the subject of economics, it is important that students are given opportunities to observe how economic science can help them to understand events in the real world. This anthology is designed to meet such a need.

The volume is divided into five major units. Unit 1 introduces several general concepts involving economic analysis. At the heart of economics is the notion of "opportunity cost," the idea that in choosing one economic alternative, we must forgo other choices. What, for example, is the opportunity cost of a human life? How might a knowledge of economic reasoning assist us in making daily decisions?

Unit 2 presents articles that treat economic issues from a microeconomic perspective. Microeconomics studies the way in which market values are established through the interaction of consumers (households) and producers (firms). For instance, what role does the Internet play in the choices consumers make and the size of business enterprises? How do mergers affect the business climate? How does government regulation of industry affect market competition?

Issues involving work and income distribution are examined in unit 3. You will find that this is an area of intense controversy, particularly as it relates to government programs that attempt to alter the distribution of income and wealth. Questions raised include: What are the causes of growing income disparities in America? What role do unions play in the U.S. economy? What should be done about the U.S. health care crisis? How does corporate outsourcing affect job opportunities?

Broader economic issues are the focus of the next two units, which involve macroeconomics (unit 4) and the global economy (unit 5). The economy-wide perspective of macroeconomics leads us to consider ways of gauging an economy's health, vis-à-vis levels of employment, the degree of price stability, and the rate of economic growth over time. Readings selected for this unit raise questions of great consequence to the United States. For example, what is the current outlook for the U.S. economy? How do tax cuts and changes in the money supply affect the economy? Should we be concerned about the growing federal deficit?

Finally, unit 5 examines recent changes in the world economy. In the last decade we have witnessed a series of unforeseen events: the globalization of the world economy; the aftershocks of the 9/11 terrorist attacks; the rush by many former communist states to embrace the market system; and the impoverishment of many developing countries burdened by staggering international obligations. How did such developments come about, and what do they portend as the global economy enters a new century?

In this edition of *Annual Editions: Economics 34/e* there are *World Wide Web* sites that can be used to further explore the topics.

Whether you are currently pursuing studies in economics or are just a casual reader eager to learn more about some of the major economic issues of the day, you will find *Annual Editions: Economics 34/e* to be one of the most useful and up-to-date anthologies available. Your input can be valuable for the next edition. Please offer your opinions by filling out and returning to us the postage-paid *article rating form* on the last page of this book.

Don Cole
Editor

Contents

Preface   iv

Topic Guide   xii

Internet References   xiv

UNIT 1
Introduction

Unit Overview   xvi

1. **How Much for a Life? Try $3 Million to $5 Million,** Peter Passell, *The New York Times,* January 29, 1995
Much economic reasoning is based on the **opportunity cost** principle, the idea that any decision involving scarce resources must involve costs in terms of **foregone alternatives** elsewhere. Peter Passell applies this principle to an age-old question: What is the value of a human life?   3

2. **More, Bigger, Faster,** Amar Bhidé, *Across the Board,* September/October 2004
Economist Joseph Schumpeter once insisted that the process of **creative destruction**—through which old industries are continuously being replaced by new ones—was an essential fact about capitalism. In this article Amar Bhidé demonstrates how capitalism will thrive as long as we can **create new wants**—and **new products** to meet them.   6

3. **Counter-Terrorism: The Private Cost of More Security,** Peter Navarro, *Los Angeles Times,* September 8, 2002
Peter Navarro argues that the greater danger that **terrorism** poses to America may be purely economic. The danger lies in a severe **productivity shock** that could lead to a gross domestic product trillions of dollars below what it otherwise would be.   10

UNIT 2
Microeconomics

Unit Overview   12

4. **Smoke Signals,** *The New York Times,* New Jersey Sunday Edition, January 10, 1999
One of the more useful concepts in microeconomics is **demand elasticity**, which measures the responsiveness of consumer demand to changes in prices. Several years ago the New Jersey legislature doubled the state cigarette tax in an effort to reduce smoking. This article examines the impact that this has had on cigarette sales in both New Jersey and nearby states.   14

The concepts in bold italics are developed in the article. For further expansion, please refer to the Topic Guide and the Index.

5. **Jousting for Television's Holy Grail,** Neil Munro, *National Journal,* June 8, 2002

The **cable TV industry** is beating its two rivals in the battle to control **the fate of digital TV.** Neil Munro describes efforts of the cable TV industry, consumer electronics firms, TV broadcasters, and TV and movie producers to control the course of digital TV.   **16**

6. **Bruised in Bentonville,** Andy Serwer, *Fortune,* April 18, 2005

In business, there is big and there is **Wal-Mart,** the world's largest company. Studies show that the market power that Wal-Mart exerts depresses wages, dominates suppliers, polices the culture, and disrupts communities. Andy Serwer asks: **Can the world's biggest company adjust?**   **18**

7. **Airlines,** Giovanni Bisignani, *Foreign Policy,* January/February 2006

Bankruptcies, terrorism, and high oil prices have rocked the airline industry while customers complain about bad services and long lines. **Are the airlines doomed?** Giovanni Bisignani believes air travel will survive, but not without major changes in the way the industry is organized.   **21**

8. **Modernizing U.S. Antitrust Law: The Role of Technology and Innovation,** Thomas A. Hemphill, *Business Economics,* April 2005

Maintaining and promoting a competitive economic environment and protecting consumer welfare are the central objectives of **antitrust policy.** Thomas A. Hemphill examines ways in which **technological and market innovation** contribute to antitrust goals.   **24**

9. **The Real Price of Gas,** *International Center for Technology Assessment,* November 1998

The retail price Americans pay for gasoline appears to be low in comparison with prices prevailing in most other nations. Adding in the many **external costs** that consumers pay indirectly by way of increased taxes, insurance costs, and retail prices in other sectors, this study estimates the **real per gallon price to be in excess of $15.**   **29**

10. **The Truth About Oil,** Jon Birger, *Fortune,* October 3, 2005

Pain at the pump has quite a few Americans upset. Chances are, though, they are angry about the wrong things. Jon Birger examines **five myths many people believe about today's oil pinch**—and what the real story is.   **31**

11. **The Eco-Economic Revolution: Getting the Market in Sync with Nature,** Lester R. Brown, *The Futurist,* March/April 2002

Because the economy is largely dependent on the consumption of fossil fuels that result in carbon emission byproducts, concerns exist about the economy's ability to reduce these emissions without sacrificing output and employment. **Lester Brown shows how responsible policies might benefit both the environment and economy.**   **34**

12. **Congested Parks—A Pricing Dilemma,** Dan M. Bechter, *Monthly Review,* (Federal Reserve Bank of Kansas City), June 1971

Overcrowding at public parks creates a **classic microeconomic dilemma:** people face insufficient parking space, which must be allocated through adjusting park fees.   **42**

The concepts in bold italics are developed in the article. For further expansion, please refer to the Topic Guide and the Index.

UNIT 3
The Economics of Work and Income

Unit Overview   **48**

13. **Building a More-Humane Economy,** Robert D. Atkinson, *The Futurist,* May/June 2006
    According to Robert D. Atkinson, *achieving a more-humane economy* requires neither an anticorporate crusade nor a simple-living, back-to-nature movement. Rather, it entails promoting *more humane high-performance work organizations* and robust and sustained *productivity growth* that will enable people to work less without earning less.   **50**

14. **The Rich Get (Much) Richer,** Steven Rattner, *BusinessWeek,* August 8, 2005
    The notorious *income gap keeps widening.* Over the past three decades the share of income going to the top 1% of U.S. households has nearly doubled, while the share garnered by the top 0.01%—the 13,000 or so households with an average income of $10.8 million in 2002—has multiplied nearly four times. Steven Rattner suggests ways to reduce this imbalance.   **55**

15. **Outsourcing Jobs: The Myths and Realities,** Martin N. Baily and Diana Farrell, *Current,* February 2005
    The authors maintain that *the debate over outsourcing* is misplaced because the issue is not globalization, but instead the way nations allocate the benefits of economic integration. They suggest various ways in which public policy can help disadvantaged workers.   **56**

16. **Laid Off and Left Out,** Bob Herbert, *The New York Times,* May 25, 2006
    In this review of Louis Uchitelle's new book, "The Disposable American: Layoffs and Their Consequences," Bob Herbert says that there is no doubt that the better-educated and better-trained worker gets better jobs. But the reality is that there are not enough good jobs available to meet the demand for them.   **60**

17. **Multiple Minimums,** John M. Broder, *The New York Times Upfront,* February 20, 2006
    While the U.S. Congress has not raised the *federal minimum wage* for almost 10 years, some states have taken action. John M. Broder analyzes the possible impacts of these minimum wage increases and how they might affect the equality of life among unprofessional workers.   **61**

18. **The Gender Gyp,** Thomas N. Bethell, *AARP Bulletin,* July–August 2005
    Because they tend to have greater longevity than men, women are more likely to need income for decades after their earning years draw to a close. Thomas N. Bethell shows why *Social Security is all the more important for women.* While for men it is primarily a worker retirement program, for women it becomes a family insurance plan.   **63**

19. **The Health Care Crisis and What to Do About It,** Paul Krugman and Robin Wells, *The New York Review of Books,* March 23, 2006
    Americans spend some 16 percent of gross domestic product on health care, while other advanced nations spend far less. Yet, in general, judging by life span and infant mortality, most developed nations are healthier than the United States. Paul Krugman and Robin Wells present some ideas about *how to improve the quality of care for every dollar spent.*   **67**

The concepts in bold italics are developed in the article. For further expansion, please refer to the Topic Guide and the Index.

UNIT 4
Macroeconomics

Unit Overview   76

20. **Countdown to a Meltdown,** James Fallows, *The Atlantic Monthly,*
    July/August 2005
    James Fallows *imagines what the U.S. economy might look like in 2016.* He
    uses the scenario he creates to pinpoint challenges with which the country must
    deal with now.   79

21. **Seizing Intangibles for the G.D.P.,** Louis Uchitelle, *The New York
    Times,* April 9, 2006
    Louis Uchitelle asserts that when it comes to measuring how much the American
    economy produces and who gets what share of the pie, the federal government's
    most celebrated statistic—*the gross domestic product*—leaves something to be
    desired.   90

22. **The Elephant in the Room,** Aidan Rankin, *The Ecologist,* December/
    January 2005
    According to Aidan Rankin, the *pursuit of economic growth* makes global and
    regional inequalities more obvious and extreme. And yet policy makers and po-
    litical campaigners remain in thrall to the idea that the *"trickle down effect"* might
    one day take place, and that an *invisible hand* might somehow fashion order
    out of economic chaos.   91

23. **Social Spending and Economic Growth, Interview with Peter
    Lindert,** *Challenge,* July/August 2004
    Prevailing opinion holds that big government and high taxes reduce economic
    growth. But Peter Lindert in his book "Growing Public: Social Spending and Eco-
    nomic Growth Since the Eighteenth Century" disagrees. He shows how states
    that spend a lot on social programs grow no more slowly than those that spend
    little.   93

24. **Why Are Taxes So Complicated and What Can We Do About It?,**
    William G. Gale, *The Brookings Review,* Winter 1999
    Since virtually everyone agrees that taxes should be easy to understand, admin-
    ister, and enforce, *why are taxes so complicated*? The author suggests that
    people also agree that taxes should be fair, should be conducive to economic
    prosperity, should raise sufficient revenue to finance government spending, and
    should respect the privacy of individuals.   97

25. **The Tax Reform Revolution,** Murray Weidenbaum, *USA Today,*
    January 2005
    Murray Weidenbaum maintains that the *four approaches to tax reform*—flat,
    USA, national sales, and valued-added—are all variations on the same theme.
    All would shift the base of federal taxation *from income to consumption* while
    simplifying the process of complying with tax law.   100

26. **Tax Reform R.I.P.,** Robert J. Samuelson, *The Washington Post,*
    May 12, 2004
    The *appeal of tax breaks* is that they give the appearance of reducing the gov-
    ernment's size, even as government interference in the economy increases. A tax
    system (such as that of the United States) that has a huge number of such breaks
    cannot be simple, will contain many contradictions, and is ultimately "unfair." 104

The concepts in bold italics are developed in the article. For further expansion, please refer to the Topic Guide and the Index.

27. **Link Between Taxation, Unemployment Is Absent,** Jonathan Weisman, *The Washington Post,* March 15, 2004
Following federal tax increases in 1993, the U.S. unemployment rate dropped steadily for seven years. When taxes where cut in 2001, the jobless rate rose and in 2003 (when taxes were cut again) unemployment increased again. Jonathan Weisman contends that the *relationship between taxes and unemployment* is far more complicated than many people (including politicians) understand.

105

28. **What Should Central Banks Do?,** Frederic S. Mishkin, *Review (Federal Reserve Bank of St. Louis),* November/December 2000
In the last 20 years, there has been substantial rethinking about *how central banks should do their job.* Frederic Mishkin discusses seven basic principles that can serve as useful guides for central banks to achieve their objectives.

106

29. **How Does Monetary Policy Affect the U.S. Economy?,** *FRBSF Economic Letter,* January 30, 2004
This article discusses how *Federal Reserve policy actions* affect real interest rates, which in turn affect aggregate demand and ultimately output, employment, and inflation.

116

30. **It's His Economy Now—And Yours,** Justin Fox, *Fortune,* November 28, 2005
As *Ben Bernanke replaces Alan Greenspan* as chairman of the Federal Reserve System, a number of large issues face America—stagnant pay, a pension crisis, and a troubled health care system, among them. Justin Fox argues that the trouble is that these are matters that Bernanke won't be able to do anything about.

119

31. **Banking Consolidation,** *FRBSF Economic Letter,* June 18, 2004
As *megamergers* continue to shape the structure of the *U.S. banking industry*, this article looks at the economic drivers behind them and highlights some important policy implications.

122

32. **Bank ATMs and ATM Surcharges,** *FRBSF Economic Letter,* December 16, 2005
The *automated teller machine (ATM)* has become a part of everyday life and processes in excess of 30 million transactions per day. This article examines various reasons for the recent proliferation of ATMs, and the *pricing schemes* that accompany them.

125

33. **Toward a Cashless Society,** David R. Warwick, *The Futurist,* July/August 2004
Until recently, it appeared that America was headed toward the use of a *completely electronic payments system.* David Warwick argues that the *benefits that might result from ending the use of cash* could include major reductions in taxes, vastly improved public services, and the total eradication of many of the most serious and violent crimes.

128

The concepts in bold italics are developed in the article. For further expansion, please refer to the Topic Guide and the Index.

UNIT 5
The Changing Global Economy

Unit Overview   **132**

34. **Update on the State of the Future,** Jerome C. Glenn and Theodore J. Gordon, *The Futurist,* January/February 2006
The authors assert that global prospects for improving the overall health, wealth, and sustainability of humanity are increasing, but slowly. In the years ahead, **globalization** will present humanity with **both challenges and opportunities** as increased connectivity highlights the strengths and shortcomings as a global community.   **135**

35. **As Job Exports Rise, Some Economists Rethink the Mathematics of Free Trade,** Jeff Madrick, *The New York Times,* March 18, 2004
The standard tenets of **free trade** strongly support the case for outsourcing. Most economists believe that the benefit of lower prices gained from free trade far exceed the cost of lost jobs or lower wages. Recent studies take issue with this view.   **139**

36. **Is the Current Account Deficit Sustainable?,** *The NBER Digest,* December 2004
Some economists and politicians are concerned about America's **current account deficit**, which has risen to a level near 6 percent of GDP. A study by the National Bureau of Economic Research argues that the risks of a high and rising deficit may be more serious than just a few years ago.   **141**

37. **The High-Tech Threat from China,** Jeffrey E. Garten, *Business-Week,* January 31, 2005
The news is full of headlines about **China**—its rising trade surplus, ballooning currency reserves, relentless search for oil, and tensions with the United States over textiles and intellectual property rights. Jeffery E. Garten cautions that one development has been seriously underreported—the possibility that China may become a **technological superstate.**   **143**

38. **Building Blocks,** Christian Caryl, *Newsweek International,* December 12, 2005
The Association of Southeast Asian Nations (ASEAN) is considering broadening its membership to include China, Japan, and South Korea. Christian Caryl considers what further integration of this part of the global economy might mean for world trade.   **144**

39. **Where the Money Went,** James S. Henry, *Across the Board,* March/April 2004
How did **developing countries** end up owing $2.5 trillion? James S. Henry argues that Western institutions haven't exactly been innocent bystanders.   **146**

40. **Asymmetric Globalization: Global Markets Require Good Global Politics,** Nancy Birdsall, *Brookings Review,* Spring 2003
In the global game, economic power matters. In the last two decades, most **developing countries** took steps to open and liberalize their markets. Nancy Birdsall asks: what are the implications of market-led globalization for the world's poor nations?   **151**

The concepts in bold italics are developed in the article. For further expansion, please refer to the Topic Guide and the Index.

41. **Will the World Run Dry? Global Water and Food Security,** Mark W. Rosegrant, Ximing Cai, and Sarah A. Cline, *Environment,* September 2003

Demand for the world's increasingly scarce water supply is rising rapidly, challenging its availability for food production and putting global food security at risk. The authors say that **the impending water crisis** can be averted, but only if fundamental reform of the water sector is undertaken now.   **156**

42. **Do Global Attitudes and Behaviors Support Sustainable Development?,** Anthony A. Leiserowitz, Robert W. Kates, and Thomas M. Parris, *Environment,* November 2005

Many advocates of sustainable development recognize that a transition to **global sustainability**—meeting human needs and reducing hunger and poverty while maintaining the life-support systems of the planet—will require changes in human values, attitudes, and behaviors. This article reports on what is currently known about such attitudes and behaviors.   **165**

43. **Eliminating Child Labor,** Miriam Wasserman, *Regional Review,* Second Quarter 2000

Much of the developing world continues to rely on **child labor.** Miriam Wasserman asks: Can we learn from the U.S. experience about what is required for its elimination?   **180**

Index   **187**
Test Your Knowledge Form   **190**
Article Rating Form   **191**

The concepts in bold italics are developed in the article. For further expansion, please refer to the Topic Guide and the Index.

Topic Guide

This topic guide suggests how the selections in this book relate to the subjects covered in your course. You may want to use the topics listed on these pages to search the Web more easily.

On the following pages a number of Web sites have been gathered specifically for this book. They are arranged to reflect the units of this *Annual Edition*. You can link to these sites by going to the student online support site at *http://www.mhcls.com/online/*.

ALL THE ARTICLES THAT RELATE TO EACH TOPIC ARE LISTED BELOW THE BOLD-FACED TERM.

Antitrust policy

8. Modernizing U.S. Antitrust Law: The Role of Technology and Innovation

Banking industry

29. How Does Monetary Policy Affect the U.S. Economy?
30. It's His Economy Now—And Yours
31. Banking Consolidation
32. Bank ATMs and ATM Surcharges
33. Toward a Cashless Society

Chinese economy

15. Outsourcing Jobs: The Myths and Realities
20. Countdown to a Meltdown
34. Update on the State of the Future
37. The High-Tech Threat from China
38. Building Blocks
40. Asymmetric Globalization: Global Markets Require Good Global Politics

Common resource problem

11. The Eco-Economic Revolution: Getting the Market in Sync with Nature
12. Congested Parks—A Pricing Dilemma

Competition

2. More, Bigger, Faster
5. Jousting for Television's Holy Grail
6. Bruised in Bentonville
7. Airlines
8. Modernizing U.S. Antitrust Law: The Role of Technology and Innovation
10. The Truth About Oil
31. Banking Consolidation

Consumers

2. More, Bigger, Faster
4. Smoke Signals
6. Bruised in Bentonville
7. Airlines
9. The Real Price of Gas
10. The Truth About Oil
40. Asymmetric Globalization: Global Markets Require Good Global Politics

Corporate responsibility

6. Bruised in Bentonville
10. The Truth About Oil
13. Building a More-Humane Economy
15. Outsourcing Jobs: The Myths and Realities
16. Laid Off and Left Out
34. Update on the State of the Future

Cost-benefit analysis

1. How Much for a Life? Try $3 Million to $5 Million

Deficit

3. Counter-Terrorism: The Private Cost of More Security
20. Countdown to a Meltdown

23. Social Spending and Economic Growth, Interview with Peter Lindert
36. Is the Current Account Deficit Sustainable?

Discrimination

6. Bruised in Bentonville
18. The Gender Gyp

Elasticity

4. Smoke Signals

Environmental economics

9. The Real Price of Gas
10. The Truth About Oil
11. The Eco-Economic Revolution: Getting the Market in Sync with Nature
41. Will the World Run Dry? Global Water and Food Security
42. Do Global Attitudes and Behaviors Support Sustainable Development?

European Union

7. Airlines
13. Building a More-Humane Economy
34. Update on the State of the Future

Fiscal policy

20. Countdown to a Meltdown
22. The Elephant in the Room
23. Social Spending and Economic Growth, Interview with Peter Lindert
24. Why Are Taxes So Complicated and What Can We Do About It?
26. Tax Reform R.I.P.
27. Link Between Taxation, Unemployment Is Absent

Free-rider problem

3. Counter-Terrorism: The Private Cost of More Security

Health care

19. The Health Care Crisis and What to Do About It
23. Social Spending and Economic Growth, Interview with Peter Lindert

Income distribution

13. Building a More-Humane Economy
14. The Rich Get (Much) Richer
15. Outsourcing Jobs: The Myths and Realities
16. Laid Off and Left Out
17. Multiple Minimums
18. The Gender Gyp
34. Update on the State of the Future
39. Where the Money Went

Inflation

28. What Should Central Banks Do?
29. How Does Monetary Policy Affect the U.S. Economy?
30. It's His Economy Now—And Yours

International trade and finance

15. Outsourcing Jobs: The Myths and Realities
16. Laid Off and Left Out
34. Update on the State of the Future
35. As Job Exports Rise, Some Economists Rethink the Mathematics of Free Trade
36. Is the Current Account Deficit Sustainable?
37. The High-Tech Threat from China
38. Building Blocks
39. Where the Money Went
40. Asymmetric Globalization: Global Markets Require Good Global Politics
41. Will the World Run Dry? Global Water and Food Security
43. Eliminating Child Labor

Internet

2. More, Bigger, Faster
8. Modernizing U.S. Antitrust Law: The Role of Technology and Innovation

Labor-management relations

6. Bruised in Bentonville
13. Building a More-Humane Economy
15. Outsourcing Jobs: The Myths and Realities
16. Laid Off and Left Out
17. Multiple Minimums

Less-developed countries

39. Where the Money Went
40. Asymmetric Globalization: Global Markets Require Good Global Politics

Market failures

3. Counter-Terrorism: The Private Cost of More Security
9. The Real Price of Gas
11. The Eco-Economic Revolution: Getting the Market in Sync with Nature
12. Congested Parks—A Pricing Dilemma
17. Multiple Minimums
18. The Gender Gyp
19. The Health Care Crisis and What to Do About It
40. Asymmetric Globalization: Global Markets Require Good Global Politics

Minimum wage

17. Multiple Minimums

Monetary policy

28. What Should Central Banks Do?
29. How Does Monetary Policy Affect the U.S. Economy?
30. It's His Economy Now—And Yours

Opportunity costs

1. How Much for a Life? Try $3 Million to $5 Million

Poverty

14. The Rich Get (Much) Richer
16. Laid Off and Left Out
17. Multiple Minimums
42. Do Global Attitudes and Behaviors Support Sustainable Development?

Productivity

3. Counter-Terrorism: The Private Cost of More Security
13. Building a More-Humane Economy

21. Seizing Intangibles for the G.D.P.
22. The Elephant in the Room
23. Social Spending and Economic Growth, Interview with Peter Lindert
34. Update on the State of the Future

Protectionism

14. The Rich Get (Much) Richer
15. Outsourcing Jobs: The Myths and Realities
16. Laid Off and Left Out
20. Countdown to a Meltdown
35. As Job Exports Rise, Some Economists Rethink the Mathematics of Free Trade
38. Building Blocks
40. Asymmetric Globalization: Global Markets Require Good Global Politics

Renewable resources

11. The Eco-Economic Revolution: Getting the Market in Sync with Nature
41. Will the World Run Dry? Global Water and Food Security
42. Do Global Attitudes and Behaviors Support Sustainable Development?

Scale economies

6. Bruised in Bentonville
31. Banking Consolidation

Social Security System

18. The Gender Gyp

Stock markets

20. Countdown to a Meltdown
30. It's His Economy Now—And Yours

Super stores

6. Bruised in Bentonville

Taxation

24. Why Are Taxes So Complicated and What Can We Do About It?
26. Tax Reform R.I.P.
27. Link Between Taxation, Unemployment Is Absent

Telecommunications industry

5. Jousting for Television's Holy Grail
20. Countdown to a Meltdown

Unemployment

13. Building a More-Humane Economy
15. Outsourcing Jobs: The Myths and Realities
16. Laid Off and Left Out
17. Multiple Minimums
20. Countdown to a Meltdown
27. Link Between Taxation, Unemployment Is Absent
35. As Job Exports Rise, Some Economists Rethink the Mathematics of Free Trade

User fees

12. Congested Parks—A Pricing Dilemma

Work life balance

13. Building a More-Humane Economy

Internet References

The following Internet sites have been carefully researched and selected to support the articles found in this reader. The easiest way to access these selected sites is to go to our student online support site at *http://www.mhcls.com/online/*.

AE: Economics

The following sites were available at the time of publication. Visit our Web site—we update our student online support site regularly to reflect any changes.

General Sources

AmosWEB
http://www.amosweb.com

This site seeks to be the premier Internet site for instructional economic information. Main features include a glossary of over 500 economic terms and concepts, a reading room, and an interactive question-and-answer resource.

The Dismal Scientist
http://www.dismal.com

Often referred to as the "best free lunch on the Web," this is an excellent site with many interactive features. It provides access to economic data, briefings on the current state of the economy, and original articles on economic issues.

UNIT 1: Introduction

Economics: Complete Guide to Economic Resources on the Web
http://economics.miningco.com

This frequently updated resource "mines the Net" for information on economic subjects. It includes a large number of links and online articles from economics magazines and journals.

Litigation Analytics: How Much for a Human Life?
http://www.humanlifevalue.com/index.html

"How much is a human life worth?" This site provides an interesting interactive exercise involving this question.

UNIT 2: Microeconomics

CEO Express—Business and Financial News
http://www.ceoexpress.com

A comprehensive source of news on business, finance, and technology, this site provides users with extensive tools for researching companies through direct links to the home pages of *Fortune* 500 and many other firms.

Corporate Watch
http://www.corpwatch.org

Corporate Watch is an online magazine and resource center designed to provide an array of tools for investigating and analyzing the activities of transnational corporations.

Internet Public Library: Business and Economics Reference
http://ipl.org/ref/RR/static/bus0000.html

This comprehensive reference library on the production, distribution, and consumption of goods and services includes many subtopics about consumer issues, employment, business and industry, and labor and the workplace.

New York Times Business Connections
http://www.nytimes.com/library/cyber/reference/busconn.html

This page of links to business and economics sites on the Web was prepared for use by journalists of the *New York Times* for their own research purposes. It includes links to such categories as Markets, Companies, Business News, Banking and Finance, and Government.

Small Business Administration
http://www.sbaonline.sba.gov

The U.S. Small Business Administration provides financial, technical, and management assistance to 23 million small businesses.

UNIT 3: The Economics of Work and Income

Center on Budget and Policy Priorities
http://www.cbpp.org

This nonpartisan research organization and policy institute conducts research and analysis on a range of government policies and programs, with an emphasis on those affecting low- and moderate-income people.

Joint Center for Poverty Research
http://www.jcpr.org

This site examines what it means to be poor and to live in America. Issues considered include changing labor markets, the causes of inequality, family functioning, the impact of concentrated urban poverty, and implications for public policy.

Today's Unions
http://www.aflcio.org

The AFL-CIO Web page provides access to a large number of topics concerning ways in which labor unions might improve the lives of working families.

The Urban Institute
http://www.urban.org

The Urban Institute investigates national social and economic problems and analyzes solutions.

U.S. Department of Health and Human Services
http://www.hhs.gov

The Department of Health and Human Services is the U.S. government's principal agency for protecting the health of all Americans and providing essential human services, especially for those who are least able to help themselves.

U.S. Department of Labor
http://www.dol.gov

This Department of Labor Web site includes information about the department and its agencies, labor laws and trends, press releases, and texts of regulations.

UNIT 4: Macroeconomics

Citizens for Tax Justice
http://www.ctj.org

Citizens for Tax Justice is a research and advocacy organization that "seeks to give ordinary people a greater voice in the development of tax laws."

Congressional Budget Office

http://www.cbo.gov

The Congressional Budget Office seeks to provide "objective, timely, nonpartisan analyses needed for economic and budget decisions and with the information and estimates required for the Congressional budget process."

Federal Reserve Board

http://www.federalreserve.gov

The Web site of the Federal Reserve Board (the Fed) links to all the Federal Reserve Banks and other federal agencies. It provides access to the Fed's "Beige Book," a report published eight times each year on current economic conditions by the Federal Reserve district.

History of Money

http://www.ex.ac.uk/~RDavies/arian/llyfr.html

An award-winning site that provides a comprehensive chronology of money from ancient times to the present day, this page includes articles on the Origins of Banking, Money in North American History, Britain and the European Monetary Union, and Third World Debt in the 20th Century.

The Public Debt

http://www.publicdebt.treas.gov/opd/opd.htm

Features of this site include estimates of "daily amounts to the penny of the debt," interest costs of the outstanding public debt, and long-term trends.

UNIT 5: The Changing Global Economy

The European Union in the United States

http://www.eurunion.org

Here is a comprehensive Web site for those interested in the nature and origin of the European Union. Topics include EU policies and legislation, information on member states, and EU–U.S. relations.

Institute for International Economics

http://www.iie.com

Since its founding in 1981, the Institute for International Economics has provided objective analysis of key international economic problems and has proposed concrete solutions.

Inter-American Development Bank (IDB)

http://www.iadb.org

The Inter-American Development Bank was established in 1959 to help accelerate economic and social development in Latin America and the Caribbean. This site offers access to IDB reports and information on member countries.

North American Free Trade Association (NAFTA)

http://www.nafta-sec-alena.org

NAFTA's objective is "to provide accurate and timely information to U.S. exporters experiencing market access barriers in Canada or Mexico."

Organization for Economic Co-operation and Development (OECD)

http://www.oecd.org

The Web site of the OECD page provides information on OECD activities, news, and documentation. One interesting feature is links to the Center for Co-operation with Non-members.

Sustainable Development.Org

http://www.sustainabledevelopment.org

Extensive links at this site lead to such sustainable development categories as agriculture, energy, environment, finance, health, micro enterprise, public policy, and technologies.

United Nations Development Programme (UNDP)

http://www.undp.org

The UNDP helps people in 174 countries to help themselves by focusing on poverty elimination, environmental regeneration, job creation, and the advancement of women.

World Resources Institute

http://www.wri.org

The World Resources Institute provides information and practical proposals for policy and institutional change that will foster environmentally sound, socially equitable development.

We highly recommend that you review our Web site for expanded information and our other product lines. We are continually updating and adding links to our Web site in order to offer you the most usable and useful information that will support and expand the value of your Annual Editions. You can reach us at: *http://www.mhcls.com/annualeditions/*.

UNIT 1
Introduction

Unit Selections

1. **How Much for a Life? Try $3 Million to $5 Million**, Peter Passell
2. **More, Bigger, Faster**, Amar Bhidé
3. **Counter-Terrorism: The Private Cost of More Security**, Peter Navarro

Key Points to Consider

- Is life priceless? Explain your answer in terms of the opportunity cost principle.

- To what extent does the success of capitalism depend upon the creation of new wants?

- What are the economic implications of the 9/11 attacks?

Student Web Site

www.mhcls.com/online

Internet References

Further information regarding these Web sites may be found in this book's preface or online.

Economics: Complete Guide to Economic Resources on the Web
  http://economics.miningco.com
Litigation Analytics: How Much for a Human Life?
  http://www.humanlifevalue.com/index.html

Value	Change	%Change
3,006.62	38.97 ▲	1.31%
2,649.71	33.35 ▲	1.27%
807.90	2.93 ▲	0.36%
10,744.54	96.03 ▲	0.90%
1,367.40	13.28 ▲	0.98%
626.42	4.70 ▲	0.76%
61.33	0.49 ▼	0.79%

Economics concerns the decisions we face in meeting our material needs. Examples of such decisions can be found everywhere: college students confront rising tuition costs; a local business firm announces that it will lay off workers; a newspaper editorial comments on the merits of a national health care system; the U.S. Congress debates proposals to reform taxes. Like a view on a very clear day, a list of all possible economic problems appears to have no end.

Beginning students of economics often wonder why this is so. Why are the 6 billion citizens of the planet not able to find a way to meet their needs for material existence? More than a half century ago, the British economist Lionel Robbins provided an interesting answer to this question. He suggested that we are unable to do all the things we may wish to do for the simple reason that our economic resources—human talents, the natural endowment, and the stock of capital—are finite. Robbins defined "the economic problem" as one of scarcity: Our resources are scarce because the number of possible uses to which they might be put in meeting our material needs is unlim-

ited. Economics, therefore, ultimately concerns the hard choices we must make, both private and public, about ways to employ these resources. Because such choices always carry a price (or "opportunity cost") in terms of alternatives foregone, economics leads us to consider the costs and benefits of things we choose to do.

This unit offers different perspectives on the subject of resource limits and opportunity costs. First, Peter Passell raises an age-old question: What is the value of a human life? People sometimes chide economists for knowing "the cost of everything and the value of nothing." Yet, as Passell demonstrates, economic reasoning has great usefulness in understanding why people do the things they do, even—indeed, especially—when those things involve risky behaviors. When smokers light up, for example, they are making economic decisions (however subconsciously) about the value of the risks they incur. In effect, they are placing a value on their own lives. One of the tasks economists have is to remind us that no behavior is without cost and that at times these costs can be substantial.

1

Then, Amar Bhidé demonstrates how a principle known as *creative destruction* (originally developed by Joseph Schumpeter many years ago) applies to U.S. capitalism today. Bhidé shows how capitalism thrives as long as we can create new wants—and new products to meet them.

Finally, the unit concludes with an article in which Peter Navarro considers the possible costs of providing more security, in view of the September 11, 2001 attacks on the World Trade Center. He argues that the greatest danger terrorism poses to America may be purely economic, in the form of "productivity shocks."

How Much for A Life?
Try $3 Million to $5 Million

Even so, risk experts say some safety laws just aren't worth it.

PETER PASSELL

You've watched in horror a dozen times: Scenes of barely recognizable aircraft parts strewn across smoldering moonscapes, with the occasional shoe or child's toy the only reminders of lives snuffed out in unimaginable terror. And no doubt you've wondered when it would be your turn, a thought quickly shrugged away but never truly forgotten.

Flying, everyone knows, is a risky business. Any expense that makes it safer thus seems an expense worth making. And the only question most people ask after a crash is how to get the regulators to get off their duffs before the next one.

But the truth comes in shades of gray, not black and white. Americans' obsession with the tiny probability of dying in an airline accident is, at best, a distraction from the reality that commercial aviation is one of the great blessings of the age. At worst, it is an invitation to expensive and even self-defeating fixes, a symptom of our inability to cope sensibly with risk. But Republican conservatives in Congress are now pressing for a more sharp-penciled analysis of the cost of government health and safety regulations.

Just how safe is flying in America? Based on the experience of the last two decades, Arnold Barnett, a management professor at the Massachusetts Institute of Technology, sets the probability of dying from unnatural causes on your next commercial jet flight at about one in seven million. A flier who boards a jet each day can thus expect to meet the grim reaper every 19,000 years.

The propeller planes linking hundreds of small cities to big airports are three or four times as dangerous. But that only brings the odds of ending up a grim statistic to one in two million. The chance of suffering a heart attack while waiting for the conveyor belt to mangle your luggage is much greater.

The yawning gap between the actual and imagined risk of flying no longer surprises specialists in risk analysis, who make careers of explaining why people who brush aside the dangers of driving on icy highways or gorging on cookie dough ice cream are so ready to believe that portable phones cause brain cancer. But a comparison of the way risk analysts think about safety with the way Government balances risk against potential gain is sobering.

Probabilities alone don't offer much insight into which chances are worth taking. That question, suggests the brave new science of risk analysis, can be answered only by weighing the cost of avoiding a statistical death against the subjective value of life.

Try that one again. Assume for the sake of argument that it would cost $500 per car to put anti-skid brakes in each of the 10 million cars sold this year—a total of $5 billion. Assume that installing the gadgets on this year's fleet would ultimately save 5,000 lives, or $1 million per life. Assume that, on average, people value their lives at up to $5 million. Since the $1 million cost of saving a life is less than the $5 million value of life, the safety feature must be worth buying.

Sounds O.K., at least until the part about the value of life being $5 million. Who is to say that a life is worth $5 million rather than $500 million?

One answer is Americans couldn't afford to spend $500 million. Kip Viscusi, an economist at Duke University, estimates that if the entire gross national product were devoted to making life safer, there would only be $55 million available to prevent each accidental death. So, at least in this limited sense, life must be worth less than $55 million.

More to the point, people voluntarily accept the risk of death in return for money all the time. Dozens of studies have imputed a value to life from data on the extra wages required to lure workers to perform dangerous jobs. If, for example, it takes an extra $100,000 in lifetime earnings to persuade miners to cope with one extra chance in a hundred of premature death underground, miners must implicitly value their lives at no more than 100 times $100,000 or $10 million.

Dozens of other studies have focused on the cost of safety devices that are voluntarily purchased in order to assay how much people are willing to spend to reduce the probability of accidental death. If smoke detectors cost $20 and are widely seen as reducing the risk of a fiery death by one chance in 10,000, buyers must value their lives at least 20 times 10,000, or $200,000.

How Much Is a Saved Life Worth?

Safety regulations are rarely free of cost. If seat belts cost, say $50 per car, and equipping a million cars with seat belts will save 1,000 lives, the regulators must be assuming that lives are worth at least $50,000 a piece.

Here are estimates of the minimum value of a life that are built into a sampling of Government regulations. Figures take into account the medical and hospital costs avoided because lives were saved, but they ignore other benefits of the regulations, like prevention of property damage and injuries that do not result in death.

Automobiles	Reduce lead content of gasoline from 1.1 to 0.1 grams per gallon	No net cost
	Child restraints in cars	$1.3 million
	Dual master cylinders for car brakes	$7.8 million
Ejection systems for the B-58 bomber		$22 million
Flashing lights at **railroad crossings**		$730,000
Sea walls to protect against 100-year storm surges		$96 million
Asbestos	Banned in brake linings	$230,000
	... in automatic transmission parts	$1.2 billion
Radiation	Safety standards for X-ray equipment	$400,000
	... for uranium mine tailings	$190 million

These studies hardly produce uniform answers—nor do risk analysts expect them to. After all, people have very different "tastes" for risk. But researchers are still willing to generalize. Most middle-income Americans, they say, usually act as if their lives are worth $3 million to $5 million based on what they demand in extra pay for dangerous jobs and what they spend for safety devices.

A few Federal agencies, notably the Department of Transportation, evaluate new health and safety regulations by comparing an estimate of the cost per life that would probably be saved against a benchmark figure. But most are too savvy to be caught putting a value on life. And in some cases, the law actually bars consideration of cost in deciding how safe is safe enough.

The result is a hodgepodge of cost-effective regulations mixed with inconceivably expensive ones. At one extreme are rules that actually save money as well as lives. Mandatory childhood immunization programs, for example, cost less than treating the diseases. At the other extreme are rules that probably save only a statistical fraction of a life, and at enormous cost. Strict controls on benzene emissions by the tire makers run to an estimated $340 billion per life spared.

The most wasteful rules, however, are the ones that do save dozens of lives but at farcical cost. Draconian controls on toxic wastes from a variety of manufacturing plants, as well as cleanup standards for abandoned uranium mines and chemical waste sites, fit the category. Indeed, with cleanup obligations on the books that would cost government and industry several hundred billion dollars to meet over the next decade, risk researchers argue that the net impact of the programs on life expectancy may actually be perverse.

How so? The affluent live longer than the poor, at least in part because they have the will and the means to lead more secure lives. Not only are they more likely to visit a doctor before a cough turns into pneumonia, they can afford fresh vegetables, health clubs and bicycle helmets for their kids.

Hence the life-lengthening effects of requiring auto makers to install anti-skid brakes or preventing trace chemicals from ending up in drinking water must be weighed against the life-shortening effects of reducing living standards in order to pay the bill.

Mr. Viscusi estimates that the break-even point in what specialists have dubbed "risk-risk" calculations is around $10 million. Thus by his reckoning, regulations that reduce private spending by more than $10 million per statistical life saved are probably self-defeating.

Where does airline safety fit in this picture? When pressed to mandate life-preserving technology for commercial aircraft, the Federal Aviation Agency has generally acted with one eye on the economics. According to a 1984 study, smoke detectors required in airplane lavatories save lives for about a half-million dollars each. Emergency floor lighting runs to approximately $1 million per life saved—well under the $3 million to $5 million benchmark for the value of life. Still, some of the most hotly debated proposals suggest just how seductive bad ideas can be.

Infants can't use ordinary seat belts, so they are more vulnerable than adults in survivable airplane accidents unless they are strapped into special child seats. But there is a big catch here: Airlines insist that parents buy tickets for children if kids are to be assured seats of their own. So if Washington had demanded child restraints in response to petitions from safety groups in the 1980's, an estimated one-fifth of the infants who now fly in relative safety would be priced out of the air and end up traveling at greater risk in autos. On balance, more lives would be lost in cars than saved in planes.

A parallel question—one hardly ever asked—is whether aircraft manufacturers voluntarily spend too much on safety. If free markets worked according to Hoyle, one might expect Boeing and Airbus to sell less-safe planes, were it profitable to do so. But since aircraft makers and airlines—not to mention product liability lawyers—are deeply reluctant to acknowledge that there is any acceptable trade-off between cost and safety, such calculations are apparently never made in any systematic way.

What is apparent, though, is that commercial aviation is now so safe and the system that keeps it safe is so complex that the rare fatal accident offers little insight into how flying could be made safer at reasonable cost. Take the case of USAir and its subsidiaries, which suffered seven deadly accidents in seven years—a frequency of mishaps that Mr. Barnett of M.I.T. calculates had only a 2 percent probability of being purely coincidental. Add the fact that USAir was apparently guilty of an embarrassing number of safety and training miscues, including the failure to refuel a plane before take-off, and it is understandable why many travelers are looking for other ways to get to Pittsburgh.

But like the clusters of rare cancers that occasionally make headlines, clusters of airline accidents are harder to interpret than it might at first seem. Much depends on how the universe of possible coincidences is defined. For while the probability that chance alone generated USAirs unenviable safety record was just 1 in 50, there was a probability of 1 in 8 that some major airline that was no more dangerous than its competitors would crack up seven planes in seven years. One in 8 is still daunting odds, but not quite a smoking gun.

Even if one concedes that USAir must have been doing something disastrously wrong, it is hard to pinpoint what it was doing disastrously wrong. While it is gratifying to see that USAir pilots are now on notice to double-check fuel gauges before take-off, it is far from clear that the carrier's safety lapses were more serious than those of competitors with spotless accident records.

Safe air travel is worth some money and trouble, of course. And, no doubt, the tens of thousands of people who earn their paychecks keeping it safe will come up with some affordable ideas on how to make it safer. But the fact that many Americans who can't spot the difference between a wart and a melanoma know all about aircraft de-icing techniques and Doppler radar says more about their fears than about their knowledge of risk.

More, Bigger, Faster

Capitalism will thrive as long as we can create new wants—and products to meet them.

AMAR BHIDÉ

China isn't to blame for the so-called jobless recovery. Neither is India. But those counting on exports or offshoring's efficiency to jumpstart the stagnant U.S. economy are off-base as well. The United States—and its corporations—can't rely only on running a tighter ship.

The long-run prosperity of the West depends on the capacity of its entrepreneurial individuals and firms to create and satisfy new consumer wants. When the new-want capacity is in good repair, job "losses"—through improvements in the efficiency of domestic production or through outsourcing to low-wage countries—enhance standards of living. If this capacity is impaired, neither the low road of protection nor the high road of free trade will take the country in the right direction.

At least in the United States, most policymakers understand that in the long run, economic growth requires productivity growth: For per-capita living standards to increase, so must per-capita output. What is less well understood is that productivity growth requires the creation and satisfaction of new wants, not just the more efficient provision of existing wants.

An artist may increase her productivity by developing more efficient techniques that speed her output of paintings. Alternatively, she may create a market for a new oeuvre that commands higher prices. She may produce exactly the same number of canvases as before, but her *economic* output and productivity increase.

That type of market creation—on a larger scale, of course—is critical. Currently, discussions of productivity tend to focus on increases in efficiency and ignore the development of new markets, which is a dead end: Economies cannot sustain growth in productivity and living standards simply through efficiency. Sure, in the short run, increased efficiency does reduce costs, and as costs decline, people consume more of the good or service. But eventually, the law of diminishing utilities sets in: Sated consumers refuse to buy more even if prices continue to decline. After that, further increases in production efficiencies must come at the expense of the demand for labor.

In principle, societies could accommodate reductions in the demand for labor by increasing the time for everyone's leisure. Over the last century, economic growth has helped reduce working hours and increase vacations. But somehow, beyond a

certain point, societies seem unable to accommodate reductions in labor demand by spreading the work around: Consider France's less-than-successful efforts to control unemployment by mandating working-hour reductions across the nation.

Automobiles helped create a market that did not previously exist.

It is the entrepreneurial activity of creating and satisfying new wants that keeps the system humming. The new-want process employs the labor and purchasing power released by increased efficiencies, and it creates incentives for *continued* increases in efficiencies: Producers who satisfy old wants have to keep economizing on their use of labor because they must compete for employees (and share of consumers' wallets) with the producers who satisfy new wants.

Outsourcing jobs to low-wage countries resembles efficiency improvement in its symbiotic relationship to the satisfaction of new wants. It improves living standards in the United States, provided the human capital released here can be used to make new goods and services. Otherwise, as with improvements in efficiency, outsourcing is all too likely to reduce the demand for domestic labor.

Non-Destructive Creation

In the twentieth century, the United States enjoyed, according to one expert, a ten-and-a-half-fold increase in real per-capita GDP. This was driven by, in part, more efficient methods of production of existing goods; innovations such as tractors, threshing machines, fertilizers, pesticides, and hybrid seeds led to vast improvements in agricultural productivity. As productivity increases reduced costs and increased the affordability of food, per-capita consumption grew.

But the increase in the consumption of food and other existing goods is only part of the story. Few of the goods and services consumed these days bear much resemblance to the goods and services of the late nineteenth century. Some of the new goods replaced the goods consumed by our forebears. Cars and buses replaced horses and stagecoaches. Steamships grounded sailing ships, and ready-to-eat cereal pushed homemade porridge off breakfast tables. As did the improvements in agricultural productivity, many of the new products reduced costs and, therefore, prices.

Economist Joseph Schumpeter insisted that this "creative destruction" of stagecoaches, porridge, and candles is an "essential fact about capitalism." But in fact, many new twentieth-century products did not displace existing products—rather, they created new markets and satisfied new wants. Air-conditioners reduced temperatures in previously uncooled factories, stores, and office buildings. Airplanes did not reduce the demand for automobiles—people flew when they would not have driven. New drugs and vaccines offered cures for diseases for which treatments did not previously exist. In 1938, *The New York Times* lamented that the typewriter was "driving out writing with one's own hand," yet global consumers continue to buy some fourteen billion pencils annually, enough to circle the world sixty-two times.

Moreover, even those apparently destructive new products also created new markets because of features that satisfied a different set of wants than did the products they made obsolete. For instance, mass-produced automobiles provided much faster and not just cheaper transportation than did horse carriages, so people could live in spacious houses located at some distance from their workplace. Automobiles thus helped create a market for commuting (and suburban housing) that did not previously exist.

The IT innovations of the late twentieth century have followed the same pattern as earlier decades' electromechanical innovations. The digital revolution has certainly involved some substitution. Calculators displaced slide rules, microprocessor-based workstations displaced mini-computers, and CDs displaced cassette recorders. But there has been at least as much non-destructive creation. Consider the ubiquitous personal computer, now used by two-thirds of the U.S. population. PCs and other new computer architectures did not blow away the traditional mainframe computer in a gale of creative destruction. The PC's killer business application, the spreadsheet, did not displace any existing mainframe-based applications—rather, it allowed users, many of whom had not previously used computers extensively, to perform analyses and simulations that they would not have otherwise performed. Similarly, the enormous growth of the home PC market did not reduce the demand for mainframe computers until the last few years.

Predictions that mechanization would create mass unemployment didn't come true.

The role of PCs in expanding the pie rather than destroying existing markets apparently represents a common feature of the digital revolution. New communications services—e-mail, newsgroups, and "chat"—provided a critical mass of users for the Internet and online services such as America Online. These services have not obviated traditional phone lines—indeed, they have helped *increase* demand; cities continue to require new area codes.

And those new products that *have* displaced old products have often done so *after* they have created a new market. For instance, as I discovered in the course of a consulting study for a now-defunct typewriter manufacturer, U.S. shipments of word-processing units grew fourteen-fold between 1977 and 1981. But because word processors increased primary demand by satisfying some hitherto-unmet want, U.S. sales of typewriters remained steady at around a million units a year during this period. Similarly, one day, cell phones may make land-line phones obsolete—but not before consumers have purchased hundreds of millions of units in applications where land-line phones had not been used.

Thanks to innovations that created markets for new goods and services, predictions that mechanization and mass production would create mass unemployment didn't come true. True, changes in production technologies put many artisans out of work, and between 1900 and 1960, productivity improvements on the farm cut U.S. agricultural employment in half. But the labor released by farm and workshops was quickly absorbed by factories established to serve new markets: In that same sixty-year period, total employment more than doubled. Plus, the assembly-line worker earned more than the farmer or skilled artisan. And although manufacturing-sector wages stagnated after the 1970s, overall U.S. employment and income have continued to rise. As fresh wants have arisen—in, for instance, information technology—new industries have expanded or sprouted to fill them.

The Role of Imports

The last three decades have seen dramatic growth in imports from low-wage countries. And, like efficiency improvements in the production of existing goods, imports have fostered the growth of U.S. industries that satisfy new needs. Just as low-cost groceries helped consumers purchase Model Ts, cheap TV sets from the Far East have allowed U.S. households the wherewithal to purchase PCs powered by Intel microprocessors and Microsoft software. And just as surplus farm labor provided employees for Henry Ford's assembly lines, engineers who would have otherwise been employed by American TV manufacturers were available for employment by IT companies.

Long-run synergies do not, however, ensure that new industries' job gains will always offset the jobs lost in existing industries. And when job losses exceed gains, outsourcing—rather than efficiency improvements—gets blamed. In truth, apart from a few specific industries such as toys and bicycles, far fewer jobs are lost to imports than to efficiency improvements in industries where demand has been stagnant. So curbs on outsourcing would save few jobs.

Some free-traders pin their hopes on forcing low-wage countries to open their markets to U.S. exports. But exports to low-wage countries cannot compensate for the migration of jobs to these regions. A Chinese worker earning 40 cents an hour simply cannot buy the same goods and services as someone earning just the legal U.S. minimum wage of $5.15. Moreover, workers in developing countries spend only a small portion of their income on U.S.-made products. As Chinese employees' incomes grow, the nation's imports of goods from other low- or middle-income countries increase faster than imports from countries with high wages. So whereas China's annual trade surplus with the United States exceeds $120 billion, its trade with India (where per-capita GDP is about half of China's) shows a deficit. And even in those products such as automobiles and washing machines, for which foreign companies dominate the Chinese market, labor and transportation costs often favor local manufacturers.

It's a safe bet that in the long run, employment in existing industries will continue to decline.

The U.S. trade balance has been in deficit since 1976, though in those years U.S. exporters have faced markets abroad that are more, not less, open. We can't count on any further reductions in tariff and non-tariff barriers leading to an upsurge in export-related jobs. "New" jobs in "new" industries must replace the old jobs lost to efficiency gains and outsourcing.

Reasons for Optimism

It's a safe bet that in the long run, whatever happens to outsourcing, employment in existing industries will continue to decline. And no one can predict when new industries will start adding jobs faster than old industries shed them. Public policies cannot speed things up: Tax cuts and easy money might, in the short run, stimulate "old" economy demand for automobiles and housing, but they cannot induce consumers to use Short Messaging Services on their cell phones, or to buy Segway Human Transporters, or to adopt any number of technologies hailed as the next big thing.

Nevertheless, because of the new-want machine that we have developed over the last hundred years, the long-run prospects are excellent. On the supply side, innovation has become everybody's business. In the nineteenth century, inventions were made and developed by a few individuals. For instance, automobile pioneers were one- or two-man shows: Karl Benz and Gottlieb Daimler in Germany, Armand Peugeot in France, the Duryea brothers of Springfield, Mass. And one- or two-man outfits couldn't develop products for mass consumption—just think of early automobiles, expensive contraptions owned by a few buffs who rode around the countryside terrifying horses. In the twentieth century, the task of converting inventions into mass-market products came to pervade business and society. Planned and unwitting collaborations allowed products that initially only kind-of-sort-of worked to reach commercial critical mass. When Altair, believed by many to be the first personal computer, was introduced in 1975, its aficionados derived less

practical use from their machines than did the turn-of-the-century automobile buffs. Lacking basic input or output devices (such as keyboards and printers), Altairs could not even scare horses. A procession of individual entrepreneurs, followed by large companies like IBM, Microsoft, and Intel, turned this oddity into a ubiquitous tool.

The innovation system also favors the non-destructive creation of goods and services that satisfy new wants. As Harvard's Clay Christensen has pointed out, innovative products usually start up by serving a function that existing products do not. An innovator that tries to take market share away from existing products faces resistance from the businesses that face the threat of substitution as well as from users who have invested in the old regime. (For instance, movie theaters have been reluctant to switch over to higher-quality digital projection systems.) Overcoming this resistance reduces profitability and makes the funding requirements prohibitive for many entrepreneurs. And large, established companies prefer to develop businesses that increase their total sales rather than cannibalize existing revenues.

On the demand side, we haven't—and won't—run out of new wants to satisfy. It's true that, rising obesity notwithstanding, we can't eat much more than we already do, meaning that any new food products must replace old food products. We may also have exhausted our "free" time—cellular phones that may not displace land lines do absorb the time that we might otherwise devote to quiet reverie. But although it would be foolhardy to make firm predictions about what great new markets lurk around the corner, opportunities for satisfying new wants hardly have been exhausted.

On the demand side, we haven't— and won't—run out of new wants to satisfy.

Expenditures on health care, for instance, are almost certain to expand. Modern medicine has found cures for many diseases and increased U.S. life expectancies from forty-seven years in 1900 to seventy-seven today. No treatments exist, however, for a great many other diseases, and current life expectancies are well below any theoretical limit for the human lifespan. The aging of the population similarly provides ample opportunities for goods and services that enhance the quality of the lives of older citizens. Among the young and would-be-young, the desire to look and feel good has sustained many new businesses—indeed, new sectors altogether. The number of health clubs in the United States has jumped 50 percent in the last four years, with membership topping 36 million in 2002. Businesses have also created non-destructive sales by finding new ways to tickle the senses—for instance, by selling ringer tones and faceplates to enhance cellular phones. Such consumption might not please all tastes, but they have maintained the growth of the modern shopping basket in the past and likely will continue to do so in the future.

The fine condition of the new-want machine is good news for the integration of nearly a billion Chinese and Indian workers into the labor markets of the developed world. To be sure, the speed and magnitude of this integration are unprecedented and will hurt some U.S. workers and communities. But on balance, it represents an opportunity for continued prosperity on both sides of the trade rather than a threat to American livelihoods. As long as we continue playing the new-want game, everyone will win.

AMAR BHIDÉ is a professor of business at Columbia University and author of, most recently, *The Origin and Evolution of New Businesses.*

COUNTER-TERRORISM:
The Private Cost of More Security

PETER NAVARRO

The greatest danger that terrorism poses to America may be purely economic, the threat of weapons of mass destruction notwithstanding. The danger lies in a severe "productivity shock" that could lead to a gross domestic product trillions of dollars below what it otherwise should be.

The most obvious source of this shock lies in a deficit-producing shift from butter to guns in the federal budget as we wage war against terrorism. Cuts in education and infrastructure spending will directly lower productivity even as deficit-driven higher interest rates indirectly cut productivity by crowding out investment in the private sector.

But the more subtle, potentially more serious productivity shock may come from a federally mandated substitution of "protective" for "productive" capital in the private sector. That is, money spent for more fences, guards and surveillance equipment at the expense of new machinery, technology and software. Over the next several years, this capital substitution will probably accelerate as a security-conscious White House and Congress impose a new layer of regulations the likes of which we haven't seen since the 1970s.

Since Sept. 11, some corporations have voluntarily put capital into protection. But the levels of counter-terrorism spending have been far below what one might have expected, particularly in light of the legal liabilities that corporations may face for failing to protect their employees and customers. Moreover, with the exception of a few sectors like petroleum, which have adopted plans to safeguard facilities from terrorist attacks, there has been little coordinated action by corporate leadership.

This relative inaction in the private sector poses an ideological problem for the Bush administration, one that has provoked considerable differences of opinion across federal bureaucracies. To understand why President Bush finds himself between a conservative rock and a pragmatic hard place, it's important to know why the private sector has failed to shoulder its fair share of the counter-terrorism burden.

First, corporate executives have been reluctant to invest in new plant machinery, let alone in protective devices, during these recessionary times. Corporations that have significantly boosted counter-terrorism spending, like Boeing, can either afford to or have no other option because of their risk exposure.

Second, some industry stakeholders have simply let others carry the burden. Bush's initial response to this "free rider" problem was classically conservative. Rather than jam new regulations down industry's throat, government should form "patriotic" partnerships with business to develop voluntary counter-terrorism obligations. But after months of corporate foot-dragging, Bush now understands that free riders will continue to shirk their duty absent federal mandates.

The recent skirmish between Bush and Congress over the chemical industry's failure to regulate itself illustrates the underlying policy conflict. The industry was initially asked to devise plans to prevent a terrorist attack on chemical plants from sending waves of toxic fumes into a major urban area. But free riders run rampant in this industry.

Of the nation's 15,000 chemical companies, only about 10% even participate in the industry's trade association. Moreover, the sector's profit margins are very low. Finally, the industry has been in almost constant regulatory warfare with the government. As a result of the chemical sector's go-slow approach to managing the terrorist threat, the Bush administration had to cancel a much ballyhooed June rollout of the president's voluntary partnerships.

Democratic Sens. Jon Corzine of New Jersey and Harry Reid of Nevada quickly used the opportunity to push legislation that would achieve what volunteerism hadn't. Outflanked, Bush tacked. Amazingly, he is moving forward on using the Environmental Protection Agency, a favorite target during his 2000 presidential campaign, to crack down on the chemical industry.

The skirmish raises a broader policy question: How best to proceed with the design, implementation and enforcement of a complex and costly layer of new counter-terrorism regulations? Unfortunately, the answer so far has many unsettling parallels with the mistakes of the regulation-heavy 1970s.

During that decade, the federal government churned out new, strict regulations on everything from clean air to water purity to occupational health and safety. We now know that their poor initial design and implementation were a major cause of a decade of lost productivity and painfully slow economic growth.

A basic problem was that overzealous bureaucrats and politicians adopted a broad range of "command and control" standards that left little maneuvering room for industry. For example, the EPA required new power plants to use expensive "best available control technology" whether or not the new plants could meet new emission standards by simply burning lower-sulfur coal.

We eventually learned that it was cheaper to use market mechanisms to bring about the desired regulatory effects. Tools like pollution and emissions credits and "smog markets" have allowed industry to meet standards in a less costly manner and not succumb to the free-rider problem.

Despite this 1970s lesson, Congress and the White House appear to be moving toward costly command-and-control mandates to get the counter-terrorism protection they deem necessary. The irony is that a corporate leadership seemingly as devoid of a co-operative spirit, patriotism and vision as it is of ethics is driving the movement.

The stakes are high. If productivity levels drop to 1970s levels again, our GDP will be at least $2 trillion lower than it otherwise would be in 10 years. Yes, this estimate is wildly at odds with the Bush administration's, which doesn't anticipate a major productivity shock. There are, however, no glasses rose-colored enough to produce honestly the administration's assessment. It's not just the disparate fiscal, monetary, regulatory and military forces that Sept. 11 has set in motion. It is also the almost breathtaking scope of the regulatory counter-terrorist checklist.

This list ranges from strengthened background checks, vulnerability assessments, bolstered plant security and tighter enforcement of immigration laws to stockpiling vaccines, establishing readiness plans in case of another terrorist attack and running a national health surveillance network. Also included are tasks like retrofitting nuclear power plants to survive a terrorist air assault, installing air filters in major buildings to combat bioterrorism and possibly equipping hazardous waste trucks with automatic braking systems to thwart sabotage and suicide bombers.

If there is any reassuring news in all this, it is this: If we allow our creativity to blossom, as we did during the space race, and if we practice our 1970s regulatory lessons, we can prosecute the war on terrorism cost-effectively while developing and deploying the new technologies necessary to outrun terror. The space program is an instructive precedent: Every dollar spent yielded seven tax dollars reaped from commercial spinoffs. If we could ensure that our counter-terrorist research and development cut in both military and civilian ways, we may be able to overcome any productivity losses resulting from our war against terrorism.

PETER NAVARRO teaches macroeconomics at the Graduate School of Management at UC Irvine.

UNIT 2
Microeconomics

Unit Selections

4. **Smoke Signals**, *The New York Times*
5. **Jousting for Television's Holy Grail**, Neil Munro
6. **Bruised in Bentonville**, Andy Serwer
7. **Airlines**, Giovanni Bisignani
8. **Modernizing U.S. Antitrust Law: The Role of Technology and Innovation**, Thomas A. Hemphill
9. **The Real Price of Gas**, *International Center for Technology Assessment*
10. **The Truth About Oil**, Jon Birger
11. **The Eco-Economic Revolution: Getting the Market in Sync with Nature**, Lester R. Brown
12. **Congested Parks—A Pricing Dilemma**, Dan M. Bechter

Key Points to Consider

- Why is the concept of demand elasticity important, and how might it be used?

- What role do economics of scale play in the success of large corporations? Is Wal-Mart too big?

- What is the "real" price of gasoline? What is the truth about the oil industry today?

- What is "eco-economics," and how might policies be developed to aid both the environment and the economy?

Student Web Site

www.mhcls.com/online

Internet References

Further information regarding these Web sites may be found in this book's preface or online.

CEO Express—Business and Financial News
http://www.ceoexpress.com

Corporate Watch
http://www.corpwatch.org

Internet Public Library: Business and Economics Reference
http://ipl.org/ref/RR/static/bus0000.html

New York Times Business Connections
http://www.nytimes.com/library/cyber/reference/busconn.html

Small Business Administration
http://www.sbaonline.sba.gov

While there are many ways to subdivide the science of economics, the most common one distinguishes between macroeconomics and microeconomics. Macroeconomics is the study of the economy "in the large"; it concerns such broad issues as how gross domestic product (GDP), unemployment, inflation, and economic growth are determined. Microeconomics—the subject of this unit—involves the study of the economy "in the small"; it investigates the economy in terms of its separate components and focuses on the individual decision-making processes of consumers and producers in a market setting.

The primary roots of modern microeconomics can be traced to Adam Smith's *An Inquiry into the Nature and Causes of the Wealth of Nations* published in 1776. In this work Smith shows how individuals, acting in their own self-interest, serve the best interests of a market economy. Smith's argument (which is generally accepted by most economists today) provides the basis for a laissez-faire political philosophy—the belief that noninterference by government in the workings of a market system promotes the greatest good for the greatest number of people.

With the intensification of both domestic and global competition in recent years, companies are compelled to adopt new strategies (never foreseen in the days of Adam Smith), which include consideration of the size of the targeted market, superior access to resources and customers, and restrictions on competitor's options. The ability of a single firm to pursue such strategies depends, of course, on the nature of its market environment. Microeconomic analysis shows that this can range from a perfectly competitive environment (of numerous small, price-taking firms) to a monopolized one (containing a single, price-making seller).

This unit begins with several articles that illustrate specific microeconomic concepts: "the laws of supply and demand," "demand elasticity," "e-commerce," "economics of scale," and "monopoly power." These concepts are used to answer a series of very interesting questions, including: Why is it that recent efforts to discourage smoking may impose a greater burden on cigarette consumers than producers? Is Wal-Mart too big? Is the airline industry doomed?

The remaining articles of this unit deal with the microeconomics of public policy. First Thomas Hemphill shows how techno-

logical innovation contributes to the goals of antitrust policy. The article entitled "The Real Price of Gas" demonstrates how the failure to account for "externalities" understates the price of gasoline. Next, Jon Birger examines five current myths about the oil industry. Then, Lester Brown shows how policies might be developed to benefit both the environment and the economy. Finally, Dan Bechter investigates a classic microeconomic dilemma: the overcrowding of public parks, which often results in the imposition of fees for what might otherwise be regarded as a "free good."

Smoke Signals

Doubling of Cigarette Tax Sends Some Smokers Across State Lines, but Many into Abstinence

Smokers in New Jersey took such a shellacking at the cash register last year that they stopped buying cigarettes in numbers never seen before. How many stopped smoking is a separate question.

Since the state cigarette tax doubled last Jan. 1, sales have declined about 12 percent, Treasury Department data show. While some sales have been chased across state borders, public health experts estimate that at least two-thirds of the decline reflects a decrease in smoking.

"Wow, that's a whole lot more than we predicted," said Larry Downs, director of New Jersey Breathes, a coalition of antismoking organizations. Before the increase, Mr. Downs said, consumption had been dropping by 2 to 4 percent a year. "Something's going on," he continued. "I'll give you 4 percent for people buying cigarettes elsewhere and I'll take the 8 percent drop."

Mr. Downs said the tax increase had set up "a real-life public health experiment": While New Jersey's tax rose to 80 cents a pack from 40 cents, neighboring states maintained their rates— Pennsylvania at 31 cents a pack, New York at 56 cents and Delaware at 24 cents. Len Fishman, the state Commissioner of Health and Senior Services, said the initial wallop was meant to drive down sales, even though most of the new revenue finances health care.

"We were hoping a dramatic increase would decrease consumption," Mr. Fishman said. "We did predict that there would be a reduction in the number of people who smoke." He said that in his travels around the state, "a lot of people have told me that they quit, and a lot told me that this was the straw that broke the camel's back."

The tax increase placed New Jersey behind only Alaska and Hawaii, at $1 a pack, and Washington State, at 82.5 cents. (On Jan. 1, California's tax rose to 87 cents a pack.) The sticker shock was compounded last month by a price increase, 45 cents a pack at wholesale and about 60 cents at the counter, from tobacco manufacturers.

The two hits raised prices by about 50 percent. At Wawa convenience stores, for example, premium brands cost $3.32 a pack, up from $2.22 before the tax increase.

Revenue from tax stamps from Jan. 1 through June 30, the end of the 1998 fiscal year, were about 13 percent below what they would have been had sales remained at their 1997 levels; when the effect of volume discounts was taken into account, the decline in cigarette sales was about 12 percent, Treasury Department officials said.

Preliminary figures for the current fiscal year show similar decreases. When the tax took effect, cigarette revenue was already falling; in the fiscal year 1997 revenue dropped 2 percent. Had that dropoff continued, 1998 revenue through November would have been about $433.3 million, or 54.2 million cartons. Instead, revenue was $379.4 million, or 47.4 million cartons. The gap, then, represents about 6.8 million cartons, and there is no way to know how many were bought in other states.

In New York, cigarette tax revenue from January to November 1998 was 0.3 percent below collections for the same period in 1997. Pennsylvania reported a 1.4 percent increase in 1998. In Delaware, where revenue was already increasing at a rate of 3 percent a year, the first half of 1998 saw a 10 percent increase over the first half of 1997. Pennsylvania's additional revenue through November represents about 1.2 million more cartons than were sold from January to November 1997, but sales were declining—by 1.8 percent in the 1997 fiscal year—and if that decline had continued, the extra tax collections would represent about 2.9 million more cartons.

Delaware's extra sales through November, assuming a continued 3 percent increase, exceeded 500,000 cartons. While researchers have consistently found dropoffs in smoking after price increases, they cannot know exactly what role prices have played. There have been few large, one-time price increases, and no precedent for a tax increase as large as New Jersey's.

Mr. Fishman cites the example of Massachusetts, which raised its tax 25 cents a pack in 1992 and registered a 12.5 percent decline in sales the next year.

"Talking about price increases can be tricky," Mr. Fishman said. "If you have gradual increases, you lose some of the impact. A state with a high tax may have had less of an increase over the years."

It is especially hard to measure the effects of cigarette prices on underage buyers. Many studies have concluded that price has a greater effect on children and teenagers than on adults. But a recent analysis by economists at Cornell University, using data on students who were eighth graders in 1988, found that price increases had very little effect on whether they took up smoking.

And while the smoking rate among adults has been inching down—to 23.2 percent of adults nationwide and 21.5 percent in New Jersey, according to the Federal Centers for Disease Control and Prevention—it has sharply risen among teenagers and children. In its most recent published survey of high school seniors, taken in 1997, the University of Michigan's Institute for Social Research found that 24.6 percent were daily smokers, a figure that has steadily climbed from a low point of 18.1 percent in 1988.

In New Jersey, the centers' 1997 survey of 9th to 12th graders found that 38 percent had smoked a cigarette in the previous month and 19 percent were daily smokers.

Mr. Fishman said his department had predicted a decline of 10 to 12 percent in smoking among children and teenagers as a result of the tax increase and that its effects would become clearer this spring, when the state surveys middle-school students.

It will be longer yet before the manufacturers' price increase, which took effect only in late November, shows measurable results. But Rich Herbeck, co-owner of Irwin Tobacco and Candy, a distributor in Trenton, said that even though the increase was nationwide, it was sending New Jerseyans across the bridges just as the tax hit had done last January.

"People were so shocked by it that they're looking for any method to save money," Mr. Herbeck said.

Jousting for Television's Holy Grail

Neil Munro

In the romantic chronicles of the Middle Ages, the chaste and pure-hearted knights would couch their lances and sally forth into the unknown in search of the Holy Grail from which Jesus drank.

But these days, the search for the Holy Grail is confined, like so much else, to the realm of television—digital television, to be exact. And the sallying forth is being led by lobbyists encircling the Federal Communications Commission and Congress. It is within those two bodies that three factions are seeking to control the fate of digital television—essentially the computerized TV signals that are needed for high-definition TV sets and for the further use of TV sets for other functions, such as online shopping. So far in this battle, the cable-TV industry is triumphing over its two rivals—the local broadcasters and the TV manufacturers. The cable industry's pending prize is what some participants describe as the modern Holy Grail—the revenue-generating power to sway more than 100 million consumers as they turn on their digital televisions in their living rooms for entertainment, advertising, online shopping, banking services, news, and much more.

The cable-TV industry is winning this prize because it has spent nearly $60 billion over six years to juice up old cable-TV wires to serve as the nation's primary broadband network—or, to use a more comprehensible image, as the nation's cyberspace shopping mall. The industry, represented by the National Cable & Telecommunications Association, is in such a good position that even deregulatory-minded Republicans on the Hill are publicly warning the industry to behave itself.

"You'll see Congress intervening if cable uses its inherent advantage unfairly," predicted Ken Johnson, a senior spokesman for Rep. W.J. "Billy" Tauzin, R-La., the chairman of the House Energy and Commerce Committee.

The primary losers are the consumer-electronics firms that make TV sets. They find themselves relegated to the status of taxi drivers. Their highly sophisticated, but essentially dumb, digital TVs will allow consumers to zip around this cyber-mall, but they won't be able to offer any guidebooks, shopping tips, programming, product tie-ins, or advertising. The greatest part of the advertising and goods-peddling will instead emerge from the digital "set-top" box, which is controlled by the cable-TV industry.

The nation's TV broadcasters are also losers, partly because they sought more rent-free space in the TV cyber-mall than they're going to get. Roughly speaking, Congress's current "must-carry" rules require the cable companies to give a single cable-TV slot to each local broadcast station, an NBC or ABC affiliate, for example, to ensure that residents see the local station's mix of entertainment, advertising, and news. But the TV broadcasters wanted two—the existing one for their old analog-TV signals and a new one for their new digital-TV signals. The FCC, however, has made it clear that each broadcaster will get two channels only temporarily, while the broadcasters transition from old analog- to new digital-TV signals. But the two will not be permanent. That means the broadcasters will have to pay the cable companies for any second channel. Besides, without control over the set-top box, which provides the software brains for the digital TV, the broadcasters will be limited in their ability to extract more money from channel-hopping pedestrians who wander into their channel in the infinitely large online mall.

There is a fourth large player in this drama, namely the producers who make movies and television series. The final financial arrangements between these producers, the broadcasters, and the cable companies have yet to be decided. Piracy poses the major problem for the producers. Unless the digitized movies and TV shows are somehow protected against digital pirates—the professional types in Hong Kong and elsewhere, as well as the amateurs everywhere else—the producers will see prospective online customers buying perfect copies of their product at rock-bottom prices.

This drama has a host of bit players, too—the companies offering satellite television; the software and video-game developers such as Microsoft; the telecommunications firms selling Internet access via phone or wireless; and the publicly funded TV stations eager to offer arts and educational programming using digital signals. No final outcome to this tangled business battle, however, will be possible until consumers start using digital-TV services. So far, only 2 percent of the 70-plus million households in the United States have TVs capable of receiving digital signals, partly because digital TVs cost more than ordinary analog TVs.

But because of past and current investments, analysts expect progress over the next year or two. For example, many broadcasters have already begun investing in digital-TV equipment, ensuring more digital-TV broadcasts in the coming months. Also, the TV set makers are pushing down the price of digital TVs, perhaps to $1,700 per set by the end of the year, while producers are more willing to show new movies on digital TV. These trends might create a long-awaited snowball effect, much to the benefit of all the related industries, supporters of digital TV say.

Emergencies, in Digital

There's a national security reason for the government to subsidize the rollout of digital TV, says John Lawson, the president and CEO of the Association of Public Television Stations. Current emergency broadcast systems can be overloaded, but digital TV "can be a very powerful and flexible component of an emergency communications system."

Getting this capability, he estimates, would cost the government $200,000 for each broadcast site, plus about $300 for each receiver of the signals. The broadcast sites could include the 365 publicly funded TV stations, plus the 1,400 commercial stations. Receivers could be installed in police stations, schools, and other local government offices.

Of course, this proposal would help the association's member stations, which have already invested $758 million in digital-TV gear that remains under-used because few consumers have bought digital TVs, he said. Additional uses for digital-TV signals would help speed the purchase by consumers, and by schools, of digital TVs, thus allowing owners of the sets to receive his member stations' various art and educational shows in digital-TV format, he said.

To get from here to there, the association has hired consultant James Lee Witt, President Clinton's successful director of the Federal Emergency Management Agency. The association also has seven in-house lobbyists, and "we're making the rounds" on Capitol Hill, Lawson said.

— Neil Munro

To speed things along, Michael Powell, chairman of the FCC, issued a detailed letter in April urging the various industry players to voluntarily commit to a series of goals, such as the inclusion of five digital-TV channels on each cable-TV network. And since last year, Tauzin has brought the various industry players to a roundtable to work out their differences. So far, the letter and the roundtable have called for voluntary action by industry members, said Johnson, Tauzin's spokesman. "It is painfully slow, but we are making progress," he said.

But this reliance on volunteerism may be temporary. "Everyone recognizes that Congress is insistent on this transition [from analog to digital TV] taking place," Johnson said. "Either the affected industries work collaboratively or Congress and the FCC will do it for them, either through regulation or legislation."

Faced with this threat, each industry highlights its accomplishments and spotlights the others' shortcomings. Dennis Wharton, senior vice president for communications at the National Association of Broadcasters, says that 422 of his association's 1,300 member stations are already broadcasting digital signals. But, he said, few cable-TV companies are carrying these digital signals to viewers' living rooms, and too few digital TVs have been sold. The broadcasters already face a government deadline for digital broadcasting, and "we've argued that cable operators and TV set manufacturers should have similar pressure to make this transition a success." For example, "if there was a rule that [new] digital-TV sets were required to have this digital-TV tuning device [to receive digital signals] by a certain date, that would advance the transition rapidly," he said.

The 12 largest manufacturers of TV sets "are at the table trying to figure out how we can make this happen," said Jenny Miller, a spokeswoman for the Consumer Electronics Association. Powell's April letter called on the TV industry to include digital tuners in all new TV sets by January 2006, with lesser goals for January 2004 and 2005. The government's first priority, however, should be shortcomings in the cable sector, Miller said. For example, the cable-TV companies' set-top boxes don't preserve consumers' home recording rights, and are designed to "potentially control everything" that the consumer sees via the digital-TV set, including Internet services and the program guide that alerts viewers to programs they might like to see, she said.

But Robert Sachs, president and CEO of the NCTA, says, "The 10 largest cable companies are enthusiastically endorsing the Powell plan, and by January next year, would carry up to five high-definition [digital] signals." There's also plenty of competition to allay fears of the cable-TV industry's clout, he said, with 20 million households already getting satellite TV, in comparison to the 70 million households that get cable TV.

If industry is going to get digital TV out into the marketplace, consumers need cheaper digital TVs, he said. Sachs said that the producers who make TV programs must be assured that their work will not be pirated. To help the producers make their products available, the cable-TV industry has included anti-piracy protections in its set-top boxes, he said.

Amid this competition, there is harmony on one point—that all the industries are out to maximize their own position and weaken their rivals'. The electronics manufacturing companies, said one cable-industry official, "want to leverage our infrastructure, the one we built with our money, to derive revenue from our investment." The broadcasters are loath to meet the congressional deadlines for digital-TV broadcasts, because that would force them to give the existing nondigital channels back to the government for other uses, said an official lined up against the broadcast industry. And the cable companies don't want to lose any control over the set-top boxes, because that would weaken their ability to generate revenue from digital-TV consumers, said an executive from the electronics industry.

Such jockeying is inevitable. After all, according to Marc Smith, a spokesman for the NCTA, digital TV is indeed the Holy Grail for these competing industries.

NEIL MUNRO can be reached at nmunro@nationaljournal.com.

Bruised in Bentonville

For Wal-Mart, the customer has always been king. But lately the retailer has realized that it has other constituents—and some are mad as hell. Can the world's biggest company adjust?

ANDY SERWER

By some financial measures, the No. 1 company in the FORTUNE 500 had a pretty good year in '04. Wal-Mart yet again defied the laws of large numbers, with sales climbing 10% to an astonishing $288 billion. Profits rose 13%, to more than $10 billion, in spite of a soft Christmas season.

And yet Wal-Mart is embattled as it has never been before. Sex-discrimination litigation, wage and pay disputes, fights with unions, and other workplace problems have left the company at loggerheads with plaintiffs' lawyers, federal investigators, and even the chattering classes. From Chicago to New Orleans to California to New York (never mind Quebec and Mexico), news that Wal-Mart is coming to town is now often greeted with protests. Every week, it seems, a new untoward story comes to light: a multimillion-dollar settlement with immigration authorities over illegal workers; the resignation of a top company officer after allegations of financial improprieties; lawsuits delaying construction of dozens of Supercenters in California, a market critical to the company's growth. With characteristic zeal and efficiency, Wal-Mart has marched itself straight into a management and public relations quagmire.

As with most things at Wal-Mart, the problem goes back at least in part to Sam Walton, the visionary founder and leader of the company until he died in 1992. Sam disdained the press, publicists, and government relations, regarding them as wasteful distractions. Focus on serving the customers, Sam said, and everything else will take care of itself. Even after the company grew large enough to draw criticism as a destroyer of small-town America, Wal-Mart's buyers and merchandisers were moneymakers and heroes, and its lawyers and personnel execs were cost centers and zeros.

But now Wal-Mart is the biggest company in the world—inevitably a global symbol of business power—and it can't get away with such corporate isolationism anymore. It has other constituencies that need to be taken care of—millions of employees and local citizens, for example. Yet Sam's successors too often have followed the letter of his rules, not the spirit. He might have been an obsessive merchandiser, but Sam never would have put stonewalling the outside world above growing the company. "I think if Sam were alive today he wouldn't be jumping for joy over all the external communications we have to do," says Jay Allen, Wal-Mart's senior vice president of corporate affairs. "But he would see the need for it now."

The flat stock price is attributable in part to what one analyst calls "headline risk."

Until recently the company was unable even to admit that its world had changed, that it must address these problems. It is starting to do so now, but it has dug itself such a hole that so far it has not had much success. Wal-Mart has hired legions of publicists, lobbyists, and lawyers, and its senior executives have taken to giving tub-thumping speeches in defense of its actions. But the company's stock price is stuck where it was six years ago.

Defining Wal-Mart's problems isn't easy. Some have occurred because the company, now with 1.6 million employees worldwide, is just so big. Like other giant institutions (the military and post office come to mind), it is bound to have bad apples. Some problems stem from an ingrained attitude that the bottom line supersedes all. Some are the result of actions by antagonists such as unions. Still others seem to be the product of simple tone-deafness.

It is difficult, too, to assess the impact these problems have had on Wal-Mart's business. True, the company built or expanded 242 Supercenters in the U.S. last year—each producing an estimated $79.5 million in revenues on average, according to Morgan Stanley—and plans to build 240 to 250 more this year. But it has also had to scrap or delay plans to build stores in California, Illinois, and New York. Each unbuilt store is a marginal hit to revenues. And whenever there is a unionizing action or local friction over a new store, the company sends out lawyers, PR people, and anti-union teams—a marginal increase in costs. The flat stock price is attributable in part to what Deutsche Bank analyst Bill Dreher calls "headline risk." The overhang of a potential multibillion-dollar settlement from a gender-discrimination class-action lawsuit couldn't be helping matters much either.

To combat its problems, Wal-Mart has employed a variety of tactics, including carrots, sticks, money, lawyers, and jawboning. That's appropriate, given that it faces all manner of difficulties, but its actions can appear muddled and uncoordinated too.

Facing a raft of cases alleging workplace malfeasance, for instance, Wal-Mart is litigating some and settling others. On its website the company acknowledges that it is the subject of "more than 40 pending wage-and-hour cases seeking class certification status." Those are generally complaints in which employees claim managers tolerated or required off-the-clock work; the company is fighting the claims. On the other hand, the company recently paid a record $11 million settlement to U.S. Immigration and Customs Enforcement, settling a four-year-old federal investigation into the hiring of hundreds of illegal immigrants to clean floors at 60 stores around the country. The biggie, though, is the class-action gender-discrimination lawsuit certified last year, which could encompass the claims of 1.6 million women who have worked at Wal-Mart since 1998. The lawsuit alleges that women are underpaid and underpromoted relative to their male peers. It is the largest civil rights class ever certified and could potentially cost the company billions. For the time being, Bentonville is fighting this one tooth and nail.

As for employee misconduct, Wal-Mart CEO Lee Scott says he's now taking a hard line. "The world has changed, and so you have to react more dramatically and more aggressively, in a less forgiving, harsher way," he said in a recent interview. That seems to apply to the highest levels of the company. On March 25 board member Tom Coughlin, the onetime head of Wal-Mart's stores division, stepped down as a director. According to an SEC filing, Coughlin resigned because of a disagreement with the company over an investigation into alleged unauthorized use of corporate gift cards and reimbursements valued between $100,000 and $500,000.

"The world has changed, and so you have to react more dramatically and more aggressively, in a less forgiving, harsher way."

When it comes to unions, Wal-Mart's stance is implacable. And this fight may provide the clearest example yet of how the company's adherence to the old ways of doing business is hurting it in the present.

In the mid-1990s, Wal-Mart's growth slowed, and CEO David Glass and chairman Rob Walton saw the need to move beyond selling dry goods to middle America. They decided to bet on the Supercenter concept of huge stores as large as 200,000 square feet that include a full supermarket. They would plop down these Supercenters everywhere, in Texas, Florida, and New York. And they began eyeing California, too, where the company had a small presence. The plan was a smash hit. Within a matter of years, Wal-Mart became a giant in the supermarket business, and the company's stock took off again. Supermarkets like Kroger, Albertsons, Safeway, and Winn-Dixie (now in bankruptcy) came under tremendous pressure, and so

did the union representing many of the workers in those stores, United Food and Commercial Workers.

In 2002, Wal-Mart announced it would build up to 40 Supercenters in California. To compete, California grocery-store managements began looking to pare costs. The following year Safeway presented to its workers a contract that slashed medical benefits and wages. Safeway workers went out on strike. Soon thereafter the two other major chains in Southern California—Kroger, which owns Ralphs supermarkets, and Albertsons—locked out UFCW members at their stores. What followed was a bitter strike/lockout that left more than 60,000 grocery workers out of work until February 2004. In the end it was a draw—benefits were cut, but not as severely as management had wanted.

Today Wal-Mart has only three Supercenters in California (another three are under construction), compared with, for instance, more than 200 in Texas and more than 100 in Florida. Why so few? In part it's because lawsuits funded by local businesses and UFCW chapters are holding back construction. The lawsuits take advantage of California's tough Environmental Quality Act, which requires studies not only of wildlife and air quality but also of potential economic decay caused by store closings.

Wal-Mart officials say the suits will slow but not stop them. "The horse-and-buggy industry wasn't permitted to crush the car," argues Scott. "The candle lobby wasn't allowed to stop electric lights. Ultimately that's what this debate is all about."

There is a softer side to Wal-Mart's battle plan, though. For the first time the company is publicizing the millions of dollars it contributes to local community organizations. It is running a national TV image-advertising campaign. It has started a website, walmartfacts.com, to rebut its critics. It has engaged another PR firm, Hill & Knowlton, and it has hired dozens of communications specialists and dropped them into regional offices, state capitals, and Washington, D.C.

And not a minute too soon. Lots of big companies develop image problems, and a few even become part of a broad cultural debate (think McDonald's and nutrition policy). But Wal-Mart at this point seems to have moved into a league of its own. After a long critique of the company was published in the *New York Review of Books*, of all places, Scott responded with an open letter to the publication's readers. The University of California at Santa Barbara hosted a conference last April titled "Wal-Mart: A Template for 21st-Century Capitalism?" As you might imagine, the discussion was in no way Wal-Mart friendly. The conference's organizer, Nelson Lichtenstein, proposed this central thesis: Throughout U.S. history there has usually been one dominant company that essentially sets a benchmark living wage for the American worker. "Today that company is Wal-Mart, but its pay is so low, it can't be considered a living wage," Lichtenstein says.

On this point, Wal-Mart management says, there is a tradeoff. The more than a million Americans working at Wal-Mart are paid wages that might be higher, but if they were, Wal-Mart's goods would cost more, to the detriment of the 296 million of us who can shop at Wal-Mart. There is something coldly reductionist, though, about Wal-Mart's paying its workers so little that the only store where they can afford to shop is Wal-

Mart. It brings to mind an old Bob & Ray routine, a fictitious interview with one Hudley Pierce, CEO of the Great Lakes Paper Clip Co. When asked how his employees can possibly live on a wage of 14 cents a week, Pierce responds, "We don't pry into the personal lives of our employees. But as I understand it, our people live in caves on the edge of town, and they forage for food." Wal-Mart argues that retailing has always been a low-wage sector, and that the company has actually raised the standard in this business.

Away from university campuses and journals of opinion, though, can Wal-Mart find a way to stem the tide of criticism? "I look at it this way," says Jay Allen. "Thirty percent of the country don't care one way or the other about Wal-Mart. Thirty percent love us. Thirty per cent have sincere questions about us. And 10% hate us. We need to focus on the 30% that have sincere questions about us and work to answer their questions."

Wal-Mart is learning, but in some cases it's still bungling. Last year it raised public ire in Inglewood, Calif., when it attempted to circumvent local laws and essentially construct a Su-

percenter in the dead of night. Locals got wind of the project, organized, and voted it down. Plans for a store there have been scrapped. "What we did in Inglewood was wrong," says Allen. "We have to learn from those mistakes."

Scott is having to defend his company in the pages of the *New York Review of Books*, of all places.

But is it doing so? In Dunkirk, Md., a local ordinance was passed recently limiting the size of a store to 75,000 square feet to keep out big-box retailers. Wal-Mart has proposed building a 74,998-square-foot store there—and then erecting a 22,689-square-foot garden center right next door. That's following the letter of the law, but isn't it violating the spirit?

"We are going to find a way to serve customers," Allen says.

Airlines

Bankruptcies, terrorism, and high oil prices have rocked the airline industry. Customers complain about bad service and long lines. Are airlines doomed? Not a chance. The global economy cannot function without air travel. But the industry that emerges from the coming shakeout will need a whole new set of wings.

GIOVANNI BISIGNANI

"The Airline Industry Is Going to Collapse"

Never. Given the headlines of the past few years, it's not surprising that people think airlines are on the brink of disaster. Household names such as Canadian, Swissair, and TWA have disappeared. During the past five years, the industry has hemorrhaged more than $1 million *an hour*, racking up losses in excess of $43 billion. But total collapse is not on the horizon. More than 2 billion people fly each year, a number that grows by nearly 6 percent annually. More than $3.2 trillion worth of cargo is transported by air each year. Simply put, globalization, as we know it, would cease without the airline industry.

It is true, however, that many airlines are limping along. Today, 50 percent of the U.S. airline industry has filed for bankruptcy, including major players such as Delta, Northwest, and United Airlines. Last year alone, North American carriers lost well in excess of $8 billion. But the rest of the world doesn't have it so bad. European airlines are breaking even, with some even turning a profit. And Asian carriers are actually enjoying their fifth consecutive year in the black, with $1 billion in profits in 2005. To be sure, in a competitive industry with tight profit margins, every airline faces challenges staying aloft. But U.S. airlines have it far worse than most, because of hypercompetitive domestic markets and a labor force that is reluctant to change with the industry.

Countless businesses have been buoyed by the lowering of trade barriers, but airlines suffer because they still face enormous hurdles. The airline industry was among the first to operate globally, but it is still waiting for the benefits of globalization. Do we purchase cars or medications based on the nationality of a company's shareholders? If an Egyptian can spend a night at a Singaporean hotel in Hamburg, why can't an Australian fly a Brazilian airline from Mexico City to Miami? Airlines support 29 million jobs and $2.9 trillion worth of economic activity worldwide. Few industries so vital to the health of the global economy remain so restricted by archaic ownership rules.

"The Airline Industry Can Never Be Profitable"

Not so. A complex mix of factors has led to the industry's current state of crisis. For starters, an enormous amount of an airline's costs is fixed. Ten percent of costs go to monopoly suppliers such as airports and air navigation services. Labor is stubbornly difficult to control, accounting for an average of 20 percent of costs in Asia, 30 percent in Europe, and 38 percent in the United States. And one expense that is extremely volatile for airlines—the price of oil—has skyrocketed. Fuel is now a $97 billion bill that takes up an average of 25 percent of costs. If last year's oil prices were at the 2002 level of $25 a barrel, airlines would have made a profit of 5 percent. Airlines have responded with deeper cost-cutting and streamlining, but it's like fighting a serious illness with cosmetic surgery.

Airlines would become profitable if they were run like an equally strategic global industry, telecommunications. As the telecom sector was deregulated in the 1990s, key markets, such as Britain, Germany, and Japan, saw the price they could offer consumers decline by 30 percent or more. Airlines experienced the same drop in prices. So why is the global telecommunications industry so healthy while airlines continue to lose billions? Again, the answer is consolidation. A handful of telecommunication companies have developed into global businesses. Look at the British company Vodafone, which operates under its own brand in practically every major market in the world. No airline is allowed to approach anywhere near that model of success. Most countries remain content to treat airlines like cash cows, forever milking them with national prerogatives and taxes that raise the cost of doing business. Profitability will not be possible until governments get out of the way and allow airlines to join the globalized world that they were instrumental in creating.

"The Demand for Air Travel Remains Soft"

No. Despite severe shocks in recent years—including the attacks of Sept. 11, 2001, and outbreaks of avian flu—the demand for air travel is at record levels and is expected to grow an average of 6 percent each year for the foreseeable future. People need to fly. More important, people want to fly. World air travel declined only twice in the past three decades. The first time was during the first Gulf War, when four major American airlines went bankrupt; the second was 2001 through 2003. Less than two months after the World Health Organization gave the all-clear for travelers in SARS-affected regions, the number of passengers flying into Hong Kong's airport had more than made up for losses during the scare.

If history is a guide, the world's airline industry will double in size every 15 years. That means that by 2020, passenger numbers will grow from 2 billion to 4 billion. Cargo will increase from 39.5 million tons to 79 million tons. Moreover, air traffic typically grows at twice the rate of gross domestic product. Therefore, in booming economies, the demand for air travel will be particularly high. Air India has ordered 68 Boeing planes, one of the largest aircraft orders ever. And new, no-frills airlines such as Kingfisher and SpiceJet have taken off in India, where passenger demand is expected to grow by almost 12 percent annually during the next four years. The rate will be even higher in China. Nearly 30 million Chinese traveled abroad last year; the World Tourism Organization predicts that figure will exceed 100 million in 15 years. Its inbound traffic will increase too, as China becomes the No. 1 destination for foreigners with 137 million visitors expected in 2020.

"It's Never Been Safer to Fly"

Yes, but some regions are less safe than others. Despite financial difficulties, airlines still offer the safest form of transportation. In 2004, 428 people lost their lives in air accidents. But airlines carry 2 billion passengers annually. Compare that to 1945, when 9 million people flew with a similar number of fatalities. Airlines have steadily become safer over the course of decades.

But the reality today is that the record differs greatly from region to region. The accident rate in Africa, for example, is almost seven times higher than the global average. African skies carry only 4.5 percent of total global traffic, yet they account for 25 percent of accidents. As with other industries, many countries in the developing world simply don't have enough money or staff to devote to safety oversight. Moreover, airlines with limited resources often operate older aircraft, which require more rigorous maintenance. Still, for most of the world, safety has never been better. The first international standards audit for airline safety management is making improvements in all regions. Although only two years old, already 140 airlines, representing 70 percent of global traffic, have signed on to this industry-run program.

The same cannot be said for security. There is no doubt that airline security has been stepped up since the 2001 terrorist attacks, particularly in the U.S. domestic market. But, governments' failure to harmonize measures around the world makes this progress more cumbersome than necessary. Travelers are familiar with the hassle of long airport security lines. But they may be less aware of the complex data processing that goes on behind the scenes. Many governments require airlines to submit passenger information in advance of arrival, and ask for similar data in multiple formats to different divisions within the same department. Out of a $5.6 billion security bill each year, more time and money is spent by airlines on battling bureaucracy than helping governments guard against terrorism.

"Airlines Need More Regulation"

Absolutely not. Many people mistakenly believe that deregulation is at the root of airlines' troubles. They think the only solution to save the industry is to re-regulate, throw up barriers to market access, and turn airlines into something akin to a utility. But governments never truly deregulated airlines in the first place; they've only installed half-measures that offer the illusion of unfettered competition. Carriers remain at the mercy of monopoly suppliers—airports and air traffic control—that account for a bill of more than $42 billion each year.

Airlines do not need handouts, special treatment, or government subsidies. They simply need the basic freedom to do business like any other business—to serve markets where they exist, to merge or consolidate where it makes sense, and to make money or go bankrupt and die if necessary. Instead, airlines are stuck with absurd 60-year-old ownership rules that largely prevent them from consolidating across borders. This antiquated bilateral system was designed during an era in which many carriers were run by the state and international air travel was reserved for the elite. Airlines were beholden to Cold War foreign policy. That simply won't work in a world where airlines are intensely competitive businesses operating a mass transit system for billions of travelers.

Governments need to review the international regulatory framework that controls air transport. Airlines ostensibly operate in a free market, but so far only Europe has truly liberalized. There has been some successful cross-border consolidation, with the merger of Air France and KLM in 2003 and Lufthansa's gradual takeover of Swiss. But even they were cumbersome arrangements that didn't allow for maximum economic benefit. The United States and the European Union are in negotiations to permit greater airline access across the Atlantic. Such an "open skies" deal will help, but governments could lift restrictions on the flow of commerce even further.

"Low-Cost Airlines Will Save the Industry"

Not Really. Any frequent flyer knows that air travel has never been cheaper. Relative newcomers such as the United States' JetBlue, Malaysia's Air Asia, and Brazil's GOL have burst onto the scene in the middle of the airline industry's greatest financial crisis—and have met with success. Southwest is the most profitable airline in the United States, and Ireland's Ryanair consistently posts net profit margins of more than 20 percent. These airlines have forced change that is good for consumers and for the industry. Passengers can increasingly find comparable fares on major carriers and young upstarts.

Airlines are in a race to evolve into a low-cost industry, but the low-cost airlines alone won't be equipped to get us there. Their model works most successfully only on voyages that are less than three hours. These flights also often avoid major hubs. By doing so, they can't connect into networks that span the world. Furthermore, these airlines began with a big cost advantage because they didn't have the legacy of decades of labor negotiations. This edge will erode as time progresses, as operations develop complexity and costs creep into the process.

The cost gap between low-cost carriers and the major airlines has narrowed from 93 percent to 66 percent in just three years. The success of Southwest and Ryanair are exceptions in the low-cost sector. Most of their competitors don't generate enough money to cover their costs of capital. And even though some low-cost carriers may be profitable, many more go bankrupt. More likely, low-cost and traditional airlines will coexist—or merge. That will become even more evident as competition in the industry heats up.

"There Is No Room for Innovation in Air Travel"

Wrong. There are already fresh ideas to make flying more pleasurable and efficient in the future. The concept of all premium-class flights is gaining speed. Traditional carriers such as Lufthansa, as well as startups Eos and Maxjet, operate on strategic trans-Atlantic routes with planes that offer only luxury seating. Boeing recently completed the world's longest nonstop flight, a 23-hour trip eastward from Hong Kong to London. Airlines from 13 countries have placed orders for the double-decker, 555-passenger Airbus A380, which is scheduled to fly commercial passengers this year. Some of these planes may include private bedrooms and spa services. Virgin Atlantic CEO Richard Branson has proposed sending tourists into space, and he plans someday to use plant waste to fuel his fleet. And a handful of startups are building ultralight jet planes that could service small regional airports as air taxis.

Some airports have already evolved from utilitarian flight terminals to grand shopping malls. The economic returns from filling a passenger's time in the airport with good food and shopping has helped reduce the need for high landing fees. The next step is to ease a passenger's ability to move through an airport. Today, you may be asked to pull out your passport and ticket as many as five times to board a plane. Biometric technology that scans your face and matches it to your flight information will someday offer a one-stop check-in. Long lines at airports could become history.

Twenty years ago, no one could have imagined that Dubai International Airport would be a hub for global travel. In 2025, the busiest markets could be locations that seem on the periphery today. Airline traffic in Asia could easily replace North America and Europe in size and importance. We will probably have fewer carriers. And not every country will have its flag on an aircraft tail. If unleashed, commercial forces will find the best way to safely and inexpensively move people and goods around the planet. Ultimately, for the airline industry, that is the only way to fly.

GIOVANNI BISIGNANI is director general and CEO of the International Air Transport Association, a trade organization that represents 265 commercial airlines, including most major carriers.

Modernizing U.S. Antitrust Law: The Role of Technology and Innovation

THOMAS A. HEMPHILL

A ntitrust law is an important feature of the U.S. business environment, profoundly affecting the strategies and actions of firms of all sizes and in many industries. Furthermore, antitrust litigation can adversely affect the competitive outlook for a publicly-traded company that finds itself in the unenviable role of defendant. From time to time, the U.S. Congress has undertaken major reviews of current legislation to adapt it to emerging challenges in the economy. Thus, in July, 2004, the U.S. Antitrust Modernization Commission ("Commission") held its first public meeting in Washington, D.C. The Commission, a result of federal legislation passed in November 2002, is statutorily charged with four specific duties (Antitrust Modernization Commission Act, 2002):

- To examine whether the need exists to modernize the antitrust laws and to identify and study related issues;
- To solicit views of all parties concerned with operation of the antitrust laws;
- To evaluate the advisability of proposals and current arrangements with respect to any issues so identified; and
- To prepare and to submit to Congress and the President a report containing detailed findings and conclusions, together with recommendations for legislative or administrative action not later than three years after the first meeting of the Commission.

The bipartisan Commission has twelve members, with four appointed by the President, two each by the majority and minority leader of the Senate, and two each by the Speaker and the minority leader of the House of Representatives. The Commission is charged with reporting its findings to Congress by April 2007. This is the sixth time in U.S. history that such a national study commission or committee has been charged with making such a wide-spread review of U.S. antitrust law (Foer, 2003).[1]

As can be seen by its statutory charge, this Commission has no specific mandate or focus on any aspect of the federal antitrust laws. However, the Congressman who sponsored the bill creating the Commission, House Judiciary Committee Chairman F. James Sensenbrenner, Jr. (R-Wis.), attended the Commission's first public meeting (held on July 15, 2004). Addressing the Commissioners, Congressman Sensenbrenner

called for the Commission to study the following areas of antitrust policy concern: how the antitrust laws operate in the modern, information-driven economy; the intersection between antitrust law and intellectual property law; conflicts between U.S. and foreign antitrust law; the relationship between federal and state antitrust enforcement; the application of antitrust laws in regulated industries; and the length of time taken to conduct reviews of mergers (Antitrust Modernization Commission, 2004). To help establish its review and study agenda, the Commission proposed a Federal Register notice calling for public comment to be received by September 30, 2004 (Antitrust Modernization Commission, 2004).[2]

In this article, I will focus on identifying the major competition-related areas of technology and innovation which have been recommended for study in the public comments received by the Commission and conclude by offering personal recommendations on where the Commission should focus its efforts in these particular areas of study. But first, as a primer for those not as familiar with antitrust policy and law, I will briefly review the economic and social philosophy underlying essential U.S. antitrust statutes.

U.S. Antitrust Policy and Law

Antitrust policy, representing the philosophical foundation of the antitrust statutes, has historically consisted of economic, political, and social goals, all delineated in legislative histories or judicial interpretations.[3] Most American scholars of antitrust policy have identified four general objectives of antitrust policy that have emerged over the last century:

- the protection and preservation of a competitive economic environment;
- the protection of consumer welfare by prohibiting deceptive and unfair business practices;
- the protection of small, independent business firms from the economic pressures exerted by competition from big business;
- the preservation of small-town American values and customs.

Depending on one's disciplinary perspective, antitrust law may be viewed differently. In the case of Robert H. Bork (1978), a legal scholar, it is a form of business regulation. Contrarily, Irving M. Stelzer, an economist, views the antitrust laws as an effective tool for avoiding government regulation, thus leaving resource allocation to competitive markets rather than assigning it to public regulators (Stelzer, 1997). Furthermore, Stelzer makes a convincing case for the proposition that the absence of competition in the marketplace is more likely to result in direct regulation of prices and profits or direct government provision of a good or service. When antitrust policy fails to prevent the creation or maintenance of private monopoly power through unfair business practices, says Stelzer, direct regulation is the usual government response in a society built on democratic capitalism.

Maintaining and promoting a competitive economic environment and protecting consumer welfare are at the heart of the Sherman Act of 1890 and the Clayton Act of 1914, the essential legislation governing U.S. antitrust policy. These are considered the central objectives of antitrust policy as enforced by the U.S. Department of Justice's (DOJ) Antitrust Section and the Federal Trade Commission (FTC).[4] In general, the Sherman Act proscribes illegal acts of combining or conspiring to restrain trade (i.e., cartels and monopolizing behavior, rather than simply a "monopoly"); the Clayton Act enjoins various practices "that may be substantially to lessen competition, or to tend to create a monopoly." The economic reasoning behind these statutes argues that consumers will be best served by firms that compete vigorously for their purchases, thereby eliminating collusion and the maintenance of higher-than-normal product or service prices. Under Section 5 of the FTC Act of 1914, the FTC is authorized to investigate business conduct, practices, and the management of companies and to define what methods of competition are unfair and thus unlawful. This expansion in the interpretation of the earlier antitrust statutes was a legislative response to a growing recognition of certain business methods that could be used to exploit or mislead consumers.

In general, the language of the antitrust statutes is intentionally vague, allowing for the federal antitrust agencies to exercise their authority to interpret and enforce the laws according to the economic philosophy of the administration in power.[5] Specific changes in the antitrust statutes pertaining to business conduct or practices statutorily codified are rare and occur only in response to an overwhelming need for business management and public/private enforcement guidance. Not surprisingly, the theories of industrial organization economists are strongly incorporated into the enforcement policies of federal antitrust agencies, as well as the growing body of academic knowledge in the business fields of marketing science and organizational theory/strategy. As economics and management science have evolved, the contours of antitrust doctrine and enforcement policy have followed suit.

The modern interpretation of the antitrust statutes (especially Section 2 of the Sherman Act) emphasizes that modern firms may compete on the basis of "superior products" or "business acumen" and legally maintain a monopoly position (U.S. v. Grinnel Corp., 1966). This public policy emphasis on encouraging managerial and technological innovation is supported by both federal antitrust agencies in their enforcement of enabling statutes and by Congress in enacted legislation which encourages certain competitor collaborations.[6] Supporting an objective of facilitating an innovative market environment falls comfortably into the realm of an "economic" goal (i.e., the enhancement of consumer welfare and market efficiency), certainly in line with the post–1970s emphasis in antitrust enforcement. Simultaneously, encouraging innovation also addresses traditional societal political concerns for diffusion of private power and maximum opportunity for individual enterprise (Shenefield and Stelzer, 1999).

Technology and Innovation Issues

Throughout the 1990s, in speeches given by officials of the federal antitrust enforcement agencies, jointly published FTC-DOJ industry guidelines, and trial arguments of their attorneys, the federal antitrust agencies have focused on an emerging public policy objective: encouraging technological and market innovation (Beard and Kaserman, 2002). As then-chairman of the FTC, Robert F. Pitofsky, commented, "Innovation is more and more the central arena in which competition plays out. [It] is the hot issue for the foreseeable future (*Business Week*, 2000)."

As mentioned earlier, the Commission requested public comments recommending competition issues that the members should consider for its review and study agenda. As a result of this Notice, 35 interested parties, representing think tanks, industry and business associations, corporations, non-profit advocacy groups, academicians, business economists, and practicing antitrust attorneys, responded with suggested issues and questions that the Commission members should pursue. In this article, the comments relating to issues pertaining to technological change and market innovation will be presented, then categorized as a result of an analysis of the comments received (with representative sources cited).

Clarify the Interface Between Intellectual Property Rights and Antitrust Law

According to the Business Roundtable (2004), the antitrust laws and the intellectual property laws share a common objective: the enhancement of consumer welfare through the promotion of innovation. The antitrust laws promote innovation largely through promoting vigorous competition to stimulate innovation. The intellectual property laws stimulate innovation by enabling innovators to profit from their work. The different legal regimes sometimes come into conflict, principally where the antitrust laws arguably limit the exercise of the rights conferred by the intellectual property laws. In its comments, the U.S. Chamber of Commerce (2004) posits that antitrust enforcement should be consistent with intellectual property policy.

In its comments, Sun Microsystems, Inc. (2004) recommends that the Commission study whether antitrust law and policy should require standards-setting organizations to adopt procedures and intellectual property rights policies that require disclosure—particularly of the intellectual property to be incorporated in a proposed standard and relevant license terms—early in the standard development process and prior to voting on the standard in question (referred to as *ex ante* adoption). Sun also recommends that consideration should be given to permitting standards development working groups to discuss these matters so that informed decisions can be made on the desirability of incorporating intellectual property rights in the design of the standard.

Furthermore, the following questions might be considered by the Commission as a means to stimulate competition and innovation, and to protect intellectual property rights:

- Should legislation be enacted to create a new administrative procedure to allow post-grant review of and opposition to patents? (American Bar Association, 2004)[7]
- Should the appropriate decision-makers consider possible harm to competition—along with other possible benefits and costs—before extending the definition of patentable subject matter? (American Bar Association, 2004)
- Does the evolution of intellectual property rights in recent years raise the risk that protection of monopoly in the name of innovation will unduly reduce the role of competition? Should there be a dedicated court for intellectual property (American Antitrust Institute, 2004)?
- In what ways should conflicts between the goals of intellectual property and antitrust law be resolved? Should the U.S. Court of Appeals for the Federal Circuit ("Federal Circuit") be abolished or modified (American Antitrust Institute, 2004)?[8]
- Should compulsory licensing of intellectual property rights for the stated purpose of promoting competition be an acceptable practice (Association for Competitive Technology, 2004)?

The Antitrust Laws, Dynamic Markets and the Network Economy

Given the rapid changes in technology today and the ease by which new technologies and firms can produce and market products, many firms with a dominant market position may be "transient monopolies." The Commission is recommended to review the application of the antitrust laws to dynamic markets and determine how to best apply those laws to these new markets (Zywicki, 2004). Furthermore, the use of static, price-based theory in antitrust analysis of high technology industries may not be adequate to assess competition. Such industries raise difficult questions in assessing competition (Coleman, Pleatsikas, and Teece, 2004):

- How does one determine the "relevant" market to assess competition?

- What does market power and monopoly power mean in such markets?
- How should one analyze the likely impact of a particular action (such as a merger) on innovation?

The increasing prevalence of networks in the modern economy (e.g., banking, mobile telecommunications, and digital databases) has generated debate about antitrust law and policy. With network effects, consumers and businesses may reap significant advantages that flow from the many consumers that utilize the same provider or platform. As a consequence, competition in industries in which network effects are important and in which competing networks are not interoperable may be "winner-take-all" (or "winner-take-most"). In addition, once one firm (or standard) starts to look as though it may become the winner, the market can quickly "tip" to favor it, as buyers in search of the advantages of network effects jump on the bandwagon of the likely winner (American Bar Association, 2004).

Some have suggested that network effects raise new considerations for antitrust law because externalities promote anticompetitive practices such as lying and predation. As with other issues in antitrust, however, network effects can often be procompetitive and provide increased consumer benefits (Freedom Works Foundation, 2004).

Moreover, concerns have been raised about inefficient "lock-in," which constrains consumer choice to products of the dominant firm or an inferior technology path (called "path dependence"), even though superior alternatives may exist. Real-world markets, however, are very dynamic; and there is little evidence of detrimental lock-in (Freedom Works Foundation, 2004).

Considering the competitive dynamics of this new economy, the American Antitrust Institute (2004) asks a relevant question: Does the growth of network industries require any change in antitrust policy or analysis?

Assessing the Need for Legislative or Administrative Action

The comments and questions submitted by the interested parties provide a strong basis for the Commission to investigate important technology and innovation issues that are perplexing antitrust enforcers and corporations in the United States today. The issue of intellectual property rights and antitrust law affecting the very important de jure standards-setting process exercised in high-technology industries remains contentious—creating an increasingly chilly environment for standard development activities. Furthermore, the dynamic market approach to antitrust analysis, of particular relevance in rapidly evolving, high technology industries, can have a profound affect on whether the evidence supports a finding of an antitrust violation. Finally, the competitive importance of information and communications technology industries opens up a number of questions about the interpretation of antitrust analysis in the network-based economy.

Dennis W. Carlton, a University of Chicago industrial organization economist and member of the Commission, stated quite succinctly his idea of the best approach for the Commission members to successfully execute their Congressional charge:

> There have been a few, not a lot, [of] studies of the effectiveness of the antitrust laws, and I think one of the useful functions we could perform in coming up with a list of priorities is … identifying where we think our antitrust laws have worked well and … also [uncovering] evidence of where it [antitrust law] worked poorly. (Antitrust Modernization Commission, October 20, 2004., p. 38.)

Not surprisingly, changes in the antitrust laws are rare—and purposely so. They tend to be incorporated in agency policy and court holdings, which recognize empirically-based theories developed in the nation's economics departments and business schools. In his comments submitted to the Commission, Bork (2004) offers advice to Commission members which they should consider as they execute their Congressional charge:

> The antitrust laws, in my opinion, are performing well, in fact better than at any time in the past seventy-five years. It follows that I think there is very little need for 'modernization.'
>
> This is not to say that all cases are being decided correctly, but such mistakes as are being made are due more to the human element, which can never be eradicated, than to any systematic flaws in antitrust doctrine.

I agree with Dennis Carlton: where there is evidence that antitrust law has not performed well (i.e., the results of antitrust law, policy, and enforcement have not provided the anticipated economic benefits), the Antitrust Modernization Commission should focus its legislative and administrative recommendations on remedying these deficiencies. Early indications are that the Commission will be actively soliciting public comments throughout the three-year investigative process. For those economists, attorneys, industry executives, and academics still perplexed by many of the antitrust issues related to technology and innovation, 2007 cannot come too soon.

Notes

1. Other study commissions, described in Foer (2003), have included: The Temporary National Economic Committee (1938–41), The Report of the Attorney General's National Committee to Study the Antitrust Laws (1955), The White House Task Force Report on Antitrust Policy (the "Neal Report") (1967–69), The National Commission for Review of Antitrust Laws and Procedures (NCRALP) (1977–79), and the International Competition Advisory Committee ("ICPAC") (1998–2000).
2. See 69 Fed. Reg. 43,969 (July 23, 2004).
3. From the perspective of economists of the Chicago School, efficiency should be the only objective of antitrust policy.
4. The DOJ may bring both criminal and civil charges against defendants, while the FTC only civil charges. The state attorneys general may bring both criminal and civil charges to bear against a defendant, while private litigants (persons and companies) can only bring civil antitrust charges against a defendant, both at the state and federal levels. Nearly 95 percent of all antitrust enforce-

ment actions are initiated by private litigants. As pertains to compensation in civil cases, treble damages assessed against the defendant(s) are the norm.
5. The judiciary also has the authority to interpret the meaning of the antitrust statutes in their rulings (Shenefield and Stelzer, 1999).
6. See the National Cooperative Research and Production Act (NCRPA) of 1993. The NCRPA has two major technology policy goals: first, to increase the number of R&D and production joint ventures entered into by U.S. firms and second, to increase the global competitiveness of the United States in key technology areas of research, development, and production.
7. The American Bar Association drew its questions from Federal Trade Commission (2003).
8. The Federal Circuit was created in 1982 to promote uniformity in patent law. It has exclusive jurisdiction over appeals from the U.S. Patent and Trademark Office with respect to patent applications and from judgments in civil actions for patent infringements.

References

American Antitrust Institute. 2004. "Comments of the American Antitrust Institute on the Issues to be Included on the Commission's Agenda," September 30, @**http://www.antitrustinstitute.org/results.cfm** (accessed November 27, 2004).

American Bar Association. 2004. "Report of the Section of Antitrust Law of the American Bar Association to the Antitrust Modernization Commission," September 30, **http://www.abnet.org** (accessed November 27, 2004).

Antitrust Modernization Commission Act. 2002. Subtitle D, Public Law 107–273, November 2, **http://www.amc.gov** (accessed November 25, 2004).

Antitrust Modernization Commission. July 15, 2004. Public Meeting Transcript. Washington, D.C., **http://www.amc.gov** (accessed November 25, 2004).

Antitrust Modernization Commission. October 20, 2004. Public Meeting Transcript. Washington, D.C., **http://www.amc.gov** (accessed March 29, 2005).

Association for Competitive Technology. 2004. "Prevent Antitrust Suits from Undermining Intellectual Property and Stifling Innovation," No specific date cited. **http://www.actinline.org** (accessed November 25, 2004).

Beard, T. Randolph and David L. Kaserman. 2002. "Patent Thickets, Cross-Licensing, and Antitrust." *Antitrust Bulletin* 47:345–368.

Bork, Robert H. 1978. *The Antitrust Paradox*. New York: Basic Books.

Bork, Robert H. 2004. "Comments on the Status of the Antitrust Laws," No specific date cited. **http://www.amc.gov** (accessed November 25, 2004).

Business Roundtable. 2004. "Comments of the Business Roundtable Regarding Commission Issues for Study," September 29, **http://www.amc.gov** (accessed November 25, 2004).

Business Week. 2000. "Antitrust for the Digital Age," May 15, 46–48.

Coleman, Mary, Chris Pleatsikas, and David J. Teece. 2004. "Issues for Consideration: The Treatment of Innovation in Antitrust Cases," September 29, **http://www.amc.gov** (accessed November 25, 2004).

Federal Trade Commission. 2003. *To Promote Innovation: The Proper Balance of Competition and Patent Law and Policy*. October.

Foer, Albert A. 2003. "Putting the Antitrust Modernization Commission into Perspective," *Buffalo Law Review* 51:1029–1051.

Freedom Works Foundation. 2004. "Written Comments on the Antitrust Modernization Commission's Request for Public

Comment," July 23, **http://www.amc.gov** (accessed November 25, 2004).

Shenefield, John H. and Irwin M. Stelzer. 1999. *The Antitrust Laws: A Primer*, 3rd ed. Washington, DC: The AEI Press.

Stelzer, Irwin M. 1997. "A Conservative Case for Regulation." *The Public Interest* (Summer) 85–97.

Sun Microsystems, Inc. 2004. "Comments Regarding Commission Issues for Study," September 30, **http://www.amc.gov** (accessed November 25, 2004).

U.S. Chamber of Commerce. 2004. "Suggestions from the U.S. Chamber of Commerce Regarding Antitrust Issues that are Appropriate for Commission Study," September 30, **http://www.amc.gov** (accessed November 25, 2004).

Zywicki, Todd J. 2004. "Comments Regarding Commission Issues for Study," September 20, **http://www.amc.gov** (accessed November 25, 2004).

THOMAS A. HEMPHILL is a visiting instructor in the Department of Strategic Management and Public Policy in the School of Business at The George Washington University, Contact tomhemphill@comcast.net.

From *Business Economics*, Vol. 40, issue 2, April 2005. Copyright © 2005 by National Association for Business Economics (NABE). Reprinted by permission.

The Real Price of Gas

Executive Summary

This report by the International Center for Technology Assessment (CTA) identifies and quantifies the many external costs of using motor vehicles and the internal combustion engine that are not reflected in the retail price Americans pay for gasoline. These are costs that consumers pay indirectly by way of increased taxes, insurance costs, and retail prices in other sectors.

The report divides the external costs of gasoline usage into five primary areas: (1) Tax Subsidization of the Oil Industry; (2) Government Program Subsidies; (3) Protection Costs Involved in Oil Shipment and Motor Vehicle Services; (4) Environmental, Health, and Social Costs of Gasoline Usage; and (5) Other Important Externalities of Motor Vehicle Use. Together, these external costs total $558.7 billion to $1.69 trillion per year, which, when added to the retail price of gasoline, result in a per gallon price of $5.60 to $15.14.

Tax Subsidies

The federal government provides the oil industry with numerous tax breaks designed to ensure that domestic companies can compete with international producers and that gasoline remains cheap for American consumers. Federal tax breaks that directly benefit oil companies include: the Percentage Depletion Allowance (a subsidy of $784 million to $1 billion per year), the Nonconventional Fuel Production Credit ($769 to $900 million), immediate expensing of exploration and development costs ($200 to $255 million), the Enhanced Oil Recovery Credit ($26.3 to $100 million), foreign tax credits ($1.11 to $3.4 billion), foreign income deferrals ($183 to $318 million), and accelerated depreciation allowances ($1.0 to $4.5 billion).

Tax subsidies do not end at the federal level. The fact that most state income taxes are based on oil firms' deflated federal tax bill results in undertaxation of $125 to $323 million per year. Many states also impose fuel taxes that are lower than regular sales taxes, amounting to a subsidy of $4.8 billion per year to gasoline retailers and users. New rules under the Taxpayer Relief Act of 1997 are likely to provide the petroleum industry with additional tax subsidies of $2.07 billion per year. In total, annual tax breaks that support gasoline production and use amount to $9.1 to $17.8 billion.

Program Subsidies

Government support of US petroleum producers does not end with tax breaks. Program subsidies that support the extraction, production, and use of petroleum and petroleum fuel products total $38 to $114.6 billion each year. The largest portion of this total is federal, state, and local governments' $36 to $112 billion worth of spending on the transportation infrastructure, such as the construction, maintenance, and repair of roads and bridges. Other program subsidies include funding of research and development ($200 to $220 million), export financing subsidies ($308.5 to $311.9 million), support from the Army Corps of En-

gineers ($253.2 to $270 million), the Department of Interior's Oil Resources Management Programs ($97 to $227 million), and government expenditures on regulatory oversight, pollution cleanup, and liability costs ($1.1 to $1.6 billion).

Protection Subsidies

Beyond program subsidies, governments, and thus taxpayers, subsidize a large portion of the protection services required by petroleum producers and users. Foremost among these is the cost of military protection for oil-rich regions of the world. US Defense Department spending allocated to safeguard the world's petroleum resources total some $55 to $96.3 billion per year. The Strategic Petroleum Reserve, a federal government entity designed to supplement regular oil supplies in the event of disruptions due to military conflict or natural disaster, costs taxpayers an additional $5.7 billion per year. The Coast Guard and the Department of Transportation's Maritime Administration provide other protection services totaling $566.3 million per year. Of course, local and state governments also provide protection services for oil industry companies and gasoline users. These externalized police, fire, and emergency response expenditures add up to $27.2 to $38.2 billion annually.

Environmental, Health and Social Costs

Environmental, health, and social costs represent the largest portion of the externalized price Americans pay for their gasoline reliance. These expenses total some $231.7 to $942.9 billion every year. The internal combustion engine contributes heavily to localized air pollution. While the amount of damage that automobile fumes cause is certainly very high, the total dollar value is rather difficult to quantify. Approximately $39 billion per year is the lowest minimum estimate made by researchers in the field of transportation cost analysis, although the actual total is surely much higher and may exceed $600 billion.

Considering that researchers have conclusively linked auto pollution to increased health problems and mortality, the CTA report's estimate of $29.3 to $542.4 billion for the annual uncompensated health costs associated with auto emissions may not adequately reflect the value of lost or diminished human life. Other costs associated with localized air pollution attributable to gasoline-powered automobiles include decreased agricultural yields ($2.1 to $4.2 billion), reduced visibility ($6.1 to $44.5 billion), and damage to buildings and materials ($1.2 to $9.6 billion). Global warming ($3 to $27.5 billion), water pollution ($8.4 to $36.8 billion), noise pollution ($6 to $12 billion), and improper disposal of batteries, tires, engine fluids, and junked cars ($4.4 billion) also add to the environmental consequences wrought by automobiles.

Some of the costs associated with the real price of gasoline go beyond the effects of acquiring and burning fuel to reflect social conditions partially or wholly created by the automobile's preeminence in the culture of the United States. Chief among these conditions is the growth of urban sprawl. While monetizing the impact of sprawl may prove a challenging endeavor, several researchers have done significant work on the subject. The costs of sprawl include: additional environmental degradation (up to $58.4 billion), aesthetic degradation of cultural sites (up to $11.7 billion), social deterioration (up to $58.4 billion), additional municipal costs (up to $53.8 billion), additional transportation costs (up to $145 billion), and the barrier effect ($11.7 to $23.4 billion). Because assessment of the costs of sprawl is somewhat subjective and because study of the topic remains in a nascent stage, the CTA report follows the lead of other researchers in field of transportation cost analysis and reduces the total of the potential cost of sprawl by 25% to 50% to arrive at a total of $163.7 to $245.5 billion per year.

Other External Costs

Finally, external costs not included in the first four categories amount to $191.4 to $474.1 billion per year. These include: travel delays due to road congestion ($46.5 to $174.6 billion), uncompensated damages caused by car accidents ($18.3 to $77.2 billion), subsidized parking ($108.7 to $199.3 billion), and insurance losses due to automobile-related climate change ($12.9 billion). The additional cost of $5.0 to $10.1 billion associated with US dependence on imported oil could rise substantially, totaling $7.0 to $36.8 billion, in the event of a sudden price increase for crude oil.

Recommendations

The ultimate result of the externalization of such a large portion of the real price of gasoline is that consumers have no idea how much fueling their cars actually costs them. The majority of people paying just over $1 for a gallon of gasoline at the pump has no idea that through increased taxes, excessive insurance premiums, and inflated prices in other retail sectors that that same gallon of fuel is actually costing them between $5.60 and $15.14. When the price of gasoline is so drastically underestimated in the minds of drivers, it becomes difficult if not impossible to convince them to change their driving habits, accept alternative fuel vehicles, support mass transit, or consider progressive residential and urban development strategies.

The first step toward getting the public to recognize the damage caused by the United States' gasoline dependence is getting the public to recognize how much they are paying for this damage. The best way, in turn, to accomplish this goal is to eliminate government tax subsidies, program subsidies, and protection subsidies for petroleum companies and users, and to internalize the external environmental, health, and social costs associated with gasoline use. This would mean that consumers would see the entire cost of burning gasoline reflected in the price they pay at the pump. Drivers faced with the cost of their gasoline usage up front may have a more difficult time ignoring the harmful effects that their addiction to automobiles and the internal combustion engine have on national security, the environment, their health, and their quality of life.

The Truth About Oil

Pain at the pump has plenty of Americans ticked. Chances are, though, they are angry about the wrong things. Here are five myths many people believe about today's oil pinch—and what the real story is.

JON BIRGER

A fellow road warrior pulls up to the pumps at Fillup's Food Store in Panama City, Fla. He looks at the nearly $3-a-gallon price of unleaded, and then with one word sums up the feelings of drivers nationwide: "Crazy."

Crazy indeed. Not that long ago, though, it would have been madness to suggest that oil could go from $18 a barrel to $65 in four years—and even crazier to suggest that such a run-up wouldn't spark a painful recession, with consumers spurning trips to the shopping mall and businesses crippled by cost hikes. Conventional wisdom has held that there are price thresholds that can't be breached without affecting spending habits. In 2003, for instance, Republican pollster Frank Luntz spoke of $2-a-gallon gasoline as a "magic number" that, if crossed, would harm Republican reelection hopes. Well, gas passed $2 a gallon a month before the 2004 election, and the oil guy in the White House still won. Two bucks wasn't so magic after all.

A sustained run of $3 gas could be what finally kicks the legs out from under the U.S. consumer—already, Wal-Mart is blaming lackluster sales on high gas prices—but it's hard to know for sure. After all, so much of the conventional wisdom on oil has been wrong. That's a problem, because if the U.S. is ever to make progress on treating its oil addiction, it needs to understand its source.

Myth No. 1: Gas Stations Are Gouging Consumers.

REALITY: If consumers are getting gouged, then gas station owners are being impaled. When gasoline prices spike, as they have in the wake of Hurricane Katrina, windfall profits rarely accrue to gas station owners. Kim Do, owner of a Coast station in Pleasanton, Calif., reports that in the immediate aftermath of the storm, she lost 8 to 10 cents on every gallon of gas she sold. "Customers are very angry—they call my prices a rip-off," Do says. "I tell them, 'I'm just like you.'" In fact, because retail prices are stickier than wholesale ones, gas stations make the fattest profits when prices are *falling*—a point made in a recent study by Berkeley economist Severin Borenstein.

Pumping gasoline is a dog-eat-dog business even when prices are normal, especially with Costco and Wal-Mart now muscling in. Low profit margins on gas are why so many gas stations double as convenience stores. "The objective is to get you to fill up on coffee, not gasoline," quips Gene Guilford, director of the Independent Connecticut Petroleum Association (ICPA).

Those low margins can turn into no margins when there's a sudden rise in gas prices. Metropolitan service stations don't have much inventory stored in their underground tanks. That means they're buying gasoline from wholesalers at least once a day and are just as vulnerable as their customers to rising prices. What's more, most independent stations can't pass along all their costs because they compete with the likes of Chevron and Valero, which do have large inventories of lower-priced gasoline by virtue of being big refiners. During price spikes, the majors use this advantage to underprice fuel, relatively speaking, in hope of gaining market share. In Connecticut, for instance, the ICPA figures the retail price of gasoline should have been $3.31 cents a gallon on Sept. 7, adding up all the taxes and costs. But the actual retail average was $3.08. No matter: On Sept. 8, Connecticut attorney general Richard Blumenthal announced he was looking into price gouging by gas stations.

What about Big Oil? Aren't the giants guzzling profits? Sure, but there is nothing sinister about that—no cabal of cigar-chomping oil barons plotting how to squeeze the world for their evil ends. Yes, a few crooked traders were able to game the California energy markets for a time in 2001. But in a market as big and wide-open as oil, there are thousands of traders all over the world making the action. Unlike California power prior to the crisis, oil is a freely traded commodity. The markets, not the magnates, set the price.

Myth No. 2: Hedge Funds Are Inflating the Price of Oil.

REALITY: No, it's the Trilateral Commission in cahoots with the World Bank. Just kidding. Still, even many sophisticated people believe that hedge funds are driving up prices. Sean Cota, a Vermont heating-oil dealer who sits on the executive

Pump Primer

Gas prices vary by state because of differing tax and emissions rules. Here is a representative gallon, circa Sept. 7.

Distribution and marketing costs	$0.07
Credit card fees	$0.09
State excise tax	$0.18
Federal excise tax	$0.18
Dealer markup	$0.20
State and local sales tax	$0.23
Refinery cost and profits	$0.89
Crude oil cost	$1.54
Retail price	$3.38

committee of the Petroleum Marketers Association of America, points out that average daily trading volumes in NYMEX crude oil and heating oil futures have risen dramatically—61% and 36%, respectively—since 2000. When the trading volume of oil grossly exceeds consumption, he argues, that is a sign that hot money is firing up the market. "Prices are now being set by fear and greed, not by supply and demand," he concludes. His estimate: At least $20 of the current $65 price of oil is a byproduct of speculation by hedge funds and investment banks. Germany's Economy Minister, Wolfgang Clement, recently put the figure at $18, a sentiment echoed by Chancellor Gerhard Schröder.

That is not, however, an accurate reading of how financial markets operate. Take Cota's concerns about excessive trading volumes. Futures trading in all commodities far surpasses the amount consumed by end users. And according to NYMEX, hedge funds account for less than 3% of volume in oil futures (a figure Cota disputes). In any case, basic market theory states that high volume leads to more, not less, efficient pricing. That's why thinly traded stocks tend to be more volatile—and vulnerable to manipulation—than heavily traded names like Microsoft or GE.

"People make these kinds of arguments because they have their own ideas about where prices should be," says Stephen Figlewski, a finance professor at New York University's Stern School of Business and founding editor of the *Journal of Derivatives*. "Oil producers think prices should be high, and oil consumers think they should be low. But if the price isn't where they want it, the one thing they all agree on is that it must be someone else's fault." The truth is that emotion—fear of dwindling supply—drives oil prices harder than speculation ever will.

There have been a dozen or so oil shocks, and each time, cheaper oil has returned.

Even if speculators were dominating trading of oil and gas futures, it's still not clear that would lead to higher prices. Futures require two to tango. A hedge fund cannot purchase a contract to buy oil at $65 a barrel in November if someone else isn't prepared to take the bearish side of that bet. That someone else can be an oil company looking to offset some risk or another

hedge fund looking to profit from falling fuel prices. Data from the Commodity Futures Trading Commission show that the week before Katrina sidelined much of the Gulf oil industry, 14% of all short, or bearish, positions on crude oil were held by "noncommercial traders"—a subset that includes hedge funds and banks. This same group held only a slightly larger share—16%—of long, or bullish, positions. "For every hedge fund that's made money, I know a lot that have lost money," says Morgan Stanley chief economist Stephen Roach.

Still dubious? Consider this: The average hedge fund has gained only 2.1% year so far this year. The average managed futures fund (the type most likely to invest in oil) has actually lost money, dropping 6.6%. Why? Because many have been shorting oil, according to Merrill Lynch hedge fund analyst Mary Ann Bartels. So if hedge funds really are driving up oil prices, they're doing a lousy job of profiting from it.

Myth No. 3:
We're Running Out of Oil.

REALITY: This one is true. Sort of. Unlike wind or water, oil is not a renewable resource. So by definition we're using it up, in the same way that we are all dying all the time. The real question is, When will it become impossible (or impossibly expensive) to recover enough to meet demand? Answering that question is not easy. New discoveries and new drilling technologies have transformed the science of exploration, which is why global reserves have doubled since 1980 (to 1.3 trillion barrels) even as consumption has soared.

There's no shortage of oil experts, however, who say that the industry cannot keep up the pace, and that the age of ever-expanding reserves is over. These "peak oil" theorists argue that we need to prepare for an era in which supply trails demand, particularly given the fast-growing needs of China and India. The guru of the peak-oil set—and author of its latest manifesto—is Matt Simmons. A leading energy banker in Houston, Simmons spent years poring over oilfield engineering reports and concluded that some of the world's most important fields are thinning out. "I believe the Middle East has no spare capacity," he says. He's even more pessimistic about some newer fields like those in Russia and the deep waters of the Gulf of Mexico.

Simmons is no kook—his book on the subject, *Twilight in the Desert*, is a must-read in energy circles. But there is a Chicken Little aspect to the peak-oil viewpoint. There have been a dozen or so oil shocks over the past 60 years—all replete with handwringing over in-the-ground reserves—and cheaper oil has returned each time. "The one thing I've learned," says Roach, "is that oil is a mean-reverting commodity." This time around, Roach expects high fuel prices to dent consumption—he's predicting a downturn in travel and other discretionary spending—while spurring oil companies to dig deeper and farther afield for oil.

The analysts at Cambridge Energy Research Associates have done their own painstaking global survey of oil production, and they couldn't disagree with Simmons more. In their view, production could rise 16 million barrels a day by 2010, leaving a comfortable gap between supply and demand.

The real problem with the peak-oil argument has less to do with engineering than with philosophy. It lacks imagination. Thirty years ago few thought it would be possible to produce price-competitive oil from Canadian oil sands. Today the cost of producing that oil is about $20 a barrel and is still falling. Similarly, you can't rule out the idea that today's speculative energy technologies will become cost-efficient by the time Middle East oil production starts to wane. "The peak-oil argument underestimates the potential for technological progress," says Economy.com's Thorsten Fischer, who expects oil to fall to about $40 a barrel by next year. Simmons thinks prices could triple by 2010.

Peak-oil theory also overlooks alternative explanations for why oil exploration hasn't been terribly fruitful in recent years. It may be that there is oil to be found, but investors haven't given oil companies the requisite incentives to find it. Blame the dot-com boom. Having been burned by accounting cheats and profitless wonders, post-2000 investors demanded cash flow, dividends, and stock buybacks. So despite booming profits and revenues, Exxon Mobil spent less on capital and exploration in 2004 than in 2003. And the $11.7 billion figure for 2004 was $3 billion less than the company earmarked for dividends and buybacks. Of course, $65 oil has a way of changing priorities. After years of stagnation, drilling-rig counts have soared 36% since April 2004. There are 2,895 active rigs worldwide, according to Baker Hughes, the most since 1986.

Myth No. 4: The U.S. Is Running Out of Refining Capacity.

REALITY: So what? It's fair to say that in recent months supply has been straining to meet demand and that U.S. refineries had to work flat-out just to convert enough crude into gas to keep the pumps filled. Then Katrina came, knocking out 20% of the industry. But America's struggle to ramp up capacity—we haven't built a new refinery in 30 years, though many existing ones have expanded—does not mean doom. There are many products that the U.S. happily consumes in which we are not self-sufficient—think kiwi fruit or funny t-shirts.

The U.S. should easily be able to import gasoline and other refined petroleum products from India, the Caribbean, South America, and other places where labor costs, NIMBYism, and environmental regulations don't cripple new construction. The Department of Energy projects that worldwide refining capacity will increase 61% over the next 20 years. Says Fischer: "There's little reason to build a new refinery in the U.S. if you can do it faster and cheaper overseas." And while not all overseas refineries can produce gasoline that meets our environmental standards, who doesn't want to sell into the U.S. market? New plants will be, and already are, designed to meet American requirements.

Finally, if oil companies don't want to build, their customers may beat them to it: In mid-September, Virgin Group founder Richard Branson announced plans for a $2 billion refinery that will help his airline defray the high cost of jet fuel.

Myth No. 5: The Government Must Intervene to Bring Down Energy Prices.

REALITY: Nooooo! The last time the U.S. went down that road, in the 1970s, the end result was gas lines, shortages—and little change in prices. But evidently they don't teach much history in politician school anymore—a frightening number of elected officials seem ready to re-embrace price controls. U.S. Senators Carl Levin (D-Michigan) and Maria Cantwell (D-Washington) want to give President Bush the power to set gasoline prices. In Massachusetts, secretary of state William Galvin has proposed a moratorium on natural-gas price increases. Hawaii's Republican governor has signed a law imposing limited price controls on gas; it will be interesting to see how much gas is left for the state to control.

A confidence-boosting release of some crude from the Strategic Petroleum Reserve might help to calm tempers, but all in all, the best thing the U.S. can do to bring down oil prices is—nothing. Ask yourself, Which is more likely to deliver cheaper oil: bureaucratic controls or all those new drilling rigs that went up only because of the incentive provided by high prices?

Of course, "I did nothing!" won't fly as a campaign slogan. And in fact, there are things the U.S. could be doing to treat our oil addiction. Because here's another uncomfortable truth: The U.S. now imports almost 60% of the oil it consumes each year, and that figure will only grow. One unfortunate result: Prickly characters like Hugo Chavez have us over a metaphorical barrel.

For starters, Congress could raise fuel-efficiency standards for cars. Even a 10% improvement would save the equivalent of two million barrels a day by 2025—more than we now import from Saudi Arabia or Venezuela. We could reverse policies that encourage consumption, like the absurd tax incentives for small businesses to buy pickups and SUVs. We could ease some of the moratoriums on domestic oil and gas exploration. We could think harder about how to diversify supply; displace oil from uses not associated with transportation; and kick-start, through the wise use of market incentives, the journey toward a future beyond oil.

Years of relatively cheap oil—and low gasoline taxes—have allowed the U.S. to get away with being extraordinarily inefficient in our use of energy; we don't get nearly as much economic activity out of a barrel as our economic peers. The U.S. will never be self-sufficient in oil, even if we pave Alaska and drain the Gulf. But we can, and should, get more for our oil bucks. The U.S. is vulnerable to oil tremblors like the kind we are experiencing now because we have made a series of decisions—about taxes, subsidies, housing, transport, lifestyles—that have led precisely to this point. With the Gulf still damp from Katrina, it's time to ask if we can do it better.

FEEDBACK jbirger@fortunemail.com

The Eco-Economic Revolution

Getting the Market in Sync with Nature

If we want economic progress to continue, we must systematically restructure the global economy to make it environmentally sustainable. Here's a description of a future eco-economy, along with tips on future industries and job possibilities.

LESTER R. BROWN

Today's global economy has been shaped by market forces, not by the principles of ecology. Unfortunately, by failing to reflect the full costs of goods and services, the market provides misleading information to economic decision makers at all levels. This has created a distorted economy that is out of sync with the earth's ecosystem—an economy that is destroying its natural support systems.

An economy is sustainable only if it respects the principles of ecology. These principles are as real as those of aerodynamics. If an aircraft is to fly, it has to satisfy certain principles of thrust and lift. So, too, if an economy is to sustain progress, it must satisfy the basic principles of ecology. If it does not, it will decline and eventually collapse. There is no middle ground. An economy is either sustainable or it is not.

The market does not recognize basic ecological concepts of sustainable yield, nor does it respect the balances of nature. For example, it pays no attention to the growing imbalance between carbon emissions and nature's capacity to "fix" carbon, much less to the role of burning fossil fuels in creating the imbalance. For most economists, a rise in carbon dioxide levels is of little concern. For an ecologist, such a rise—driven by the use of fossil fuels—is a signal to shift to other energy sources in order to avoid rising temperatures, melting ice, and rising sea level.

An eco-economy would be one that satisfies our needs without jeopardizing the prospects of future generations to meet their needs. Creating such an economy is not a trivial undertaking; it is nothing less than an Environmental Revolution.

Ecology over Economics

Ecologists understand the processes that support life on Earth. They understand the fundamental role of photosynthesis, the concept of sustainable yield, the role of nutrient cycles, the hydrological cycle, the sensitive role of climate, and the intricate relationship between the plant and animal kingdoms. They know that the earth's ecosystems supply services as well as goods and that the former are often more valuable than the latter.

A sustainable economy respects the sustainable yield of the ecosystems on which it depends: fisheries, forests, rangelands, and croplands. A particular fishery can sustain a catch of a certain size, but if the demands on the fishery exceed the sustainable yield by even 2% a year, the fish stocks will begin to shrink and will eventually disappear. As long as the harvest does not exceed the sustainable yield, it can be sustained in perpetuity. The same is true for forests and rangelands.

Nature also relies on balances. These include balances between soil erosion and new soil formation, between carbon emissions and carbon fixation, and between trees dying and trees regenerating.

Nature depends on cycles to maintain life. In nature, there are no linear flow-throughs, no situations where raw materials go in one end and garbage comes out the other. In nature, one organism's waste is another's sustenance, and nutrients are continuously cycled. This system works. Our challenge is to emulate it in the design of the economy.

Ecologists appreciate the role of photosynthesis, the process by which plants convert solar energy into the biochemical energy that supports life on the earth. Anything that reduces the photosynthetic product, such as desertification, the paving of productive land, or the acidification of lakes by acid rain, reduces the productivity of the earth in the most fundamental sense.

Despite this long-standing body of ecological knowledge, national governments have expanded economic activity with little regard for sustainable yields or the fragile balances in nature. Over the last half century, the sevenfold expansion of the global economy has pushed the demand on local ecosystems beyond the sustainable yield in country after country. The fivefold growth in the world fish catch since 1950 has pushed the demand of most oceanic fisheries past their ability to produce fish sustainably. The sixfold growth in the worldwide demand for paper is shrinking the world's forests. The doubling of the world's herds of cattle and flocks of sheep and goats since 1950 is damaging rangelands, converting them to desert.

The clear-cutting of a forest may be profitable for a logging firm, but it is economically costly to society.

An ecologist not only recognizes that the services provided by ecosystems may sometimes be worth more than the goods, but that the value of services needs to be calculated and incorporated into market signals if they are to be protected. Although calculating services is not a simple matter, any reasonable estimate is far better than assuming that the costs are zero, as is now the case. For example, a forest in the upper reaches of a watershed may provide services—such as flood control and the recycling of rainfall inland—that are several times more valuable than its timber yield. Unfortunately, market signals do not reflect this, because the loggers who are cutting the trees do not bear the costs of the reduction in services. National economic policies and corporate strategies are based largely on market signals. The clear-cutting of a forest may be profitable for a logging firm, but it is economically costly to society.

Another major failure of the market to provide reliable information comes when governments subsidize the depletion of resources or environmentally destructive activities. For example, over several decades the U.S. Forest Service used taxpayer money to build roads into national forests so that logging companies could clear-cut forests. This subsidy only artificially lowered the costs of lumber and paper, and it led to flooding, soil erosion, and the silting of streams and rivers. In the Pacific Northwest, it destroyed highly productive salmon fisheries. And all this destruction was underwritten by taxpayers.

In a world where the demands of the economy are pressing against the limits of natural systems, relying on distorted market signals to guide investment decisions is a recipe for disaster. Historically, for example, when the supply of fish was inadequate, the price would rise, encouraging investment in additional fishing trawlers. When there were more fish in the sea than we could ever hope to catch, the market worked well. Today, with the fish catch often exceeding the sustainable yield, investing in more trawlers in response to higher prices will simply accelerate the collapse of these fisheries.

A similar situation exists with other natural systems, such as aquifers, forests, and rangelands. Once the climbing demand for water surpasses the sustainable yield of aquifers, the water tables begin to fall and wells go dry. The market says drill deeper wells. Farmers engage in a competitive orgy of well drilling, chasing the water table downward. On the North China Plain, where 25% of the country's grain is produced, this process is under way. In Hebei Province, data for 1999 show 36,000 wells, mostly shallower ones, being abandoned during the year as

55,000 new, much deeper wells were drilled. In Shandong Province, 31,000 were abandoned and 68,000 new wells were drilled.

In an eco-economy, drilling additional wells would be banned once a water table showed signs of falling. Instead of spending money to dig deeper wells, investments would be channeled into measures to boost water efficiency and to stabilize population in order to bring water use into balance with the sustainable supply.

Evidence is accumulating that our global economy is slowly undermining itself on several fronts. If we want economic progress to continue, we have little choice but to systematically restructure the global economy in order to make it environmentally sustainable.

Imagining the Scope of Change

Converting our economy into an eco-economy is a monumental undertaking. There is no precedent for transforming an economy shaped largely by market forces into one shaped by the principles of ecology.

The scale of projected economic growth outlines the dimensions of the challenge. The growth in world output of goods and services from $6 trillion in 1950 to $43 trillion in 2000 has caused environmental devastation on a scale that we could not easily have imagined a half century ago. If the world economy continued to expand at 3% annually, the output of goods and services would increase fourfold over the next half century, reaching $172 trillion.

Building an eco-economy in the time available requires rapid systemic change. We will not succeed with a project here and a project there. We are winning occasional battles now, but we are losing the war because we do not have a strategy for the systemic economic change that will put the world on an environmentally sustainable development path.

Although the concept of environmentally sustainable development evolved a quarter century ago, not one country has a strategy to build an eco-economy—to restore carbon balances, to stabilize population and water tables, and to conserve its forests, soils, and diversity of plant and animal life. We can find individual countries that are succeeding with one or more elements of the restructuring, but not one that is progressing satisfactorily on all fronts.

Nevertheless, glimpses of the eco-economy are clearly visible in some countries. For example, 31 countries in Europe, plus Japan, have stabilized their population size, satisfying one of the most basic conditions of an eco-economy. Europe has stabilized its population within its food-producing capacity, leaving it with an exportable surplus of grain to help fill the deficits in developing countries. China—the world's most populous country—now has lower fertility than the United States and is moving toward population stability.

Denmark is the eco-economy leader. It has stabilized its population, banned the construction of coal-fired power plants, banned the use of non-refillable beverage containers, and is now getting 15% of its electricity from wind. In addition, it has restructured its urban transport network; now 32% of all trips in

Today's Economy vs. Tomorrow's Eco-Economy

Today's Economy	Eco-Economy
Shaped by market forces.	Respects principles of ecology.
Unsustainable: Maximizes profit regardless of consequences to the ecosystem.	Sustainable: Respects carrying capacity of systems; e.g., does not exceed sustainable oceanic fish catch.
Disregards nature's services.	Recognizes ecosystems' natural services.
Consumes dwindling supply of fossil fuels.	Relies on renewable resources such as wind, solar, and geothermal energy.
Pollutes the environment and destabilizes climate.	Minimal pollution, climate-neutral.
Carbon-based auto industry dependent on oil from politically unstable Middle East.	Hydrogen-based fuel-cell auto industry not reliant on specific country source.
Contributes to noisy, congested, and polluted cities.	Will create rail-centered, bicycle-friendly cities that offer less stress and pollution, more exercise.
Likely to decline in not-too-distant future as natural supplies deteriorate.	Will create major new industries; e.g., the wind industry will bring income and jobs from manufacturing, installation, and maintenance.

Source: *Eco-Economy*

Copenhagen are on bicycle. Denmark is still not close to balancing carbon emissions and fixation, but it is moving in that direction.

An eco-economy would be one that satisfies our needs without jeopardizing the prospects of future generations to meet their needs.

Other countries have also achieved specific goals. A reforestation program in South Korea, begun more than a generation ago, has blanketed the country's hills and mountains with trees. Costa Rica has a plan to shift entirely to renewable energy by 2025. Iceland, working with a consortium of corporations led by Shell and DaimlerChrysler, plans to be the world's first hydrogen-powered economy.

So we can see pieces of the eco-economy emerging, but systemic change requires a fundamental shift in market signals—signals that respect the principles of ecological sustainability. Unless we are prepared to shift taxes from income to environmentally destructive activities, such as carbon emissions and the wasteful use of water, we will not succeed in building an eco-economy.

Restoring the balances of nature in energy production depends on shifting from a carbon-based economy to a hydrogen-based one. Even the most progressive oil companies, such as BP and Royal Dutch/Shell, that are talking extensively about building a solar/hydrogen energy economy are still investing overwhelmingly in oil, with funds going into climate-benign sources accounting for a minute share of their investment.

Reducing soil erosion to the level of new soil formation will require changes in farming practices. In some situations, it will mean shifting from intense tillage to minimum tillage or no tillage. Agroforestry will loom large in an eco-economy. Restoring forests that recycle rainfall inland and control flooding means reversing decades of tree cutting and land clearing with forest restoration, an activity that will require millions of people planting billions of trees.

Building an eco-economy will affect every facet of our lives. It will alter how we light our homes, what we eat, where we live, how we use our leisure time, and how many children we have. It will give us a world where we are a part of nature, instead of estranged from it.

Restructuring the Economy

We can now see what an eco-economy looks like. Instead of running on fossil fuels, it will be powered by renewable sources of energy, such as wind and sunlight, and by geothermal energy from within the earth. It will be hydrogen-based instead of carbon-based. Cars and buses will run on fuel-cell engines powered by electricity produced with an electrochemical process using hydrogen as the fuel instead of internal combustion engines. With fuel cells powered by hydrogen, there is no climate-disrupting carbon dioxide or noxious health-damaging pollutants; only water is emitted.

In the new economy, atmospheric carbon dioxide levels will be stable. In contrast to today's energy economy, where the world's reserves of oil and coal are concentrated in a handful of countries, energy sources in the eco-economy will be widely dispersed—as widely distributed as sunlight and wind. The world's heavy dependence on the Middle East for much of its energy will likely decline as the new climate-benign energy sources and fuel-cell engines take over.

The energy economy will be essentially a solar/hydrogen economy with various energy sources deriving from the sun used either directly for heating and cooling or indirectly to produce electricity. Wind-generated electricity, which is likely to be the lowest-cost source of energy, will be used to electrolyze water, producing hydrogen. This provides a means of both storing and transporting wind energy. Initially, existing natural gas pipelines will be used to distribute hydrogen. But over the longer term, both natural gas and oil pipeline networks can be adapted to carry hydrogen as the world shifts from a carbon-based to a hydrogen-based economy.

The transport systems of cities have already begun to change. Instead of the noisy, congested, polluting, auto-centered transport

Declining Industries in an Eco-Economy

Industry	Description
Coal mining	The 7% decline in world coal burning since it peaked in 1996 will continue in the years ahead.
Oil pumping	Projections based on shrinking oil reserves indicate production will peak and start declining in the next 5-20 years. Concern about global warming could bring the decline closer.
Nuclear power	Although public concern focuses on safety issues, it is the high cost that is ensuring the industry's decline.
Clear-cut logging	The rapid spread in eco-labeling of forest products will likely force logging firms to change to sustainable harvesting or be driven out of business.
Manufacture of throwaway products	As efforts to close the materials cycle intensify, many throwaway products will either be banned or taxed out of existence.
Automobile manufacturing	As world population urbanizes, the conflict between the automobile and the city will intensify, reducing dependence of automobiles.

Source: *Eco-Economy*

Examples of Expanding Industries in an Eco-Economy

Industry	Description
Fish farming	Although growth will slow from the double-digit rate of the last decade, rapid expansion is likely to continue.
Bicycle manufacturing	Because bicycles are affordable, nonpolluting, quiet, require little parking space, and provide much-needed exercise in exercise-deprived societies, they will become increasingly common.
Wind-farm construction	Wind-electricity generation, including off-shore wind farms, will grow rapidly over the next few decades, until wind is supplying most of the world's electricity.
Wind-turbine manufacturing	Today the number of utility-scale wind turbines is measured in the thousands, but soon it will be measured in the millions, creating an enormous manufacturing opportunity.
Hydrogen generation	As the transition from a carbon-based to a hydrogen-based energy economy progresses, hydrogen generation will become a key industry.
Fuel-cell manufacturing	As fuel cells replace internal-combustion engines in automobiles and begin generating power in buildings, a huge market will evolve.
Solar-cell manufacturing	For many of the 2 billion people living in rural Third World communities who lack electricity, solar cells will be the best bet for electrification.
Light-rail construction	As people tire of the traffic congestion and pollution associated with the automobile, cities in industrial and developing countries alike will be turning to light rail to provide mobility.
Tree planting	As efforts to reforest the earth gain momentum and as tree plantations expand, tree planting will emerge as a leading economic activity.

Source: *Eco-Economy*

systems of today, cities will have rail-centered transport systems, and they will be bicycle- and pedestrian-friendly, offering more mobility, more exercise, cleaner air, and less frustration.

Urban transport systems will have the same components as they do today: automobile, rail, bus, and bicycle. The difference will be in the mix. As more city planners recognize the inherent conflict between the automobile and the city, cleaner and more efficient transport systems will develop. Urban personal mobility will increase as automobile use and traffic congestion decline.

The materials sector of the eco-economy will look far different, too, as it shifts from the linear economic model, where materials go from the mine or forest to the landfill, to the reuse/recycle model, yielding no waste and nothing for the landfills.

One of the keys to reversing the deforestation of the earth is paper recycling; the potential here has been only partly realized. A second key is developing alternative energy sources that will reduce the amount of wood used as fuel. In addition, boosting the efficiency of wood burning can measurably lighten the load on forests.

Another promising option is the use of carefully designed, ecologically managed, and highly productive tree plantations. A small area devoted to plantations may be essential to protecting forests at the global level. Plantations can yield several times as much wood per hectare as can a natural forest.

In the economy of the future, the use of water will be in balance with supply. Water tables will be stable, not falling. The economic restructuring will be designed to raise water productivity in every facet of economic activity.

In this environmentally sustainable economy, harvests from oceanic fisheries, a major source of animal protein in the human diet, will be reduced to the sustainable yield. Additional demand will be satisfied by fish farming. This is, in effect, an aquatic version of the same shift that occurred during the transition from hunting and gathering to farming. The freshwater, herbivorous carp polyculture on which the Chinese rely heavily for their vast production of farmed fish offers an ecological model for the rest of the world.

A somewhat similar situation exists for rangelands. One of the keys to alleviating the excessive pressure on rangelands is to feed livestock the crop residues that are otherwise being burned for fuel or for disposal. This trend, already well under way in India and China, may hold the key to stabilizing the world's rangelands.

And finally, the new economy will have a stable population. Over the longer term, the only sustainable society is one in which couples have an average of two children.

Creating New Industries

Describing the eco-economy is obviously a somewhat speculative undertaking. In the end, however, it is not as open ended as it might seem, because the eco-economy's broad outlines are defined by the principles of ecology.

What is not so clear is how ecological principles will translate into economic design. For example, each country has a unique combination of renewable energy sources that will power its economy. Some countries may draw broadly on all their renewable energy sources, while others may concentrate heavily on one that is particularly abundant, such as wind or solar energy. A country with a wealth of geothermal energy may choose to structure its energy economy around this subterranean energy source.

Building a new economy involves phasing out old industries, restructuring existing ones, and creating new ones. World coal use is already being phased out, dropping 7% since peaking in 1996. It is being replaced by efficiency gains in some countries, by natural gas in others (such as the United Kingdom and China), and by wind power in others (such as Denmark).

The automobile industry faces a major restructuring as it changes power sources, shifting from the gasoline-powered internal combustion engine to the hydrogen-powered fuel-cell engine. This shift from the explosive energy that derives from igniting gasoline vapor to a chemical reaction that generates electricity will require both a retooling of engine plants and the retraining of automotive engineers and automobile mechanics.

The new economy will also bring major new industries, ones that either do not yet exist or that are just beginning. Wind electricity generation is one such industry. Now in its embryonic stage, it promises to become the foundation of the new energy economy. Millions of turbines soon will be converting wind into electricity, becoming part of the global landscape. In many countries, wind will supply both electricity and, through the electrolysis of water, hydrogen. Together, electricity and hydrogen can meet all the energy needs of a modern society.

In effect, there will be three new subsidiary industries associated with wind power: turbine manufacturing, installation, and maintenance. Manufacturing facilities will be found in scores of countries, industrial and developing. Installation, which is basically a construction industry, will be more local in nature. Maintenance, since it is a day-to-day activity, will be a source of ongoing local employment.

The robustness of the wind turbine industry was evident in 2000 and 2001 when high-tech stocks were in a free fall worldwide. While high-tech firms as a group were performing poorly, sales of wind turbines were climbing, pushing the earnings of turbine manufacturers to the top of the charts. Continuing growth of this sector is expected for the next few decades.

As wind power emerges as a low-cost source of electricity and a mainstream energy source, it will spawn another industry: hydrogen production. Once wind turbines are in wide use, there will be a large, unused capacity during the night when the demand for electricity drops. With this essentially free electricity, turbine owners can turn on the hydrogen generators and convert the wind power into hydrogen, ideal for fuel-cell engines. Hydrogen generators will start to replace oil refineries. The wind turbine will replace both the coal mine and the oil well. Both wind turbines and hydrogen generators will be widely dispersed as countries take advantage of local wind resources.

Changes in the world food economy will also be substantial. Some of these, such as the shift to fish farming, are already under way. The fastest-growing subsector of he world food economy during the 1990s was aquaculture, expanding at more than 11% a year. Fish farming is likely to continue to expand simply because of its efficiency in converting grain into animal protein.

Even allowing for slower future growth in aquaculture, fish farm output will likely overtake beef production before 2010. Perhaps more surprising, fish farming could eventually exceed the oceanic fish catch. Indeed, for China—the world's leading consumer of seafood—fish farming already supplies two-thirds of the seafood, while the oceanic catch accounts for the other third. With this development, new jobs will be created: aquatic ecologist, fish nutritionist, and marine veterinarian.

Another growth industry of the future is bicycle manufacturing and servicing. Because the bicycle is nonpolluting, frugal in its use of land, and provides the exercise much needed in sedentary societies, future reliance on it is expected to grow. As recently as 1965, the production of cars and bikes was essentially the same, but today more than twice as many bikes as cars are manufactured each year. Among industrial countries, the urban transport model being pioneered in the Netherlands and Denmark, where bikes are featured prominently, gives a sense of the bicycle's future role worldwide.

As bicycle use expands, interest in electrically assisted bikes is also growing. These bikes are similar to existing bicycles, except for a tiny battery-powered electric motor that can either power the bicycle entirely or assist elderly riders or those living in hilly terrain, and their soaring sales are expected to continue climbing in the years ahead.

Just as the last half century has been devoted to raising land productivity, the next half century will be focused on another growth industry: raising water productivity. Virtually all societies will be turning to the management of water at the watershed level in order to manage available supply most efficiently. Irrigation technologies will become more efficient. Urban wastewater recycling will become common. At present, water tends to flow into and out of cities, carrying waste with it. In the future, water will be used over and over, never discharged. Since water does not wear out, there is no limit to how long it can be used, as long as it is purified before reuse.

Another industry that will play a prominent role in the new economy, one that will reduce energy use, is teleconferencing. Increasingly for environmental reasons and to save time, individuals will be "attending" conferences electronically with both audio and visual connections. This industry involves developing the electronic global infrastructure, as well as the services, to make teleconferencing possible. One day there may be thousands of firms organizing electronic conferences.

New Jobs in the Eco-Economy

Restructuring the global economy will create not only new industries, but also new jobs—indeed, whole new professions and new specialties within professions. For example, as wind becomes an increasingly prominent energy source, thousands of wind meteorologists will be needed to analyze potential wind sites, monitor wind speeds, and select the best sites for wind farms. The better the data on wind resources, the more efficient the industry will become.

Wind engineers will be hired to design customized wind turbines. The appropriate turbine size and design can vary widely according to site. It will be the job of wind engineers to tailor designs to specific wind regimes in order to maximize electricity generation.

Environmental architecture is another fast-growing profession. Among the signposts of an environmentally sustainable economy are buildings that are in harmony with the environment. Environmental architects design buildings that are energy- and materials-efficient and that maximize natural heating, cooling, and lighting. In a future of water scarcity, watershed hydrologists will be in demand. It will be their responsibility to understand the hydrological cycle, including the movement of underground water, and to know the depth of aquifers and determine their sustainable yield. They will be at the center of watershed management regimes.

As the world shifts from a throwaway economy, engineers will be needed to design products that can be recycled—from cars to computers. Once products are designed to be disassembled quickly and easily into component parts and materials, comprehensive recycling is relatively easy.

Technologies used in recycling are sometimes quite different from those used in producing from virgin raw materials. Within the U.S. steel industry, for example, where nearly 60% of all steel is produced from scrap, the technologies used differ depending on the feedstock. Steel manufactured in electric arc furnaces from scrap uses far less energy than traditional open-hearth furnaces using pig iron. Recycling engineers will be responsible for closing the materials loop, converting the linear flow-through economy into a comprehensive recycling economy.

In countries with a wealth of geothermal energy, it will be up to geothermal geologists to locate the best sites either for supplying power plants or for tapping directly to heat buildings.

Retraining petroleum geologists to master geothermal technologies is one way of satisfying the likely surge in demand for geothermal geologists.

If the world is to stabilize population sooner rather than later, it will need far more family-planning midwives in Third World communities. This growth sector will be concentrated largely in developing countries, where millions of women lack access to family planning. The same family-planning counselors who advise on reproductive health and contraceptive use can also play a central role in controlling the spread of HIV.

> ## In scale, the Environmental Revolution is comparable to the Agricultural and Industrial Revolutions that preceded it.

Another pressing need, particularly in developing countries, is for sanitation-system engineers who can design sewage systems not dependent on water, a trend that is already under way in some water-scarce countries. As it becomes clear that using water to wash waste away is a reckless use of a scarce resource, a new breed of sanitation engineers will be in wide demand. Washing waste away is even less acceptable today as marine ecosystems are overwhelmed by nutrient flows. Apart from the ecological disruption of a water-based disposal method, there are also much higher priorities in the use of water, such as drinking, bathing, and irrigation.

Yet another new specialty that is likely to expand rapidly in agriculture as productive farmland becomes scarce is that of the agronomist who specializes in multiple cropping and intercropping. This position requires expertise both in the selection of crops that can fit together well in a tight rotation in various locales and in agricultural practices that facilitate multiple cropping.

Investing in the Environmental Revolution

Restructuring the global economy so that economic progress can be sustained represents the greatest investment opportunity in history. The conceptual shift is comparable to that of the Copernican Revolution in the sixteenth century. In scale, the Environmental Revolution is comparable to the Agricultural and Industrial Revolutions that preceded it.

The Agricultural Revolution involved restructuring the food economy, shifting from a nomadic lifestyle based on hunting and gathering to a settled lifestyle based on tilling the soil. Although agriculture started as a supplement to hunting and gathering, it eventually replaced these practices almost entirely. The Agricultural Revolution entailed clearing one-tenth of the earth's land surface of either grass or trees so it could be plowed. Unlike the hunter-gatherer culture that had little effect on the earth, this new farming culture literally transformed the surface of the earth.

Expanding Professions in an Eco-Economy

Profession	Description
Wind meteorologists	Wind meteorologists will play a role in the new energy economy comparable to that of petroleum geologists in the old one.
Family-planning midwives	If world population is to stabilize soon, literally millions of family-planning midwives will be needed.
Foresters	Reforesting the earth will require professional guidance on what tree species to plant where and in what combination.
Hydrologists	As water scarcity spreads, the demand for hydrologists to advise on watershed management, water sources, and water efficiency will increase.
Recycling engineers	Designing consumer applications so they can be easily disassembled and completely recycled will become an engineering specialty.
Aquacultural veterinarians	Until now, veterinarians have typically specialized in either large animals or small animals, but with fish farming likely to overtake beef production by 2010, marine veterinarians will be in demand.
Ecological economists	As it becomes clear that the basic principles of ecology must be incorporated into economic planning and policy making, the demand for economists able to think like ecologists will grow.
Geothermal geologists	With the likelihood that large areas of the world will turn to geothermal energy both for electricity and for heating, the demands for geothermal geologists will climb.
Environmental architects	Architects are learning the principles of ecology so they can incorporate them into the buildings where we will live and work.
Bicycle mechanics	As the world turns to the bicycle for transportation and exercise, bicycle mechanics will be needed to keep the fleet running.
Wind-turbine engineers	With millions of wind turbines likely to be installed in the decades ahead, there will be strong worldwide demand for wind-turbine engineers.

Source: *Eco-Economy*

The Industrial Revolution has been under way for two centuries, although in some countries it is still in its early stages. At its foundation was a shift in sources of energy from wood to fossil fuels, a shift that set the stage for a massive expansion in economic activity. Indeed, its distinguishing feature is the harnessing of vast amounts of fossil energy for economic purposes. While the Agricultural Revolution transformed the earth's surface, the Industrial Revolution is transforming the earth's atmosphere.

The additional productivity that the Industrial Revolution made possible unleashed enormous creative energies. It also gave birth to new lifestyles and to the most environmentally destructive era in human history, setting the world firmly on a course of eventual economic decline. The Environmental Rev-

olution resembles the Industrial Revolution in that each is dependent on the shift to a new energy source. And like both earlier revolutions, the Environmental Revolution will affect the entire world.

There are differences in scale, timing, and origin among the three revolutions. Unlike the other two, the Environmental Revolution must be compressed into a matter of decades. And while the other revolutions were driven by new discoveries and advances in technology, this revolution is being driven more by our instinct for survival.

There has not been an investment situation like this before. The amount that the world spends now each year on oil, the leading source of energy, provides some insight into how much it could spend on energy in the eco-economy. In 2000, the world used nearly 28 billion barrels of oil, some 76 million barrels per day. At $27 a barrel, the total comes to $756 billion per year. How many wind turbines, solar rooftops, and geothermal wells will it take to produce this much energy?

One big difference between the investments in fossil fuels and those in wind power, solar cells, and geothermal energy is that the latter will supply energy in perpetuity. These "wells" will not run dry. If the money spent on oil in one year were invested in wind turbines, the electricity generated would be enough to meet one-fifth of the world's needs.

Investments in the infrastructure for the new energy economy, which would eventually have to be made as fossil fuels are depleted, will obviously be huge. These include the transmission lines that connect wind farms with electricity consumers and the pipelines that link hydrogen supply sources with end users. Much of the infrastructure for the existing energy economy—the transmission lines for electricity and the pipelines for natural gas—can be used in the new energy economy as well. The local pipeline distribution network in various cities for natural gas can easily be converted to hydrogen.

For developing countries, the new energy sources promise to reduce dependence on imported oil, freeing up capital for investment in domestic energy sources. Although few countries have their own oil fields, all have wind and solar energy. In terms of economic expansion and job generation, these new energy technologies are a godsend.

Investments in energy efficiency are also likely to grow rapidly simply because they are so profitable. In virtually all countries, industrial and developing, saved energy is the cheapest source of new energy. Replacing inefficient incandescent light bulbs with highly efficient compact fluorescent lamps offers a rate of return that stock markets are unlikely to match.

There are also abundant investment opportunities in the food economy. It is likely that the world demand for seafood, for example, will increase at least by half over the next 50 years, and perhaps much more. If so, fish-farming output—now 31 million tons a year—will roughly need to triple, as will investments in fish farming. Although aquaculture's growth is likely to slow from the 11% a year of the last decade, it is nonetheless likely to be robust, presenting a promising opportunity for future investment.

A similar situation exists for tree plantations. At present, tree plantations cover some 113 million hectares (280 million acres). An expansion of these by at least half, along with a continuing rise in productivity, is likely to be needed both to satisfy future demand and to eliminate one of the pressures that are shrinking forests. This, too, presents a huge opportunity for investment. No sector of the global economy will be untouched by the Environmental Revolution. In this new economy, some companies will be winners and some will be losers. Those who anticipate the emerging eco-economy and plan for it will be the winners. Those who cling to the past risk becoming part of it.

LESTER R. BROWN is board chairman of the Worldwatch Institute and president of the Earth Policy Institute, 1350 Connecticut Avenue, N.W., Washington, D.C. 20036. Telephone 1-202-496-9290; email epi@earth-policy.org; Web site www.earth-policy.org.

This article draws from his book, *Eco-Economy: Building an Economy for the Earth* (W.W. Norton, 2001, paperback), which is available from the Futurist Bookstore for $15.95 ($14.50 for Society members), cat. no. B-2382.

Originally published in the March/April 2002 issue of *The Futurist*, pp. 23–32. Used with permission from the World Future Society, 7910 Woodmont Avenue, Suite 450, Bethesda, Maryland 20814. Telephone: 310/656-8274; Fax: 301/951-0394; http://www.wfs.org.

Congested Parks—A Pricing Dilemma

DAN M. BECHTER

In the last year or two, newspapers and magazines have been calling attention to the problems caused by record numbers of people crowding into some of our national parks.[1] Yellowstone and Yosemite are receiving most of the publicity, but other national recreation areas are suffering similar popularity troubles. Many state and local parks, too, are being strained to accommodate rapidly increasing attendance. It is easy to conclude that these congestion difficulties justify creating new public parks and expanding outdoor recreation facilities in existing ones. Additions to supply would seem appropriate, considering the rising demand. Yet, the apparently inadequate recreational capacities of various public parks may reflect something other than a lag in adjustment of supply to demand. Governments may be distorting the recreation market by charging too little for the recreational use of public parks. Such an improper pricing practice would be misallocating resources. Some groups would be benefiting—perhaps those that are not intended to—at the expense of others. Economic analysis helps show the nature and probable consequences of the park crowding problem. It also helps reveal the complex and indirect influences on public park fees, the choices of consumers, and the markets for all recreational goods and services.

When Demand Crowds Supply

Overflowing visitation at a public park provides a textbook display of a shortage. Park crowding means insufficient park space—or types of park space, such as camping space, driving space, fishing space, etc.—to satisfy outdoor recreationists. They want more. Their wants, however, depend directly on what they must pay. The existence of a shortage says only that the quantity demanded exceeds the quantity supplied at the going price. Excessive park crowding, therefore, reflects a park entry or a park privilege fee that is below the one that equates the amount of park space consumers want to the amount available. Chart 1 clarifies the explanation.

Chart 1 shows a set of demand and supply relationships for camping spaces in a hypothetical public park. Demand curve D_1D_1 shows that the lower the price, the larger the number of park camping spaces desired on an average summer day.[2] Vertical line S_{1S1} indicates the number of camping spaces in the park—assumed to be an invariable quantity in the very short run. Now, suppose park officials set the camping fee at \$1. Clearly,

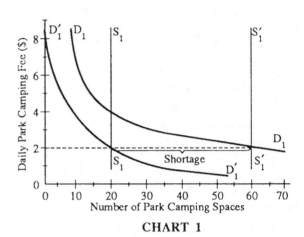

CHART 1

quantity demanded (60 spaces) exceeds quantity supplied (20 spaces), or a shortage of 40 spaces prevails at that price.

What happens to the 40 camping families whom the park cannot accommodate? Those who can return home may disappointedly do so. Others may not show up, having heard about or previously experienced the shortage. Still others may try to squeeze and shoehorn into the camping area, or pitch their tents in unauthorized areas of the park. Some may find other public or private places to camp nearby. The remainder may stay in motels, sleep along the road, or drive all night.

As can be seen, selling a good or service below the market-clearing price—where demand equals supply, or \$4, in the example simply requires other forms of rationing or adjustment, such as first come, first served, which places a premium on arrival time. Some of these adaptations, in effect, increase the cost of the outdoor recreation experience. They make the consumer spend extra time and money guaranteeing himself participation in the leisure activity. Other adjustments, such as crowding into available space, make outdoor recreation less fun.

The shortage shown in Chart 1—or any market shortage, for that matter—can be reduced by (a) increasing price, (b) increasing supply, (c) decreasing demand, or (d) a combination of the preceding. Before considering these solutions, consider a part of what is going on outside the park.

Chart 2 shows another set of supply and demand curves—those for camping spaces on private land near the hypothetical public park. Currently, entrepreneurs are making 18 such spaces available, charging the going-market price of $2.50. Note that quantity demanded equals quantity supplied at this price—no shortage here. On a day of normal demand, everyone who wants to camp in a private area can do so. Some of this demand for private camping spaces depends, of course, on overflow from the public park. Assuming that campers prefer locations within the park to those outside, it might seem strange that some are willing to pay the extra half dollar charged by private campgrounds. It must be remembered, however, that the park cannot satisfy demand at $2. Also, note that a sizable portion of the left tail of demand curve D_1D_1 (Chart 1) lies above $4, indicating that several campers are willing to pay more than this amount for places inside the park. Some of these people certainly would be willing to locate outside for less when the park is full.

Now, consider each of the solutions to the shortage of public park camping spaces. Suppose first that the park authorities raise their camping fee to $4 (Chart 1). The shortage immediately disappears. Everyone wanting a space at this price within the park finds one, because quantity demanded declines from 60 to 20 spaces. In addition, because of the increase in the park's camping fee, more people will decide in favor of the less expensive private facilities. Demand curve D_2D_2 for private camping spaces (Chart 2) will shift over to $D'_2D'_2$. For awhile, there will be a shortage of private camping spaces, and campground owners may raise their prices. Eventually they will expand, or new private campgrounds will open. This is what curve $S'_2S'_2$ shows—the number of camping spaces private landowners will supply, given the opportunity to adjust to various prices. As can be seen, the market price settles at $3 a space where quantity demanded = quantity supplied = 29 spaces.[3] ($S'_2S'_2$ slopes upward to the right, showing that costs per space increase as space is increased.) Furthermore, the market for motel rooms, and other markets, will be affected. This example only looks at the market for the most obvious substitute for public camping spaces.

Suppose that instead of increasing price, the park officials increase the number of camping spaces from 20 to 60 in Chart 1, shifting supply out to $S'_1S'_1$. Again, the shortage disappears. As a result, however, the private campgrounds may be driven out of business. (In Chart 2, D_2D_2 shifts left—not shown.) Other markets, too, are affected.

Instead of increasing the number or the price of park camping spaces, the park authorities (Federal, state, or municipal) may try to alleviate the crowding—the shortage situation—by reducing demand for these spaces. (D_1D_1 would shift left to $D'_1D'_1$ in Chart 1.) This could be done by allowing the quality of the park facilities to run down. Or, another public park could be established nearby, thereby relieving the pressure on the existing one. Subsidization of private campgrounds, to lower their costs and to encourage their expansion and improvement, offers still another means of reducing the demand for space in the hypothetical public park.

Each of these alternatives affects the outdoor recreation market differently. If camping conditions in the public park are allowed to deteriorate, for example, the demand for private campground space in the vicinity might rise as the desirability

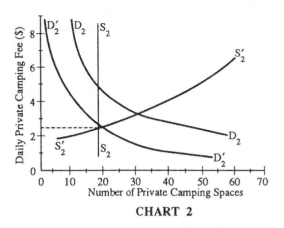

CHART 2

of these private areas increases relative to those in the park. On the other hand, the region may become less attractive as an outdoor recreation area, especially if the whole park deteriorates, and private enterprise also may suffer declines in demand. Creating more public parks or subsidizing private outdoor recreation areas in the region should, at least in the short run, decrease demand for space in individual parks. In the region as a whole, however, such measures will likely encourage more outdoor recreation by reducing its time-and-money cost to consumers.

How Many People?
How Much Per Person?

Since undue crowding caused by an economic shortage can be so easily eliminated by increasing price, one wonders why this quick and obvious solution is not chosen. Alternatively, when "idle" space seems plentiful in the park, why not develop it for the more intensive recreational purposes that consumers want? Clearly, certain obstacles must be barring the wholesale use of these prescriptions. Indeed, several less apparent economic considerations make it difficult to determine the desirable amount of park use. Still other socioeconomic factors affect decisions of how to best allocate this use among outdoor recreationists.

Principles of Private Pricing

As a starting point, it proves helpful to think of how a public park would be managed if it were a privately owned enterprise. Microeconomic analysis proceeds from the axiom that an individual economic unit behaves in ways that it believes to be in its own self-interest. The theory of the firm treats profits as a measure of self-interest, and economists have found that the simple assumption that business enterprises act to maximize profits explains much of firm behavior. Assume that this objective—profit maximization—guides the park managers. Under such an assumption, what can one expect?

The owners may conclude that their land and water holdings would yield higher profits if used for purposes other than, or in addition to, outdoor recreation. With profit maximization as their goal, they may choose to turn the park into a farm, a strip mine, an oil field, or a residential area. Is this bad? Maybe, but the free country, free market philosophy argues that consumers, with their dollar votes, should direct the use of resources. In an idealized economic system, higher profit levels serve to stimulate production of those goods and services that society wants most. However, market imperfections and an excessive discounting of the value of resources to future generations leave our economy well shy of this idealized state. Consequently, profit signals cannot always be relied on to allocate resources in society's best interest.

In the absence of information on such shortcomings, the most profitable use of resources is presumed to be the most economically desirable. Thus, if private interests would operate resources differently from the government, the public use may have a questionable economic basis. The government should be able to defend its choice of uses by establishing the presence of considerations not fully reflected in profits and by showing that including these considerations favors using the resources in a less profitable manner. Otherwise—putting this back into context—if the government cannot show that the net economic benefits of a public park at least equal those society receives by allowing the same area of land and water to be operated for the top competing purpose, the park cannot be justified.[4]

Returning to the question of pricing, suppose that businessmen do operate the parkland as an outdoor recreation area. To keep things simple, let the rental of camping spaces be the park's sole market activity. The profit-maximizing owners will need to know (a) the demand for their camping spaces, and (b) the amount it costs them to supply varying numbers of camping spaces.

Complexities appear quickly. The relationship between price and quantity demanded is complicated by the fact that the quality of the product depends on the number of people buying it. Up to a point, the representative camper may enjoy the camping experience more as the number of other campers in the park increase. He likes their company. Eventually, however, increases in the number of campers reduce the camper's total satisfaction. He dislikes crowding.[5] Assuming the quality of camping first rises then falls with the number of campers, so does the amount the camper is willing to pay (Chart 3).

It is apparent that demand depends implicitly on supply. In the short run, a fixed amount of parkland cannot supply various quantities of a constant quality of camping spaces. Campers want more than just a place to sleep. They also want open, natural spaces around them. When more camping spaces are supplied, less open space remains. Because of the crowding phenomenon, quantity demanded may become unresponsive to reductions in price once certain degrees of congestion are reached. The profit-maximizing park owners would never reduce prices under such circumstances, of course.

In their cost calculations, the park owners will allow for upkeep.[6] As more camping spaces are rented, the cost of maintaining each additional one may decline as certain economies are realized. On the other hand, the least expensive ways of supplying camping spaces may be exhausted early. Also, as the number of camping spaces grows, the cost of maintaining the quality (of the decreased quantity) of open space might increase, perhaps dramatically, as certain critical levels of camping pressure

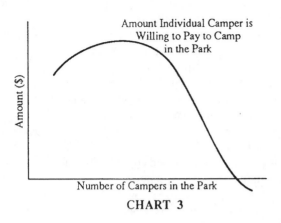

CHART 3

are reached. For example, the park's wildlife—a prime attraction to campers—may cease to reproduce without sufficient space and seclusion.

Taking all internal cost and demand considerations into account, owners maximize profits at that price and quantity where further reductions in price would increase revenues from camping space rentals by less than the cost of supplying these additional spaces.

Principles of Public Pricing

For the economy as a whole, economic efficiency requires using resources to produce each good or service up to the point where the marginal social benefit of each good or service equals its marginal social cost. Achieving this goal is rendered impossible by insurmountable measurement problems. Rules for economic efficiency serve best to indicate when one resources use comes closer to the ideal than another. The preceding discussion argues that, because of the crowding phenomenon, the demand for camping spaces in a particular park will be downward sloping—park owners cannot rent any number of camping spaces at some competitive market price. Moreover, parks often possess unique features and are located unequal distances from the homes of their visitors. This product differentiation also implies that a downward sloping demand curve faces each park. Thus, under such monopolistically competitive conditions, if all of society's costs of park use are borne by the park owners, and if all of society's benefits of park use are received by the park visitors, it necessarily follows that the profit-maximizing price will limit park use (camping) more than is desirable. In other words, private owners will stop short of the point where the resource cost of supplying the last camping space exactly equals what society is willing to pay for it.[7]

This leads directly to the obvious but important corollary; *Under conditions of monopolistic competition where all costs and benefits of park use are internal, the socially optimal amount of park congestion exceeds that which would be permitted by unregulated private enterprise.* People may complain of crowded conditions in a public park, but that *in itself* does not justify limiting visitation. So long as the discomforts of crowding are internalized—that is, so long as they are reflected in a lower-than-otherwise price—the park visitor has no economic grounds for complaint (assuming he fully anticipates the situation).

People who do not visit a park may benefit from those who do. Juvenile delinquency, for example, may be reduced by providing city park and recreation areas. These external benefits can be regarded as negative costs, reducing marginal social costs, perhaps to the extent that a negative price—a payment to those who use the park—is called for.[8] Conceivably, therefore, society's interest could be served by subsidizing park crowds, if not more parks.

On the other hand, and much more likely to be the case for parks located outside the city, the benefits that nonvisitors receive may well be *inversely* related to the number of park visitors. The more people who drive to the park, for example, the more highway congestion and air pollution for everyone. Nonvisitors also may benefit from a park's provision of natural habitat for wildlife, its protection of rare plants and animals, and its preservation of unique natural and historical areas.[9] As already noted, greater visitor pressure can reduce park quality. To the extent that added visitation decreased the benefits that nonvisitors get from the park, park visits increase in cost to society. In the camping space example, external benefits of nonuse increase the economically appropriate price and decrease the desirable level of camping. If government officials ignore these external costs and benefits in their pricing of park services, they can end up behaving less in the public interest than would private owners.

A Pricing Dilemma

The theory of optimal pricing is, of course, far easier than its practice. It is one thing to say that all costs and benefits should be identified and measured, another to figure out how. These difficulties are important, but not the topic of concern here. Rather, this section focuses on an obstacle that keeps park officials from charging the economically appropriate price for park use even when that price is known—public opinion.

The conditions reported at some popular public parks do not suggest an equilibrium in quantity demanded and quantity supplied. True, as shown earlier in this article, congestion is sometimes economically desirable and can be expected to cause complaints of crowding. But when people are turned away, and when overuse threatens the park's survival, something must be out of kilter. Park authorities seem to be both encouraging visitation with low fees, and discouraging visitation by not adequately expanding recreation facilities and by otherwise limiting—in nonprice fashions—the activities of the visitors.

Public opinion forces this strange behavior. In theory, at least, economists can usually fit public opinion into the pricing system fairly easily by translating it into dollar values that society places on the activities in question.[10] In this case, however, public opinion is against the pricing system. People strongly resist public park fees and the use of these fees to allocate park use. Americans apparently feel that public parks are theirs to use free of charge (or at nominal cost) as a right of part ownership. Strangely, they do not seem to feel this way about the Na-

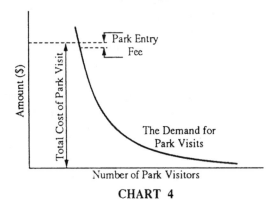

CHART 4

tion's highways (we have gasoline taxes as well as turnpike tolls).[11]

Related to the ownership argument is the redistributive argument that entry fees would have to be raised substantially to adequately limit visitation, and that this would discriminate against the poor. It might seem unreasonable or unlikely that the demand for a one-day park visit, for sightseeing only, would be inelastic between carload entry fees of just a few dollars up to $100 or more. But this may well be the case for parks like Yellowstone, because such large increases in entry fees may amount to relatively small percentage increases in the total cost of the park visit (Chart 4). Pointing this out, however, also implies that very few poor people presently can afford to visit such parks anyway. Park-type outdoor recreation is perhaps best thought of as a luxury. Most people would agree that those who want a luxury should pay for it. Yet, the under-pricing of park-type recreation subsidizes the leisure activities of the affluent—they own the boats, the trailers, the camping equipment, and so on.[12]

Until attitudes change, government officials face great resistance to increases in public park entry and use fees. Perhaps much of this resistance would decrease if proper pricing methods were used. Accelerating park deterioration and other costs of excessive crowding certainly call for changes in the pricing of park recreation. Paradoxically, governments appear to be working in the wrong direction. New highways to parks, for example, lower the time and money cost of a visit. The golden Eagle Passport—a $10 annual permit that admits the purchaser and his passengers or his family to more than 3,000 designated Federal outdoor recreation areas—encourages more visitation.

Some groups, besides visitors, obviously benefit from park subsidies. Vested interests point to the regional activity generated by park use. Owners and employees of lodging places, restaurants, bait and tackle stores, and many other kinds of businesses and concessions, do not want to give up what is actually a subsidy to them. They logically reason that, if parks increase fees, the demand for complementary goods and services they sell will decline. Manufacturers of boats, automobiles, and other outdoor recreation equipment also benefit from the subsidization of park use.

Other groups suffer. It can be argued, for example, that the subsidization of park recreation reduces the demand for outdoor sports events, bowling, and all other activities that consumers consider substitutes. Ronald F. Lee writes, "... for most people, there is no substitute for a visit to a national park." A visit to a national park may be a unique experience, but that does not mean it has no substitutes. Most Americans already substitute other things—staying home, for example—for national park visits. And, if the price of visiting national parks is increased, even more people will substitute other leisure activities.[13]

Further Complexities and Ideas

Most public parks of any size supply several different types of outdoor recreation. Many of these compete with one another for available park space. One example of this has already been given—open space competes with park use. But water skiing competes with fishing, picnicking with camping, and so on. A park contains, therefore, several sub-markets, and as such it can supply any one of many, many, different types of park use mixes. Some activities use more resources than others, and these should be priced higher. In practice, it may be extremely difficult and expensive to collect for each activity engaged in by a park visitor. But it might be possible to approximate his cost by charging him on the basis of the time he spends in the park and the equipment he takes in. Perhaps simply multiplying time by total weight by a price for a standard "user unit" would do the job. This would (1) discourage long stays, (2) discourage autos, campers, boats, and other heavy equipment, and (3) permit a relatively low entry price for visitors willing to travel light within the park and willing to stay only a short period.[14]

Seasonal park congestion could also be relieved by varying visitation fees by time of year. Although used to some extent, this method of pricing is largely untapped. The advance reservation idea probably favors certain groups over others, although it does have the advantage of guaranteeing space. Unfortunately, one likely outcome of a reservation system in situations where demand exceeds supply is a black market or scalpers' market in tickets. Why not use the pricing system directly instead of driving it underground?

The cost of park-type outdoor recreation must be borne by someone. This includes not only the direct operating costs, but the opportunity costs of the resources as well. In instances where it is practical and where external costs and benefits are not significant, charging the user enough to cover these costs seems warranted. Privately owned recreation areas do this. For this reason, Professor Milton Friedman would have governments get out of the noncity park business:

> If the public wants this kind of activity enough to pay for it, private enterprises will have every incentive to provide such parks. And, of course, there are many private enterprises of this nature now in existence. I cannot myself conjure up any neighborhood effects [externalities] or important monopoly effects that would justify governmental activity in this area.[15]

But most people, it seems safe to say, simply do not trust private enterprise to preserve the natural beauty of some national and state parks. Many park resource development decisions are irreversible, and the long-run consequences of a misguided short-run profit motive could be severe. On the other hand, public ownership does not guarantee development of resources in the long-run best interest of society either.

Reading Questions

1. How may government distort the public parks recreation market?

2. Discuss and evaluate various alternatives for alleviating a shortage of public park camping spaces.

3. Compare the principles of private pricing and public pricing for recreational use of parks.

4. What is the equity impact of underpricing park recreation?

Notes

1. See, for example, Paul Friggens, "Last chance for Yellowstone?" *Reader's Digest,* March 1971, pp. 190–96.

2. Assume away (as unnecessarily complicating here) the likelihood that campers prefer some of the park's campsites to others.

3. A more complete treatment of these adjustments would include probable increases in the demand for park camping spaces brought about by increases in the price of private camping spaces, and so on, back and forth, until an equilibrium is reached.

4. In choosing from alternative uses of resources, it is wrong to say that "other factors besides economics must be considered." Economics is the study of man's choices from competing alternatives. By definition, therefore, nothing else matters. The trick is to identify and appropriately include all important economic consideration, both current and future, when calculating benefits and costs. The confusion arises because many people commonly but incorrectly use the word "economics" as if it were synonymous with "profits," or "private enterprise." A few months ago on a television special about a national park, for example, it was reported that the reconsideration of plans for a new airport represented a victory for conservation over economics. Not at all. It represented a reassessment of the net benefits from building the airport. (Conservationists were responsible for bringing about this reassessment, to be sure.) For the time being, society has decided that it would be worse off—all things considered—with the airport.

5. The desire for privacy will vary among campers, and with the type of camping area. Two campers (or camping parties) in the same park may be one too many for some individuals, especially if the park is a wilderness area.

6. Private owners would allow a profitable park to run down over time only so long as, or to the extent which, the costs of doing so—losses in future profits due to lower future demand—were less than the costs of maintaining park quality. Time preference—the values owners place on future dollars versus present dollars—matters here.

7. Because owners must reduce prices on all spaces in order to rent more spaces, the additional or marginal revenue from renting one more camping space is less than the price at which it is rented. Profits decline with increased "sales" once marginal cost exceeds marginal revenue. Logically, therefore, profits are less than the maximum where price equals marginal cost.

8. It sounds strange, but why not? If, for example, it is found that children who participate in junior baseball are less likely to get sick, less likely to turn to crime, and less likely to go on welfare, might it not make sense to expand such programs even if it requires giving the participants some dollar inducement?

9. Birds that nest in a park, for example, fly, feed, and sing far outside its boundaries. (On the other side of the ledger, park wildlife can damage crops and otherwise increase the cost of farming and ranching.) Benefits are sometimes less obvious. Relatively few people have ever seen a whooping crane, but millions derive pleasure from reading and hearing about it fight for survival.

10. These values need not be expressed to the dollar. Thus we now adequately protect the bison because the gains from doing so exceed the costs by some unmeasured—but not infinite—amount. But we continue to reduce the chances of survival of the bald eagle and osprey—and other species—because the necessary costs of more protection have been judged greater than the gains.

11. On highways too, however, improper pricing results in crowded conditions. See Gabriel Roth, *Paying for Roads: The Economics of Traffic Congestion* (Baltimore: Penguin Books, 1967).

12. Two experts in outdoor recreation write: "By and large, the supply of free public parks in the United States is less adequate in crowded city areas where people are poor than it is in suburban and higher income residential areas, where the people concerned are more nearly able to pay for their own outdoor recreation. On a state or national basis, the discrepancy is even worse; the really poor people do not own the private automobiles which are necessary to get to most state parks and to all national parks and national forests, nor can they, in most cases, afford the other travel costs of such visits. The argument that free public parks help the poor is almost wholly myth." Marion Clawson and Jack L. Knetsch, *The Economics of Outdoor Recreation* (Baltimore: Resources for the Future; Johns Hopkins Press, 1966), p. 271.

13. The quote is from Mr. Lee's book, *Public Use of the National Park System,* 1872–2000 (Washington: Department of Interior, National Park Service, U.S. Government Printing Office, 1968), p. 87.

14. Some parks currently do not permit visitors to stay indefinite periods of time. This is consistent with the philosophy that it is better for society if five people spend one day in the park than if one person spends five days. If this point of view is accepted, a fee rising *progressively* with length of stay is called for.

15. *Capitalism and Freedom* (Chicago: University of Chicago Press, 1962), p. 31.

MR. BECHTER is presently the Vice President of the Federal Reserve Bank of Richmond.

Reprinted with permission from *Monthly Review* (Federal Reserve Bank of Kansas City), June 1971, pp. 80–81.

UNIT 3
The Economics of Work and Income

Unit Selections

13. **Building a More-Humane Economy**, Robert D. Atkinson
14. **The Rich Get (Much) Richer**, Steven Rattner
15. **Outsourcing Jobs: The Myths and Realities**, Martin N. Baily and Diana Farrell
16. **Laid Off and Left Out**, Bob Herbert
17. **Multiple Minimums**, John M. Broder
18. **The Gender Gyp**, Thomas N. Bethell
19. **The Health Care Crisis and What to Do About It**, Paul Krugman and Robin Wells

Key Points to Consider

- In what sense are the rich getting richer and the poor poorer? What role might job outsourcing play in this trend?

- Why might Social Security be more important for women than for men? Is raising the minimum wage a good idea?

- In what sense is the U.S. health care system in a state of crisis, and what might be done about this?

Student Web Site

www.mhcls.com/online

Internet References

Further information regarding these Web sites may be found in this book's preface or online.

Center on Budget and Policy Priorities
http://www.cbpp.org

Joint Center for Poverty Research
http://www.jcpr.org

Today's Unions
http://www.aflcio.org

The Urban Institute
http://www.urban.org

U.S. Department of Health and Human Services
http://www.hhs.gov

U.S. Department of Labor
http://www.dol.gov

Economic justice means different things to different people. For some, the fairest way to distribute income and wealth is to "allow the market to decide," so that rewards are provided strictly on the basis of the human and property resources that individuals contribute to the economy. Others maintain that such an arrangement is inherently unfair; since people differ in their natural abilities, inheritances, age, race, sex, and licks, resources tend to be distributed in a highly unequal fashion. A market system tends to penalize those whose resources are insufficient to enable them to achieve adequate living standards.

Economists generally agree that complete equality in the distribution of income and wealth is undesirable, since then there would be no financial incentive to induce people into more difficult undertakings. However, there is widespread disagreement within the economics profession on two questions. First, if inequality is to serve as an incentive to great efficiency in the use of resources, exactly how unequal should the distribution of income and wealth be? Secondly, what is the proper role of government in modifying the way in which a market economy distributes its rewards?

In the United States—as in all highly developed capitalist countries—there are large differences in the distribution of income and wealth. American households in the top 20 percent of the population earn almost half of the total U.S. income, while those in the bottom 20 percent earn less than 4 percent of the total. Differences in the distribution of wealth are even greater. In 2005 the bottom 40 percent of the U.S. population essentially had zero wealth, while the top fifth accounted for 85 percent of all the American wealth. While most Americans are better off today (in terms of the absolute amount of income and wealth available) than they might have been, say, 50 years ago, there are certain trends that disturb those concerned about issues of inequality. One of these is a decline (since the mid-1970s) in the purchasing power of median household earnings and a rise (since the early 1980s) in the extent of poverty.

Readings selected for this unit identify some major issues in current debates on the subject of income as well as the possible roles of government in promoting economic justice. In the first article, Robert Atkinson outlines certain conditions necessary for the creation of a more-humane economy. Steven Rattner then examines causes of and possible cures for the widening of the U.S. income gap. The next two articles offer varying perspectives on the effects of job outsourcing and layoffs. Martin Baily and Diana Farrell suggest ways in which public policy might help workers who are disadvantaged by the "outsourcing" of work by businesses. Bob Herbert says that while the U.S. workforce needs better access to education and

training, there is no guarantee that there will be a sufficient number of good jobs available.

Government programs aimed at redressing specific economic imbalances are the subject of the next essays. First, John Broder analyzes possible implications of raising the minimum wage for nonprofessional workers. The first minimum wage law was passed in 1938 during the Great Depression, when millions lived in poverty. There has been a debate ever since between those who say minimum wage hikes hurt job creation (particularly for the young and unskilled), and those who see it as a guarantee of basic living standards for workers.

Next, Thomas Bethell shows why, as a result of the fact that they have greater longevity than men, women are all the more dependent on Social Security. While for men Social Security is primarily a worker retirement program, for women it becomes a family insurance plan. In the last article of this unit, Paul Krugman and Robin Wells ask: Why is the U.S. health care system in a state of crisis, and what might be done about this?

Building a More-Humane Economy

With the emergence of a new economy based on the growth of knowledge jobs and higher productivity, the challenge now is to create a society that satisfies our deeper human needs and wants.

ROBERT D. ATKINSON

Many people fear that the benefits of the New Economy—increased productivity and the material gains it brings—are outweighed by its pitfalls—rapid change, lost jobs due to automation and outsourcing, and disrupted lives. Their faith in the future can only be restored when the benefits of higher productivity translate into a significantly better and more-humane economy for individuals, not just for corporations or nations.

As economist John Maynard Keynes wrote in 1930 in an essay entitled "Economic Possibilities for Our Grandchildren," technology that steadily boosts productivity could one day liberate us from toil. What Keynes and others longed for, and indeed predicted, was a future focused on life, not just work. However, productivity needed to reach a level that would enable people to live the good life without excessive hours of backbreaking or mind-numbing work. Unlike Karl Marx and other utopians, Keynes realized that liberation from toil would have to wait until productivity greatly improved.

That dreamed-of future may at last be in our sights, and advanced, postindustrial economies may now be entering a period where we can think of the organization of the economy, and indeed of society itself, not as an end in itself but as a means for people to live more fulfilled, meaningful, and enjoyable lives. Many people work in unfulfilling, boring, and hard jobs because that work needs to be done and the production system requires the work to be organized this way. But as the economy evolves, work is likely to evolve to be more interesting and fulfilling. Regardless of the type of work, many people work long hours. Increasing productivity will mean we can work less without earning less.

Such a vision may seem hopelessly utopian, particularly given that many people seem to be working longer, under greater stress. But today's New Economy is unleashing a host of forces that could enable a more-humane economy in which people can enjoy more-satisfying work even as they work less.

The Digital Economy: Realizing Its Potential

The rise of the digital economy, which saw a massive boost with the Internet boom, has been responsible for the turnaround in productivity growth after 1995. But the digital economy boom has only just begun. Many companies (47% of manufacturers and 39% of nonmanufacturers) believe they have reached less than half the efficiency gains that could be made possible thanks to the new technologies, according to the Institute for Supply Management, a U.S.-based association for purchasing and supply professionals.

In the future, we will see more and more routine information processes become digitized, such as movie tickets sold at self-serve kiosks, standard government forms in interactive online formats, and all types of financial transactions, institutional and personal, conducted virtually.

One reason why the infotech revolution is boosting productivity is because it is turning consumers into producers, or "prosumers," as Alvin Toffler termed them. A soccer mom who pumps her own gas, paying for it with the flash of a smart card, does not work for the gas station, but she increases the gas station's productivity. Mom benefits by receiving a lower-costing fill-up than at a full-service station; the station owner benefits by selling more gas with fewer employees. Add in Mom buying airline tickets, filing income taxes, and paying bills online and a host of other prosumer activities, and it's easy to get a sense of what a powerful force this will be.

The digital revolution has produced enormous benefits. But five things will have to happen to the technology system for it to achieve its full promise.

1. Technologies need to be more accessible—i.e., easier to use for more people. Most people in industrialized societies do not think twice about plugging an electrical appliance into a wall socket, nor do they have to get out a manual to start the car. But such easy familiarity with older technologies is not yet the case for a large number of digital technologies. When a network connection breaks down or a not-so-intuitive program freezes up, productivity comes to a screeching halt.

2. Technologies need to keep improving. New and better technology will help the digital economy reach its full potential. Voice, handwriting, and optical recognition

features would allow humans to better interact with computers. Intelligent agents that routinely filter and retrieve information based on users' preferences would make the Internet experience more productive as well as more pleasant. Expert-system software would help in making decisions in medicine, engineering, finance, and other fields. High-definition displays would accelerate the adoption of e-book readers. And batteries that last longer would make mobile devices much more usable.

3. The technologies need to converge. It is funny to see so many "road warriors" carrying around cell phones, laptop computers, PDAs, etc. At home, it's just as bad, with a host of unconnected electronic appliances—stereos, MP3 players, televisions, telephones, computers, printers and peripherals, and so on. Networking many of these devices wirelessly has helped overcome the problem, but full, seamless convergence of operations would vastly improve usability and digital transformation.

4. Processes need further disintermediation. The more that customers handle their own transactions online without inefficient layers of intermediaries between them and the goods and services they need, the more productive the economy will be. The travel industry, for instance, has witnessed a reduction of travel agents thanks to online reservation services; banks have replaced many human tellers with cash machines. Government at all levels needs to make sure that they don't give in to demands from offline intermediaries for protectionist legislation against online competitors.

5. The technologies need to be ever-present. The adoption of productivity-enhancing technologies needs to be ubiquitous. When we get to 75% of the population being online and 50% of the population using key applications such as electronic bill payment, as well as wider penetration of high-speed broadband connection, we will pass a critical inflection point. The cyberworld will begin to dominate, rather than cyber-business and traditional business existing in parallel worlds.

Advancing digital transformation is crucial because it is the key source of productivity advancement, and that in turn is the key to enabling workers to work less while earning more. As the economy gets more productive, companies become more knowledge driven, and people become more prosperous, workers could increasingly expect more rewarding occupations, more leisure, and more-livable communities. The first part of the twentieth century focused on production and investment; in the last half of the twentieth century, the economy focused on mass consumption. Now, we are moving toward an economy focused on enabling people to live good lives: more-satisfying workplaces, less work time, more time to enjoy away from work, more civic involvement, and more choices about where to live, thus leading to the creation of more-livable communities.

Creating a More-Humane Workplace

Achieving this more-humane economy requires neither an anticorporate crusade nor a simple-living, back-to-nature movement. Rather, it entails promoting more humane high-performance work organizations and robust and sustained productivity growth that will enable people to work less without earning less.

Public policy could play a significant role. In 2000, the Occupational Safety and Health Administration indicated that all workplace rules should be applied to home offices, including the ridiculous idea that every home with a telecommuter would need lighted exit signs. Clearly the industrial-age laws need to be reformed for information-age workplaces. Millions of workers want flexible hours, nonhierarchical project teams, and the ability to telecommute more than they want the old protections of rigid hours, wages, work conditions, and management-labor bargaining.

Labor laws need to be modernized to reflect today's social and economic realities, empowering the high-performance knowledge workers while continuing to protect the right of workers in traditional jobs to organize in collective bargaining units. One solution might be to create a set of workplace rules specifically for productivity-growing high-performance workplaces. Employers could be given considerably more flexibility for creating employee work teams as well as involvement teams.

High-performance work organizations also require higher skills. But like so many chicken-or-egg issues, if workers do not have the skills to work in the more demanding high-performance work systems, employers will continue to organize production in the old ways that simplify work, giving employees little reason to upgrade their skills. And employers have a disincentive to invest in worker training if they believe that investment is likely to soon move on to greener pastures. To increase both the demand and supply of high-performance skills, government could boost funding for adult education and workforce development programs and provide seed funding for collaborative industry training ventures. Not only will these policies boost productivity, but they will also encourage more firms to move to high-performance workplaces.

The high-performance work organization does have its limits, however. Even if all employers wanted to organize work in more-satisfying ways, it is simply impossible for many jobs, such as tollbooth attendants. In many cases the best approach will be to support efforts to automate these kinds of bad jobs. Some have argued that automation of lower-skill jobs will only reduce the demand for low-skill workers and reduce their wages. But in fact, it would lead to an economy with a larger share of more-skilled and highly paid jobs, thus raising incomes for workers.

Getting More Time for the Rest of Life

While most workers want more-satisfying work, many also want less work. Luckily, the New Economy could provide the means for people to work less without reducing their incomes.

Vacation Days by Law

Spain	30
France	30
Ireland	28
Japan	25
Belgium	24
Norway	21
United Kingdom	20
Germany	18
Canada	10
United States	0

High productivity has "bought" little free time in the United States, where government currently does not require business to offer it.

Source: *Work to Live: The Guide to Getting a Life* by Joe Robinson (Perigee, 2003)

The twentieth century saw the enactment of laws to limit workweeks and stipulate additional pay for overtime. But even with shorter workweeks, incomes continued to grow as increased automation enabled productivity to grow. So by the 1950s, the future of leisure looked bright.

However, since then, increased productivity has not been translated into more hours of leisure time. In part, this is because, according to economist Robert Gordon, only the highest-earning 10% of workers have seen their incomes increase faster than productivity. Much of the economic benefit of productivity growth in the United States has gone into the pockets of the richest 1% of wage earners, including CEOs, entertainers, professional athletes, attorneys, and doctors. In the last 25 years, these highest earners have gained more income than the bottom 50% of wage earners combined.

Other countries, have been more successful in ensuring that the benefits of productivity gains were shared widely. For example, in the late 1980s and early 1990s, Germany saw somewhat less growth than the United States did, but a significantly greater number of people benefited from it, enabling them to cut back on their work hours.

Moreover, even for Americans whose incomes went up, but not as fast as productivity, most chose to consume the increased fruits of higher productivity in the form of more products and services. They bought more stuff, and the consumer society flourished. Wages began to grow faster in the mid-1990s, but leisure did not. As Americans made more money, they used it to purchase more goods and services. A host of new products and services (e.g., widescreen televisions, cell phones, computers) had been created that people felt they needed, or at least wanted. And the pressures to consume come both from society at large (keeping up with the Joneses) and from the increased competitiveness of the global economy.

As a result, in contrast to other advanced economies, average annual work hours in the United States increased, from 1,883 hours in 1980 to 1,966 hours in 1997, creating what some refer to as a crisis of leisure time. Americans now work almost two weeks a year more than the Japanese, long derided as worka-

holic salarymen. And Americans take few vacation days (13) compared with Japanese (25 days) and Europeans (37 for the French, 42 days for Italians).

The United States also has a greater share of its total population in the workforce, thanks largely to the increased participation of women and to a workforce that retires later (age 65.1 on average) than other advanced countries (e.g., age 59.3 in France).

The benefit of this hard work is that the United States has the highest per capita income in the world. The cost, however, is stress, exhaustion, neglected children, and the loss of community.

The rise of the 24-hour global company has exacerbated the conflict between corporate values and family values. In a hyper-competitive economy, the ideal employee is the one who is always available, not the one who is constantly juggling family responsibilities. Even at Eli Lilly—a company with a reputation for being one of the most family-friendly—a 1995 survey found that just 36% of workers said it was possible to get ahead and still devote sufficient time to their families. Such perceptions often reflect reality. One study found that employees who took family and medical leaves had fewer promotions and smaller wage gains.

Increased time devoted to work has led to decreased time for families, particularly in time devoted to parenting. The impacts of this parenting deficit are profoundly troubling. About one-third of all U.S. adolescents have contemplated suicide; half are at moderate or high risk of abusing drugs, failing in school, getting pregnant, or otherwise seriously damaging their lives. While the risks are exacerbated by poverty, "in survey after survey, young adolescents from all ethnic and economic backgrounds lament their lack of parental attention and guidance," reports the Carnegie Council on Adolescent Development.

This work overload among U.S. workers is coming at the expense of not just time spent with children, but also time devoted to civic activity. In Bowling Alone (2000), social scientist Robert Putnam details how voter turnout, knowledge about current affairs, and civic organizational activity have all fallen sharply since the early 1960s. For example, each additional 10 minutes per day stuck in traffic reduces workers' involvement in community affairs by 10%.

The increase in work time, especially among women, has deleterious effects on social capital. Many of those women who were homemakers in the 1950s and 1960s were the nation's best social capitalists, keeping school organizations, reading clubs, and neighborhood associations afloat. Now when they are not working, they are busy keeping the family going.

Many economic conservatives argue that Americans are working more because they choose to. While a few hard-charging professionals may enjoy 60-plus hour workweeks, evidence suggests that most Americans want to reduce their work hours. About half of the respondents in a *Washington Post* poll said they would work fewer hours or fewer days per week, with about 20% saying they would not work at all if they could do so and live as well. While several years ago only about 10% of workers said they would prefer more time off instead of more work, nearly a third now would prefer more time off, while the numbers are even higher among women with kids (41%), Gen

X'ers (40%), those with long commutes (44%), and those making more than $60,000 per year (45%).

In an attempt to help workers better balance work and family, companies are increasingly giving them more options such as flextime, job sharing, on-site child care, and telecommuting. But more and more workers are saying that this is not enough. They do not merely want flexibility for their work—they want to devote less time to work. The Employment Policy Foundation, a nonprofit workplace-research organization, found that time off has become the most-valued benefit a company can offer its employees. One solution now used by 27% of employers is to lump sick, vacation, and personal days into one category, so that workers can take any of these days off, for any reason, with their supervisor's approval.

A small share of companies are making even more radical changes, such as adopting a 30-hour workweek. Ron Healey, the founder and CEO of 30/40, has convinced a growing list of skeptical CEOs to cut the workweek, including switching to six-hour shifts while still paying workers for a full eight-hour day. Healey says the added expense of hiring more workers pays off because they are more productive, happier, and—most importantly—loyal to the company. He argues that absenteeism is eliminated and workers are more productive since they waste less time.

Balanced Lives, Livable Workplaces and Communities

Creating an economy in which people will be able to better balance work and family will take more than individuals acting as autonomous agents in the labor market. And anyway, most individuals do not have the choice to work a 35-hour week, since the norm, reinforced by U.S. law, is 40 hours.

The first key to creating a more family-friendly economy is to put productivity growth at the center of national economic policies. Robust productivity growth is the means by which society can afford to consume more leisure while also experiencing rising real incomes. This means that policy makers need to enact policies to boost research and development, education and workforce training, digital adoption, and investment in new capital equipment, including software.

Second, companies, individuals, and government all need to take steps to ensure that a share of increased productivity can go to "buying" leisure. Legislation requiring that employers provide at least three weeks of paid vacation is a place to start. In addition, policies to allow workers to take time off instead of time-and-a-half wages, to encourage telecommuting, and to significantly reduce traffic congestion can all help people spend more time with their families.

While ensuring a better balance between work and non-work activities is important for all workers, it is especially important for families with young children. Yet, the trend in the United States over the last three decades has been for new mothers to work. The percentage of mothers of one-year-olds who worked full or part time grew from 17% in 1965 to 58% by 2001. Many families cannot afford to have one parent stay at home during the first year of the child's life, and the impacts are felt not just in families, but throughout society. Good parenting is an investment that brings society-wide benefits. Children who are raised well are less likely to be a drain on societal resources (e.g., be in jail, have poor health, etc.) and are more likely to become more-productive workers.

Publicly supported universal full-day preschool and after-school programs is a popular solution in policy circles, but it's probably not the best. One survey found that most U.S. parents (72%) would rather stay home and raise their children than work, if money were not an issue. Working couples often choose to work different schedules so at least one parent is available to be with the children. This practice seems to confirm the preference of working parents for avoiding commercial day care if possible. Support for child care appears to better fit people's needs as workers than their needs as parents, not to mention the needs of their children. The United States could start by providing six months of paid leave for new parents and adopting legislation modeled on a recent law in the United Kingdom that requires companies to seriously consider reasonable requests from parents with children under age 6 to work flexibly unless there is a compelling business reason that would preclude them from granting the request.

The New Economy is not just making work more productive and satisfying; it is also allowing people greater choice in where they want to live, which could encourage community and civic involvement.

People tend to live in big metros because that is where jobs are. Historically, cities have arisen and grown as centers of commerce, largely because firms, suppliers, and customers all need to be near each other. Agglomerations of people, infrastructure, and industry allowed for the efficient production, transport, and distribution of goods and services.

In the factory-based industrial economy, a large share of people lived in industrial cities in the Midwest and Northeast because that was where the factories were. In the corporate, mass-production economy, people spread out in the South and West, with most people in suburbs and central cities of large metropolitan areas. However, just as where people lived and worked in the past changed along with economies, this is happening once again. The New Economy is giving people and companies more locational freedom. An increased share of the economy consists of processing information in digital form, so less economic activity needs to be near natural resources or even big population centers.

Where will it be? In the New Economy, companies increasingly look to move to and expand where knowledge workers live. Because they are in greater demand and are able to be particular about who they work for, knowledge workers can live in places that provide a high quality of life in addition to a good job. The result is that for the first time in history it is possible to conceive of a society where a significant share of people live not where the jobs are, but rather where they want, with the jobs following them. And increasingly that choice is small towns or rural areas, with 60% of Americans preferring to live there.

There are several things governments can do to help create a more human-centered distribution of economic activity. Governments can use the location of government jobs to foster more-balanced growth. Where state and federal governments choose to locate their jobs can play an important role in regional development. In addition, when the federal government is making decisions as to closing certain facilities, such as military bases, one of the factors it should use in making the decision is whether the facility is in a large, booming metropolitan area.

But governments need to do more than just move their own jobs to smaller cities; they also need to establish policies to encourage private companies to do the same. One thing that government could do to support the transition to enable more workers to work and live in smaller communities is to phase out farm subsidies and reinvest the savings in innovative rural development efforts.

Are a Humane Economy and a Productive Economy in Conflict?

Today, in the face of growing global competition, pro-business conservatives argue that focusing on living the good life will reduce efficiency and competitiveness. In contrast, civil society liberals and progressives argue that the relentless drive toward efficiency dampens the human spirit, fails to meet human needs, and spoils the environment. Efforts to boost productivity, they argue, support the interests of the powerful, not the people.

Luckily, the conservatives and the liberals are both wrong. In the New Economy, increased efficiency and a more-humane economy can go hand-in-hand. The key challenge is to boost productivity rapidly but in a way that offers more-humane work environments and more time for leisure.

Increased productivity can create a more-humane economy. Higher productivity leads to higher wages and lower prices, which allow people to work less while maintaining or increasing incomes. Moreover, automating unpleasant and unsatisfying jobs shifts the overall mix of jobs toward more-satisfying ones. Finally, productivity growth creates the wealth that is necessary for the kind of public investments needed to foster a more-livable society.

The relationship works both ways: In an economy that is increasingly powered by knowledge, a more-humane economy can boost productivity. People are more productive when they are able to establish a healthier balance between work and non-work activities. One study found that companies supporting flexible work arrangements such as flextime, telecommuting, and job sharing had 3.5% higher market value than companies with no workplace flexibility.

We have come a long way from the days of efficiency expert Frederick Taylor and treating workers like cogs in a machine. Maybe the humane economy that John Maynard Keynes foresaw 75 years ago is finally at hand.

ROBERT D. ATKINSON is vice president and director of the Technology and New Economy Project at the Progressive Policy Institute, 600 Pennsylvania Avenue, S.E., Suite 400, Washington, D.C. 20003. Telephone 202-608-1239; e-mail ratkinson@ppionline.org; Web site www.ppionline.org.

This article draws from his book *The Past and Future of America's Economy: Long Waves of Innovation that Power Cycles of Growth* (Edward Elgar, 2004; paperback edition, 2005), which is available from the Futurist Bookshelf, www.wfs.org/bkshelf.htm.

The Rich Get (Much) Richer

The top 1% take a fatter slice now than at any time since the 1920s

STEVEN RATTNER

Hooray for *The New York Times* and *The Wall Street Journal* for returning the problems of class in America to the front page. Shame on the rest of us, passive witnesses to the emergence of a second Gilded Age, another Roaring Twenties, in which the fruits of economic success have gone not to the broad populace but to a slim sliver at the top. For this handful, life is a sweet melange of megafortunes, grand houses, and massive yachts. Meanwhile, the bottom 80% endures economic stagnation, including real wages that haven't risen in 14 months, according to the Bureau of Labor Statistics.

Much of the recent commentary has focused on class mobility, the opportunity for individuals to move up the ladder. But trumpeting mobility as a reason for ignoring growing income inequality is a chimera. Even if mobility is high—a questionable assertion—it is hardly a consolation for those who remain at the bottom, gazing across a growing distance at the more successful.

We can debate a lot of economic data but not income inequality. Every serious study shows that the U.S. income gap has become a chasm. Over the past 30 years, the share of income going to the highest-earning Americans has risen steadily to levels not seen since shortly before the Great Depression.

JUST HOW DRAMATIC A SHIFT over the past three decades? Economists Thomas Piketty and Emmanuel Saez calculated (using data from the Internal Revenue Service, hardly a hotbed of partisanship) that the share of income going to the top 1% of households nearly doubled, to 14.7% in 2002, up from a low of 7.7% in the early 1970s. By comparison, the income share for the top 1% peaked at 19.6% in 1928 before beginning its long slide. What is particularly alarming is that at every step up the ladder, the disparity has progressively widened. Over the past 30 years, the share of income garnered by the top 10% of Americans has grown by about a third; the share of the top 0.01%—the 13,000 or so households with an average income of $10.8 million in 2002—has multiplied nearly four times.

What's to blame for this sorry situation? Certainly globalization has taken its toll. Cheaper labor in emerging markets means relentless wage pressure on U.S. workers. Meanwhile, the fruits of American success in fast-growing services and technology remain available only to the slice of our workforce with the necessary skills. Other factors, such as an increasingly regressive tax code, have also played a role.

Growing inequality helps explain why so many Americans feel so vulnerable even as the overall economy continues to expand. Moods understandably darken when many have to take second jobs and go into debt to improve their living standards. These pressures are exacerbated by another evident trend: greater income insecurity, a result of the decreasing percentage of Americans who have certainty of pension and health-care benefits to cushion them against a loss of wages.

The renewed attention to the glacial progress of all but a few has drawn fire from an eclectic mix of those who say it isn't true, those who say it is true but it doesn't matter, and those who say we don't know enough to know whether it's true, so let's not worry about it. But a common thread among these naysayers is the fear that fretting about income disparities could lead to the redistributionist and suffocating slow-growth policies of Old Europe.

We can follow their advice and do nothing and hope that America's rising tide eventually will lift all boats proportionately—something that has not occurred in 30 years. Or we can believe in growth capitalism while also worrying that most Americans are being left behind. As Brad DeLong, an economist at University of California at Berkeley recently wrote, historical data suggest that growth and less income inequality are not mutually exclusive objectives.

Sadly, there is no magic bullet. We need to provide more education and training to fix our problem of too many low-skilled workers. We don't need to become tax-code Robin Hoods, but we can be vigilant about tax plans—like virtually all of President George W. Bush's—that widen the gulf between haves and have-nots. Finally, we can provide more protection for those at risk, such as better wage insurance to cushion the effects of globalization.

If we don't pursue policies to fix inequality, social pressures may force unwise, even extremist moves, like protectionism. Income inequality is now wider in America than anywhere else in the industrialized world and on a par with that of a Third World country. Is this the American Dream?

STEVEN RATTNER is managing principal of private investment firm Quadrangle Group and former deputy.

Outsourcing Jobs

The Myths and Realities

Martin N. Baily and Diana Farrell

With the digital revolution and the dramatic fall in international telecommunications costs comes the prospect that white collar jobs, long insulated from global competition, can be performed offshore in countries where labor can be had for as little as one-tenth its cost in the United States. Call-center agents, data processors, medical technicians and software programmers are all finding their jobs at risk from the nation's growing trade in services with emerging markets. In fact, offshoring is often blamed for the agonizingly slow pace of job growth in the United States during the current economic recovery.

Even free-trade advocates have wavered in their convictions that open is always better. Pessimists warn that millions of Americans will lose their jobs to an army of disciplined, educated Indian and Chinese workers. In response, Congress's 2004 omnibus spending bill included a provision that prohibits federal agencies from outsourcing some kinds of work to private companies that use workers in foreign countries. Twenty-three states are considering similar restrictions, and at least four have already passed them.

The debate over outsourcing, which cast a long shadow over this year's election campaign in the Midwest, is misplaced, however, because the issue is not globalization, but the way nations allocate the benefits of economic integration. Trade in labor services, like other international trade, benefits the United States as a whole by making the economic pie bigger and raising the standard of living. Outsourcing jobs abroad can help keep companies profitable, thereby preserving other jobs in the United States. The cost savings can be used to lower prices, and in some cases to offer consumers better service. And by increasing their productivity, offshoring enables companies to invest more in the new technologies that will create jobs at home. With the world's most flexible and innovative economy, the United States is uniquely positioned to benefit from the trend.

Of course, what is good for the economy as a whole is not good for every individual. History and common sense confirm that outsourcing will cost some workers their jobs. But this painful reality does not weaken the case for free trade. The United States could enjoy the benefits of free trade in services while protecting individuals with programs that help workers make the transition to new jobs. These programs might include job retraining opportunities and generous mandated severance packages, portable health and pension benefits, and wage insurance.

How the United States Benefits

We looked into what happens to a dollar of U.S. corporate spending when a company moves a service job to India. We found that, far from being a zero-sum game, offshoring is a story of mutual gain, benefiting both countries. The receiving economy (India) captures 33 cents, in the form of wages paid to local workers, profits earned by local outsourcing providers and their suppliers, and taxes collected from second- and third-tier suppliers to the outsourcing companies.

But the gains to the U.S. economy are much larger. The most obvious source of value is the cost savings enjoyed by U.S. companies. For every dollar of corporate spending that moves offshore, American businesses save 58 cents. Companies can reinvest the savings in new business opportunities, pay additional dividends to shareholders, or both. Moreover, because wages are lower in the relevant foreign labor markets, companies can hire more (as well as better-qualified) workers to do the same job, and spend more on supervision and training. Some companies have found that offshore workers are more highly motivated and perform better, particularly in low-skilled jobs that lack prestige and suffer from high turnover at home. One British bank's call-center agents in India process 20 percent more transactions than their counterparts in the United Kingdom and have a 3 percent higher accuracy level.

Consumers benefit, too, as companies are forced to pass on savings in the form of lower prices—much as they now benefit from trade in goods. New research by Catherine Mann of the Institute for International Economics found that the globalization of computer manufacturing has reduced the cost of hardware by as much as 30 percent, thereby boosting demand and adding roughly $230 billion to the U.S. GDP since 1995. Trade in services will do the same. A medical technician in India, for instance, can read an MRI scan at a fraction of the cost of a comparable analysis in the United States.

Transferring that position to India may cause an American technician to be laid off, but lower prices for these lifesaving technologies enable more sick people to receive scans.

How It Works

Offshoring yields benefits for the U.S. economy in other ways as well. First, Indian companies that sell the services will also import goods and services—everything from telecommunications equipment to legal and financial expertise. A call center in Bangalore is likely to be filled with HP computers, Microsoft software and telephones from Lucent, and to be audited by PricewaterhouseCoopers. We estimate that for every dollar of corporate spending that moves abroad, offshore companies buy five cents' worth of goods and services from the United States. On top of that, young Indian workers employed by outsourcing firms buy imported goods. Thanks to these corporate and individual buyers, exports from the United States to India stood at $5 billion in 2003, up from $3.7 billion in 2000.

In addition, the U.S. economy benefits because many Indian outsourcing firms are owned in whole or in part by U.S. companies, including General Electric and EDS, that repatriate their earnings. In this way, another four cents of every dollar spent abroad returns to the United States.

All told, the direct benefits to the United States from corporate savings, added exports and repatriated profits total 67 cents—twice the benefit to India. But the gains don't end there. Corporate savings may be invested in new businesses in the United States, and that investment will boost productivity as well as creating jobs. Based on historical experience, these new jobs will, on average, add more value than the ones lost: carriage makers were replaced by auto assemblers, and farmers by processed food factory workers.

Indeed, this has been the pattern in recent decades as manufacturing jobs moved offshore. U.S. manufacturing employment shrank by two million in the past 20 years—but net employment increased by 43 million jobs in other areas, including educational and health services, professional and business services, trade and transport government, leisure and hospitality, and financial services. Over the same period, domestic manufacturing output increased despite the decline in the number of manufacturing workers, because factories became much more productive. Higher productivity means a higher national income and a higher standard of living.

The pattern is likely to be repeated as jobs in call centers, back-office operations, and information technology services go offshore. Opportunities will appear to redeploy labor and invest capital to generate higher-value-added occupations will appear. The Bureau of Labor Statistics estimates that between 2000 and 2010, the United States economy will create 22 million jobs (net of jobs lost), mostly in business services, health care, social services, transportation and communications.

The Bureau of Labor Statistics also predicts that computer-related occupations—often thought to be at high risk of offshoring—will be among the fastest-growing domestic job categories. While code writing can be done abroad, many other IT functions like systems integration cannot. In addition, there will undoubtedly be jobs created in areas we can't even imagine today. Thirty years ago, for example, no one could have guessed the coming ubiquity of the cellular phone, an industry now employing nearly 200,000 workers in the United States.

The view that new jobs will be created as old jobs disappear is based on repeated experience. For example, in the 1990s, trade expanded rapidly, with increases in offshoring of both manufacturing and service jobs. At the same time, overall employment soared, unemployment fell to 4 percent, and real wages rose.

Lori Kletzer, an economist at the University of California (Santa Cruz), found that between 1979 and 1999, 69 percent of nonmanufacturing workers who lost jobs due to free trade found new ones within one year, and on average earned 96.2 percent of their old wages. These figures, combined with the fact that 72 cents of every dollar spent offshore had previously been spent on U.S. wages, implies that the additional value to the United States economy of redeploying workers would be 45 to 47 cents. This is a conservative estimate, based on historical figures of job loss due to trade. White-collar employees at risk of offshoring today are generally more highly educated and might be expected to find new jobs faster than workers in the service sector as a whole.

Thus, far from being bad for the United States, offshoring creates net value for the economy—to the tune of $1.12 to $1.14 for every dollar that goes abroad.

Offshoring in Context

Offshoring's impact on employment needs to be put in perspective. Forrester Research predicts that by 2015, roughly 3.4 million business-processing jobs for U.S. firms will be performed abroad. Although this number may seem large, it is only a small piece of the jobs picture.

Employment in the United States today totals more than 150 million. Technological change, economic recessions, shifts in consumer demand and other shocks generate continual job turnover. Each month, roughly 2 million Americans change jobs. Even the most pessimistic predictions of job loss due to offshoring will be far lower.

The number of service jobs likely to be lost to offshoring is also small compared to the number of workers who lose jobs through mass layoffs prompted by corporate mergers and restructuring, even when the economy is growing. In 1999 alone—at the peak of the 1990s boom—1.15 million workers lost their jobs due to corporate restructuring. Job churn is part of life, even in a growing economy.

Competitive economies with flexible labor markets can cope with the natural process of job creation and destruction, and the U.S. economy is arguably in the best position of any to do so. According to the Organization for Economic Cooperation and Development, the United States has the highest rate of reemployment of any OECD country by a factor of almost two. Most workers who lose their positions find another within six months. Over the past 10 years, 3.5 million private-sector jobs have been created each year on average—and job growth was fastest among high-wage jobs.

A flexible job market will enable the U.S. to create jobs faster than outsourcing eliminates them. Consider how the American semiconductor industry reinvented itself after losing out to Japanese competitors that entered the market during the late 1980s. The Japanese quickly dominated the memory chip segment of the industry, and spurred a public outcry over "unfair" Japanese competition and the loss of high-paying jobs at home. The big U.S. players—Intel, Texas Instruments and Motorola—all exited the memory business.

But this prompted American companies to invest more aggressively in the production of microprocessors and logic products—the next growth wave in semiconductors. Intel became the dominant global player in microprocessors; Texas Instruments became dominant in digital signal processors, the brains in mobile phones, while Motorola gained a strong position in communications devices. Throughout this shift toward higher-value-added activities, the total number of U.S. jobs in semiconductors and closely related electronics held constant at around half a million.

Separating Fact from Fiction

A number of myths and half-truths muddle the public debate over white-collar offshoring. Virtually all economists have concluded that trade contributes to economic growth. But skeptics argue that trade in services is somehow different from trade in goods, and will be less beneficial to the U.S. economy.

That's implausible, however, given the strength of U.S. service industries. The United States continues to run a trade surplus in services, even with India. Indeed, it can boast of the most productive service sector of any country in the world. American banks, law firms, accounting firms, information technology integrators and management consultants (to name a few service businesses) have established themselves as global competitors. As a result, it has been Washington's policy to demand more openness on the part of other countries in these areas. What's more, the depreciating dollar will undoubtedly help boost service exports even higher.

Others argue that the number of workers in China and India is so large that integrating them into the global economy will lead to persistent unemployment in the United States and Europe. Certainly, both of these emerging economies have a large supply of productive workers. But they also have fast-growing appetites for goods and services. The great majority of their enormous workforces will be producing for their own economies. Provided China and India allow their currency exchange rates to adjust to market forces, they will not be a net drain on economic activity or jobs in the rest of the world.

Technology Replacing People

The notion that China and India are taking work from the United States because of their low wages is equally untenable. The truth is that many jobs in India today are viable only in a low-wage environment and could not exist in the United States. Thus, the fact that a half-million people are now employed in India's outsourcing industry does not mean that there could be 500,000 more jobs in the United States. Without offshoring, companies would scale back or stop offering premium services like round-the-clock customer help. Moreover, technology is putting many U.S. jobs at risk even without offshoring. Automated voice-response systems are replacing call-center workers, online hotel and airline booking systems are replacing live operators and travel agents and imaging software is replacing data-entry workers.

A related myth is the notion that service-sector offshoring is responsible for the anemic job creation during this economic recovery. More than two million jobs in the United States have been lost since 2000. But nearly all of those jobs were in manufacturing, not services. Moreover, employment in information technology, which is allegedly one of the sectors hardest hit by offshoring, has actually grown since 1999. While it is true that 70,000 computer programmers have lost their jobs, more than 115,000 higher-paid software engineering jobs were created during the period. Jobs for computer support specialists and systems analysts and administrators grew by roughly 83,000.

The Challenge for Policymakers

Arguments about the greater good and the long-term health of the economy do not, of course, ease the plight of the people who do lose their jobs or find themselves in lower-wage employment. While free trade creates wealth and improves a nation's average standard of living, not everyone benefits—particularly not in the short-term. Today, globalization is creating a higher level of turnover in the work force than ever before. Rather than pursuing a single career with just one or two companies, as workers in previous generations could expect, most people today will have many employers, and a growing number will switch their careers as well. Job change is a much larger part of life than it used to be, and the challenge for policymakers is to lubricate the transition.

A stable number of workers who lose their jobs because of free trade do not easily find new ones, or must accept jobs with lower wages. From 1979 to 1999, roughly 30 percent of the people who were laid off as a result of cheap imports in sectors other than manufacturing had not found jobs a year later. And for the majority who did find new jobs, the wages varied considerably. On average, wages in the new jobs were about the same as the wages in the jobs that had been lost. But hardly anybody is average: 55 percent took lower-paid jobs, and about 25 percent took pay cuts of 30 percent or more.

Public policy can help such workers make the transition. Job-retraining programs and continuing-education grants can help workers gain new skills as the economy evolves. Mandated severance packages could help, too; increased portability of health benefits and pension plans between jobs is essential. Tax credits might be offered to companies that hire workers who lost their jobs because of trade.

Wage insurance also would help. For a small percentage of the savings from offshoring, companies could purchase insurance covering the wage losses of displaced workers. Building upon an insurance proposal that Lori Kletzer and Robert Litan of the Brookings Institution developed for workers displaced by trade in manufacturing, we estimate that for as little as 4 to 5 percent of the savings companies realize from offshoring, they could insure all full-time workers who lost jobs as a result.

The program would compensate workers for 70 percent of the difference between the wage rate they received on the jobs they lost and the wage rates they received on the new jobs, as well as offer health care subsidies for up to two years.

These policies would make the U.S. labor force more flexible, allowing the economy's wealth-creation engine to flourish. Protectionism, by contrast, might save a few jobs in the short run, but would stifle innovation and job creation in the long run. And as a practical matter, protectionism makes little sense, given how enmeshed the U.S. economy already is with the rest of the world.

In early 2004, Congress debated an amendment to a trade bill that would have prohibited federal agencies from contracting with companies that outsource abroad. But it found that under the terms being discussed, procurement for the Department of Defense would grind to a halt. The amendment that finally passed was a weaker version that hardly constrains any activity. Similarly, Ohio considered a law to prohibit state contracts from going to companies with ties abroad—only to find that it would exclude virtually all of the current contractors in the state.

Facilitating change, not stopping it, must be the policymakers' goal.

MR. BAILY is a senior advisor to the McKinsey Global Institute. **MS. FARRELL** is director of the Institute. From "Is Your Job Headed for Bangalore?" by Martin N. Baily and Diana Farrell, *The Milken Institute Review,* Fourth Quarter, 2004, pages 33–41.

Laid Off and Left Out

Bob Herbert

You don't hear much from the American worker anymore. Like battered soldiers at the end of a lost war, ordinary workers seem resigned to their diminished status.

The grim terms imposed on them include wage stagnation, the widespread confiscation of benefits (including pensions they once believed were guaranteed), and a permanent state of employment insecurity.

For an unnecessarily large number of Americans, the workplace has become a hub of anxiety and fear, an essential but capricious environment in which you might be shown the door at any moment.

In his new book, "The Disposable American: Layoffs and Their Consequences," Louis Uchitelle tells us that since 1984, when the U.S. Bureau of Labor Statistics started monitoring "worker displacement," at least 30 million full-time workers have been "permanently separated from their jobs and their paychecks against their wishes."

Mr. Uchitelle writes on economic issues for *The Times*. In his book, he traces the evolution of that increasingly endangered species, the secure job, and the effect that the current culture of corporate layoffs is having on ordinary men and women.

He said he was surprised, as he did the reporting for the book, by the extensive emotional fallout that accompanies layoffs. "There's a lot of mental health damage," he said. "The act of being laid off is such a blow to the self-esteem. Layoffs are a national phenomenon, a societal problem—but the laid-off workers blame themselves."

In addition to being financially strapped, laid-off workers and their families are often emotionally strapped as well. Common problems include depression, domestic strife and divorce.

Mr. Uchitelle's thesis is that corporate layoffs have been carried much too far, that they have gone beyond a legitimate and necessary response to a changing economy.

"What started as a necessary response to the intrusion of foreign manufacturers into the American marketplace got out of hand," he writes. "By the late 1990's, getting rid of workers had become normal practice, ingrained behavior, just as job security had been 25 years earlier."

In many cases, a thousand workers were fired when 500 might have been sufficient, or 10,000 were let go when 5,000 would have been enough. We pay a price for these excesses. The losses that accrue to companies and communities when many years of improving skills and valuable experience are casually and unnecessarily tossed on a scrap heap are incalculable.

"The majority of the people who are laid off," said Mr. Uchitelle, "end up in jobs that pay significantly less than they earned before, or they drop out altogether."

At the heart of the layoff phenomenon is the myth, endlessly repeated by corporate leaders and politicians of both parties, that workers who are thrown out of their jobs can save themselves, can latch onto spiffy new jobs by becoming better educated and acquiring new skills.

"Education and training create the jobs, according to this way of thinking," writes Mr. Uchitelle. "Or, put another way, a job materializes for every trained or educated worker, a job commensurate with his or her skills, for which he or she is appropriately paid."

That is just not so, and the corporate and political elite need to stop feeding that bogus line to the public.

There is no doubt that the better-educated and better-trained get better jobs. But the reality is that there are not enough good jobs currently available to meet the demand of college-educated and well-trained workers in the United States, which is why so many are working in jobs for which they are overqualified.

A chapter in "The Disposable American" details the plight of exquisitely trained airline mechanics who found themselves laid off from jobs that had paid up to $31 an hour. Mr. Uchitelle writes: "Not enough jobs exist at $31 an hour—or at $16 an hour, for that matter—to meet the demand for them. Jobs just don't materialize at cost-conscious companies to absorb all the qualified people who want them."

The most provocative question raised by Mr. Uchitelle is whether the private sector is capable of generating enough good jobs at good pay to meet the demand of everyone who is qualified and wants to work.

If it cannot (and so far it has not), then what? If education and training are not the building blocks to solid employment, what is? These are public policy questions of the highest importance, and so far they are being ignored.

Multiple Minimums

Congress hasn't raised the federal minimum wage in years, but many states are increasing theirs

JOHN M. BRODER

While Congress has not raised the federal minimum wage in almost 10 years, some states have taken action on their own: Nearly half of the civilian labor force now lives in states where the minimum wage is higher than the rate set by the federal government.

Seventeen states and the District of Columbia have set minimum wages that exceed the federal minimum of $5.15 an hour. And this year, lawmakers in dozens of the remaining states will debate raising their minimum wages.

The federal minimum wage was last raised in 1997. Since then, efforts to increase it have been opposed by lawmakers and business groups who argue that a higher rate raises costs and, as a result, slows the creation of entry-level jobs and particularly hurts young and unskilled workers.

In response, labor unions and community groups have increasingly focused their efforts on the states. And in some areas, "living wage" movement shave helped raise minimum wages on a local level. In Santa Fe, N.M., a living-wage ordinance has boosted the minimum to $9.50 an hour.

A Long Debate

Opinion polls show wide public support for an increase in the federal minimum wage, which falls far short of the income needed to place a family above the federal poverty level. Even the president of Wal-Mart, the country's largest private employer, endorses an increase, saying that workers who are earning the federal minimum can't afford to shop at his stores.

"The public is way ahead of Washington," says Bill Samuel, legislative director of the AFL-CIO, a federation of labor unions. "They see this as a matter of basic fairness, the underpinning of basic labor law in this country, a floor under wages so we're not competing with Bangledesh."

The minimum wage has been fiercely debated since it was established in 1938 as part of the Fair Labor Standards Act under President Franklin D. Roosevelt. Opponents argue that it is a government intrusion into the employer-employee relationship. An increase, they say, drives up labor costs across the board and freezes out unskilled and first-time workers, whom employers may decide not to hire as a result of the increased costs.

According to the U.S. Bureau of Labor Statistics, in 2004, about 2 million americans—2.7 percent of the overall workforce—earned the minimum-wage requirements.) They were generally young (half were under 25, and a quarter were teenagers), unmarried, and without a high school diploma.

Advocates of an increase point out that inflation has made the minimum wage worth less today in terms of purchasing power than at any time since 1955. They also say that raising it does not cause job losses. Tim Nesbitt, former president of the Oregon AFL-CIO, says that even with a minimum wage of $7.25 an hour, one of the nation's hightest, Oregon has had twice the rate of job growth as the rest of the country.

The battle is expected to be particularly intense this year in Ohio, one of two states (the other is Kansas) that has a minimum wage below the federal level. Ohio's minimum is $4.25 an hour for small employers, some farms, and most restaurants. A proposed constiutional amendment would raise it to $6.85.

How Much for a Burger?

Rick Cassara, a Cleveland restaurant owner, says that he opposes a mandated wage increase. "It exerts upward pressure on all wages and prices," he says. "If the minimum wage is $7 and I have pay $8 or $9 to hire a dishwasher, then the cooks are going to say they want more. How much can I charge for that hamburger?"

In 2004, voters in Nevada and Florida approved ballot initiatives to raise the minimum wage to $6.15. And in Claifornia, where the minimum wage is $6.75, a $1-an-hour increase is being debated.

For many workers, increases in the minimum wage may not make enought of a difference. Noemi Rodreiguez, a single mother in New York City, says the minimum wage, which was recently raised from $6.50 to $6.75 an hour in New York, means falling short. Rodriguez, 21, now makes $8 an hour as chief photo technician at a chain drugstore. Six months ago, she says, "I earned the minimum wage when I started here, and I was still going hungry. It's not enough to pay utilities, buy food, and take care of my baby."

Background

The first minimum-wage law passed in 1938 during the Depression, when millions lived in poverty. There has been a debate ever since between those who say minimum-wage hikes hurt job creation, particularly for the young and unskilled, and those who see it as a guarantee of basic living standards for workers.

JOHN M. BRODER is Los Angeles bureau chief for *The New York Times*; with additional reporting by Jon Gertner and Anthony Ramirez.

The Gender Gyp

No wonder women are worried about Social Security. They have a lot more to lose.

THOMAS N. BETHELL

I t's true what you've heard: women are different from men. Look at a snapshot of our economy. Although times are changing, women still are less likely than men to join the work force (which doesn't mean they're working any less hard at home, they're just not getting paid for it). Women who do go to work are generally paid less than men, and they're less likely to have any kind of pension plan. They're far more likely to leave employment for long stretches, to raise kids—often as single mothers—or to care for aging parents. And, as a rule, they live longer than men.

These facts have far-reaching consequences. Women are less likely to be able to accumulate savings while working (or, of course, while out of the work force). But because of their greater longevity, they're more likely to need income for decades after their earning years draw to a close. And in old age they're likely to end up alone, with few resources to draw upon.

That's where Social Security comes in.

"Social Security looks very different from a woman's perspective," says Nancy Duff Campbell, co-president of the National Women's Law Center. "For men it's mainly a worker retirement program. For women it's a family insurance plan."

'We need what the name says—"security"— not more risks. There's risks enough in this life without thinking up new ones.'
—Erma Jean Mingo

Janice Thomas, a former nurse now raising two children, sees firsthand how it works for the elderly parishioners she encounters doing pastoral outreach work at a church in Washington. "I know how important Social Security is to the women I visit with," she says. "They'd be lost without it." She'd like to see the program strengthened—for example by providing credit for years spent raising a family—but mostly she wants to see no changes that could expose more women to the risk of ending their lives in poverty.

"As a neonatal and pediatric nurse in Atlanta, I saw the effects of poverty at the beginning of life," she says. "Social Se-

curity guards against it at the end. To weaken that protection would be criminal."

While 80 percent of men get benefits as retired workers, only 39.7 percent of women do. Most women—60.3 percent—get benefits at least in part as a spouse or former spouse of a retired, disabled or deceased worker. Social Security is designed to meet their needs in four ways:

1. It uses a progressive benefit formula that replaces a higher proportion of earnings for people with low lifetime earnings. That's particularly important protection for women working in low-wage jobs and for women who leave the work force to raise families or care for aging parents and then re-enter it later.
2. Its annual cost-of-living adjustment (COLA) fully protects benefits—whether paid to a retired worker, a spouse or a survivor—against inflation and maintains their purchasing power over time. That's vital protection for longer-living women (who account for 71 percent of all beneficiaries age 85 and up).
3. It helps women who haven't been working but who are married to a worker by paying them a benefit when the working spouse retires (generally 50 percent of the worker's benefit). When the retired worker dies, his widow gets a lifelong benefit equal to his benefit.
4. It pays survivor benefits to women whose husbands die or become disabled during their working years, helping them meet the cost of raising children. Although politicians speak of Social Security as a program for retirees, it helps more than 5.3 million children—making it the nation's most important safety net for them.

That's how the program saved César Moreno Pérez's mother when her husband, a California farm worker, died in 1994, leaving her to care for their eight children. Social Security survivor benefits kept the family out of poverty and helped César to graduate from the University of California at Berkeley. Today, he works as a policy analyst for the Labor Council for Latin American Advancement.

"My grandmother worked most of her life in the fields and depends totally on her Social Security check," he says. "For my mother it will be the same story when she can't work in the fields anymore. Social Security doesn't make anyone rich, but by keeping people out of poverty it helps them keep their dignity."

Social Security isn't perfect. Lawmakers could do more to help women by taking steps such as improving benefits for dual-earning spouses and by providing a "family service credit" for the years when a woman leaves employment to raise or care for a family. But such changes would increase Social Security's overall costs, so they're unlikely to gain traction at a time when many politicians claim that Social Security faces insolvency and that our first priority should be to shrink the program.

Social Security's critics argue that the current program has shortcomings affecting African American families. They claim that African American men die younger and their families would be better off if some of the money had been in private accounts that could be left to heirs. Yet the private account may not contain enough money for the monthly benefits that Social Security provides to widows and surviving children. In addition, African American families rely more on Social Security's disability benefits, which private accounts generally cannot match.

'The right place for risk is a 401(k) or an IRA— not Social Security.'

—Shannon Huhn

Despite the scary talk about Social Security's future, the program's trustees anticipate that revenues over the next 75 years will probably fall short of expenses by about 2 percent of taxable payrolls. Economists and politicians have suggested various ways to close that gap and keep the program solvent without slashing benefits. [See "What's the Big Idea?" *AARP Bulletin*, April.]

Strengthening the program is the approach favored by Shannon Huhn, a commercial real estate broker in Laguna Beach, Calif. She remembers her grandmother moving in with her family when Huhn was a teenager. "She had come to America as an Irish immigrant, she was widowed at a fairly young age, and Social Security—along with our family—was her safety net," Huhn recalls. "Now we're told that Social Security is underfunded. We should shore it up, not redesign it in a way that puts basic retirement income at risk. The right place for risk is a 401(k) or an IRA—not Social Security."

President Bush is campaigning for a very different plan. Rather than shore up the present program, the two proposals he has thus far embraced would shrink it by (1) encouraging workers to divert some of their payroll contributions into private investment accounts, and (2) reducing benefits, compared to what's promised under current law, for all but the poorest workers. [See "Future Shock," *AARP Bulletin*, June.]

The mechanics are complex, but the basic thinking is simple: The hope is that private investment accounts would do well enough to offset the reduced benefits. Meanwhile, Social Security would gradually become a much smaller program.

What Women Get

Social Security Now	Private Accounts
Defined benefits. Social Security provides predetermined benefits to disabled and retired workers, their dependents and surviors.	**Benefits not defined.** Benefits will depend on investment success and how the market is doing when a person retires.
Survivor and disability insurance. This insurance is equal, on average, to a $400,000 life insurance policy and a $350,000 disability policy—important protection for spouses and children.	**Limited insurance.** Proposals reduce survivor benefits for all but low-wage workers. A worker whose career is cut short by death or disability may not have much in a private account.
Better benefits for lower earners. Social Security's progressive formula pays comparatively higher benefits to women with low, lifetime earnings, a help to child rearers and caregivers.	**Lower benefits for most workers.** Under price indexing defined benefits would be reduced for all but lowest income earners. Private accounts would depend on how much a worker pays in.
Inflation protection. Automatic annual cost-of-living adjustment (COLA) fully protects the purchasing power of benefits—an important protection for longer-living women.	**Inflation risk.** Inflation at just 2.5% per year would cut the value of an annuity by 40% in 20 years. Few private annuities carry even partial inflation protection—it's often capped at 3%.
Protection for divorced women. If a wage earner and a spouse divorce (after at least 10 years of marriage), the spouse is eligible for benefits.	**Protection for divorced women unclear.** Proposals don't say whether a private account holder must share access, setting the stage for legal struggles.

Sources: Social Security Administration, National Women's Law Center

Bush argues that private accounts will be a better investment than Social Security. Campaigning in Kentucky on June 2, he said: "Right now, when we collect your money, if you're a youngster out there working hard and paying into the system, you'll be displeased to know you get about a 1.8 percent return on your money, which is pitiful … Heck, you can put your money in T-bills and do better than that."

Mary Katharine Ham, editor of the *Insider*, a Heritage Foundation quarterly publication, echoes the president's argument: "Granted, my Social Security money does gain 1.76 percent. That's better than the 0 percent sock-drawer rate but less than the amount it would earn in a simple savings account—and much less than it would earn if I could invest it in bonds or stock index funds."

But others argue that it's misleading to talk about Social Security as an investment, since its purpose is to provide insurance—and you wouldn't talk about home insurance, for example, as an investment.

The key issue is how switching to a private investment account would affect women—and the answer is, it depends. If you work in a low-wage job or take time out to raise children, you're unlikely to be able to build up much of an account. When you retire, if you convert your account into an annuity—an insurance policy that provides annual income in monthly payments—a small balance in the account would mean small payments. If the stock market is down when you retire, the account may be even lower than expected—further reducing the annuity (which will also be reduced by administrative fees).

Moreover, annuities are based on life expectancy—which works against women. To illustrate: If a man and a woman arrive at retirement with equal amounts in their accounts, the woman will get a lower monthly payment—typically about 8 to 13 percent lower—because the insurer assumes she'll live longer. Terms vary from company to company, but for an annuity purchased at age 65 with a $100,000 investment account, a man might get about $700 a month, a woman about $610.

'Social Security doesn't make anyone rich, but by keeping people out of poverty it helps them keep their dignity.'

—César Moreno Pérez

So, whether a woman gets an annuity as a former worker or as a spouse, she'll get lower monthly payments than a man. And, as time goes on, the purchasing power of her annuity will shrink. A typical annuity purchased at age 65 will lose at least 40 percent of its value by the time she reaches age 85. Few annuities carry any inflation protection, and those that promise partial protection (often capped at a certain percentage) do so by reducing the amount of the monthly payment. No annuities carry the full protection of Social Security's COLAs.

In short, a private investment account can work for those who have considerable money to put into it and who are not concerned about inflation protection. But for others, this could be a risky way to build basic retirement income.

It's too risky when compared with the assured benefits that Social Security provides, says Erma Jean Mingo, retired and living in San Diego after 40 years as a public school teacher and assistant principal in Denver. "I follow the Social Security debate every hour on the hour," she says. "For generations Social Security has helped families like mine overcome the disadvantages we came up against. My father worked hard all his life—and then he lived on his Social Security. My brother is disabled; he lives on his Social Security. We need what the name says—'security'—not more risks. There's risks enough in this life without thinking up new ones."

Women will also be affected by another part of Bush's plan—reduced benefits (compared with what's promised under present law) for all but the poorest workers, those making below about $20,000 today. By linking benefits to prices instead of wages, the plan would cut benefits for everyone else—in other words, for about 70 percent of workers under 55 today. That means that benefits payable to the surviving widows and children of such workers would be cut, too, because they're based on the worker's benefit. Thus, shrinking Social Security by cutting wage earners' benefits would have a domino effect.

'As a pediatric nurse, I saw the effects of poverty at the beginning of life. To weaken protection at the end would be criminal.'

—Janice Thomas

Proponents of this approach argue that scaling back benefits for all but the poor is necessary because Congress has made promises it can't keep, sending Social Security toward eventual insolvency. Others, however, believe that moderate revenue increases and benefit adjustments can keep the program in balance. The president's proposal for price indexing is "an unnecessary and unfair benefit cut on the middle class," according to AARP Director of Policy John Rother.

There's a strong case to be made that most women can't afford to see their old-age security jeopardized by benefit cuts. Without Social Security, 53 percent of all women over 65 would be poor (compared with 12.4 percent now). Social Security provides 90 percent or more of total income for more than four in 10 single (including widowed) women over 65.

For minorities, there's even more at stake. More than six in 10 single African American and Hispanic women receive 90 percent or more of their income from Social Security. And even with Social Security's help, nearly half (44 percent) of African American and more than half (58 percent) of Hispanic elderly women living alone are poor.

"Given these circumstances," says Maya Rockeymoore, research director for the Congressional Black Caucus Foundation, "the guiding principle for lawmakers should be 'First, do no harm.'"

'I'd like to believe I'm planning my own life so I'll never have to depend on Social Security. But you never know what will happen.'

—Patricia Huggins

Looking ahead, will fewer women need to rely on Social Security in their old age? If so, policy decisions that have the effect of increasing risk and gradually shrinking benefits might not seem so harsh. But many experts agree that, based on key indicators, women's reliance on Social Security will remain high. Among the indicators:

- Work force participation rates remain lower for women in the 25-to-54 age range (75 percent versus 91 percent for men).
- Women earn less than men (about 76 cents on the dollar).
- The typical woman's 401(k) balance is 40 percent lower than the typical man's ($10,000 vs. $17,000).

- Social Security's actuaries estimate that, 40 years from now, 40 percent of women will rely at least in part on spousal benefits for their income.
- The Gerontological Society of America forecasts that poverty rates among those women who become eligible for Social Security benefits in 2020 will be unchanged from 1991.

It's hard to argue that Social Security is outliving its usefulness for women. "I'd like to believe I'm planning my own life so I'll never have to depend on Social Security," says Patricia Huggins, an aerobics instructor and massage therapist in Washington. "But you never know what will happen, which is why we need to be able to count on it. I've worked with older women in nursing homes living on fixed incomes who absolutely rely on Social Security, and I think the onset of old age is challenging enough without living in fear of not having enough to live on."

THOMAS N. BETHELL, a writer-editor in Washington, has been following Social Security issues for many years.

The Health Care Crisis and What to Do About It

PAUL KRUGMAN AND ROBIN WELLS

Thirteen years ago Bill Clinton became president partly because he promised to do something about rising health care costs. Although Clinton's chances of reforming the US health care system looked quite good at first, the effort soon ran aground. Since then a combination of factors—the unwillingness of other politicians to confront the insurance and other lobbies that so successfully frustrated the Clinton effort, a temporary remission in the growth of health care spending as HMOs briefly managed to limit cost increases, and the general distraction of a nation focused first on the gloriousness of getting rich, then on terrorism—have kept health care off the top of the agenda.

But medical costs are once again rising rapidly, forcing health care back into political prominence. Indeed, the problem of medical costs is so pervasive that it underlies three quite different policy crises. First is the increasingly rapid unraveling of employer-based health insurance. Second is the plight of Medicaid, an increasingly crucial program that is under both fiscal and political attack. Third is the long-term problem of the federal government's solvency, which is, as we'll explain, largely a problem of health care costs.

The good news is that we know more about the economics of health care than we did when Clinton tried and failed to remake the system. There's now a large body of evidence on what works and what doesn't work in health care, and it's not hard to see how to make dramatic improvements in US practice. As we'll see, the evidence clearly shows that the key problem with the US health care system is its fragmentation. A history of failed attempts to introduce universal health insurance has left us with a system in which the government pays directly or indirectly for more than half of the nation's health care, but the actual delivery both of insurance and of care is undertaken by a crazy quilt of private insurers, for-profit hospitals, and other players who add cost without adding value. A Canadian-style single-payer system, in which the government directly provides insurance, would almost surely be both cheaper and more effective than what we now have. And we could do even better if we learned from "integrated" systems, like the Veterans Administration, that directly provide some health care as well as medical insurance.

The bad news is that Washington currently seems incapable of accepting what the evidence on health care says. In particu-

lar, the Bush administration is under the influence of both industry lobbyists, especially those representing the drug companies, and a free-market ideology that is wholly inappropriate to health care issues. As a result, it seems determined to pursue policies that will increase the fragmentation of our system and swell the ranks of the uninsured.

Before we talk about reform, however, let's talk about the current state of the US health care system. Let us begin by asking a seemingly naive question: What's wrong with spending ever more on health care?

1.

Is health care spending a problem?

In 1960 the United States spent only 5.2 percent of GDP on health care. By 2004 that number had risen to 16 percent. At this point America spends more on health care than it does on food. But what's wrong with that?

The starting point for any discussion of rising health care costs has to be the realization that these rising costs are, in an important sense, a sign of progress. Here's how the Congressional Budget Office puts it, in the latest edition of its annual publication *The Long-Term Budget Outlook*:

> Growth in health care spending has outstripped economic growth regardless of the source of its funding.... The major factor associated with that growth has been the development and increasing use of new medical technology.... In the health care field, unlike in many sectors of the economy, technological advances have generally raised costs rather than lowered them.

Notice the three points in that quote. First, health care spending is rising rapidly "regardless of the source of its funding." Translation: although much health care is paid for by the government, this isn't a simple case of runaway government spending, because private spending is rising at a comparably fast clip. "Comparing common benefits," says the Kaiser Family Foundation, changes in Medicare spending in the last three decades has largely tracked the growth rate in private health insurance premiums. Typically, Medicare increases have been lower than those of private health insurance.

Second, "new medical technology" is the major factor in rising spending: we spend more on medicine because there's more that medicine can do. Third, in medical care, "technological advances have generally raised costs rather than lowered them": although new technology surely produces cost savings in medicine, as elsewhere, the additional spending that takes place as a result of the expansion of medical possibilities outweighs those savings.

So far, this sounds like a happy story. We've found new ways to help people, and are spending more to take advantage of the opportunity. Why not view rising medical spending, like rising spending on, say, home entertainment systems, simply as a rational response to expanded choice? We would suggest two answers.

The first is that the US health care system is extremely inefficient, and this inefficiency becomes more costly as the health care sector becomes a larger fraction of the economy. Suppose, for example, that we believe that 30 percent of US health care spending is wasted, and always has been. In 1960, when health care was only 5.2 percent of GDP, that meant waste equal to only 1.5 percent of GDP. Now that the share of health care in the economy has more than tripled, so has the waste.

This inefficiency is a bad thing in itself. What makes it literally fatal to thousands of Americans each year is that the inefficiency of our health care system exacerbates a second problem: our health care system often makes irrational choices, and rising costs exacerbate those irrationalities. Specifically, American health care tends to divide the population into insiders and outsiders. Insiders, who have good insurance, receive everything modern medicine can provide, no matter how expensive. Outsiders, who have poor insurance or none at all, receive very little. To take just one example, one study found that among Americans diagnosed with colorectal cancer, those without insurance were 70 percent more likely than those with insurance to die over the next three years.

In response to new medical technology, the system spends even more on insiders. But it compensates for higher spending on insiders, in part, by consigning more people to outsider status—robbing Peter of basic care in order to pay for Paul's state-of-the-art treatment. Thus we have the cruel paradox that medical progress is bad for many Americans' health.

This description of our health care problems may sound abstract. But we can make it concrete by looking at the crisis now afflicting employer-based health insurance.

2.

The unraveling of employer-based insurance

In 2003 only 16 percent of health care spending consisted of out-of-pocket expenditures by consumers. The rest was paid for by insurance, public or private. As we'll see, this heavy reliance on insurance disturbs some economists, who believe that doctors and patients fail to make rational decisions about spending because third parties bear the costs of medical treatment. But it's no use wishing that health care were sold like ordinary consumer goods, with individuals paying out of pocket for what they need. By its very nature, most health spending must be covered by insurance.

The reason is simple: in any given year, most people have small medical bills, while a few people have very large bills. In 2003, health spending roughly followed the "80–20 rule": 20 percent of the population accounted for 80 percent of expenses. Half the population had virtually no medical expenses; a mere 1 percent of the population accounted for 22 percent of expenses.

Here's how Henry Aaron and his coauthors summarize the implication of these numbers in their book *Can We Say No?*: "Most health costs are incurred by a small proportion of the population whose expenses greatly exceed plausible limits on out-of-pocket spending." In other words, if people had to pay for medical care the way they pay for groceries, they would have to forego most of what modern medicine has to offer, because they would quickly run out of funds in the face of medical emergencies.

So the only way modern medical care can be made available to anyone other than the very rich is through health insurance. Yet it's very difficult for the private sector to provide such insurance, because health insurance suffers from a particularly acute case of a well-known economic problem known as adverse selection. Here's how it works: imagine an insurer who offered policies to anyone, with the annual premium set to cover the average person's health care expenses, plus the administrative costs of running the insurance company. Who would sign up? The answer, unfortunately, is that the insurer's customers wouldn't be a representative sample of the population. Healthy people, with little reason to expect high medical bills, would probably shun policies priced to reflect the average person's health costs. On the other hand, unhealthy people would find the policies very attractive.

You can see where this is going. The insurance company would quickly find that because its clientele was tilted toward those with high medical costs, its actual costs per customer were much higher than those of the average member of the population. So it would have to raise premiums to cover those higher costs. However, this would disproportionately drive off its healthier customers, leaving it with an even less healthy customer base, requiring a further rise in premiums, and so on.

Insurance companies deal with these problems, to some extent, by carefully screening applicants to identify those with a high risk of needing expensive treatment, and either rejecting such applicants or charging them higher premiums. But such screening is itself expensive. Furthermore, it tends to screen out exactly those who most need insurance.

Most advanced countries have dealt with the defects of private health insurance in a straightforward way, by making health insurance a government service. Through Medicare, the United States has in effect done the same thing for its seniors. We also have Medicaid, a means-tested program that provides health insurance to many of the poor and near poor. But nonelderly, nonpoor Americans are on their own. In practice, only a tiny fraction of nonelderly Americans (5.3 percent in 2003) buy private insurance for themselves. The rest of those not covered by Medicare or Medicaid get insurance, if at all, through their employers.

Employer-based insurance is a peculiarly American institution. As Julius Richmond and Rashi Fein tell us in *The Health Care Mess,* the dominant role of such insurance is the result of historical accident rather than deliberate policy. World War II caused a labor shortage, but employers were subject to controls that prevented them from attracting workers by offering higher wages. Health benefits, however, weren't controlled, and so became a way for employers to compete for workers. Once employers began offering medical benefits, they also realized that it was a form of compensation workers valued highly because it protected them from risk. Moreover, the tax law favored employer-based insurance, because employers' contributions weren't considered part of workers' taxable income. Today, the value of the tax subsidy for employer-based insurance is estimated at around $150 billion a year.

Employer-based insurance has historically offered a partial solution to the problem of adverse selection. In principle, adverse selection can still occur even if health insurance comes with a job rather than as a stand-alone policy. This would occur if workers with health problems flocked to companies that offered health insurance, while healthy workers took jobs at companies that didn't offer insurance and offered higher wages instead. But until recently health insurance was a sufficiently small consideration in job choice that large corporations offering good health benefits, like General Motors, could safely assume that the health status of their employees was representative of the population at large and that adverse selection wasn't inflating the cost of health insurance.

In 2004, according to census estimates, 63.1 percent of Americans under sixty-five received health insurance through their employers or family members' employers. Given the inherent difficulties of providing health insurance through the private sector, that's an impressive number. But it left more than a third of nonelderly Americans out of the system. Moreover, the number of outsiders is growing: the share of nonelderly Americans with employment-based health insurance was 67.7 percent as recently as 2000. And this trend seems certain to continue, even accelerate, because the whole system of employer-based health care is under severe strain.

We can identify several reasons for that strain, but mainly it comes down to the issue of costs. Providing health insurance looked like a good way for employers to reward their employees when it was a small part of the pay package. Today, however, the annual cost of coverage for a family of four is estimated by the Kaiser Family Foundation at more than $10,000. One way to look at it is to say that that's roughly what a worker earning minimum wage and working full time earns in a year. It's more than half the annual earnings of the average Wal-Mart employee.

Health care costs at current levels override the incentives that have historically supported employer-based health insurance. Now that health costs loom so large, companies that provide generous benefits are in effect paying some of their workers much more than the going wage—or, more to the point, more than competitors pay similar workers. Inevitably, this creates pressure to reduce or eliminate health benefits. And companies that can't cut benefits enough to stay competitive—such as GM—find their very existence at risk.

Rising health costs have also ended the ability of employer-based insurance plans to avoid the problem of adverse selection. Anecdotal evidence suggests that workers who know they have health problems actively seek out jobs with companies that still offer generous benefits. On the other side, employers are starting to make hiring decisions based on likely health costs. For example, an internal Wal-Mart memo, reported by *The New York Times* in October, suggested adding tasks requiring physical exertion to jobs that don't really require it as a way to screen out individuals with potential health risks.

So rising health care costs are undermining the institution of employer-based coverage. We'd suggest that the drop in the number of insured so far only hints at the scale of the problem: we may well be seeing the whole institution unraveling.

Notice that this unraveling is the byproduct of what should be a good thing: advances in medical technology, which lead doctors to spend more on their patients. This leads to higher insurance costs, which causes employers to stop providing health coverage. The result is that many people are thrown into the world of the uninsured, where even basic care is often hard to get. As we said, we rob Peter of basic care in order to provide Paul with state-of-the-art treatment.

Fortunately, some of the adverse consequences of the decline in employer-based coverage have been muted by a crucial government program, Medicaid. But Medicaid is facing its own pressures.

3.

Medicaid and Medicare

The US health care system is more privatized than that of any other advanced country, but nearly half of total health care spending nonetheless comes from the government. Most of this government spending is accounted for by two great social insurance programs, Medicare and Medicaid. Although Medicare gets most of the public attention, let's focus first on Medicaid, which is a far more important program than most middle-class Americans realize.

In *The Health Care Mess* Richmond and Fein tell us that Medicaid, like employer-based health insurance, came into existence through a sort of historical accident. As Lyndon Johnson made his big push to create Medicare, the American Medical Association, in a last-ditch effort to block so-called "socialized medicine" (actually only the insurance is socialized; the medical care is provided by the private sector), began disparaging Johnson's plan by claiming that it would do nothing to help the

% of GDP

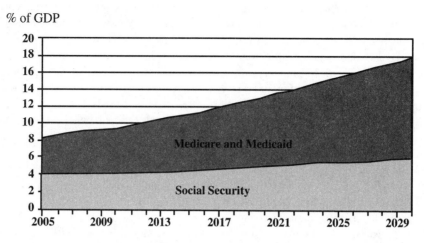

Source: Congressional Budget Office.

Figure 1 Social Security, Medicare, and Medicaid as a Percentage of GDP

truly needy. In a masterful piece of political jujitsu, Johnson responded by adding a second program, Medicaid, targeted specifically at helping the poor and near poor.

Today, Medicaid is a crucial part of the American safety net. In 2004 Medicaid covered almost as many people as its senior partner, Medicare—37.5 million versus 39.7 million.

Medicaid has grown rapidly in recent years because it has been picking up the slack from the unraveling system of employer-based insurance. Between 2000 and 2004 the number of Americans covered by Medicaid rose by a remarkable eight million. Over the same period the ranks of the uninsured rose by six million. So without the growth of Medicaid, the uninsured population would have exploded, and we'd be facing a severe crisis in medical care.

But Medicaid, even as it becomes increasingly essential to tens of millions of Americans, is also becoming increasingly vulnerable to political attack. To some extent this reflects the political weakness of any means-tested program serving the poor and near poor. As the British welfare scholar Richard Titmuss said, "Programs for the poor are poor programs." Unlike Medicare's clients—the feared senior group—Medicaid recipients aren't a potent political constituency: they are, on average, poor and poorly educated, with low voter participation. As a result, funding for Medicaid depends on politicians' sense of decency, always a fragile foundation for policy.

The complex structure of Medicaid also makes it vulnerable. Unlike Medicare, which is a purely federal program, Medicaid is a federal-state matching program, in which states provide on average about 40 percent of the funds. Since state governments, unlike the federal government, can't engage in open-ended deficit financing, this dependence on state funds exposes Medicaid to pressure whenever state budgets are hard-pressed. And state budgets are hard-pressed these days for a variety of reasons, not least the rapidly rising cost of Medicaid itself.

The result is that, like employer-based health insurance, Medicaid faces a possible unraveling in the face of rising health costs. An example of how that unraveling might take place is South Carolina's request for a waiver of federal rules to allow it to restructure the state's Medicaid program into a system of private accounts. We'll discuss later in this essay the strange persistence, in the teeth of all available evidence, of the belief that the private sector can provide health insurance more efficiently than the government. The main point for now is that South Carolina's proposed reform would seriously weaken the medical safety net: recipients would be given a voucher to purchase health insurance, but many would find the voucher inadequate, and would end up being denied care. And if South Carolina gets its waiver, other states will probably follow its lead.

Medicare's situation is very different. Unlike employer-based insurance or Medicaid, Medicare faces no imminent threat of large cuts. Although the federal government is deep in deficit, it's not currently having any difficulty borrowing, largely from abroad, to cover the gap. Also, the political constituency behind Medicare remains extremely powerful. Yet federal deficits can't go on forever; even the US government must eventually find a way to pay its bills. And the long-term outlook for federal finances is dire, mainly because of Medicare and Medicaid.

The chart in figure 1 illustrates the centrality of health care costs to America's long-term budget problems. The chart shows the Congressional Budget Office's baseline projection of spending over the next twenty-five years on the three big entitlement programs, Social Security, Medicare, and Medicaid, measured as a percentage of GDP. Not long ago advocates of Social Security privatization tried to use projections like this one to foster a sense of crisis about the retirement system. As was pointed out last year in these pages,[1] however, there is no program called Socialsecuritymedicareandmedicaid. In fact, as the chart shows, Social Security, whose costs will rise solely because of the aging of the population, represents only a small part of the problem. Most of the problem comes from the two health care programs, whose spending is rising mainly because of the general rise in medical costs.

To be fair, there is a demographic component to Medicare and Medicaid spending too—Medicare because it only serves Americans over sixty-five, Medicaid because the elderly, although a minority of the program's beneficiaries, account for most of its spending. Still, the principal factor in both programs' rising costs is what the CBO calls "excess cost growth"—the persistent tendency of health care spending per beneficiary to grow faster than per capita income, owing to advancing medical technology. Without this excess cost growth, the CBO estimates that entitlement spending would rise by only 3.7 percent of GDP over the next twenty-five years. That's a significant rise, but not overwhelming, and could be addressed with moderate tax increases and possibly benefit cuts. But because of excess cost growth the projected rise in spending is a crushing burden—about 10 percent of GDP over the next twenty-five years, and even more thereafter.

Rising health care spending, then, is driving a triple crisis. The fastest-moving piece of that crisis is the unraveling of employer-based coverage. There's a gradually building crisis in Medicaid. And there's a long-term federal budget crisis driven mainly by rising health care spending.

So what are we going to do about health care?

4.

The "consumer-directed" diversion

As we pointed out at the beginning of this essay, one of the two big reasons to be concerned about rising spending on health care is that as the health care sector grows, its inefficiency becomes increasingly important. And almost everyone agrees that the US health care system is extremely inefficient. But there are wide disagreements about the nature of that inefficiency. And the analysts who have the ear of the Bush administration are committed, for ideological reasons, to a view that is clearly wrong.

We've already alluded to the underlying view behind the Bush administration's health care proposals: it's the view that insurance leads people to consume too much health care. The 2004 *Economic Report of the President*, which devoted a chapter to health care, illustrated the alleged problem with a parable about the clothing industry:

> Suppose, for example, that an individual could purchase a clothing insurance policy with a "coinsurance" rate of 20 percent, meaning that after paying the insurance premium, the holder of the insurance policy would have to pay only 20 cents on the dollar for all clothing purchases. An individual with such a policy would be expected to spend substantially more on clothes—due to larger quantity and higher quality purchases—with the 80 percent discount than he would at the full price.... The clothing insurance example suggests an inherent ineffi-

ciency in the use of insurance to pay for things that have little intrinsic risk or uncertainty.

The report then asserts that "inefficiencies of this sort are pervasive in the US health care system"—although, tellingly, it fails to match the parable about clothing with any real examples from health care.

The view that Americans consume too much health care because insurers pay the bills leads to what is currently being called the "consumer-directed" approach to health care reform. The virtues of such an approach are the theme of John Cogan, Glenn Hubbard, and Daniel Kessler's *Healthy, Wealthy, and Wise*. The main idea is that people should pay more of their medical expenses out of pocket. And the way to reduce public reliance on insurance, reformers from the right wing believe, is to remove the tax advantages that currently favor health insurance over out-of-pocket spending. Indeed, last year Bush's tax reform commission proposed taxing some employment-based health benefits. The administration, recognizing how politically explosive such a move would be, rejected the proposal. Instead of raising taxes on health insurance, the administration has decided to cut taxes on out-of-pocket spending.

Cogan, Hubbard, and Kessler call for making all out-of-pocket medical spending tax-deductible, although tax experts from both parties say that this would present an enforcement nightmare. (Douglas Holtz-Eakin, the former head of the Congressional Budget Office, put it this way: "If you want to have a personal relationship with the IRS do that [i.e., make all medical spending tax deductible] because we are going to have to investigate everybody's home to see if their running shoes are a medical expense.") The administration's proposals so far are more limited, focusing on an expanded system of tax-advantaged health savings accounts. Individuals can shelter part of their income from taxes by depositing it in such accounts, then withdraw money from these accounts to pay medical bills.

What's wrong with consumer-directed health care? One immediate disadvantage is that health savings accounts, whatever their ostensible goals, are yet another tax break for the wealthy, who have already been showered with tax breaks under Bush. The right to pay medical expenses with pre-tax income is worth a lot to high-income individuals who face a marginal income tax rate of 35 percent, but little or nothing to lower-income Americans who face a marginal tax rate of 10 percent or less, and lack the ability to place the maximum allowed amount in their savings accounts.

A deeper disadvantage is that such accounts tend to undermine employment-based health care, because they encourage adverse selection: health savings accounts are attractive to healthier individuals, who will be tempted to opt out of company plans, leaving less healthy individuals behind.

Yet another problem with consumer-directed care is that the evidence says that people don't, in fact, make wise decisions when paying for medical care out of pocket. A classic study by the Rand Corporation found that when people pay medical expenses themselves rather than relying on insurance, they do cut back on their consumption of health care—but that they cut back on valuable as well as questionable medical procedures, showing no ability to set sensible priorities.

Table 1 International Health Comparisons

	Canada	France	UK	US
Health spending per capita, 2002	$2,931	$2,736	$2,160	$5,267
Private share of spending	30%	24%	17%	55%
Life expectancy	79.7	79.2	78.1	77.1
Infant mortality per 1,000 births	5.2	4.5	5.0	6.8
Physicians per 1,000 people	2.1	3.3	2.0	2.7
Nurses per 1,000 people	9.9	7.0	9.0	8.1
Hospital beds per 1,000 people	3.2	4.2	3.9	2.9

Source: Organization for Economic Cooperation and Development, OECD Health Data 2004

But perhaps the biggest objection to consumer-directed health reform is that its advocates have misdiagnosed the problem. They believe that Americans have too much health insurance; the 2004 *Economic Report of the President* condemned the fact that insurance currently pays for "many events that have little uncertainty, such as routine dental care, annual medical exams, and vaccinations," and for "relatively low-expense items, such as an office visit to the doctor for a sore throat." The implication is that health costs are too high because people who don't pay their own medical bills consume too much routine dental care and are too ready to visit the doctor about a sore throat. And that argument is all wrong. Excessive consumption of routine care, or small-expense items, can't be a major source of health care inefficiency, because such items don't account for a major share of medical costs.

Remember the 80–20 rule: the great bulk of medical expenses are accounted for by a small number of people requiring very expensive treatment. When you think of the problem of health care costs, you shouldn't envision visits to the family physician to talk about a sore throat; you should think about coronary bypass operations, dialysis, and chemotherapy. Nobody is proposing a consumer-directed health care plan that would force individuals to pay a large share of extreme medical expenses, such as the costs of chemotherapy, out of pocket. And that means that consumer-directed health care can't promote savings on the treatments that account for most of what we spend on health care.

The administration's plans for consumer-directed health care, then, are a diversion from meaningful health care reform, and will actually worsen our health care problems. In fact, some reformers privately hope that George W. Bush manages to get his health care plans passed, because they believe that they will hasten the collapse of employment-based coverage and pave the way for real reform. (The suffering along the way would be huge.)

But what would real reform look like?

5.

Single-payer and beyond

How do we know that the US health care system is highly inefficient? An important part of the evidence takes the form of international comparisons. Table 1 compares US health care with the systems of three other advanced countries. It's clear from the table that the United States has achieved something remarkable. We spend far more on health care than other advanced countries—almost twice as much per capita as France, almost two and a half times as much as Britain. Yet we do considerably worse even than the British on basic measures of health performance, such as life expectancy and infant mortality.

One might argue that the US health care system actually provides better care than foreign systems, but that the effects of this superior care are more than offset by unhealthy US lifestyles. Ezra Klein of *The American Prospect* calls this the "well-we-eat-more-cheeseburgers" argument. But a variety of evidence refutes this argument. The data in Table 1 show that the United States does not stand out in the *quantity* of care, as measured by such indicators as the number of physicians, nurses, and hospital beds per capita. Nor does the US stand out in terms of the quality of care: a recent study published in *Health Affairs* that compared quality of care across advanced countries found no US advantage. On the contrary, "the United States often stands out for inefficient care and errors and is an outlier on access/cost barriers."[2] That is, our health care system makes more mistakes than those of other countries, and is unique in denying necessary care to people who lack insurance and can't pay cash. The frequent claim that the United States pays high medical prices to avoid long waiting lists for care also fails to hold up in the face of the evidence: there are long waiting lists for elective surgery in some non-US systems, but not all, and the procedures for which these waiting lists exist account for only 3 percent of US health care spending.[3]

So why does US health care cost so much? Part of the answer is that doctors, like other highly skilled workers, are paid much more in the United States than in other advanced countries. But the main source of high US costs is probably the unique degree to which the US system relies on private rather than public health insurance, reflected in the uniquely high US share of private spending in total health care expenditure.

Over the years since the failure of the Clinton health plan, a great deal of evidence has accumulated on the relative merits of private and public health insurance. As far as we have been able to ascertain, all of that evidence indicates that public insurance of the kind available in several European countries and others such as Taiwan achieves equal or better results at much lower cost. This conclusion applies to comparisons within the United States as well as across countries. For example, a study conducted by researchers at the Urban Institute found that

> per capita spending for an adult Medicaid beneficiary in poor health would rise from $9,615 to $14,785 if the person were insured privately and received services consistent with private utilization levels and private provider payment rates.[4]

The cost advantage of public health insurance appears to arise from two main sources. The first is lower administrative costs. Private insurers spend large sums fighting adverse selection, trying to identify and screen out high-cost customers. Systems such as Medicare, which covers every American sixty-five or older, or the Canadian single-payer system, which covers everyone, avoid these costs. In 2003 Medicare spent less than 2 percent of its resources on administration, while private insurance companies spent more than 13 percent.

At the same time, the fragmentation of a system that relies largely on private insurance leads both to administrative complexity because of differences in coverage among individuals and to what is, in effect, a zero-sum struggle between different players in the system, each trying to stick others with the bill. Many estimates suggest that the paperwork imposed on health care providers by the fragmentation of the US system costs several times as much as the direct costs borne by the insurers.

The second source of savings in a system of public health insurance is the ability to bargain with suppliers, especially drug companies, for lower prices. Residents of the United States notoriously pay much higher prices for prescription drugs than residents of other advanced countries, including Canada. What is less known is that both Medicaid and, to an even greater extent, the Veterans' Administration, get discounts similar to or greater than those received by the Canadian health system.

We're talking about large cost savings. Indeed, the available evidence suggests that if the United States were to replace its current complex mix of health insurance systems with standardized, universal coverage, the savings would be so large that we could cover all those currently uninsured, yet end up spending less overall. That's what happened in Taiwan, which adopted a single-payer system in 1995: the percentage of the population with health insurance soared from 57 percent to 97 percent, yet health care costs actually grew more slowly than one would have predicted from trends before the change in system.

If US politicians could be persuaded of the advantages of a public health insurance system, the next step would be to convince them of the virtues, in at least some cases, of honest-to-God socialized medicine, in which government employees provide the care as well as the money. Exhibit A for the advantages of government provision is the Veterans' Administration, which runs its own hospitals and clinics, and provides some of the best-quality health care in America at far lower cost than the private sector. How does the VA do it? It turns out that there are many advantages to having a single health care orga-

nization provide individuals with what amounts to lifetime care. For example, the VA has taken the lead in introducing electronic medical records, which it can do far more easily than a private hospital chain because its patients stay with it for decades. The VA also invests heavily and systematically in preventive care, because unlike private health care providers it can expect to realize financial benefits from measures that keep its clients out of the hospital.

In summary, then, the obvious way to make the US health care system more efficient is to make it more like the systems of other advanced countries, and more like the most efficient parts of our own system. That means a shift from private insurance to public insurance, and greater government involvement in the provision of health care—if not publicly run hospitals and clinics, at least a much larger government role in creating integrated record-keeping and quality control. Such a system would probably allow individuals to purchase additional medical care, as they can in Britain (although not in Canada). But the core of the system would be government insurance—"Medicare for all," as Ted Kennedy puts it.

Unfortunately, the US political system seems unready to do what is both obvious and humane. The 2003 legislation that added drug coverage to Medicare illustrates some of the political difficulties. Although it's rarely described this way, Medicare is a single-payer system covering many of the health costs of older Americans. (Canada's universal single-payer system is, in fact, also called Medicare.) And it has some though not all the advantages of broader single-payer systems, notably low administrative costs.

But in adding a drug benefit to Medicare, the Bush administration and its allies in Congress were driven both by a desire to appease the insurance and pharmaceutical lobbies and by an ideology that insists on the superiority of the private sector even when the public sector has demonstrably lower costs. So they devised a plan that works very differently from traditional Medicare. In fact, Medicare Part D, the drug benefit, isn't a program in which the government provides drug insurance. It's a program in which private insurance companies receive subsidies to offer insurance—and seniors aren't allowed to deal directly with Medicare.

The insertion of private intermediaries into the program has several unfortunate consequences. First, as millions of seniors have discovered, it makes the system extremely complex and obscure. It's virtually impossible for most people to figure out which of the many drug plans now on offer is best. This complexity, coupled with the Katrina-like obliviousness of administration officials to a widely predicted disaster, also led to the program's catastrophic initial failure to manage the problem of "dual eligibles," i.e., older Medicaid recipients whose drug coverage was supposed to be transferred to Medicare. When the program started up in January, hundreds of thousands of these dual eligibles found that they had fallen through the cracks, that their old coverage had been canceled but their new coverage had not been put into effect.

Second, the private intermediaries add substantial administrative costs to the program. It's reasonably certain that if seniors had been offered the choice of receiving a straightforward drug benefit directly from Medicare, the vast majority would have chosen to pass up the private drug plans, which wouldn't have been able to offer comparable benefits because of their administrative expenses. But the drug bill avoided that embarrassing outcome by denying seniors that choice.

Finally, by fragmenting the purchase of drugs among many private plans, the administration denied Medicare the ability to bargain for lower prices from the drug companies. And the legislation, reflecting pressures from those companies, included a provision specifically prohibiting Medicare from intervening to help the private plans get lower prices.

In short, ideology and interest groups led the Bush administration to set up a new, costly Medicare benefit in such a way as to systematically forfeit all the advantages of public health insurance.

6.

Beyond reform: How much health care should we have?

Imagine, for a moment, that some future US administration were to push through a fundamental reform of health care that covered all the uninsured, replaced private insurance with a single-payer system, and took heed of the VA's lessons about the advantages of integrated health care. Would our health care problems be solved?

No. Although real reform would bring great improvement in our situation, continuing technological progress in health care still poses a deep dilemma: How much of what we can do *should* we do?

The medical profession, understandably, has a bias toward doing whatever will bring medical benefit. If that means performing an expensive surgical procedure on an elderly patient who probably has only a few years to live, so be it. But as medical technology advances, it becomes possible to spend ever larger sums on medically useful care. Indeed, at some point it will become possible to spend the entire GDP on health care. Obviously, we won't do this. But how will we make choices about what not to do?

In a classic 1984 book, *Painful Prescription: Rationing Hospital Care*, Henry Aaron and William Schwartz studied the medical choices made by the British system, which has long operated under tight budget limits that force it to make hard choices in a way that US medical care does not. *Can We Say No?* is an update of that work. It's a valuable survey of the real medical issues involved in British rationing, and gives a taste of the dilemmas the US system will eventually face.

The operative word, however, is "eventually." Reading *Can We Say No?*, one might come away with the impression that the problem of how to ration care is the central issue in current health care policy. This impression is reinforced by Aaron and his co-authors' decision to compare the US system only with that of Britain, which spends far less on health care than other advanced countries, and correspondingly is forced to do a lot of

rationing. A comparison with, say, France, which spends far less than the United States but considerably more than Britain, would give a very different impression: in many respects France consumes more, not less, health care than the United States, but it can do so at lower cost because our system is so inefficient.

The result of Aaron et al.'s single-minded focus on the problem of rationing is a somewhat skewed perspective on current policy issues. Most notably, they argue that the reason we need universal health coverage is that a universal system can ration care in a way that private insurance can't. This seems to miss the two main immediate arguments for universal care—that it would cover those now uninsured, and that it would be cheaper than our current system. A national health care system will also be better at rationing when the time comes, but that hardly seems like the prime argument for adopting such a system today.

Our Princeton colleague Uwe Reinhardt, a leading economic expert on health care, put it this way: our focus right now should be on eliminating the gross inefficiencies we know exist in the US health care system. If we do that, we will be able to cover the uninsured while spending less than we do now. Only then should we address the issue of what not to do; that's tomorrow's issue, not today's.

7.

Can we fix health care?

Health policy experts know a lot more about the economics of health care now than they did when Bill Clinton tried to remake the US health care system. And there's overwhelming evidence that the United States could get better health care at lower cost if we were willing to put that knowledge into practice. But the political obstacles remain daunting.

A mere shift of power from Republicans to Democrats would not, in itself, be enough to give us sensible health care reform. While Democrats would have written a less perverse drug bill, it's not clear that they are ready to embrace a single-payer system. Even liberal economists and scholars at progressive think tanks tend to shy away from proposing a straightforward system of national health insurance. Instead, they propose fairly complex compromise plans. Typically, such plans try to achieve universal coverage by requiring everyone to buy health insurance, the way everyone is forced to buy car insurance, and deal with those who can't afford to purchase insurance through a system of subsidies. Proponents of such plans make a few arguments for their superiority to a single-payer system, mainly the (dubious) claim that single-payer would reduce medical innovation. But the main reason for not proposing single-payer is political fear: reformers believe that private insurers are too powerful to cut out of the loop, and that a single-payer plan would be too easily demonized by business and political propagandists as "big government."

These are the same political calculations that led Bill Clinton to reject a single-payer system in 1993, even though his advisers believed that a single-payer system would be the least expensive way to provide universal coverage. Instead, he proposed a complex plan designed to preserve a role for private health insurers. But the plan backfired. The insurers opposed it anyway, most famously with their "Harry and Louise" ads. And the plan's complexity left the public baffled.

We believe that the compromise plans being proposed by the cautious reformers would run into the same political problems, and that it would be politically smarter as well as economically superior to go for broke: to propose a straightforward single-payer system, and try to sell voters on the huge advantages such a system would bring. But this would mean taking on the drug and insurance companies rather than trying to co-opt them, and even progressive policy wonks, let alone Democratic politicians, still seem too timid to do that.

So what will really happen to American health care? Many people in this field believe that in the end America will end up with national health insurance, and perhaps with a lot of direct government provision of health care, simply because nothing else works. But things may have to get much worse before real-

ity can break through the combination of powerful interest groups and free-market ideology.

—February 22, 2006

Notes

1. "America's Senior Moment," *The New York Review*, March 10, 2005.
2. Cathy Schoen, Robin Osborn, Phuong Trang Huynh, Michelle Doty, Kinga Zapert, Jordon Peugh, and Karen Davis, "Taking the Pulse of Health Care Systems: Experiences of Patients with Health Problems in Six Countries," *Health Affairs* Web exclusive, November 3, 2005.
3. Gerard F. Anderson, Peter S. Hussey, Bianca K. Frogner, and Hugh R. Waters, "Health Spending in the United States and the Rest of the Industrialized World," *Health Affairs,* Vol. 24, No. 4 (July/August 2005), pp. 903–914.
4. "Medicaid: A Lower-Cost Approach to Serving a High-Cost Population," policy brief by the Kaiser Commission on Medicaid and the Uninsured, March 2004.

UNIT 4
Macroeconomics

Unit Selections

20. **Countdown to a Meltdown**, James Fallows
21. **Seizing Intangibles for the G.D.P.**, Louis Uchitelle
22. **The Elephant in the Room**, Aidan Rankin
23. **Social Spending and Economic Growth, Interview with Peter Lindert**, *Challenge*
24. **Why Are Taxes So Complicated and What Can We Do About It?**, William G. Gale
25. **The Tax Reform Revolution**, Murray Weidenbaum
26. **Tax Reform R.I.P.**, Robert J. Samuelson
27. **Link Between Taxation, Unemployment Is Absent**, Jonathan Weisman
28. **What Should Central Banks Do?**, Frederic S. Mishkin
29. **How Does Monetary Policy Affect the U.S. Economy?**, *FRBSF Economic Letter*
30. **It's His Economy Now—And Yours**, Justin Fox
31. **Banking Consolidation**, *FRBSF Economic Letter*
32. **Bank ATMs and ATM Surcharges**, *FRBSF Economic Letter*
33. **Toward a Cashless Society**, David R. Warwick

Key Points to Consider

- What is the current outlook for the U.S. economy? What caused the budget surpluses of the 1990s to be converted into large and growing deficits?

- How useful is G.D.P. as a measure of the economy's performance? What is meant by the "trickle down effect," and does it really work?

- How might an understanding of basic tax concepts demystify the debate over tax cuts?

- How does monetary policy affect the U.S. economy? How can people benefit from a cashless society?

Student Web Site

www.mhcls.com/online

Internet References

Further information regarding these Web sites may be found in this book's preface or online.

Citizens for Tax Justice
   http://www.ctj.org

Congressional Budget Office
   http://www.cbo.gov

Federal Reserve Board
   http://www.federalreserve.gov

History of Money
   http://www.ex.ac.uk/~RDavies/arian/llyfr.html

The Public Debt
   http://www.publicdebt.treas.gov/opd/opd.htm

Macroeconomics provides an overview of the structure of an economy and the ways in which its major components—households, businesses, and governments—are related. Topics of investigation include such large, economy-wide variables as national output, the extent of joblessness, the general level of prices, and the rate of economic growth. Macroeconomics also considers ways in which government policies might be used to promote various national goals, including high levels of employment, price stability, and an adequate expansion of output over time. Since controversy abounds over the issue of the effectiveness of such policies, macroeconomics is a subject often debated by members of the economics profession.

Prior to the 1930s, most economists (known as "classicists") believed that a market economy was capable of achieving macroeconomic goals without intervention by the government. This belief was widespread joblessness, falling incomes, bankruptcies, and political turmoil. In 1936 British economist John Maynard Keynes attacked the classical view in his *General Theory of Employment, Interest, and Money* (a book that occupies as significant a position in economic thought as Adam Smith's *Wealth of*

Nations). Keynes demonstrated (on both a theoretical and a practical level) how macroeconomic goals could be reached through the management of total spending. As Keynes's ideas gained general acceptance over the next few decades, a national consensus emerged on the need for the federal government to intervene actively in the pursuit of such goals. This view was officially sanctioned in the Employment Act of 1946, which established a federal commitment to policies aimed at achieving "maximum employment, production, and purchasing power." Keynesian demand-management occurs primarily through monetary policy (controlling the supply and availability of money and credit) and fiscal policy (altering federal spending and taxes).

Although the goals mandated by the Employment Act are relatively clear-cut, actual policy-making experience since World War II demonstrates the great difficulties that America faces in implementing them. It also reflects the limitations of both economic ideology and the political system. While many of Keynes's insights still ring true, other approaches to macroeconomics (including attention to the supply side of the economy) also have value.

The unit begins with an article in which Louis Uchitelle questions current methods for calculating gross domestic product. He shows how such methods tend to overstate the share of income going to the nation's workforce. Then, Aidan Rankin considers broad implications of growth in G.D.P. over time. Do the benefits of growth "trickle down" to everyone?

Taxes and budgets are the focus of the next articles. Peter Lindert examines long-term trends in social spending and economic growth. Then, William Gale asks: Why are taxes so complicated, and what can we do about them? Murray Weidenbaum assesses four recent proposals for tax reform, each of which would shift the bases of federal taxation from income to consumption. Robert J. Samuelson argues that tax breaks are both more complex and less efficient than one might suppose. Finally, Jonathan Weisman contends that the relationship between taxes and unemployment is far more complicated than many people (including politicians) realize. The remaining five essays focus on money, monetary policy, and the Federal Reserve System. The first article shows how Federal Reserve policy actions affect real interest rates, which in turn affect the overall economy. Justin Fox describes possible policy implications of the recent replacement of Alan Greenspan by Ben Bernanke as chairman of the Federal Reserve System. This is followed by an essay that shows how megamergers have reshaped the U.S. banking industry. This unit concludes with two articles which deal with various aspects of "e-money" (or electronic money). What does its use mean for the future of banking and of U.S. monetary institutions?

Countdown to a Meltdown

America's coming economic crisis. A look back from the election of 2016

JAMES FALLOWS

January 20, 2016, Master Strategy Memo Subject: The Coming Year—and Beyond

Sir:

It is time to think carefully about the next year. Our position is uniquely promising—and uniquely difficult.

The promise lies in the fact that you are going to win the election. Nothing is guaranteed in politics, but based on everything we know, and barring an act of God or a disastrous error on our side, one year from today you will be sworn in as the forty-sixth president of the United States. And you will be the first president since before the Civil War to come from neither the Republican nor the Democratic Party.[1] This is one aspect of your electoral advantage right now: having created our new party, you are already assured of its nomination, whereas the candidates from the two legacy parties are still carving themselves up in their primaries.[2]

The difficulty, too, lies in the fact that you are going to win. The same circumstances that are bringing an end to 164 years of two-party rule have brought tremendous hardship to the country. This will be the first time since Franklin Roosevelt took office in 1933 that so much is demanded so quickly from a new administration. Our challenge is not just to win the election but to win in a way that gives us a chance to address economic failures that have been fifty years in the making.

That is the purpose of this memo: to provide the economic background for the larger themes in our campaign. Although economic changes will be items one through ten on your urgent "to do" list a year from now, this is not the place to talk about them in detail. There will be plenty of time for that later, with the policy guys. Instead I want to speak here not just as your campaign manager but on the basis of our friendship and shared efforts these past twenty years. Being completely honest about the country's problems might not be necessary during the campaign—sounding pessimistic in speeches would hurt us. But we ourselves need to he clear about the challenge we face. Unless we understand how we got here, we won't be able to find the way out once you are in office.

Politics is about stories—the personal story of how a leader was shaped, the national story of how America's long saga has led to today's dramas. Your personal story needs no work al all. Dwight Eisenhower was the last president to enter office with a worldwide image of competence, though obviously his achievements were military rather than technological. But we have work to do on the national story.

When it comes to the old parties, the story boils down to this: the Democrats can't win, and the Republicans can't govern. Okay, that's an overstatement; but the more nuanced version is nearly as discouraging.

The past fifty years have shown that the Democrats can't win the presidency except when everything goes their way. Only three Democrats have reached the White House since Lyndon Johnson decided to leave. In 1976 they ran a pious sounding candidate against the political ghost of the disgraced Richard Nixon—and against his corporeal successor, Gerald Ford, the only unelected incumbent in American history. In 1992 they ran their most talented campaigner since FDR, and even Bill Clinton would have lost if Ross Perot had not stayed in the race and siphoned away votes from the Republicans. And in 2008 they were unexpectedly saved by the death of Fidel Castro. This drained some of the pro-Republican passion of South Florida's Cuban immigrants, and the disastrous governmental bungling of the "Cuba Libre" influx that followed gave the Democrats their first win in Florida since 1996—along with the election. But that Democratic administration could turn out to have been America's last. The Electoral College map drawn up after the 2010 census removed votes from all the familiar blue states except California, giving the Republicans a bigger head start from the Sunbelt states and the South.

As for the Republicans, fifty years have shown they can't govern without breaking the bank. Starting with Richard Nixon, every Republican president has left the dollar lower, the federal budget deficit higher, the American trade position weaker, and the U.S. manufacturing workforce smaller than when he took office.

The story of the parties, then, is that the American people mistrust the Republicans' economic record, and don't trust the Democrats enough to let them try to do better. That is why—and it is the only reason why—they are giving us a chance. But we can move from electoral to *governmental* success only with a clear understanding of why so much has gone so wrong with the economy. Our internal polls show that nearly 90 percent of the public thinks the economy is "on the wrong track." Those readings should hold up, since that's roughly the percentage of Americans whose income has fallen in real terms in the past five years.

The story we will tell them begins fifteen years ago,[3] and it has three chapters. For public use we'll refer to them by the names of the respective administrations. But for our own purposes it will be clearer to think of the chapter titles as "Cocking the Gun," "Pulling the Trigger," and "Bleeding."

1. Cocking the Gun

Everything changed in 2001. But it didn't all change on September 11.

Yes, the ramifications of 9/11 will be with us for decades, much as the aftereffects of Pearl Harbor explain the presence of thousands of U.S. troops in Asia seventy-five years later. Before 2001 about 12,000 American troops were stationed in the Middle East—most of them in Kuwait and Saudi Arabia. Since 2003 we have never had fewer than 100,000 troops in CENTCOM's theater, most of them on active anti-insurgency duty. The locale of the most intense fighting keeps changing—first Afghanistan and Iraq, then Pakistan and Egypt, now Saudi Arabia and the frontier between Turkey and the Republic of Kurdistan—but the commitment goes on.

Before there was 9/11, however, there was June 7, 2001. For our purposes modern economic history began that day.

On June 7 President George W. Bush celebrated his first big legislative victory. Only two weeks earlier his new administration had suffered a terrible political blow, when a Republican senator left the party and gave Democrats a one-vote majority in the Senate. But the administration was nevertheless able to persuade a dozen Democratic senators to vote its way and authorize a tax cut that would decrease federal tax revenues by some $1.35 trillion between then and 2010.

This was presented at the time as a way to avoid the "problem" of paying down the federal debt too fast. According to the administration's forecasts, the government was on the way to running up $5.0 trillion in surpluses over the coming decade. The entire federal debt accumulated between the nation's founding and 2001 totaled only about $3.2 trillion—and for technical reasons at most $2 trillion of that total could be paid off within the next decade.[4] Therefore some $3.6 trillion in "unusable" surplus—or about $12,000 for every American—was likely to pile up in the Treasury. The administration proposed to give slightly less than half of that back through tax cuts, saving the rest for Social Security and other obligations.

Congress agreed, and it was this achievement that the president celebrated at the White House signing ceremony on June 7. "We recognize loud and clear the surplus is not the government's money," Bush said at the time. "The surplus is the people's money, and we ought to trust them with their own money."

If the president or anyone else at that ceremony had had perfect foresight, he would have seen that no surpluses of any sort would materialize, either for the government to hoard or for taxpayers to get back. (A year later the budget would show a deficit of $158 billion; a year after that $378 billion.) By the end of Bush's second term the federal debt, rather than having nearly disappeared, as he expected, had tripled. If those in the crowd had had that kind of foresight, they would have called their brokers the next day to unload all their stock holdings. A few hours after Bush signed the tax-cut bill, the Dow Jones industrial average closed at 11,090, a level it has never reached again.[5]

In a way it doesn't matter what the national government intended, or why all forecasts proved so wrong. Through the rest of his presidency Bush contended that the reason was 9/11—that it had changed the budget as it changed everything else. It forced the government to spend more, for war and for homeland security, even as the economic dislocation it caused meant the government could collect less. Most people outside the administration considered this explanation misleading, or at least incomplete. For instance, as Bush began his second term the nonpartisan Congressional Budget Office said that the biggest reason for growing deficits was the tax cuts.[6]

But here is what really mattered about that June day in 2001: from that point on the U.S. government had less money to work with than it had under the previous eight presidents. Through four decades and through administrations as diverse as Lyndon Johnson's and Ronald Reagan's, federal tax revenue had stayed within a fairly narrow band. The tax cuts of 2001 pushed it out of that safety zone, reducing it to its lowest level as a share of the economy in the modern era.[7] And as we will see, these cuts—the first of three rounds[8]—did so just when the country's commitments and obligations had begun to grow.

As late as 2008 the trend could have been altered, though the cuts of 2003 and 2005 had made things worse. But in the late summer of 2008 Senate Republicans once again demonstrated their mastery of the basic feints and dodges of politics. The tax cuts enacted during Bush's first term were in theory "temporary," and set to expire starting in 2010. But Congress didn't have to wait until 2010 to decide whether to make them permanent, so of course the Republican majority scheduled the vote at the most awkward moment possible for the Democrats: on the eve of a close presidential election. The Democratic senators understood their dilemma. Either they voted for the tax cuts and looked like hypocrites for all their past complaints, or they voted against them and invited an onslaught of "tax and spend" attack ads in the campaign. Enough Democrats made the "smart" choice. They held their seats in the election, and the party took back the presidency. But they also locked in the tax cuts, which was step one in cocking the gun.[9]

The explanation of steps two and three is much quicker: People kept living longer, and they kept saving less. Increased longevity is a tremendous human achievement but a fiscal challenge—as in any household where people outlive their savings. Late in 2003 Congress dramatically escalated the fiscal problem by adding prescription-drug coverage to Medicare, with barely any discussion of its long-term cost. David M. Walker, the government's comptroller general at the time, said that the action was part of "the most reckless fiscal year in the history of the Republic," because that vote and a few other changes added roughly $13 trillion to the government's long-term commitments.

The evaporation of personal savings was marveled at by all economists but explained by few. Americans saved about eight percent of their disposable income through the 1950s and 1960s, slightly more in the 1970s and 1980s, slightly less and then a lot less in the 1990s. At the beginning of this century they were saving, on average, just about nothing.[10]

The possible reasons for this failure to save—credit-card debt? a false sense of wealth thanks to the real-estate bubble?[11] stagnant real earnings for much of the population?—mattered less than the results. The country needed money to run its government, and Americans themselves weren't about to provide it. This is where the final, secret element of the gun-cocking process came into play: the unspoken deal with China.

The terms of the deal are obvious in retrospect. Even at the time, economists discussed the arrangement endlessly in their journals. The oddity was that so few politicians picked up on what they said. The heart of the matter, as we now know, was this simple equation: each time Congress raised benefits, reduced taxes, or encouraged more borrowing by consumers, it shifted part of the U.S. manufacturing base to China.

Of course this shift had something to do with "unfair" trade, undereducated American workers, dirt-cheap Chinese sweatshops, and all the other things that American politicians chose to yammer about. But the "jobless recovery" of the early 2000s and the "'jobless collapse" at the end of the decade could never have occurred without the strange intersection of American and Chinese (plus Japanese and Korean) plans. The Chinese government was determined to keep the value of its yuan as low as possible, thus making Chinese exports as attractive as possible, so that Chinese factories could expand as quickly as possible, to provide work for the tens of millions of people trooping every year to Shanghai or Guangzhou to enter the labor force. To this end, Chinese banks sent their extra dollars right back to the U.S. Treasury, in loans to cover the U.S. budget deficit; if they hadn't, normal market pressures would have driven up the yuan's value.[12] This, in turn, would have made it harder for China to keep creating jobs and easier for America to retain them. But Americans would have had to tax themselves to cover the deficit.

This arrangement was called "Bretton Woods Two," after the regime that kept the world economy afloat for twenty-five years after World War II. The question economists debated was how long it could last. One group said it could go on indefinitely, because it gave each country's government what it really wanted (for China, booming exports and therefore a less dissatisfied population; for America, the ability to spend more while saving and taxing less). But by Bush's second term the warning signals were getting louder. "This is starting to resemble a pyramid scheme," the *Financial Times* warned early in 2005.[13] The danger was that the system was fundamentally unstable. Almost overnight it could go from working well to collapsing. If any one of the Asian countries piling up dollars (and most were doing so) began to suspect that any other was about to unload them, all the countries would have an incentive to sell dollars as fast as possible, before they got stuck with worthless currency. Economists in the "soft landing" camp said that adjustments would be gradual, and that Chinese self-interest would prevent a panic. The "hard landing" camp—well, we know all too well what they were concerned about.

2. Pulling the Trigger

The 2008 election, like those in 2000 and 2004, could have gone either way. If Fidel Castro had died two years earlier, the second Bay of Pigs tragedy and related "regime change" difficulties might have been dim memories by Election Day. Or if he had died a year later, the Cuban-American bloc of Florida voters would have been as reliably Republican in 2008 as in the previous fifty years. Since the red state-blue state divide was otherwise the same as in 2000 and 2004, if the Republicans had held Florida they would presumably have held the White House as well—despite mounting unease about debt, deficits, job loss, and rising U.S. casualties in Pakistan.

But by dying when he did, at eighty-two, and becoming the "October surprise" of the 2008 campaign, Castro got revenge on the Republicans who had for years supported the Cuban trade embargo. Better yet, he got revenge on his original enemies, the Democrats, too.[14] Castro couldn't have planned it, but his disappearance was the beginning—the first puff of wind, the trigger–of the catastrophe that followed.

Or perhaps we should call it the first domino to fall, because what then happened had a kind of geometric inevitability. The next domino was a thousand miles across the Caribbean, in Venezuela. Hugo Chavez, originally elected as a crusading left-winger, was by then well into his role as an outright military dictator. For years our diplomats had grumbled that Chavez was "Castro with oil," but after the real Castro's death the comparison had new meaning. A right-wing militia of disgruntled Venezuelans, emboldened by the news that Castro was gone, attempted a coup at the beginning of 2009, shortly after the U.S. elections. Chavez captured the ringleaders, worked them over, and then broadcast their possibly false "confession" that they had been sponsored by the

CIA. That led to Chavez's "declaration of economic war" against the United States, which in practice meant temporarily closing the gigantic Amuay refinery, the source of one eighth of all the gasoline used on American roads—and reopening it two months later with a pledge to send no products to American ports.

That was when the fourth—and worst—world oil shock started.[15] For at least five years economists and oilmen alike had warned that there was no "give" in the world oil market. In the early 2000s China's consumption was growing five times as fast as America's—and America was no slouch. (The main difference was that China, like India, was importing oil mainly for its factories, whereas the United States was doing so mainly for its big cars.[16]) Even a temporary disruption in the flow could cause major dislocations.

All the earlier oil shocks had meant short-term disruptions in supply (that's why they were "shocks"), but this time the long term was also in question. Geologists had argued about "peaking" predictions for years, but the concept was on everyone's lips by 2009.[17]

The Democrats had spent George Bush's second term preparing for everything except what was about to hit them. Our forty-fourth president seemed actually to welcome being universally known as "the Preacher," a nickname like "Ike" or "Honest Abe." It was a sign of how much emphasis he'd put on earnestly talking about faith, family, and firearms to voters in the heartland, in his effort to help the Democrats close the "values gap." But he had no idea what to do (to be fair, the man he beat, "the Veep," would not have known either) when the spot price of oil rose by 40 percent in the week after the Chavez declaration—and then everything else went wrong.

Anyone who needed further proof that God is a Republican would have found it in 2009. When the price of oil went up, the run on the dollar began. "Fixed exchange rates with heavy intervention [in essence, Bretton Woods Two] have enormous capacity to create an illusory sense of stability that could be shattered very quickly," Lawrence Summers had warned in 2004. "That is the lesson of Britain in 1992, of Mexico in 1994, of emerging Asia in 1997, of Russia in 1998, and of Brazil in 1998." And of the United States in 2009. It didn't help that Hugo Chavez had struck his notorious then-secret deal with the Chinese: preferential future contracts for his oil, which China needed, in return for China's backing out of Bretton Woods Two, which Chavez wanted.

There had been hints of how the falling dominoes would look as early as January of 2005. In remarks made at the World Economic Forum in Davos, Switzerland, Fan Gang, the director of China's nongovernmental National Economic Research Institute, said that "the U.S. dollar is no longer seen as a stable currency."[18] This caused a quick flurry in the foreign-exchange markets. It was to the real thing what the World Trade Center car bomb in 1993 was to 9/11.

When we read histories of the late 1920s, we practically want to scream, *Stop! Don't buy all that stock on credit! Get out of the market before it's too late!* When we read histories of the dot-com boom in the late 1990s, we have the same agonizing sense of not being able to save the victims from themselves: *Don't take out that home-equity loan to buy stocks at their peak! For God's sake, sell your Cisco shares when they hit 70, don't wait till they're back at 10!*

In retrospect, the ugly end is so obvious and inevitable. Why didn't people see it at the time? The same clearly applies to what happened in 2009. Economists had laid out the sequence of causes and effects in a "hard landing," and it worked just as they said it would.

Once the run on the dollar started, everything seemed to happen at once. Two days after the Venezuelan oil shock the dollar was down by 25 percent against the yen and the yuan. Two weeks later it was down by 50 percent. By the time trading "stabilized," one U.S. dollar bought only 2.5 Chinese yuan—not eight, as it had a year earlier.[19]

As the dollar headed down, assets denominated in dollars suddenly looked like losers. Most Americans had no choice but to stay in the dollar economy (their houses were priced in dollars, as were their savings and their paychecks), but those who had a choice unloaded their dollar holdings fast.[20] The people with choices were the very richest Americans, and foreigners of every sort. The two kinds of assets they least wanted to hold were shares in U.S.-based companies, since the plummeting dollar would wipe out any conceivable market gains, and dollar-based bonds, including U.S. Treasury debt. Thus we had twin, reinforcing panics: a sudden decline in share prices plus a sudden selloff of bonds and Treasury holdings. The T-note selloff forced interest rates up, which forced stock prices further down, and the race to the bottom was on.

Because interest rates had been so low for so long, much of the public had forgotten how nasty life could be when money all of a sudden got tight.[21] Every part of the cycle seemed to make every other part worse.

Businesses scaled back their expansion or investment plans, since borrowed money was more expensive. That meant fewer jobs. Mortgage rates went up, so buyers who might have bid on a $400,000 house could now handle only $250,000. That pushed real-estate values down; over time the $400,000 house *became* a $250,000 house. Credit-card rates were more onerous, so consumers had to cut back their spending. Some did it voluntarily, others in compliance with the Garnishee Amendments to the Bankruptcy Act of 2008. Businesses of every sort had higher fixed costs: for energy, because of the oil-price spike; for imported components, because of the dollar's crash; for everything else, because of ripple effects from those changes and from higher interest rates. Those same businesses had lower revenues, because of the squeeze on their customer base. Early in Bush's second term economists had pointed out that the U.S. stock indexes were surprisingly weak considering how well U.S. corporations had been doing.[22] The fear of just these developments was why.

Americans had lived through a similar self-intensifying cycle before—but not since the late 1970s, when many of today's adults were not even born. Back in those days the sequence of energy-price spike, dollar crash, interest-rate surge, business slowdown, and stock-market loss had overwhelmed poor Jimmy Carter—he of the promise to give America "a government as good as its people." This time it did the same to the Preacher, for all his talk about "a new Democratic Party rooted in the oldest values of a free and faithful country." When he went down, the future of his party almost certainly went with him.

The spate of mergers and acquisitions that started in 2010 was shocking at the time but looks inevitable in retrospect. When the CEOs of the three remaining U.S. airlines had their notorious midnight meeting at the DFW Hilton, they knew they were breaking two dozen antitrust laws and would be in financial and legal trouble if their nervy move failed. But it worked. When they announced the new and combined AmFly Corporation, regulators were in no position to call their bluff. At their joint press conference the CEOs said, accept our more efficient structure or we'll all declare bankruptcy, and all at once. The efficiencies meant half as many flights (for "fuel conservation") as had been offered by the previously competing airlines, to 150 fewer cities, with a third as many jobs (all non-union).[23] Democrats in Congress didn't like it, nor did most editorialists, but the administration didn't really have a choice. It could swallow the deal—or it could get ready to take over the routes, the planes, the payrolls, and the passenger complaints, not to mention the decades of litigation.

Toyota's acquisition of General Motors and Ford, in 2012, had a similar inevitability. Over the previous decade the two U.S. companies had lost money on every car they sold. Such profit as they made was on SUVs, trucks, and Hummer-style big rigs. In 2008, just before the oil shock, GM seemed to have struck gold with the Strykette—an adaptation of the Army's Stryker vehicle, so famous from Iraq and Pakistan, whose marketing campaign attracted professional women. Then the SUV market simply disappeared. With gasoline at $6 a gallon, the prime interest rate at 15 percent, and the stock and housing markets in the toilet, no one wanted what American car makers could sell.[24] The weak dollar, and their weak stock prices, made the companies a bargain for Toyota.[25]

For politicians every aspect of this cycle was a problem: the job losses, the gasoline lines, the bankruptcies, the hard-luck stories of lifetime savings vanishing as the stock market headed down. But nothing matched the nightmare of foreclosures.

For years regulators and financiers had worried about the "over-leveraging" of the American housing market. As housing prices soared in coastal cities, people behaved the way they had during the stock-market run-up of the 1920s: they paid higher and higher prices; they covered more and more of the purchase price with debt; more and more of that debt was on "floating rate" terms—and everything was fine as long as prices stayed high and interest rates stayed low.

When the market collapsed, Americans didn't behave the way economic theory said they should.[26] They behaved the way their predecessors in the Depression had: they stayed in their houses, stopped paying their mortgages, and waited for the banks to take the next step. Through much of the Midwest this was a manageable problem: the housing market had gone less berserk to begin with, and, as in the Great Depression, there was a longer-term, more personal relationship between customers and financiers. But in the fastest-growing markets—Orlando, Las Vegas, the Carolina Research Triangle, northern Virginia—the banks simply could not wait. The deal brokered at the White House Security-in-Shelter Summit was ingenious: federal purchase of one million RVs and mobile homes, many of them built at idle auto or truck factories; subsidies for families who agreed to leave foreclosed homes without being evicted by marshals, such that they could buy RVs with no payments for five years; and the use of land at decommissioned military bases for the new RV villages. But it did not erase the blogcam live broadcasts of families being evicted, or the jokes about the "Preachervilles" springing up at Camp Lejeune, the former Fort Ord, and the Philadelphia naval shipyard.

Here is how we know that, a sitting president is going to lose: he is seriously challenged in his own party's primaries.[27] So if the economic tailspin had left any doubts about the prospects for the Preacher and his party, they were removed by the clamor to run against him in the Democratic primaries of 2012. The party's biggest names were all there: the senators from New York, Illinois, and Florida; the new governors of California and Pennsylvania; the mayor of New York, when it looked as if the Olympic Games would still be held there that fall; and the actor who in his three most recent films had captured Americans' idea of how a president should look and sound, and who came closest to stealing the nomination from the incumbent.

He and the rest of them were probably lucky that their campaigns fell short—not that any politician ever believes that. The Democratic nomination in 2012 was obviously a poisoned chalice, but a politician can't help thinking that a poisoned chalice is better than no chalice at all. The barrier none of them could have overcome was the financial crisis of state and local government.

All that befell the federal budget during the collapse of 2009–2012 happened to state and local governments, too, but more so. They had to spend more—on welfare, Medicaid, jails, police officers—while taking in less. One by one their normal sources of funding dried up.[28] Revenues from the multi-state lottery and the FreedomBall drawings rose a bit. Unfortunately, the surge of spending on casino gambling in forty-three states and on legalized prostitution in thirty-one didn't benefit state and local governments, because except in Nevada those activities were confined to Indian reservations, and had only an indirect stimulative effect.

And many governors and mayors faced a reality the president could avoid: they operated under constitutions and charters that forbade deficit spending. So they had no practical choice but to tighten the clamps at both ends, cutting budgets and raising taxes. The process had begun before the crash, as politicking in most state capitols was dominated by "intractable" budget disputes.[29] When the downturn really hit, even governors who had never heard of John Maynard Keynes sensed that it was a bad idea to raise taxes on people who were being laid off and evicted. But they were obliged by law to balance their budgets. All mayors and governors knew that it would be dicey to renege on their basic commitments to education, public safety, public health, and public infrastructure. But even in hindsight it is hard to know what else they could have done. California did too much too fast in closing sixty-three of its 110 community colleges[30] and imposing $9,500 annual "user fees" in place of the previous nominal fees. Its solution to the financing crisis on its high-end campuses was defter—especially the "Great Pacific Partnership" between the University of California and Tsinghua University, in Beijing. This was a win-win arrangement, in which the Chinese Ministry of Education took over the funding of the UC Berkeley physics, computer-science, and biology laboratories, plus the genomics laboratory at UC San Francisco, in exchange for a 51 percent share of all resulting patents.

State and local governments across the country did what they could. Fee-for-service became the norm—first for "enrichment" programs in the schools, then to underwrite teachers' salaries, then for emergency police calls, then for inclusion in routine police and fire patrols. First in Minnesota, soon after in Michigan, New York, and Pennsylvania, there were awkward moments when the governor, exercising his power as commander in chief of the state National Guard, ordered the Guard's medical units to serve in hospitals that had furloughed nurses and emergency-room doctors. The Democratic president decided not to force the question of who had ultimate control over these "citizen soldiers." This averted a showdown in the short term, but became one more attack point for the Republicans about weak and vacillating Democrats. Cities within 150 miles of the Mexican border opened police-service and trash-hauling contracts to companies based in Mexico. The state of Georgia, extending a practice it had begun in the early 2000s, said that it would hire no new public school teachers except under the "Partnership for Excellence" program, which brought in cut-rate teachers from India.[31]

The chaos in public services spelled the end for the administration, and for the Democratic Party in the long run. The Democrats couldn't defend the unions. They couldn't defend pensioners. They couldn't even do much for their limousine liberals. The nation had never been more in the mood for firm leadership. When the "Desert Eagle" scored his astonishing coup in the Saudi Arabian desert just before Christmas of 2011, America knew who its next leader would be. For a four-star general to join his enlisted men in a nighttime HALO[32] special-operations assault was against all established practice. The Eagle's determination to go ahead with the stunt revealed him to be essentially a MacArthuresque ham. But the element of surprise was total, and the unit surrounded, captured, and gagged Osama bin Laden before he was fully awake.

The general's news conference the next day had the largest live audience in history, breaking the record set a few months earlier by the coronation of England's King William V. The natural grace of this new American hero was like nothing the world had seen since Charles Lindbergh landed in Paris. His politics were indistinct, but if anything, that was a plus. He was strong on defense; urgent (without details) about "lighting smart against our economic enemies"; and broadly appealing on "values"—a devout Catholic who had brought the first openly gay commandos into a front-line combat unit. ("When we were under fire, I never asked who they loved, because I knew they loved our flag.") Political pros had always assumed that America's first black president would be a Republican and a soldier, and they were right. He just didn't turn out to be Colin Powell.

The only suspense in the election was how big the win would be. By Labor Day it was clear that the Democrats might lose even the District of Columbia, whose rich residents were resentful about their ravaged stock portfolios, and whose poor residents had been cut off from Medicaid, welfare, and schools. As the nation went, so went the District, and after fifty-seven presidential elections the United States had its first across-the-board electoral sweep.

3. Bleeding

The emergencies are over. As our current president might put it, it's a war of attrition now. His administration hasn't made anything worse—and we have to admit that early on his ease and confidence were like a balm. But he hasn't made anything better, either. If not fully tired of him, the public has grown as fatalistic about the Republicans' ability to make any real difference as it already was about the Democrats'. The two-party system had been in trouble for decades. It was rigid, polarizing, and unrepresentative. The parties were pawns of special interests. The one interest group they neglected was the vast center of the American electorate, which kept seeking split-the-difference policies. Eight years of failure from two administrations have finally blown apart the tired duopoly. The hopes of our nation are bleeding away along with our few remaining economic resources.

Here is the challenge:

- Our country no longer controls its economic fundamentals.
- Compared with the America of the past, it has become stagnant, classbound, and brutally unfair.
- Compared with the rest of the world, it is on the way down. We think we are a great power—and our military is still ahead of China's. Everyone else thinks that over the past twenty years we finally pushed our luck too far.

To deal with these problems once in office, we must point out basic truths in the campaign. These truths involve the past sources of our growth: savings, investment, education, innovation. We've thrown away every one of these advantages. What we would do right now to have back the $1 trillion that Congress voted away in 2008 with the Freedom From Death Tax Act![33] A relatively small share of that money might have kept our aerospace programs competitive with Europe's[34]—to say nothing of preparing us for advances in other forms of transportation. A little more might have made our road and highway system at least as good as China's.[35] With what was left over, our companies might have been able to compete with Germany's in producing the superfast, quiet, efficient maglev trains that are now doing for travel what the jet plane did in the 1950s. Even if we couldn't afford to make the trains, with more money at least some of our states and regions might have been able to buy them, instead of just looking enviously at what China, India, and Iran have done.[36]

Or we could have shored up our universities. True, the big change came as early as 2002, in the wake of 9/11, when tighter visa rules, whatever their effect on reducing terrorism, cut off the flow of foreign talent that American universities had channeled to American ends.[37] In the summer of 2007 China applied the name "twenty Harvards" to its ambition, announced in the early 2000s, to build major research institutions that would attract international talent. It seemed preposterous (too much political control, too great a language barrier), but no one is laughing now. The Chinese mission to Mars, with astronauts from Pakistan, Germany, and Korea, indicates the scope of China's scientific ambition. And necessity has pushed China into the lead in computerized translation technology, so that foreign students can read Chinese characters. The Historic Campus of our best-known university, Harvard, is still prestigious worldwide. But its role is increasingly that of the theme park, like Oxford or Heidelberg, while the most ambitious students compete for fellowships at the Har-Bai and Har-Bei campuses in Mumbai and Beijing. These, of course, have become each other's main rivals—whether for scores on the World Ingenuity Test or in the annual meeting of the teams they sponsor at the Rose Bowl.

Or we could at last have begun to grapple with healthcare costs. We've managed to create the worst of all worlds—what the Democrats call the "30–30 problem." Thirty percent of our entire economy goes for health and medical costs,[38] but 30 percent of our citizens have no regular contact with the medical system. (Except, of course, during quarantines in avian-flu season.) For people who can afford them, the "tailored therapies" of the past decade represent the biggest breakthrough in medicine since antibiotics or anesthesia. The big killers—heart disease and cancers of the colon, lung, breast, and prostate—are now manageable chronic diseases at worst, and the big moral issues involve the question of whether Baby Boomers are living "too long." But the costs are astronomical, which raises questions of both efficiency and justice. Google's embedded diagnostic technology dramatizes our problem: based on nonstop biometric testing of the thirty-seven relevant enzymes and organ-output levels, it pipes into cell-phone implants instructions for which treatment, pill, or action to take next. The system is extremely popular—for the 10 million people who can afford it. NetJet flights to the Bahamas for organ replacement illustrate the point even more sharply, although here the breakthrough was less medical than diplomatic. The World Trade Organization, after the most contentious proceeding in its history, ruled that prohibiting commerce in human organs for transplant was an unjust trade barrier. The ruling may have caused the final, fatal split in the Republican Party (libertarians were jubilant, religious conservatives appalled), but it became the foundation of an important Caribbean industry after threats of violence dissuaded many transplant centers from operating within the United States. Meanwhile, despite the Strong America–Strong Americans Act of 2009, which tied income-tax rates to body-mass index and cigarette consumption, smoking and eating junk food have become for our underemployed class what swilling vodka was for the dispossessed in Boris Yeltsin's Russia.

All these issues involve money, and we can't avoid talking about money in this campaign. But your ability to address an even harder issue will largely determine whether you can succeed in the job the voters are about to give you.

That problem is the sense of sunset, decline, hopelessness. America has been so resilient as a society because each American has imagined that the sky was the limit. Obviously it was not for everyone, or always. From the beginning we've had a class system, and a racial-caste system, and extended periods—the 1890s, the 1930s, the 1970s, the past few years—when many more people than usual were struggling merely to survive. But the myth of equal opportunity has been closer to reality here than in any other society, and the myth itself has mattered.

My father, in explaining why it was so painful for him to see a lifetime's savings melt away after the Venezuelan crisis, told me about a political speech he remembered from his own youth. It was by Daniel Patrick Moynihan, a Harvard professor who later became a politician. In the late 1960s, when American prosperity held despite bitter political turmoil, Moynihan told left-wing students why preserving that prosperity should be important even to them. We know Europe from its novels, Moynihan said: the old ones, by Austen and Dickens and Stendahl, and the more recent ones, too. We know it as a static society. Young people, seeking opportunity, have to wait for old people to die. A whole life's prospects depend on the size of an inheritance. People know their place. America, Moynihan said fifty years ago, must never become a place like that.

That is the place we have become. Half this country's households live on less than $50,000 a year. That sounds like a significant improvement from the $44,000 household median in 2003. But a year in private college now costs $83,000, a day in a hospital $1,350, a year in a nursing home $150,000—and a gallon of gasoline $9. Thus we start off knowing that for half our people there is no chance—none—of getting ahead of the game. And really, it's more like 80 percent of the public that is priced out of a chance for future opportunity. We have made a perfect circle—perfect in closing off options. There are fewer attractive jobs to be had, even though the ones at the top, for financiers or specialty doctors, are very attractive indeed. And those who don't start out with advantages in getting those jobs have less and less chance of moving up to them.

Jobs in the middle of the skill-and-income distribution have steadily vanished if any aspect of them can be done more efficiently in China, India, or Vietnam. The K-12 schools, the universities, the ambitious research projects that could help the next generation qualify for better jobs, have weakened or dried up.[39] A dynamic economy is always losing jobs. The problem with ours is that we're no longer any good at creating new ones. America is a less attractive place for new business because it's a less attractive place, period.[40]

In the past decade we've seen the telephone companies disappear. Programming, data, entertainment, conversation—they all go over the Internet now. Pharmaceuticals are no longer mass-produced but, rather, tailored to each patient's genetic makeup. The big airlines are all gone now, and much of publishing, too. The new industries are the ones we want. When their founders are deciding where to locate, though, they'll see us as a country with a big market—and with an undereducated work force, a rundown infrastructure, and a shaky currency. They'll see England as it lost its empire. They'll see Russia without the oil reserves, Brezhnev's Soviet Union without the repression. They'll see the America that Daniel Patrick Moynihan feared.

This story is now yours to tell, and later I'll turn to notes for the stump speech. But remember that the reality of the story reaches backward, and that is why I have concentrated on the missed opportunities, the spendthrift recklessness, the warnings America heard but tuned out. To tell it that way in public would of course only make things worse, and we can't afford the recriminations or the further waste of time. The only chance for a new beginning is to make people believe there actually is a chance.

Notes

1. The last one was Millard Fillmore, a Whig. We will not emphasize this detail.

2. Also, though I never thought I'd say it, thank God for the Electoral College. In only two states, Michigan and Maine, are you polling above 50 percent of the total vote—in Michigan because of the unemployment riots, in Maine because that's what they're like. But you will probably have a strong plurality in at least forty other states, yielding a Reagan-scale electoral-vote "mandate."

3. Nothing in history ever quite "begins." Did America's problems with militant Islam begin in 2001? Or twenty years earlier, when we funded the anti-Soviet *mujahideen* in Afghanistan, who later turned their weapons against us? Or sixty years before that, with the breakup of the Ottoman Empire after World War I? Or during the Crusades? Similarly, warning signs of today's economic problems were apparent in the mid-1960s. But the big change started fifteen years ago, at the beginning of this century.

4. The federal debt consists of bills, notes, and bonds that come due at different periods—thirteen weeks, five years, twenty years. The main way to retire debt is to pay off holders on the due date. Only $2 trillion worth of debt would have matured within a decade, so only that much could be paid off. That is why the Bush administration's first budget message said, "Indeed, the President's Budget pays down the debt so aggressively that it runs into an unusual problem—its annual surpluses begin to outstrip the amount of maturing debt starting in 2007."

5. In 2005 Ben White, of *The Washington Post*, noted the coincidence of the Dow's peak and Bush's signing of the tax-cut bill.

6. Late in January of 2005 the CBO calculated that policy changes during Bush's first term had increased the upcoming year's deficit by $539 billion. Of that amount about 37 percent could be attributed to warfare, domestic security, and other post-9/11 commitments; 48 percent resulted from the tax cuts; and the rest came from other spending increases.

7. This CBO chart (omitted) illustrates the pattern. The big dive is the result of the 2001 and 2003 tax cuts.

8. In 2003 Congress approved a second round of tax cuts. In 2005, after a fifty-fifty deadlock, the Senate failed to enact a "pay as you go" provision, which would have required the administration to offset any tax cuts or spending increases by savings in the budget.

9. Through the early 2000s the Government Accountability Office issued warnings about the consequences of extending the tax cuts. This chart (omitted), from 2004, showed what would happen to the budget if the tax cuts were locked in.

10. "In the last year, the net national savings rate of the United States has been between one and two percent," the economist and then president of Harvard Lawrence Summers said in 2004, a year before the rate hit its nadir. "It represents the lowest net national savings rate in American history and, I believe, that of any major nation." Summers gave the speech five years after his appointment as Treasury secretary and five years before his nomination as chairman of the Federal Reserve Board.

11. Robert Shiller, an economist at Yale, was ahead of most other observers in predicting the collapse of the tech-stock bubble of the 1990s and the personal-real-estate bubble a decade later. In a paper for the National Bureau of Economic Research, published in 2001, he and two colleagues observed that the housing boom intensified the savings collapse. Every time homeowners heard that a nearby house had sold for an astronomical price, they felt richer, even if they had no intention of selling for years. That made them more likely to go out and spend their theoretical "gains"—and not to bother saving, since their house was doing it for them. "The estimated effect of housing market wealth on consumption is significant and large," Shiller and his colleagues concluded. If people felt rich, they spent that way.

12. As background for the speechwriters, here is the longer version of what was happening.

In normal circumstances economic markets have a way of dealing with families, companies, or countries that chronically overspend. For families or companies that way is bankruptcy. For countries it is a declining currency. By normal economic measures the American public was significantly overspending in the early 2000s. For every $100 worth of products and services it consumed, it produced only about $95 worth within our borders. The other $5 worth came from overseas. Normally an imbalance like this would push the dollar steadily down as foreigners with surplus dollars from selling oil or cars or clothes in America traded them for euros, yuan, or yen. As demand for dollars fell and their value decreased, foreign goods would become more expensive; Americans wouldn't be able to afford as many of them; and ultimately Americans would be forced to live within the nation's means.

That is in fact what happened in America's trade with Europe—and to a large extent with the oil-producing world. The euro skyrocketed in value against the dollar, and oil prices—which until the crisis of 2009 were fixed in dollars—went up too, which preserved Saudi and Kuwaiti buying power for European goods.

It didn't work this way with China. Americans bought and bought Chinese goods, and Chinese banks piled up dollars—but didn't trade them back for yuan. Instead China's central bank kept the yuan-to-dollar exchange rate constant and used the dollars to buy U.S. Treasury notes. That is, they covered the federal budget deficit. (Since Americans, on average, were saving nothing, they couldn't cover it themselves.) To a lesser extent Korean and Japanese banks did the same thing.

This was different from the situation in the 1980s and 1990s, when foreigners earned dollars from their exports and used those dollars to buy American companies, real estate, and stock. In those days foreigners invested heavily in America because (he payoff was so much greater than what they could get in Frankfurt or Tokyo. In an influential paper published in 2004 the economists Nouriel Roubini, of New York University, and Brad Setser, of Oxford University, demonstrated that this was no longer the case. Increasingly it was not individuals or corporations but foreign *governments*—in particular, state-controlled banks in Asia—that were sending money to America. And America was using it to finance the federal budget deficit.

13. The paper showed how foreign money was supporting U.S. spending.

14. We now know from the memoirs of his eldest son, Fidelito, that Castro never moderated his bitter view of the Kennedy brothers—Jack for authorizing the Bay of Pigs invasion. Bobby, for encouraging the CIA to assassinate Castro—and. by extension, their Democratic Party. Castro told his children that if the United States and Cuba ever reconciled, he dreamed of doing two things: throwing an opening-day pitch at Yankee Stadium, and addressing a Republican convention in prime time. (From *Mi Papa: The Castro I Knew*, Las Vegas: HarperCollins, 2009.)

15. The first one, starting in 1973, transformed the world more than most wars do. It empowered OPEC; enriched much of the Middle East; brought on five years of inflation, slow growth, and stock-market stagnation in the United States; pushed Japan toward a radically more energy-efficient industry; and more. The second, after the Iranian revolution of 1979, caused the inflation that helped drive Jimmy Carter from office, and spilled over into the recession of Ronald Reagan's first two years. The third, after Iraq's 1990 invasion of Kuwait, disrupted world trade enough to lay the groundwork for Bill Clinton's "It's the economy, stupid" attack against George H.W. Bush. And seven years after the shock of 2009 began, we are still feeling its effects.

16. After the first oil shock U.S. oil consumption actually fell in absolute terms. In 1973, as the first shock began, Americans consumed 35 "quads," or quadrillion BTUs, of oil. Ten years later, with a larger population and a stronger economy, they consumed only 30. But from that point on total consumption moved back up. In 2003 Americans consumed 39 quads—and *two thirds* of that oil was for transportation. Consumption for most other purposes, notably heating and power generation, actually went down, thanks to more-efficient systems. Industrial consumption was flat. So bigger cars and longer commutes did make the difference.

17. Every oil field follows a pattern of production: Its output rate starts slow and keeps getting faster until about half the oil has been pumped from the field. Then the rate steadily declines until the other half of the oil is gone. Since total world production is the aggregate of thousands of fields, it is presumed to follow a similar pattern. In 2005 the research and engineering firm SAIC released a report commissioned by the U.S. government on best guesses about the worldwide peak and what would happen when it came. "No one knows with certainty when world oil production will reach a peak," the report said, "but geologists have no doubt that it will happen." Of the twelve experts surveyed for the report, six predicted that the peak would have occurred before 2010, and three more that it would happen by 2020.

The world was not going to "run out" of oil—at least not immediately. Even at the peak, by definition, as much as had ever been pumped in history was still there to be extracted. But the rate of production, barrels per day and per year, would steadily lessen

while the rate of demand kept increasing. The report was released when oil crossed $50 a barrel; we are long into the era of oil at 30 euros, or $90.

18. "That turned out to be the next-to-last convening of the Davos conference, before the unproven but damaging accusations that it was a front for the A. Q. Khan combine.

19. What happened to America almost exactly repeated what had happened ten years earlier to Thailand, Indonesia, and other countries during the Asian panic of 1997–1998. South Korea lost 50 percent of the value of its currency in two months; Indonesia lost 80 percent over the course of a year. As in America, the collapse of each currency led to equally deep stock-market declines. The Asian crash also turned into a foreign-policy nightmare for the United States, with Prime Minister Mahathir of Malaysia leading the denunciation of U.S.-based financiers, including the "moron" George Soros, for the "'criminal" speculations that destroyed the economies of smaller nations like his. Since Malaysia and Indonesia are largely Muslim, and the financiers could be cast as part of the great shadowy U.S.-Zionist cabal, the crash worsened U.S. relations with the Islamic world.

20. Once the foreigners knew that the dollar had hit bottom, they came back to buy shares at bargain prices. But the currency run of 2009 showed the same pattern as the tech-stock crash of 2000 and, indeed, the generalized market panic of the 1930s: prices stayed depressed for years, because investors who had suffered heavy losses were understandably slow to return.

21. Let's make up flash cards for the speechwriters, so they are clear about the role of interest rates.

When interest rates go *up*, these things go *down*: stock-market prices, bond prices, housing prices, overall economic growth rates, overall investment, overall job creation.

The most important thing that goes *up* when interest rates rise is the value of the dollar. We'll save the cause and effect for our policy guys, but make sure the writers have these points straight.

For the speechwriters' benefit, let's spell this out too: Why did the dollar panic raise interest rates? Two related reasons. First, interest rates are ultimately set by supply and demand. If the Treasury can't sell enough notes at four percent to cover the deficit, it will keep raising the rate—to five, six, ten percent—until it gets the money it needs. Second, the main way a government can keep up the value of its currency is to raise interest rates, hoping to attract investments that would otherwise be made in yuan, euros, or yen.

22. In the spring of 2005, as stock averages slid week by week, W. Bowman Cutter, a managing partner of the investment-banking firm Warburg Pincus, asked, "Why are we not in a bull market now?" He said that if you looked at the traditional measures of economic strength—high corporate investment, rapid productivity improvements, strong overall growth rates—"you would have to say that 2004 was the best year of the past twenty." Interest rates at the time were still very low. "If you transposed this to any other era in history." Cutter said, "you would have a very strong bull market. Why not now? Because the market is looking to the long-term structural problems." If the market couldn't go up when conditions were promising, it had no cushion when the crisis began.

23. Jobs in the airline industry had been plummeting for years. In 2000 the eight largest carriers employed 432,000 people. Four years later a third of those jobs were gone. That meant the loss of 136,000 mainly unionized, mainly high-wage jobs, offset by a small increase in lower-paid jobs at regional and discount airlines.

24. U.S. auto companies and the U.S. auto-buying public suffered in different ways from the "slowness" of America's industry compared with Japan's, China's, and Korea's. It took Detroit companies three years to shift production from trucks and SUVs to hybrid cars; by that time the Asian brands owned the market. Also, it took the American fleet as a whole a surprisingly long time to change. The average car on America's roads is nine years old, and in the course of a decade only half of all cars are replaced. It takes a long time to work the older gas-guzzlers out of the system.

25. The rising value of the euro and the troubled state of the airline market might well have made Boeing a similar target for the new Airbus-Mitsubishi consortium—but for the Transformational Air Mobility Industrial Base Act of 2011, which converted Boeing's factories to national-defense production facilities on a par with Navy shipyards.

26. Through the boom years speculators would borrow the entire cost of a house. If they could flip" it in a year or two, the profit on the sale would offset the interest they'd paid. But after mortgage rates "floated" up above 10 percent, the calculation changed. The house's value was heading down, and the cost of covering the mortgage was heading up. If the house were just another asset, the rational choice would be to move out and give it back to the bank. But houses aren't normal assets, and that's not what people did.

27. The pattern goes back to the very beginning of the modern primary system, after World War II, and it has no exceptions. If an incumbent faces a serious, vote-getting rival for his party's nomination, he goes on to lose the White House. If not, he stays in.

28. State and local governments tax income, which was falling; property, whose value was plummeting; and retail sales, which were down as well. The blue states were somewhat cushioned against the shocks in comparison with the many red states that had declined to impose state income taxes. Those states depended on property taxes, a fast-disappearing revenue source. Also, since the Nixon years red and blue states alike had relied on federal revenue sharing. This was slashed as part of the Emergency Budget Act of 2012.

29. In 2002 the Rockefeller Institute of Government projected budget trends for the states through 2010, and found that forty-four of them were headed for long-term deficits like the ones plaguing the federal government. The difference, again, is that many states were obliged to change their policies to avoid the deficits.

30. This accelerated a trend that had begun a decade earlier in California. For instance, when the 2003 school year began, some 175,000 students could not find space in community colleges—which, like K-12 public schools, had previously offered enrollment to all eligible students.

31. Gwinnett County, near Atlanta, opened many school administrators' eyes to this possibility in 2004, when it brought in twenty-seven teachers from Hyderabad. In 2005 an examination board in England outsourced the grading of high-school achievement exams to workers in India.

32. For "high-altitude, low-opening" parachute jump. The jumpers leave the plane at 30,000 feet, free-fall for nearly two minutes, and open their chutes at 1,000 feet, a few seconds before impact. Because the airplanes are so high, they cannot be seen or heard from the ground; and the jumpers spend almost no time with their chutes visibly deployed.

33. In the spring of 2005 the Congressional Joint Committee on Taxation estimated that ending the estate tax would directly cut federal revenue by $72 billion in 2015. Other groups calculated that the total impact on the budget, including higher interest payments on a larger federal debt, would be $100 billion a year, or $1 trillion over a decade. All this tax relief flowed to the wealthiest one percent of Americans.

34. In 1990 the American aerospace industry employed 1,120,000 people. By 2004 that number had fallen by nearly half, to 593,000. During those same years the European aerospace industry was growing in both sales and work force. In 2003 Airbus overtook Boeing in world market share for commercial airliners.

35. In 2005 the American Society of Civil Engineers released a "report card" on the state of America's infrastructure—roads, dams, bridges, aviation, and so on. The overall grade was D, with the highest mark being C+, for solid-waste handling. According to the report, the most dramatic underinvestment involved the nation's roads. Simply maintaining the roads at the same level would cost $94 billion, the report said—or half again as much as actual yearly investment levels. Improving the roads would require about twice as much as the United States was spending.

36. In 2003 the city of Shanghai opened the world's fastest maglev line, whose trains average 267 miles per hour and arrive on schedule 99.7 percent of the time. An editor's note in the *Journal of the American Society of Civil Engineers* pointed out that half a dozen maglev proposals for American cities were "stalled in one stage or another of planning, permitting, or budgeting." The result, the journal's editor observed, was this: "Traffic congestion on U.S. roads worsens, energy prices fluctuate unpredictably, and, at least for the moment, China pulls ahead of the United States on the path to a safe, reliable, fast, and efficient means of transporting passengers."

37. Foreign enrollment in U.S. universities increased steadily from 1971 through 2002. It fell the next year, and has gone down ever since.

38. It was under 8 percent in 1990 and under 12 percent in 2000.

39. It's hard to remember or even to believe, but not that long ago the school system was a valuable social equalizer. More important, it was seen that way. Through the three golden decades, from the late 1940s (when the G1 Bill kicked in) to the late 1970s (when Proposition 13 passed in California), the federal government and the states put more money than ever before into elementary schools, high schools, and universities. More students than ever before finished high school; more finished college; more felt they could go further than their parents had. Proposition 13 was the California ballot measure that cut property taxes by 30 percent and then capped their future growth. It prefigured the federal tax cuts of the early 2000s, because it pushed the level of revenue below its historic "band." Before Proposition 13 California's per capita spending on public schools was high, like Connecticut's or New York's. Twenty years later it was well below the national average, just ahead of Arkansas's.

40. In the early 2000s one third of American public high school students failed to graduate on time. Niels Christian Nielsen, a member of several corporate boards in Europe and the United States, said at the University of California in 2005, "The big difference between Europe and America is the proportion of people who come out of the system really not being functional for any serious

role. In Finland that is maybe two or three percent. For Europe in general maybe fifteen or twenty. For the United States at least thirty percent, maybe more. In spite of all the press, Americans don't really get the education difference. They generally still feel this is a well-educated country and work force. They just don't see how far the country is falling behind."

JAMES FALLOWS, National correspondent for *The Atlantic*, has written three cover stories on U.S. foreign policy and Iraq: "Bush's Lost Year" (October 2004), "Blind Into Baghdad" (January/February 2004), and "The Fifty-first State?" (November 2002).

Seizing Intangibles for the G.D.P.

LOUIS UCHITELLE

The plain fact is that when it comes to measuring how much the American economy produces and who gets what share of the pie, the federal government's most celebrated statistic—the gross domestic product—leaves something to be desired.

The G.D.P. is useful, as far as it goes. It tells us how much value—often called national income—is generated each year from the production of goods and services in the United States. The G.D.P. also breaks out how much of that income goes into profits and how much into wages and salaries.

This is where the trouble is. The numbers show that the profit portion of the gross domestic product has risen mildly in recent years, while the wage-and-salary share has shrunk slightly. There is evidence, however, that because of the way the G.D.P. is calculated, the actual shift is much more pronounced.

"We know that income inequality is quite substantial," said Harry J. Holzer, a labor economist at Georgetown University, "and this new evidence suggests that it is worse than we thought."

The Bureau of Economic Analysis, which issues the G.D.P. reports each quarter, is on the case. So are two prominent economists at the Federal Reserve. They all seem to be finding that the current methods for calculating G.D.P. undercount the dollar returns from research and development. What's more, this payoff is not showing up in workers' paychecks.

The approximately $300 billion spent each year on R & D is a big concern of the bureau's economists. Until now, it has been counted as an expense, reducing the profit total within the G.D.P. Starting in September, however, the bureau will publish an experimental G.D.P. account that parallels the standard quarterly report, except for one change: R & D will be counted as capital investment rather than as an expense.

There is logic in this change. Consider the process of making and selling a dress. The cloth and thread—the raw materials—that go into the dress are an expense that must be subtracted from the sales price of the dress, once it is sold, to arrive at a profit. The automated sewing machine that makes the dress, on the other hand, is counted in the G.D.P. accounts as a capital investment because, once installed, it makes dress after dress, generating a stream of revenue. It is an investment drawn from retained earnings to generate more earnings.

Similarly, the research and development that made Prozac possible generates revenue for years, just as the sewing machine does for the dressmaker. Successful research and development yields long-term returns, and the bureau's experimental G.D.P. acknowledges as much, by classifying R & D as capital investment in the satellite account. Capital investment, in turn, counts as a contribution to profit in the G.D.P.

This reclassification leaves no doubt that workers are being left behind as the G.D.P. expands. When R & D is counted as profit, the employee compensation share of national income drops by more than one percentage point. In a $12.5 trillion economy, that's big money.

Measured in dollars, wages aren't actually falling, but workers are losing ground. "If capital income is going up and wages stay the same, then the share of total national income that goes to labor goes down," said Sumiye Okubo, an associate director of the bureau, who is directing the experimental project.

The two Fed economists—Carol A. Corrado and Daniel E. Sichel—along with an outside collaborator, Charles R. Hulten, a University of Maryland economist, go much further than Ms. Okubo and her team in arguing that the G.D.P. data should be revised. They would do more than just reclassify R & D.

In a recent research paper, "Intangible Capital and Economic Growth," they agree with Ms. Okubo's team that formal, scientific research and development should be categorized as capital investment rather than as ordinary expenses. But they say that this treatment should be extended to a host of other investments that generate revenue streams over a period of years.

They would include various intangibles, like advertising when it is used to establish a brand name that permanently lifts sales, and a retail chain's outlays to adapt existing technology to the chain's needs, as Wal-Mart did in designing a superefficient inventory control system.

Such intangibles now approach $250 billion a year, up from only $11 billion in the 1970's, the three economists calculate. If these intangibles, along with R & D, were incorporated into G.D.P. on the profit side as capital investment, labor's share of national income would decline from a fairly steady 65 percent in the 1950's, 60's and 70's to less than 60 percent today.

The long decline doesn't show up in the standard G.D.P. accounts, which ascribe nearly 65 percent of national income to labor. "The hidden earnings from these knowledge investments have not been shared equally with workers," Mr. Hulten said.

Two reasons seem likely. Some of the profit is probably going to the wealthiest Americans—the upper 1 percent whose incomes have risen sharply, in part from dividends and other forms of corporate earnings.

Then, too, most of the nation's workers are bereft of bargaining power. Unless that returns, labor's share of national income seems likely to continue its decline.

The Elephant in the Room

Economic growth is worshipped like a god—blindly and without any concern for reason.

AIDAN RANKIN

'Religion is the opium of the people' is one of Marx's best-known aphorisms. It is memorable because it tells us so much about the manipulation of faith in the industrial era, when it was often used to induce passive conformity to business interests. Before he became fixated on the class struggle, Marx showed an ecological consciousness remarkable for his time. He spoke of the need for 'the genuine resolution of the antagonism between man and nature', which is as good a definition of eco-philosophy as any. If the young Karl Marx were writing today, in the era of globalisation, it is likely that he would recognise the new opium as economic growth. For growth has become the Alpha and Omega of political discourse, the place where 'right' and 'left' converge, the goal for which activists of both camps become cheerleaders.

Economic growth has effectively become an official religion. Its theology is uncomplicated, calling to mind the 'cargo cults' that enjoyed brief popularity on South Sea islands during the mid-twentieth century. These cults did not offer salvation in the form of 'pie in the sky', but as consumer luxuries on earth delivered by miraculous ships. The ideology of growth is based on similar superstitions. It is revealing to hear economists who pride themselves on their secular rationalism speak of a 'hidden hand' directing our lives, as if economic policies and structures were not of really of human origin. Likewise, the 'trickle down effect' beloved of growth economists is as elusive as the luxury-bearing ships of the cargo cults.

Wealth does not mysteriously cascade from the rich to the poor, or from richer to poorer nations. If anything, the pursuit of economic growth makes global and regional inequalities more obvious and extreme. And yet policymakers and campaigners remain in thrall to the idea that trickle down might one day take place, and that an invisible hand might somehow fashion order out of economic chaos.

Growth is the altar before which it is legitimate to sacrifice any number of individual livelihoods, along with local communities, cultural diversity and all manner of skills, craftsmanship and accumulated wisdom. The planet itself has become the ultimate sacrificial victim, for the principles of conservation and growth are diametrically opposed and the gulf between them is growing. Economic growth has become a secular fundamentalism, placed above critical comment because to criticise it would be to question an entire worldview.

To be opposed to growth is to be politically eccentric at best. However, it is also to be a heretic or (worse still in these pseudoegalitarian times) an elitist, willing to deprive others of the 'benefits' of all the consumer goods we take for granted. Critics of growth are accused of denying their fellow humans the inalienable right to ever-increasing living standards, regardless of the planetary or social costs.

> **"If Karl Marx were writing in today's era of globalisation, it is likely he would recognise the new opium as economic growth."**

Where issues of development are concerned, the charge of elitism has the sharpest sting, and acts as the most effective silencer. The critic of growth is portrayed as standing between the world's poor and material liberation. Growth is identified with opportunity and choice for all, with 'the future' and historical inevitability. Opposition to growth is seen as restricting choice in favour of 'romantic' notions about the past. It is depicted as the preserve of privileged Canutes, trying to turn back the tide of progress. Many economists and more thoughtful politicians from all parties are profoundly worried by the environmental and social impact of continuous growth. But few dare to challenge the orthodoxies of development and progress head-on. Few bring themselves to think the apparently unthinkable—that growth itself is the root of the problem.

As well as a substitute for religion, growth has become an addiction, affecting millions of people individually and shaping mass behaviour. This was brought home to me recently by a neighbour in Yorkshire, who has lived on incapacity benefit for some years and has had difficulties with rent and household bills. On seeing my sitting room and kitchen, his response was to reel off a list of fashionable consumer goods and gadgets, expressing dismay that I did not have them and had no wish to acquire them. He claimed to be unable to 'live' without a plasma television screen.

Some readers might wish to turn this story into an argument against the benefit system, If Karl Marx were writing in today's era of globalisation, it is likely he would recognise the new opium as economic growth but this would be to miss the point entirely, for the dependency was not on welfare, but on the products of economic growth. My friend's inability to 'live' without the latest consumer goods can be likened to a heroin user's craving for the next fix. Like the addict, his satisfaction is only ever fleeting, but to feed his habit he will risk financial meltdown. This process crosses the divisions of class and income, and is replicated on a global scale as poorer regions struggle to catch up with the West.

The drug addict thinks in the short term, forgetting about the harm to his or her body or the destruction of friendship, love and trust that the habit inevitably entails. In the same way, the growth addict ignores the damage to the planet and the erosion of any sense of civilised community that arises from the relentless drive for economic expansion. The products of growth never satisfy the individual, and the pursuit of growth makes societies increasingly dysfunctional and destroys the possibility of global co-operation. Growth creates the illusion of potential abundance, but makes inevitable a dog-eat-dog competition for ever-more scarce resources. The principal casualty is the planet and the only true beneficiaries are economic elites.

Growth's hold over the modern sensibility is such that the pursuit of material abundance is assumed to be identical to the pursuit of happiness. This is despite survey after survey showing that the more 'affluent' we collectively become, the more susceptible we are to stress, insecurity and gnawing discontent. It is tempting to ascribe uncritical worship of growth to the dominant neo-liberal ideology, with its overt adulation of market forces and its indifference to environmental concerns. Yet the movements that style themselves as progressive buy in equally to the growth illusion. For, in effect, today's left subscribes to the trickle down theory just as much as the right. It clings to the belief that growth is essential, so that all should have 'access' to wealth. This approach ignores the finite nature of the earth's resources, as well as the observable truth that accelerating growth gives rise to inequalities that spiral out of control.

Most environmentalists identify with the 'progressive' wing of politics. Although the effects of growth disturb them, they still associate it with opportunity, choice and redistribution of wealth, rather than the realities of impoverishment and despoliation. Therefore, they sidestep the question of growth itself and focus on single-issue campaigns. Such an approach prolongs the delusion that we can tackle climate change, protect fragile ecosystems and the rights of indigenous peoples, or preserve local economies from the homogenising forces of globalisation—and still have a growth-based economy. Some environmental campaigners speak of 'sustainable growth', which is as much a contradiction in terms as 'democratic centralism' in the old Soviet Union. For the green movement, as much as mainstream politics, economic growth remains the elephant in the room.

It is scarcely surprising that the political class, including environmentalists, are in a state of denial. The move away from growth would be as radical as the transition from an agrarian to an industrial economy. But despite the prevalence of growth addiction, there is a politically untapped sense that something is deeply wrong with the assumptions that underpin our economy. The effects of growth mania on the environment, the climate and relations between human beings have become obvious enough to be alarming, even to those who have previously been sceptical about the ecological crisis. Here, paradoxically, there are grounds for hope. Politicians who challenge consensus and face up uncomfortable truths are respected and often successful, albeit after years in the wilderness. The most uncomfortable truth of all is that the time to address the effects of growth addiction is running out. To put it simply, we need to learn to consume less. This is something that the electorate knows in its collective bones, but we await the politician who will dare to say it.

AIDAN RANKIN is writing a book on Jainism's relevance to the West.

Social Spending and Economic Growth

Interview with Peter Lindert

Prevailing opinion holds that big government and high taxes reduce growth. Social programs are claimed to be a matter of social justice, even if they impede economic growth. But Peter Lindert in a new book argues that these claims are fiction. States that spend a lot on social programs grow no more slowly than those that spend little. He discusses his views and the evidence below.

Q The conventional wisdom, not merely among laymen but among many economists, is that the bigger the government as a proportion of one's economy, the more likely you will grow more slowly. You say there is no serious evidence to support this claim. In that case, why do so many make the claim that big government undermines growth?

A. The source is ideology and a valid theory that if governments were run badly, they would drag down economic growth.

Q. The valid theory?

A. The valid theory is that if governments did nothing but tax people on the basis of their productivity and give it to other people who were unproductive—encouraging them to be unproductive with those grants—it would make everybody work less, take less risk, and innovate less.

Q So, Is the theory valid, then? Some economists do present evidence that purports to support that theory. Not least of them is Martin Feldstein, the Harvard professor who is head of the National Bureau of Economic Research, along with some other well-known economists. What kind of empirical evidence do they present?

A. Most of it is off the mark. Most of it is evidence of what would happen in a fictitious world. When you see a computer simulation or general equilibrium model, or many common economic models with supply-and-demand curves, they are imagining a world, a world of their own creation. They are not actually using data from the real world. Now, there are other studies that suggest costs of larger government are empirically based, but many of them are still inappropriate. For example, some studies using large samples of individuals show that if people had a lower after-tax wage, they might work less. But that is not a policy experiment, one that changes the whole incentive structure of the economy. It is an isolated case that just shows how different people with different wage rates decide how much to work as individuals. So it is off the mark.

Q Explain, for the sake of clarity, what you mean when you say it is not a policy experiment.

A. Typically, studies use a data set in which people all faced one particular government's set of policies. Within that government's set of policies, people who had different wage rates decided to work different amounts. But those are all differences among individuals within one policy regime. That study cannot by its design tell us what happens if you shift the entire regime and shift all the tax rates and incentives.

Q You were going to give another example.

A. There are studies that are very close to what we would want ideally. They are also microeconomically based—that is, they are studies of how labor reacts to changed circumstances. These were the famous negative-income-tax experiments in the 1960s and '70s. Those had the virtue of really being a policy experiment for a few months' time, and they did face people with different tax systems. Now, what did those experiments show? Here is the answer: They did not show any huge effect on people's tendency to work. Furthermore, they failed to take into account other aspects of the welfare state, like health care, pensions, and so forth. Within their confines, they showed a modest loss of work if you gave people generous unemployment and welfare benefits. Now, some do not agree with my summary of these experiments. Charles Murray, the conservative author who severely criticized the welfare system, is one of these. But what he did was pick and choose among the results of these negative-income-tax experiments and picked the ones he liked. In particular, the results from Seattle and Denver seemed to show a stronger dampening effect on labor supply. But auditors found that the Seattle and Denver ones that he chose to highlight were marred by the fact that the people receiving the temporary welfare benefits had an incentive to hide some of their earnings. So they were, in fact, working more than was stated.

Q. So the empirical evidence presented, you think, has almost always been seriously flawed or did not show the results that people claimed they showed?

A. That's correct. Now, the last kind of evidence is international pooled studies where researchers compare the experience of many countries over many years. The conclusions of these studies had already begun to move in the direction of my findings that high social spending does not deter growth. While I think I have improved on their tests, Joel Slemrod, William Easterly, and others were already finding this puzzling result before I did. There was no net negative effect on GDP per capita higher government social spending per capita.

Q. When were the original studies done?

A. They are all in the 1990s. Before then, there was not a major result that had tested over many countries and many years. It is not that ideologically there was a shift in the nature of the results. There were no pooled international results before the 1990s because we did not have enough numbers.

Q What improvements did you make?

A. The improvements are technical in nature. I gave more attention to simultaneous feedback, to nonlinearity, and to differences in error variance. Let me explain a bit. On the simultaneity, in any of these studies you have to reckon that the GDP per capita itself is an influence on the policies chosen. The higher the GDP per capita, the more likely there will be higher social spending. So we cannot get the right answer unless we seriously try to take this feedback into account.

Q. So you tried to allow for that?

A. Yes, I did. Most previous studies had not. Now, my results [published in *Growing Public: Social Spending and Economic Growth Since the Eighteenth Century* (2004)] are not radically different from those of Slemrod and others, but I made this extra step.

Q. And you concentrated on social spending as opposed to, say, government spending in general per GDP, or greater growth of government spending in general?

A. Yes. And it is important in considering my study to see that not only did I leave out non-social spending, such as military spending, highways, subsidies to producer groups, and so forth. It is also different because of the way I defined the welfare state.

Q. Please explain.

A. I have realized that I have to explain in my studies what the welfare state is and is not. It is a system that generally gives relatively universal social transfers to much of the population in the form of public health, public education, worker retraining, unemployment compensation, and especially pensions. But it does not include, for the purposes of my analysis, union power, special laws to protect jobs or business groups from competition, or nationalized industries. I do not measure the impact of these because they are really separate, and I would give them some label other than welfare state. Most of them I consider by-products of past class struggles.

Q What about subsidies, like earned income tax credits or tax deductibility of mortgage interest?

A. I pay some theoretical attention to these in the book, but my statistical work did not include them. I did not view earned income tax credits as welfare expenditure. One could argue that I should have done so. I do not think it would have affected the results.

Q. What did your results show, finally?

A. When it came to the effects of larger welfare states on GDP per capita and economic growth, there were two results I need to emphasize. First, I made a hypothetical extrapolation away from what actually happened in history. I took an extreme case where a hypothetical country took 40 percent of GDP from the capitalists alone—it just soaked the rich, and even the middle. If I gave that all back in the form of unemployment compensation—yes, even my statistical patterns say that would be very costly to the level and growth rate of GDP. But then comes the second result, which is that nobody in real life ever did that. It never happened. None of the welfare states did anything as foolish as we constantly describe in our Anglo-American parables that criticize their welfare states.

Q. And those Anglo-American parables are about the danger of the welfare state? So we oversimplify and exaggerate this welfare state, creating a world that is easy to criticize because it does not exist.

A. Right. It does not really exist. These kinds of flights of fiction would be socially useful in a world that might have tried such mistakes, but they never happened and have been seriously overblown.

Q. Then what did your statistical results show?

A. Statistical results showed that the difference, other things equal, between 10 percent of GDP going into social transfers, as in the social programs in the United States or Japan, and 33 percent, as in Sweden, is indistinguishable from zero.

Q. So the conclusion, therefore, is that it has no consequence?

A. It has no consequence for GDP.

Q. For the growth or the level of GDP?

A. Either one.

Q. What period did you examine?

A. So far I have examined periods going way back to the late nineteenth century, but the most important data are between 1960 and 1995. People have asked, what if you extend it beyond 1995? Has not the day of doom suddenly arrived since then for the welfare states? And my answer is no, and you and I might want to go into that.

Q. Yes.

A. Here is what people are saying … and this is really interesting. It is just so interesting to see how social debate works in these areas. People are amazingly selective because they know the story they are after, and in their minds they will find a story that seems to work for them. So here is what happens.

People wanting to comment on welfare state versus low-budget market economies have made this debate into a contrast between Europe and America. In particular, we have seen people say, look at how much worse Germany is doing than the United States since 1995. This is very selective because Germany has special problems going back to costly reunification with East Germany. In that particular time the United States was having its high-tech boom. In such a comparison, the result looks the way one might have thought on conventional grounds—high social spending impedes growth. But we cannot be so selective. There are so many decades and so many countries to study. I can just as easily counter that one. I could say: Compare the growth rates of high-spending Sweden versus low-spending Japan since 1995, or some welfare state like Denmark or Austria versus low-spending Switzerland. In each case, the welfare states are growing faster. So would that prove that the welfare state is tremendously good for growth? Certainly not. You have to study all the experiences. It is amazing how people select what they want to hear. The bad growth in the European Union since 1995 really reflects Germany's experience, while in the raw data the rest of the EU is doing just as well on average as North America.

Q So where is the theory wrong? Why does high government spending not impede economic growth? Before breaking this down into a number of issues, let us get a general answer first.

A. Here is the overall view. Real-world democratic governments, realizing they could be thrown out of office, knew they had to design the system in such a way as to minimize the defects of high spending and taxes and add additional benefits. What defects, what benefits? This is a three-part answer. First, they have designed a mix of taxes that more pro-growth than people have realized. People are very surprised to find that Scandinavians and Europeans do not just soak the rich. To the contrary, they have the kinds of taxes that conventional mainstream North American economists say they wish they had—namely a consumption tax. Second, when it comes to the incentives for people who receive public transfers, they do not get it as wrong in the basic welfare programs as we say they do in our theories.

Q. You mean they do not create disincentives to work?

A. The disincentives to work are not nearly so bad as we have said in our classic imaginations. Third, some kinds of social transfers really have positive productivity and positive GDP effects. The best example is public health. But that is also true of some worker retraining programs and, of course, education. As a parenthesis, education does not get emphasized much in my new book because it is not controversial an aspect of the welfare state, and educational spending out of public tax money is hardly un-American. America is among the leaders in that.

Q To fill in some of the blanks here, let us get back to the first part—the tax system. When you say it is a tax system that many U.S. mainstream economists would propose, what do you mean by that?

A. When the American economists specializing in public finance and labor have been polled, they say, "We would like to avoid a taxation on capital; we would rather you tax labor a lot." And Anglo-American economists in general have long said that

it is better to tax consumption than income, because taxing income invariably means the double taxing of savings. Those are the conventional desires about a good tax system. We would like something like a flat tax, and a tax on special "sin" goods, like gasoline and alcohol. This wish list is better delivered in the welfare states than in the countries spending the least on social programs.

Q. The welfare states have big value-added taxes?
A. Yes.

Q. But they have pretty progressive income taxes?
A. Not much more than we, no. Even in the overall structure, the Swedish system is only slightly, if at all, more progressive than the British or American as of the 1980s. Now, high incomes from labor—think of physicians, in particular—are heavily taxed in Europe. If there is a wealthy group in the welfare states that is much aggrieved by the tax system, it would be top-income professionals, and doctors in particular would have the further complaint that their incomes are constrained by the public health system. Those countries' taxes on earnings made on capital are more forgiving because they did not want capital to flee. But everybody who earns from his or her own labor pays a whopping tax.

Q Now the second point. We keep seeing that the welfare state creates disincentives to work. For example, high unemployment insurance would presumably induce people not to bother to look for a job. That is not as true in the welfare states as we think it is?

A. It is not as true as people usually think it is. Their systems are more universal. They do not cut you off as fast if you get a job or your income rises. Before the mid-1990s it was America and Britain whose systems most told an unemployed single mother, "Do not work. We will tax you heavily," because they had means-tested welfare systems that restrained total spending. So the moment you got any kind of job, you lost your benefits because you moved out of the bottom 1 percent of the income spectrum. That was a defect in America that first crept in and got big in the 1960s under the "Great Society" but was also reinstated by the first Reagan administration. The minute those women got jobs, they lost the benefits. That was a mistake that the European welfare states did not make. They had a more universal sliding system. You can go partway up the scale and still be getting some benefits, so you will keep some of your extra earnings as you work. Now, in the 1990s America made significant reforms, followed by Britain in 2000, to reduce these disincentives, and they are working. One was the expansion of the earned income tax credit (EITC) in 1993; the other was welfare reform in 1996, with its work requirements. I know liberals are proud of the EITC but say welfare reform is not working. But there seems to be some job creation here that has even survived the recent recession.

The main area where we are still getting it wrong is parental leave and public day care. These are handled much better in certain European countries—Sweden is the leader. Why is that good for economic growth? It is because in an economy where everybody's earning really largely depend on their buildup of human capital, their buildup of skills, and knowing how to work within a particular firm, the chance to go back to your jobs and to have high-quality day care in Europe provides the opportunity to maintain your progress and your own skills. If you have to drop out and then come back later and search for a new job, you start at a lower level, and you never do catch up to your previous path. I wish I could tell you how much more of GDP that is worth. I cannot quantify it. But the main clue is when you look at the median wage of women relative to men. You can see that the countries that do not supply these generous programs for day care and parental leave—Britain, America and Japan—have much lower relative women's earnings. Also, in places like America, there is probably a statistical bias against all women because corporations anticipate that some of them will leave the workforce. So they do not promote them, they do not invest in them—at least as much.

Q What lessons should America learn from your studies?

A. We could look at which social areas are ones where America has done the best; and which are ones where America has done the worst and, therefore, might work hardest on changing. America has done the best in higher education. We are by far the best because we got the incentives all right. We actually had subsidies from the taxpayers because the advance of knowledge deserves some subsidy. But we forced every public institution to compete against other public institutions and the private ones. Berkeley must compete against both UCLA and Stanford in all respects—for government grants, for top faculty, for top students. Even the teachers get evaluated by their students in America, which the other countries have failed to do, to their disadvantage. Now, that is only higher education, but that is specifically the subsector for which there is the most American advantage. The biggest American disadvantage is health, in which we are near the bottom of the Organization for Economic Cooperation and Development countries.

Q. In terms of outcomes?

A. In terms of outcomes and the cost of the outcomes. So the World Health Organization has America ranking thirty-seventh in the world in the quality of its health care. In terms of outcomes, we save fewer lives with our system, and we have a much more bureaucratic and administratively costly system than the government systems that Americans usually think of as the essence of bureaucracy. It is costing us a ton, and we have higher price markups on all these services. When it comes to people saying that Medicare is in crisis—Medicare being our main government program in the health care area—yes, it is in crisis, not because there is something wrong with government health care, but it is in crisis because it has to operate within this environment of price spirals.

Q. Let us get right to the bottom line.

A. Here it is. We are trapped, and it would be good if we could get out of the trap forced on us by a kind of class warfare rhetoric. We have Democrats who will use phrases like "fat cats," and they do not like anything that looks like it is a tax on ordinary people, as opposed to just the rich. And we have Republicans who use phrases like "bloated welfare queen" and the worst one of all, "socialized medicine." This is the trap. Social programs can enhance growth if run well. They can reduce costs and provide funding and useful programs for education, human and social capital, and health. Higher taxes need not impede growth if the tax regime is developed carefully and acknowledges that ordinary people must pay their share as well as the rich. Meantime, however, we in the United States are neglecting health care reforms and the social capital of women, among other important areas. We have created an imaginary welfare state to attack, one that does not exist.

PETER LINDERT is Distinguished Professor of Economics at the University of California at Davis and a research associate of the National Bureau of Economic Research. He is author of *Growing Public: Social Spending and Economic Growth Since the Eighteenth Century,* 2 vols. (Cambridge University Press, 2004).

From *Challenge*, Vol. 47, no. 4, July/August 2004 pp. 6–16. Copyright © 2004 by M. E. Sharpe. Reprinted by permission.

Why Are Taxes So Complicated

And What Can We Do About It?

The time, money, and aggravation that tens of millions of Americans expend to understand and comply with the income tax is, it turns out, nothing new. In his 1776 *The Wealth of Nations*, Adam Smith noted that "subjecting the people to the frequent visits and the odious examination of the tax gatherers ... may expose them to much unnecessary trouble, vexation, and oppression: and though vexation is not, strictly speaking, expence, it is certainly equivalent to expence at which every man would be willing to redeem himself from it." For Americans today, the "expence" includes maintaining records, learning the law, preparing the return or hiring a preparer, corresponding with the IRS, and learning how to reduce (or cheat on) taxes.

WILLIAM GALE

How Bad Is It?

For low-income households, headaches can arise from issues regarding filing status, abandoned spouses, dependency tests, the child and dependent care tax credit, and the earned income tax credit. For individuals with higher income, complexity arises in itemizing deductions, the treatment of capital income (particularly capital gains, interest deductions, and passive losses), and the alternative minimum tax. For small business owners, issues relating to inventory, depreciation, and distinguishing various expenses can be complicated. For large corporations, tax complexity is centered on depreciation, international income, the alternative minimum tax, and coordinating with state taxes. In addition, large firms are almost continually audited; one tax expert has described the basic corporate tax return as nothing more than an "opening bid."

Stories of income tax complexity are legion. The internal revenue code contains more than five million words. In *Money Magazine*'s, recent surveys, every one of 40 to 50 tax preparers came up with a different estimate of the tax liability due on a complex, hypothetical return. The share of taxpayers who pay tax professionals to complete their tax returns rose from 42 percent in 1981 to 51 percent in 1997.

Yet the costs can easily be overblown or distorted. For many people, the tax system is not that complicated. Almost 40 percent file simplified 1040A or 1040EZ forms, and about 18 percent file the 1040 but have no itemized deductions or business income. Many people go to preparers to expedite refunds or because they prefer to spend their time on other things rather than on preparing taxes. Marsha Blumenthal and Joel Slemrod found that while the average taxpayer spent 27.4 hours on filing income tax returns and related activities, 30 percent spent less than 5 hours, and another 15 percent spent between 5 and 10 hours. About 11 percent spent 50-100 hours, and 5 percent spent more than 100 hours. About half had no out-of-pocket ex-

penses, and 17 percent paid less than $50. Costs were highest among high-income and self-employed taxpayers.

Estimates of the total cost of complying with and running the individual and corporate income tax systems in 1995 go as high as $600 billion, but the most reasonable estimates range between $75 billion and $150 billion, or about 10–20 percent of income tax revenue. Even at $75 billion—or $386 per adult per year—tax complexity imposes significant costs. Resources lost to compliance and administrative costs could be productively devoted to other activities. Complexity also generates confusion and aggravation among taxpayers, which can reduce confidence in the system. Thus, *other things equal*, social welfare would be improved by having a tax system that is simpler to comply with, administer, and enforce. Of course, other things are never equal.

Tax Trade-offs

Since virtually everyone agrees that taxes should be easy to understand, administer, and enforce, why are taxes so complicated? The answer is that people also agree that taxes should be fair, should be conducive to economic prosperity, should raise sufficient revenue to finance government spending, and should respect individuals' privacy. Many people also think tax incentives should be used to pursue social or economic policies for the poor, housing, health, the environment, and small businesses.

Trading off these goals is difficult. Sometimes the meaning of a goal is unclear. Fairness, for example, is clearly "in the eyes of the beholder." Sometimes people differ about the best way to reach a goal. Is it best to help the poor via cash payments, tax incentives to work, direct provision of health care and education, or some other way? Finally, and most importantly, the goals are mutually inconsistent, and people disagree about which goals deserve the greatest weight.

As a result, tax policy involves tradeoffs—and complexity is the result. In the end, complexity resembles pollution. Some of it is undoubtedly unnecessary, but much of it is the unfortunate byproduct of the production of goods that many people want.

For reasons of fairness, most tax systems tailor tax burdens to depend on individual characteristics. This creates complexity in several ways. It requires tracing income from the business sector to individuals. It requires reporting and documenting individual characteristics such as marital status, dependents, each person's level and composition of income and spending, and so on. And it requires tax rates that vary with individual characteristics, creating incentives to shift income to other people with lower income, such as children, or to other time periods when income might be lower.

Complexity also derives from using the tax system to house social programs that subsidize what Congress and a significant portion of the population consider to be desired activities: housing, charity, health insurance, higher education, child care, state and local governments, retirement saving, entrepreneurial activity.

Closing tax loopholes also increases complexity. Any time a provision for special treatment or social engineering arises, it must be limited. If the child care credit, for example, is not intended to subsidize ski lessons in Aspen, some line has to be drawn concerning what is allowed and what is not. The taxation of financial income is particularly difficult in this regard.

Clamping down on tax evasion often increases complexity. Given the opportunity, people sometimes cheat on their taxes. Taxes on income from wages, for example, are withheld and sent to the government by the employer. The evasion rate is around 1 percent. Taxes on income from sole proprietorships are neither withheld nor sent in by a third party. The evasion rate here exceeds 30 percent. Many tax complexities exist to limit opportunities to cheat. In the late 1980s, a new law required people who claimed the child care credit to provide the Social Security number of the care provider. This both reduced the number of child care credit claims and raised by 65 percent the amount of income reported by child care providers.

While trade-offs among consensus policy goals are an important source of complexity, political factors are another. That is, complexity can also be the result of the production of goods that only a few of us want. Politicians and interest groups have a vested interest in certain types of subsidies that reduce taxes on favored constituencies. The lavish campaign contributions received by members of the House Ways and Means Committee do not come from lobbyists deeply respectful of a tax code clean of special subsidies. There is no lobby for simplicity.

Campaign gifts received by members of the House Ways and Means Committee do not come from lobbyists respectful of a tax code clean of special subsidies.

Sometimes the tax code is used to hide subsidies that would not be supported as outright spending. Consider a "homeowner welfare program" in which taxpayers earned an entitlement to help pay their mortgages. The entitlement grew in proportion to mortgage size, interest rate, and tax rate, but anyone whose entitlement was less than $6,000 received nothing from the program. Obviously, not a very appealing idea, but not that different from the mortgage interest deduction.

And let's face it: taxpayers *like* complexity that reduces their taxes. It's just complexity that raises taxes that annoys. Thus, people will grump about the new filing requirements for capital gains or child credits, but few will volunteer to give up those cuts.

The real question is not the total amount of compliance costs, but whether society gets good value for income tax complexity. My view is that, generally, we do not. The economy-wide perspective is important here. Suppose people had to fill out ten extra lines of the tax form to receive a $1,000 tax cut. Each might regard that as "good complexity," well worth the added cost of providing a few extra pieces of information. But in the aggregate, the revenues would have to [be] raised from taxpayers, so everyone's tax "cut" would be from a higher initial tax liability and net taxes would be the same. Thus, from a social perspective, the sum of all individuals' "good complexity" would be zero or negative.

Many existing provisions designed to encourage certain activities end up either largely subsidizing activity that would have occurred anyway or creating new problems. Many of the reasons for complexity are completely inappropriate: hiding unpopular programs, special loopholes that fuel campaign contributions. It is hard to see any impact on economic growth, and the "fairness" that occurs is a very strange kind. The subsidies help one group, but at the expense of all others.

Fundamental Tax Reform and Simplicity

The complexity of existing taxes is a powerful force behind the movement to replace the income tax with a flat tax or sales tax. The new systems would shift the tax base to consumption, rather than income, flatten tax rates, eliminate all deductions and credits, and collect most or all taxes at the business level. Plan advocates promise great simplification, and it is clear that pure versions of either plan would be much simpler than the existing system. But, well, it's not that simple.

Just as the income tax has deviated from a low-rate tax, with a one-page form and three pages of instructions, the flat tax or sales tax would also be under pressure to depart from its pure form. The thousands of lobbyists now working in Washington are unlikely to pack up and go home. In short, you can repeal the tax code, but you can't repeal politics.

On paper, for example, the sales tax would be vastly simpler than the current system. But the 45 existing state sales taxes are nothing like the single-rate, no-exemption sales tax that is proposed at the national level. The states feature numerous exemptions for goods and especially services, as well as different rates for different goods.

Moreover, as Joel Slemrod has shown, it is inappropriate to analyze simplicity independently of evasion and enforcement. The sales tax rate required to replace federal taxes would be well above the 23 percent rate claimed by advocates. After correcting for mistakes in the way the proposal treats government spending, and adjusting for political factors that would erode the tax base and for a reasonable amount of tax avoidance activity, a federal sales tax could result in mark-ups at the cash register in excess of 70 percent. At these rates, the incentive to evade sales taxes (which, unlike the income tax, feature no third-party withholding to aid in compliance) and the political pressure to exempt certain goods from taxes would be strong.

No country has ever successfully run a high-rate national retail sales tax. Many have tried to implement some variant of a sales tax and have given up. European governments, and numerous conservative and liberal scholars, have concluded that sales taxes at the required rates would be unworkable.

How about the flat tax? Under such a tax, businesses pay taxes on gross sales minus the cost of materials, services, capital goods, wages, and pension contributions. Individuals pay taxes on wages and pensions, less personal exemptions. No other income is taxed, and no other deductions are allowed. Flat tax advocates claim that individual and business returns will fit on a post card. In theory, the flat tax promises to be as simple as the sales tax.

But flat tax proponents have already acknowledged the need to provide transition relief to businesses that bought assets under the old system. Various flat tax plans include deductions for mortgage interest, charity, and payroll taxes. Deductions for health insurance and state and local taxes, the earned income credit, and graduated tax rates on wage income cannot be far behind. Allowing for these items would raise the required flat tax rate to about 32 percent and complicate taxes.

More fundamentally, the flat tax makes different distinctions than the existing system does. This will create new "pressure points," and so could create a host of new compliance and sheltering issues and accentuate problems created by existing regulations. For example, the differential treatment of "interest income" and "sales" under the flat tax has led tax experts Charles McLure and George Zodrow to conclude that the business tax "contains unacceptable opportunities for abuse." As attorney Alan Feld notes, the flat tax will either generate complicated business transactions (to skirt the simple rules) or complicated tax laws (to reduce the gaming possibilities), or both.

The flat tax would cause huge changes in tax liabilities for businesses across the country. It would create situations where some businesses with large economic profits would pay no taxes and others with economic losses would face steep taxes. Amending the tax to address these issues would create complexity.

At the individual level, the flat tax would renegotiate every alimony agreement in the country. Under the flat tax, alimony payments would no longer be deductible and receipts would no longer be taxable. Another difficulty would arise from earnings that are subsequently stolen. Under the flat tax, a robbery victim is still liable for taxes—and the robber is not. Under the income tax, it is the other way around. Additional anomalies will no doubt be discovered. Each of these problems with the individual tax could be fixed—but each solution would require a bigger postcard. Even a flat tax modified along these lines would be simpler than the current system. But with a rate of 30 percent or more, a realistic flat tax may not be politically appealing.

Simplifying the Income Tax

What about tax simplification options in the existing system? To begin with, procedural changes could raise the visibility and explicit consideration of simplicity and enforcement issues in the making of tax policy. For example, the recent IRS restructuring legislation requires the IRS to report to Congress each year regarding sources of complexity in the administration of federal taxes. The Joint Committee on Taxation is required to prepare complexity analysis of new tax legislation that affects individuals or small businesses.

It is also possible to eliminate the need for certain taxpayers to file tax returns. Thirty-six countries already use a return-free system for some of their taxpayers, replacing end-of-year filing requirements with withholding throughout the year and end-of-year reconciliation by the tax agency. In recent work, Janet Holtzblatt of the Treasury Department and I found that 52 million U.S. taxpayers could be placed on a return-free system with minor changes in the structure of taxes. These families have income only from wages, pensions, Social Security, interest, dividends, and unemployment compensation; they do not itemize deductions; and they face at most a 15 percent tax rate. Although the net compliance and administrative savings may not be great (because these people already have simple returns), a return-free system could reduce the psychic costs (fear and aggravation) associated with tax filing for the affected taxpayers.

Structural reforms could also reduce complexity. Broadening the tax base by eliminating deductions and preferences and taxing capital gains as ordinary income directly removes complexity. Increased standard deductions remove many people from the tax system. Lower tax rates would reduce the value of sheltering and cheating. Increasing the number of people who face the same "basic" rate facilitates the withholding of taxes on interest and dividends at the source, further simplifying taxes and increasing compliance. In short, broadening the base and reducing the rates can be revenue-neutral, fair, and efficient, as well as simplifying. Such reforms make taxes simpler for many taxpayers and could reduce compliance costs by 10–15 percent.

Getting Serious About Simplicity

We could have much simpler taxes if we were willing to change our preferences and forgo common notions of fairness, reduce our concern with tax evasion and loopholes, eliminate a raft of targeted social and economic incentives, and reduce the extent to which taxes depend on individual characteristics. Retaining those preferences, however, does not condemn us to much of the seemingly needless complexity of the current code. While the goal of fundamental tax reform is both more distant and less likely to resolve current problems than its advocates might care to admit, the existing system could be improved and simplified with a concerted effort to take simplicity seriously as a distinct policy goal.

From *The Brookings Review*, Winter 1999, pp. 36-39. © 1999 by the Brookings Institution. Reprinted by permission.

The Tax Reform Revolution

"The four approaches to tax reform—flat, USA, national sales, and value-added—all are variations on the same theme. All would shift the base of Federal taxation from income to consumption while simplifying the process of complying with tax law."

Murray Weidenbaum

After a series of changes in tax rates and a variety of new complications in the Internal Revenue Code, the time is ripe for a basic overhaul of the Federal government's revenue system. Tinkering with individual rates or "loopholes" is not a satisfactory answer. This article attempts to move the process along by analyzing the four major alternative approaches to fundamental tax reform. Rather than promoting any single view, what follows focuses on the defining characteristics of each.

Tax reforms come in many shapes and varieties. Two main motivating factors for reform are present: to increase economic growth by encouraging savings and investment and to simplify the burdens of tax preparation.

Shifting the tax base to consumption. The most basic change in the nation's revenue structure would be to introduce a new form of Federal tax, one levied on consumption instead of income. For years, economists have debated the respective merits of income and consumption as the basis for taxation. The U.S. uses consumption taxation to a far lesser degree than most other developed Western nations.

In recent years, the traditional preference for income-based taxation has eroded. A poll of macroeconomists at 15 universities reported that 63% favored "a fundamental reform of the American tax system towards a consumption tax," with 37% opposed. Tax experts have devised—and criticized—a variety of specific consumption-based taxes. No consensus, however, has been reached on the details. It is likely that two interrelated clusters of issues—the general desirability of a tax on consumption and the specific form that it should take—will receive increased public attention in the years ahead.

Many analysts believe that taxing people on the portion of society's output that they consume is fairer than taxing them on what they contribute by working and investing. In the 19th century, economist John Stuart Mill made this point in advocating the exemption of savings as part of a "just" income tax system. In the 1940s, American economist Irving Fisher argued that the income tax involved double taxation of savings and distorted

the choice of individuals in favor of consumption. Thus, not only is the income tax unjust, it encourages consumption and leisure at the expense of thrift and enterprise.

The Treasury proposed a "spendings tax" in 1942 as a temporary wartime measure to curb inflation. The proposal quickly was rejected by Congress. A major argument against the expenditure tax—then and now—is that the exemption of savings would favor the rich since they are better able to save large portions of their income. Some believe this would lead to greater concentrations of wealth in the hands of a few. Proponents of an expenditure tax respond that it can be made as steeply progressive as desired. Moreover, the trend in income taxation since 1980 has been away from progressivity and toward a flatter, more proportional revenue structure.

Another objection to the consumption base is that it would favor the miser over the spendthrift, even when both have similar spending power or ability to pay. The response offered to this argument is that consumption uses up the resources available to the nation, while saving adds to these resources. Moreover, the fundamental way for an individual to minimize consumption tax liabilities is to consume less: the incentives to work, save, and invest are unimpaired. By contrast, the basic way to minimize the income tax is to earn less, which dampens incentives to work, save, and invest—with deleterious effects on economic growth and living standards.

In practice, much of the impact of shifting to a consumption tax base would depend on how the tax was structured. The two major categories of alternatives are expenditure (or income) taxes levied on the portion of income not saved (which conceptually is the same as consumption) and sales or value-added taxes collected on individual purchases. In essence, the first category is composed of top-down taxes, whereas the latter consists of the bottom-up variety. In theory, the base of the two types of taxes is the same—the value of goods and services purchased—and the yields could be very similar. Each of the revised tax systems could be revenue neutral, raising as much revenue as the current income tax.

In the top-down category, the two major alternatives are the flat tax and the savings-exempt income tax, the latter often referred to as the USA tax (for Unlimited Savings Allowance).

The Flat Tax. The key feature of the flat tax is that one rate would be levied on all income above a generous family deduction. In effect, the flat tax would be a form of consumption tax because the returns on saving and investment would not be taxed. The tax would be paid only on wages, salaries, and retirement income. Interest, dividends, and capital gains would be exempt for individual taxpayers based on the justification that adequate taxes had been levied at the business level. Thus, double taxation would be avoided. No deductions, however, would be allowed for interest payments, charitable contributions, or state and local taxes.

The flat tax would be much simpler than the current income tax. A key reason is the absence of "transition" rules. For example, with the substitution of a flat tax for the current income tax, the holders of municipal bonds (on which the interest is exempt from Federal income tax) would experience a substantial reduction in the market value of their portfolios. That is likely because investors buy these low-yielding "munis" for their unique tax-exempt feature—but all interest would be tax-exempt for individuals under the flat tax. Thus, the loss of this special characteristic would reduce the value of municipal bonds substantially.

Unlike the other variations of consumption taxation, the flat tax on business covers all domestic operations, including sales and exports. Likewise, all purchases (including capital equipment) are deducted from taxable revenue, including imports.

The Savings-Exempt Income Tax. The proposed USA tax (or consumed income tax, as technicians often refer to the concept) would be collected much as income taxes are now. The annual taxpayer return would continue to comprise the heart of the collection system, and a rate table accompanying the return could ensure as progressive a tax structure as Congress desires. However, one major change would be instituted. The portion of income that is saved would be exempt from taxation—until it is spent.

The difficult bookkeeping requirement to tally all consumption outlays can be finessed quite simply. Based on the notion that income equals consumption plus savings, consumption readily can be estimated, indirectly but accurately, merely by deducting savings from income.

A companion shift to the adoption of a top-down consumption tax would be the conversion of the corporate income tax to a cash-flow tax on business. A major change—and one that would encourage investment—would be to expense, or write off, all capital investments, such as purchases of production equipment and factories in the year in which they are acquired. At present, these outlays are deductible on the income tax over the useful life of the asset, which is a period of several years or even decades.

In many ways, such a business version of the consumption tax would be simpler than the existing corporate tax. For example, by focusing on cash flows, it would avoid the complicated transfer pricing arrangements under which domestic subsidiaries of foreign corporations minimize their U.S. tax payments.

Although these changes may sound quite technical, a top-down consumption tax would be a move toward simplification. In effect, the major substantive change for the individual taxpayer would be to convert the complicated Individual Retirement Accounts (IRAs) to an unrestricted savings mechanism. The individual taxpayer would decide how much to save and in what form and over what time period. Taxation based on income is by its nature more complicated than extracting revenues from consumption. Income taxation is inherently complex for many reasons. Complicated timing rules are necessary, such as depreciation allowances, capitalization of expenses, and inventory accounting. Inflation distorts the tax base by eroding the value of depreciation allowances and overstating the real value of capital gains. Being based instead on cash flow, taxation of consumption automatically avoids these difficulties.

In the case of the USA tax, transition rules are provided to avoid taxing consumption that is paid out of income previously taxed. Such a short-term complication—like some others contained in the proposed tax—are designed to maintain fairness among different categories of taxpayers. Although consumption-based taxation is designed to replace rather than supplement the existing income tax, it could increase Federal revenues over a period of time. This would come about from the higher rate of economic growth that could result from the encouragement given to savings and thus to investment. Bottom-up types of sales and value-added tax likely would generate similar effects.

An expenditure or consumption tax, as explained above, can be calculated via a top-down approach, building on the records that already are available to provide the data needed for enforcement of existing corporate and personal income taxes. In contrast, sales and value-added taxes (VAT) represent a very different way of collecting a general tax on consumption.

National Sales Tax. On the surface, a national retail sales tax seems like a very simple device for collecting revenues in place of the complicated income tax structure. However, because consumption tends to be a smaller share of income as we go up the income scale, many supporters of the sales tax recognize the need to soften the regressive impact on the poor. The required modifications inevitably introduce complications. The most widely used approach, at the state level, is to exempt categories of purchases on which the poor spend a larger proportion of their income than other citizens, such as food, housing, and medicine. Another proposal is to provide each taxpayer with a "smart card" (similar to a credit card), with credit for sales taxes based on family size. Yet another alternative is to give every taxpayer an automatic standard refund, also based on family size.

A national sales tax levied at the retail level may present special problems for small businesses. Unlike larger companies, which buy from wholesalers or directly from manufacturers, smaller enterprises often make their purchases from the same retailers as do consumers and, therefore, would have to pay the retail sales tax. Situations such as this led France and other Western European nations to move from relatively simple sales taxes to the more sophisticated but complicated VAT.

Because any sales tax (including VAT) is included in the price of purchases, it registers in all of the price indexes and, hence, exerts an inflationary force on the economy. The counter-argument is that this is a one-time effect only, occurring when the tax is enacted or increased and that the inflationary impact could be offset by appropriate changes in monetary policy (albeit at times with an adverse effect on the levels of production and employment). A study of 35 countries that introduced a VAT revealed that in only six did the new tax contribute to a faster rate of inflation.

Opponents also charge that either a national sales tax or VAT would invade the traditional area of sales taxation, that of state and local governments (46 states impose a sales tax). However, most states have come to rely on income taxes, despite heavy use of the same tax base by the Federal government.

Turning to administrative aspects, Federal imposition of a sales or value-added tax would require establishing a new tax-collection system by the government and new record keeping on the part of taxpayers. However, much of the current tax-collection system could be eliminated (except for the collection of payroll taxes for Social Security and Medicare).

Value-Added Tax. The VAT is, in effect, a comprehensive sales tax that avoids the double counting otherwise inevitable when the same item moves from manufacturer to wholesaler to retailer. In total, a VAT should be equivalent in yield to a single-stage sales tax levied at the retail level. Essentially, a firm's value added is the difference between its sales and its purchases from other firms. Value added also can be estimated by adding labor and capital inputs supplied by the firm itself—represented by wages and salaries, rent and interest payments, and profit. Although the top-down consumption tax notion remains a theoretical concept, the bottom-up VAT now is an existing tax in many countries.

Proponents of the VAT contend that it is economically neutral because, ideally, it is levied at a uniform rate on all items of consumption (unless exceptions are made to soften its regressive nature). The VAT does not distort choices among products or methods of production. Thus, shifting to a more capital-intensive and perhaps more profitable method of production does not affect the tax burden. Nor is the allocation of resources across product, market, and industry lines impacted. In these regards, the VAT is superior to the existing array of selective excise taxes.

Advocates of the value-added tax also point out that, in contrast to an income tax, there is no penalty for efficiency and no subsidy for waste. Moreover, the VAT is neutral between incorporated and unincorporated businesses and, theoretically, even between public and private enterprises. By focusing on consumption, it avoids a double-tax burden on the returns from capital. This tax starts off with no exclusions or exemptions and thus, at least initially, provides a broader and fairer tax base, one that the underground economy will have more difficulty evading.

Another argument in favor of U.S. adoption of a value-added tax is that so many other nations have implemented this form of revenue gathering. It fits in better than other taxes with the growing international character of production. The VAT has become one of the revenue workhorses of the world. It is a key component of the tax system in more than 120 countries, raising about one-fourth of the world's tax revenue. Virtually every important country in Europe imposes this tax, and it has spread throughout the Third World. France has used value-added taxation since 1948, and other members of the European Union have done so since the late 1960s or early 1970s. Canada adopted a seven percent VAT in 1991.

Unlike the situation in the U.S., though, the adoption of a tax on value added was true reform in those countries. That is, value-added taxes typically replaced an extremely inefficient form of consumption tax that already was in place: a cascading sales or turnover revenue system. Those latter taxes apply to the total amount of a firm's sales rather than only to its value added. Thus, sales taxes would be paid over the production process. Cascade-type taxes favor integrated firms (which legally can avoid one or more stages of the tax), but they severely discriminate against independent companies that operate at only one phase of the production process.

An added, widely cited reason for adopting a VAT is the anticipated foreign trade benefits. Unlike an income tax, a sales-based tax can be imposed on goods entering the country and rebated on items leaving—supposedly encouraging exports and discouraging imports. Thus, a VAT would seem to help reduce this nation's large trade deficit. However, many economists believe that fluctuations in exchange rates largely would offset these initial effects and result in little change in the balance of trade.

Opposition to VAT

Opponents of a value-added tax offer an extensive list of shortcomings. They contend that a VAT, as in the case of any consumption-based revenue source, is inherently regressive: Those least able to pay face the highest rates. That regressivity can be softened by exempting food and medicine or by offering refunds to low-income taxpayers, but such variations make the collection of the tax more complicated. They also provide opportunity for people in the underground economy to avoid paying taxes.

A variety of approaches have been suggested for collecting the new tax. The simplest is the credit method. Under this approach, the tax is computed initially on a company's total sales, and the firm is given credit for the VAT paid by its suppliers. To a substantial degree, the VAT would be self-enforced. Each company would have a powerful incentive to ensure that its suppliers paid their full share of the tax, because any underpayment would have to be made up by the next firm in the chain of production and distribution.

In practice, the collection of the VAT may not be as simple as outlined here. That would be the case if certain transactions were exempted (such as food) and if nonprofit institutions and government enterprises were treated differently from business firms. Exemptions are no minor matter in terms of the administrative complexity they generate. In France, a long and extensive debate occurred over whether or not Head & Shoulders antidandruff shampoo was a tax-exempt medicine or a cosmetic subject to the full VAT. (The product is taxable.) Food eaten at a location away from the business at which it was purchased may be tax-exempt. What happens if a McDonald's sets up tables outside of the restaurant?

The four approaches to tax reform analyzed in this article—flat, USA, national sales, and value-added—all are variations on the same theme. All would shift the base of Federal taxation from income to consumption while simplifying the process of complying with tax law. Proponents of consumption taxation believe that, from a macroeconomic viewpoint, each of the four alternatives, by expanding the pool of savings, would increase the rate of capital investment in the economy and thus enhance the prospects for economic growth. In turn, faster economic growth would raise employment opportunities and living standards while increasing the flow of revenues into the Treasury.

It may not be too surprising that many business leaders advocate a general shift to consumption as the primary tax base, and quite a few endorse one (or more) of the specific approaches to making that fundamental change. Nevertheless, consumption taxes have their critics, especially those concerned about the "distributional" effects. Each of the four approaches would alter the distribution of the Federal tax burden by income classes. As noted earlier, the bottom-up sales taxes and VAT reforms would require substantial modifications in order to avoid the regressive results that many fear. Also, the allocation of the business tax burden across industries would be different under each of the alternatives. As a general proposition, capital-intensive firms catering to industrial markets tend to favor consumption taxes. Labor-intensive companies, and especially those serving consumer markets, are far less enthusiastic, and many are quite hostile to the entire approach.

It typically takes several years for Congress to consider and enact a comprehensive tax reform. In the process, numerous changes usually are made in the original proposals on which it holds hearings. Some tax analysts believe that some combination of the four approaches to consumption taxation is likely to emerge—in the form of a tax that is flatter than the current income tax (but not flat), defers taxation on much savings (but not all), and is somewhat simpler than the status quo (but still filled with all sorts of complexities).

Several warnings are appropriate to those who would embark on fundamental reform of the Federal revenue system: None of the proposals is as simple as the proponents claim; each has substantial advantages and disadvantages; and all should be structured to raise the same amount of revenue as the tax system they replace. (That is the way professional analysts with no axe to grind compare the various reform proposals.)

MURRAY WEIDENBAUM, Economics Editor of *USA Today*, is Mallinckrodt Distinguished University Professor and honorary chairman of the Weidenbaum Center on the Economy, Government, and Public Policy, Washington University, St. Louis, Mo.

Tax Reform R.I.P.

ROBERT J. SAMUELSON

Eugene Steuerle is one of Washington's ranking policy wonks—a term used here with respect. He's forgotten more about taxes in the past 15 seconds than most of us will ever know. He arrived in Washington in 1974, worked for years at the Treasury and moved in 1989 to the Urban Institute, a think tank. Steuerle has just written a book, "Contemporary U.S. Tax Policy," that addresses the insistent question: Why is the federal tax system such a mess? The answer, in a word, is democracy.

In theory, it's easy to imagine a simple tax system with low rates, a broad tax base—the amount of taxable income—and substantial "progressivity," meaning that the rich pay higher rates. But in practice it has been elusive. Democrats and Republicans alike are too eager to use tax breaks to advance various social, economic and political agendas. The resulting tax code is so confusing, complex and contradictory that it costs taxpayers (in accounting fees and the value of their time) about $100 billion annually to complete their returns, estimates economist Joel Slemrod of the University of Michigan. In 2003 that roughly equaled the combined spending of the departments of education ($57.4 billion), homeland security ($32 billion) and state ($9.3 billion).

The appeal of tax breaks is that they give "the appearance of reducing the government's size ... even as government interference in the economy increases," writes Steuerle. But a tax system that promotes various causes (more saving, more health insurance, college attendance) cannot be simple. It brims with provisions. Goals conflict; contradictions are unavoidable. Similarly, a system that favors some taxpayers (homeowners, the elderly) must disfavor others. "Fairness" suffers.

Of course, the rich often try to skirt taxes through abusive shelters. But it's a myth that legal tax breaks mainly benefit the wealthy. The government publishes a yearly list of "tax expenditures," indicating the costs in forgone taxes of different breaks. These favor the middle and upper-middle classes. Here are some of the biggest for 2004: tax-free employer contributions to pensions and 401(k) plans, $123 billion; tax-free employer payments for health insurance, $120 billion; the deductibility of interest on home mortgages, $68 billion; charitable deductions, $43 billion; the exclusion of some Social Security benefits from income taxes, $27 billion. For the wealthy, the biggest break involves preferences for capital gains (mainly profits on stocks); in 2004, they're worth $82 billion.

All these tax breaks are immensely popular. They would be more defensible if they always made economic sense. Unfortunately, they don't. One reason Americans are building ever-larger homes for ever-smaller families is that housing is subsidized through the tax code. Similarly, the tax code subsidizes health insurance and, by shielding covered patients from many routine costs, promotes higher health spending. "The United States should have a tax system which looks like someone designed it on purpose," the late William E. Simon, Treasury secretary from 1974 to 1977, once said. Dream on.

Actually, Congress and President Reagan once made a stab at a better system. The Tax Reform Act of 1986 reduced tax rates and broadened the tax base. But the new system could survive only if politicians exercised self-restraint. It wasn't to be. Bill Clinton raised tax rates and expanded tax breaks. President Bush has gone one better. He's lowered rates and expanded preferences.

Sometimes this ceaseless competition for new tax breaks implodes. Congress is now considering a bill to repeal a provision of the corporate tax that, because it violates international trade rules, is subjecting $4 billion of U.S. exports to European tariffs. But the House and Senate versions of the bill are so stuffed with conflicting tax breaks (including ones for cruise ships, ranchers and oil companies) that the legislation has stalled.

As Steuerle notes, taxes cannot be divorced from broader budget questions. What should government do? For whom? Who pays? How much might new taxes hurt economic growth? But this is a debate we resolutely avoid. Republicans and Democrats merely echo their supporters' fondest hopes. Republicans reject any tax increases—ever. Democrats indicate that taxes need rise only on the wealthy. Considering existing budget deficits and future spending commitments, especially for retiring baby boomers, neither message is realistic.

Well, that's democracy. Tell 'em what they want to hear, not what they need to hear. Steuerle suggests that budgetary pressures—including more taxpayers triggering the alternative minimum tax—will promote sober solutions. "The grand budget compromise that must take place," he writes, "is between those who would allow retirement and health programs to continue to grow without bound and those who would continually prescribe tax cuts into the future." Based on history, that seems a triumph of hope over experience.

Link Between Taxation, Unemployment Is Absent

JONATHAN WEISMAN

When President Bill Clinton raised taxes in 1993, the unemployment rate dropped, from 6.9 to 6.1 percent, and kept falling each of the next seven years. When President Bush cut taxes in 2001, the unemployment rate rose, from 4.7 to 5.8 percent, then drifted to 6 percent last year when taxes were cut again.

It has become conventional wisdom in Washington that rising tax burdens crush labor markets. Bush castigated his political opponents last week for "that old policy of tax and spend" that would be "the enemy of job creation."

Yet an examination of historical tax levels and unemployment rates reveals no obvious correlation.

"The fact of the matter is, we have much higher rates of employment today than we did in 1954, but our level of taxation is considerably higher," said Gary Burtless, a labor economist at the Brookings Institution. "You simply can't look at total taxation to find employment levels."

The issue has become particularly relevant as Congress debates budget resolutions that would extend tax cuts that otherwise would expire over the next five years, and as Bush clashes daily with Sen. John F. Kerry (Mass.), his Democratic rival, over tax policies and job creation. The Senate voted Wednesday night to place new barriers on future tax cuts.

Republican economists—and White House officials—contend that higher marginal tax rates stifle business investment, hiring and the desire to work.

Senior Treasury Department officials said the correlation is "standard macroeconomics" dating to the Kennedy administration. Last year's surge in economic growth can be timed to the week that tax refunds arrived in American mailboxes, they said.

"The bottom line is, cuts in taxes lead to economic growth, which leads to improvements in the labor market to levels that are better than they otherwise would have been," said Mark J. Warshawsky, acting assistant Treasury secretary for economic policy.

But finding the proof in historical data is difficult, conceded Eric M. Engen, a Republican economist at the American Enterprise Institute.

"If you could hold everything else constant, yes," the correlation would be there, he said. "But everything else isn't the same. That's the big problem that economists have always had."

Engen cautioned that total tax takes are affected by economic growth as well as tax levels. A booming economy—driven not just by tax issues but also by interest rates, trade policies, inflation rates and other factors—will pump money into the government's coffers as it pushes unemployment down, he said.

Still, Burtless noted, some prominent conservative economists, including Harvard University's Martin S. Feldstein, predicted wrongly that the Clinton tax cuts would choke off the 1990s recovery and kill jobs, while the millions of new jobs that Bush said his $1.7 trillion in tax cuts would generate have not materialized. The historical disconnect does not stop there.

In 1964, federal taxation as a share of the economy stood at 17.5 percent, while unemployment was at 5.2 percent. That year, income taxes were slashed, lowering the tax rate in 1965 to 17 percent of the economy. Unemployment dropped as well, to 4.5 percent.

But then tax levels rose sharply, to 19.7 percent of the economy in 1969, while unemployment fell steadily, to 3.5 percent.

In 1981, President Ronald Reagan again slashed taxes. Taxation fell from 19.6 percent of the economy that year to 17.4 percent in 1983. The unemployment rate, however, rose over that period, from 7.6 percent to 9.6 percent. By 1989, taxation had drifted upward again, to 18.3 percent of the economy, but unemployment had fallen to 5.3 percent.

Total taxation in Sweden, including local taxes, is equal to 59.2 percent of that country's economy, the highest level in the 27-member Organization for Economic Cooperation and Development. In contrast, the U.S. total tax burden is 30.6 percent, lowest among the OECD members. Yet unemployment for the past two years in Sweden has been considerably lower than U.S. levels.

Burtless suggested that the issue is not tax levels but tax structures. Sweden has high taxation, but its generous social welfare system rewards citizens for the number of years spent working.

The Clinton tax increase was focused on upper-income households, but it included a sizable increase in the earned income credit for low-wage workers, making it more profitable for them to find and keep jobs.

What Should Central Banks Do?

This paper was prepared for the Homer Jones Lecture, Federal Reserve Bank of St. Louis, March 30, 2000. Frederic S. Mishkin is a professor at the Graduate School of Business, Columbia University and a scholar at the National Bureau of Economic Research. He thanks Dan Thornton, Bill Poole, Lars Svensson, and the participants in the Macro Lunch at Columbia University for their helpful comments. Any views expressed in this paper are those of the author only and not those of Columbia University or the National Bureau of Economic Research.

FREDERIC S. MISHKIN

Introduction

In the last twenty years, there has been substantial rethinking about how central banks should do their job. This rethinking has led to major changes in how central banks operate, and we are now in an era in which central banks in many countries throughout the world have had notable success—keeping inflation low, while their economies experience rapid economic growth. In this lecture, I outline what we think we have learned about how central banks should be set up to conduct monetary policy and then apply these lessons to see if there is room for institutional improvement in the way the Federal Reserve operates.

The lecture begins by discussing seven guiding principles for central banks and then uses these principles to outline what the role of central banks should be. This framework is then used to see how the institutional features of the Fed measure up. I will take the view that despite the Fed's extraordinarily successful performance in recent years, we should not be complacent. Changes in the way the Fed is set up to conduct its business may be needed to help ensure that the Fed continues to be as successful in the future.

Guiding Principles For Central Banks

Recent theorizing in monetary economics suggests seven basic principles that can serve as useful guides for central banks to help them achieve successful outcomes in their conduct of monetary policy. These are:

- Price stability provides substantial benefits;
- Fiscal policy should be aligned with monetary policy;
- Time inconsistency is a serious problem to be avoided;
- Monetary policy should be forward looking;
- Accountability is a basic principle of democracy;
- Monetary policy should be concerned about output as well as price fluctuations; and
- The most serious economic downturns are associated with financial instability.

We will look at each of these principles in turn.

Price Stability Provides Substantial Benefits to the Economy

In recent years a growing consensus has emerged that price stability—a low and stable inflation rate—provides substantial benefits to the economy. Price stability prevents overinvestment in the financial sector, which in a high-inflation environment expands to profitably act as a middleman to help individuals and businesses escape some of the costs of inflation.[1] Price stability lowers the uncertainty about relative prices and the future price level, making it easier for firms and individuals to make appropriate decisions, thereby increasing economic efficiency.[2] Price stability also lowers the distortions from the interaction of the tax system and inflation.[3] Price stability lowers the uncertainty about relative prices and the future price level, making it easier for firms and individuals to make appropriate decisions, thereby increasing economic efficiency.[2] Price stability also lowers the distortions from the interaction of the tax system and inflation.[3]

All of these benefits of price stability suggest that low and stable inflation can increase the level of resources productively employed in the economy, and might even help increase the rate of economic growth. While time-series studies of individual countries and cross-national comparisons of growth rates are not in total agreement, there is a consensus that inflation is detrimental to economic growth, particularly when inflation is at high levels.[4] Therefore, both theory and evidence suggest that monetary policy should focus on promoting price stability.

Align Fiscal Policy with Monetary Policy

One lesson from the "unpleasant monetarist arithmetic" discussed in Sargent and Wallace (1981) and the recent literature on fiscal theories of the price level (Woodford, 1994 and 1995) is that irresponsible fiscal policy may make it more difficult for the monetary authorities to pursue price stability. Large government deficits may put pressure on the monetary authorities to monetize the debt, thereby producing rapid money growth and inflation.

Restraining the fiscal authorities from engaging in excessive deficit financing thus aligns fiscal policy with monetary policy and makes it easier for the monetary authorities to keep inflation under control.

Time Inconsistency Is a Serious Problem To Be Avoided

One of the key problems facing monetary policymakers is the time-inconsistency problem described by Calvo (1978), Kydland and Prescott (1977), and Barro and Gordon (1983). The time-inconsistency problem arises because there are incentives for a policymaker to try to exploit the short-run tradeoff between employment and inflation to pursue short-run employment objectives, even though the result is poor long-run outcomes. Expansionary monetary policy will produce higher growth and employment in the short-run. Therefore, policymakers will be tempted to pursue this policy even though it will not produce higher growth and employment in the long-run because economic agents adjust their wage and price expectations upward to reflect the expansionary policy. Unfortunately, however, expansionary monetary policy will lead to higher inflation in the long-run, with its negative consequences for the economy.

McCallum (1995) points out that the time-inconsistency problem by itself does not imply that a central bank will pursue expansionary monetary policy that leads to inflation. Simply by recognizing the problem that forward-looking expectations in the wage- and price-setting process promotes a strategy of pursuing expansionary monetary policy, central banks can decide not to play that game. From my first-hand experience as a central banker, I can testify that central bankers are very aware of the time-inconsistency problem and are, indeed, extremely averse to falling into a time-inconsistency trap. However, even if central bankers recognize the problem, there still will be pressures on the central bank to pursue overly expansionary monetary policy and inflation may result, so that the time-inconsistency problem remains. The time-inconsistency problem is just shifted back one step; its source is not in the central bank, but rather, resides in the political process.

The time-inconsistency literature points out both why there will be pressures on central banks to pursue overly expansionary monetary policy and why central banks whose commitment to price stability is in doubt are more likely to experience higher inflation. In order to prevent high inflation and the pursuit of a suboptimal monetary policy, monetary policy institutions need to be designed in order to avoid the time-inconsistency trap.

Monetary Policy Should Be Forward Looking

The existence of long lags from monetary policy actions to their intended effects on output and inflation suggests that monetary policy should be forward looking. If policymakers wait until undesirable outcomes on inflation and output fluctuations actually arise, their policy actions are likely to be counterproductive. For example, by waiting until inflation has already appeared before tightening monetary policy, the monetary authorities will be too late; inflation expectations will already be embedded into the wage- and price-setting process, creating an inflation momentum that will be hard to contain. Once the inflation process has gotten rolling, the process of stopping it will be slower and costlier. Similarly, by waiting until the economy is already in recession, expansionary policy may kick in well after the economy has recovered, thus promoting unnecessary output fluctuations and possible inflation.

To avoid these problems, monetary authorities must behave in a forward-looking fashion and act preemptively. For example, assume that it takes two years for monetary policy to have a significant effect on inflation. Under these circumstances, even if inflation is quiescent currently (with an unchanged stance of monetary policy) and policymakers forecast inflation to rise in two years time, they must act immediately to head off the inflationary surge.

Policymakers Should Be Accountable

A basic principle of democracy is that the public should have the right to control the actions of the government: In other and more famous words, "The government should be of the people, by the people and for the people." Thus, the public in a democracy must have the capability to "throw the bums out" or punish incompetent policymakers through other methods in order to control their actions. If policymakers cannot be removed from office or punished in some other way, this basic principle of democracy is violated. In a democracy, government policymakers need to be held accountable to the public.

A second reason why accountability of policymakers is important is that it helps to promote efficiency in government. Making policymakers subject to punishment makes it more likely that incompetent policymakers will be replaced by competent ones and creates better incentives for policymakers to do their jobs well. Knowing that they are subject to punishment when performance is poor, policymakers will strive to get policy right. If policymakers are able to avoid accountability, then their incentives to do a good job drop appreciably, making poor policy outcomes more likely.

Monetary Policy Should Be Concerned with Output as well as Price Fluctuations

Price stability is a means to an end—a healthy economy—and should not be treated as an end in itself. Thus, central bankers should not be obsessed with inflation control and become what Mervyn King (1997) has characterized as "inflation nutters." Clearly, the public cares about output as well as inflation fluctuations, and so the objectives for a central bank in the context of a long-run strategy should not only include minimizing inflation fluctuations, but should also include minimizing output fluctuations. Objective functions with these characteristics have now become standard in the monetary economics literature, which focuses on the conduct of monetary policy (e.g., see the papers in Taylor, 1999).

The Most Serious Economic Downturns Are Associated with Financial Instability

A reading of U.S. monetary history (Friedman and Schwartz, 1963, Bernanke, 1983, and Mishkin, 1991) indicates that the most serious economic contractions in U.S. history, including the Great Depression, have all been associated with financial instability. Indeed, this literature suggests that financial instability is a key reason for the depth of these economic contractions. The recent financial crises and depressions in Mexico and East Asia also support this view (Mishkin, 1996, 1999a and Corsetti, Pesenti, and Roubini, 1998). Preventing financial instability is, therefore, crucial to promoting a healthy economy and reducing output fluctuations, an important objective for central banks, as we have seen above.

Implications For The Role Of A Central Bank

Armed with these seven guiding principles, we can now look at what institutional features a central bank should have in conducting its operations. We derive the following implications/criteria for the role of a central bank:

- Price stability should be the overriding, long-run goal of monetary policy;

- An explicit nominal anchor should be adopted;

- A central bank should be goal dependent;

- A central bank should be instrument independent;

- A central bank should be accountable;

- A central bank should stress transparency and communication;

- A central bank should also have the goal of financial stability.

Price Stability Should Be the Overriding, Long-Run Goal of Monetary Policy

Together, the first three principles for monetary policy outlined above suggest that the overriding, long-run goal of monetary policy should be price stability. A goal of price stability immediately follows from the benefits of low and stable inflation, which promote higher economic output. Furthermore, an institutional commitment to price stability is one way to make time-inconsistency of monetary policy less likely. An institutional commitment to the price stability goal provides a counter to time-inconsistency because it makes it clear that the central bank must focus on the long-run and thus resist the temptation to pursue short-run expansionary policies that are inconsistent with the long-run, price stability goal.

The third principle, that fiscal policy should be aligned with monetary policy, provides another reason why price stability should be the overriding, long-run goal of monetary policy. As McCallum (1990) has pointed out, "unpleasant monetarist arithmetic" only arises if the fiscal authorities are the first mover. In other words, if the fiscal authorities are the dominant player and can move first—thus setting fiscal policy exogenously, knowing that the monetary authorities will be forced to accommodate their policies to maintain the long-run government budget constraint—then fiscal policy will determine the inflation rate. Indeed, this is the essence of the fiscal theory of the price level. On the other hand, as McCallum (1990) points out, if the monetary authorities are the dominant player and move first, then it will be fiscal policy that will accommodate in order to satisfy the long-run government budget constraint and monetary policy will determine the inflation rate. An institutional commitment to price stability as the overriding, long-run goal, is just one way to ensure that monetary policy moves first and dominates, forcing fiscal policy to align with monetary policy.

The sixth guiding principle, that output fluctuations should also be a concern of monetary policy, suggests that a fanatic pursuit of price stability could be problematic because policymakers should see not only price fluctuations, but also output fluctuations as undesirable. This is why the price stability goal should be seen as overriding in the long-run but not in the short-run. As Lars Svensson (1999) states, central banks should pursue what he calls "flexible inflation targeting," in which the speed at which a central bank tries to get to price stability reflects their concerns about output fluctuations. The more heavily a central bank cares about output fluctuations, the more time it should take to return to price stability when it is not already there. However, because a "flexible inflation targeter" always sets a long-term price stability goal for inflation, the fact that a central bank cares about output fluctuations is entirely consistent with price stability as the long-run, overriding goal.

An Explicit Nominal Anchor Should Be Adopted

Although an institutional commitment to price stability helps solve time-inconsistency and fiscal alignment problems, it does not go far enough because price stability is not a clearly defined concept. Typical definitions of price stability have many elements in common with the commonly used legal definition of pornography in the United States—you know it when you see it. Thus, constraints on fiscal policy and discretionary monetary policy to avoid inflation might end up being quite weak because not everyone will agree on what price stability means in practice, providing both monetary policymakers and politicians a loophole to avoid making tough decisions to keep inflation under control. A solution to this problem, which supports the first three guiding principles, is to adopt an explicit nominal anchor that ties down exactly what the commitment to price stability means.

There are several forms that an explicit nominal anchor can take. One is a commitment to a fixed exchange rate. For example, in 1991, Argentina established a currency board that required the central bank to exchange U.S. dollars for new pesos at a fixed exchange rate of one to one. A second nominal anchor is for the central bank to have a money-growth target, as was the case in Germany. A third nominal anchor is for there to be an explicit numerical inflation goal as in inflation-targeting countries such as New Zealand, Canada, the United Kingdom, Australia, and Brazil, among others. All these forms of explicit nominal anchors can help reduce the time-inconsistency problem, as the success of countries using them in lowering and controlling inflation demonstrates (Mishkin, 1999b). These nominal anchors also help restrain fiscal policy and also are seen as an important benefit of inflation targeting in countries such as New Zealand and Canada (Mishkin and Posen, 1997, and Bernanke, Laubach, Mishkin, and Posen, 1999).

One criticism of adopting an explicit nominal anchor, such as an inflation target, is that it will necessarily result in too little emphasis on reducing output fluctuations, which is inconsistent with the guiding principle that monetary policy should be concerned with output as well as price fluctuations. However, this view is mistaken. Inflation targeting, as it has actually been practiced (Mishkin and Posen, 1997, and Bernanke, Laubach, Mishkin, and Posen, 1999), has been quite flexible and has not led to larger output fluctuations. Indeed, adoption of an inflation target can actually make it easier for central banks to deal with negative shocks to the aggregate economy. Because a decline in aggregate demand also leads to lower-than-expected inflation, a central bank is able to respond with a monetary easing, without causing the public to question its anti-inflationary resolve. Furthermore, inflation targeting can make it less likely that deflation, a fall in the price level, would occur. There are particularly valid reasons for fearing deflation in today's world, including the possibility that it might promote financial instability and precipitate a severe economic contraction. Indeed, deflation has been associated with deep recessions or even depressions, as in the 1930s, and the recent deflation in Japan has been one factor that has weakened the financial system and the economy. Targeting inflation rates of above zero, as all inflation targeters have done, makes periods of deflation less likely. The evidence on inflation expectations from surveys and interest rate levels suggest that maintaining a target for inflation above zero (but not too far above) for an extended period does not lead to instability in inflation expectations or to a decline in the central bank's credibility.

Central Banks Should Be Goal Dependent

Although there is a strong rationale for the price stability goal and an explicit nominal anchor, who should make the institutional commitment? Should the central bank independently announce its commitment to the price stability goal or would it be better to have this commitment be mandated by the government?

Here the distinction between goal independence and instrument independence made by Debelle and Fischer (1994) and Fischer (1994) is quite useful. Goal independence is the ability of the central bank to set its own goals for monetary policy, while instrument independence is the ability of the central bank to independently set the instruments of monetary policy to achieve the goals. The fifth guiding principle that the public must be able to exercise control over government actions and that policymakers must be accountable, so basic to democracy, strongly suggests that the goals of monetary policy should be set by the elected government. In other words, a central bank

should not be goal independent. The corollary of this view is that the institutional commitment to price stability should come from the government in the form of an explicit, legislated mandate for the central bank to pursue price stability as its overriding, long-run goal.

Not only is the principle of a legislated mandate and goal dependence of the central bank consistent with basic principles of democracy, but it has the further advantage that it is consistent with the second and third guiding principles—it makes time-inconsistency less likely, while making alignment of fiscal policy with monetary policy more likely. As we discussed above, the source of the time-inconsistency problem is more likely to be embedded in the political process than it is in the central bank. Once politicians commit to the price stability goal by passing central bank legislation with a price stability mandate, it becomes harder for them to put pressure on the central bank to pursue short-run expansionary policies that are inconsistent with the price stability goal. Furthermore, a government commitment to price stability also is a commitment to making monetary policy dominant over fiscal policy, ensuring a better alignment of fiscal policy with monetary policy.

An alternative way to solve time-inconsistency problems has been suggested by Rogoff (1985): Grant both goal and instrument independence to a central bank and then appoint conservative central bankers to run it, who put more weight on controlling inflation (relative to output) than does the general public. The result will be low inflation, but at the cost of higher output variability than the public desires.

There are two problems with this solution. First, having "conservative" central bankers impose different preferences from those of the public on the conduct of monetary policy is inherently undemocratic. Basic democratic principles indicate that the preferences of policymaking should be aligned with those of the society at large. Second, in the long run, a central bank cannot operate without the support of the public. If the central bank is seen to be pursuing goals that are not what the public wants, support for central bank independence is likely to erode. Thus appointment of "conservative" central bankers may not be stable in the long run and will not provide a permanent solution to the time-inconsistency problem.

The same principles that suggest that the central bank should be goal dependent, with the commitment to the price stability goal mandated by the government, also suggest that the commitment to an explicit nominal anchor should be made by the government. In the case of an exchange-rate target, the government should set the target, as in Argentina, or in the case of an inflation target, the government should set the numerical inflation goal. The fact that the government sets these targets so that the central bank as goal dependent does not mean that the central bank should be cut out of the decision-making process. Because the central bank has both prestige and expertise in the conduct of monetary policy, governments will almost always be better served by setting these targets in consultation with the central bank.

Although it is clear that the government should set the goal for the explicit nominal anchor in the long-run, it is more controversial whether it should set it in the short-run or intermediate-run. If a government, for example, set a short-run inflation or exchange rate target that was changed every month or every quarter, this could easily lead to time inconsistency in which short-run objectives would dominate. In many countries that target inflation, the Ministry of Finance, as the representative of the government, does set an annual inflation target; however, as documented in Bernanke, Laubach, Mishkin, and Posen (1999), the target rarely is changed once price stability is achieved. Thus, even though (in theory) governments could manipulate an annual inflation target to pursue short-run objectives, the transparency of goal-setting leads to a long-run approach to setting inflation targets even when it is done on an annual basis. The situation for the United States is even more complicated. Because of our congressional system, the Treasury Secretary is not the representative of Congress, in contrast to the Minister of Finance who does represent parliament in a parliamentary system. Instead the Treasury Secretary represents the executive branch. Thus, who represents the American government in setting a short- or intermediate-term target for monetary policy is not clear cut. This problem is not as severe for setting the long-run goal of monetary policy, which could be done by a congressional commission with representatives from both the executive and legislative branches, as well as from the public and the central bank. However, the difficulties of delegating the setting of shorter run targets for monetary policy in a congressional system may require that the central bank keep this responsibility.[5]

Central Banks Should Be Instrument Independent

Although the arguments above suggest that central banks should be goal dependent, the guiding principles in the previous section provide a strong case that central banks should be instrument independent. Allowing central banks to control the setting of monetary policy instruments provides additional insulation from political pressures to exploit short-run tradeoffs between employment and inflation. Instrument independence means that the central bank is better able to avoid the pursuit of time-inconsistent policies in line with the third guiding principle.

The fourth guiding principle, that monetary policy needs to be forward looking in order to take account of the long lags in the effect of monetary policy on inflation, provides another rationale for instrument independence. Instrument independence insulates the central bank from the myopia that is frequently a feature of the political process arising from politicians' concerns about getting elected in the near future. Thus, instrument independence makes it more likely that the central bank will be forward looking and adequately allow for the long lags from monetary policy actions to inflation in setting their policy instruments.

Recent evidence seems to support the conjecture that macroeconomic performance is improved when central banks are more independent. When central banks in industrialized countries are ranked from least legally independent to most legally independent, the inflation performance is found to be the best for countries with the most independent central banks (see Alesina and Summers, 1993, Cukierman, 1992, and Fischer, 1994,

among others). However, there is some question whether causality runs from central bank independence to low inflation or, rather, whether a third factor is involved, such as the general public's preferences for low inflation that create both central bank independence and low inflation (Posen, 1995).

The bottom line is that basic principles for monetary policy and democracy suggests that central banks should have instrument but not goal independence. This degree of independence for central banks is analogous to the relationship between the U.S. military and the government during the successfully prosecuted Gulf War in 1991. The military had instrument independence. It had complete control over the prosecution of the war with little interference from the government (in contrast to the less successfully waged Vietnam War). On the other hand, the military did not have goal independence. It was the Commander in Chief, George Bush, who made the decisions as to what the objectives and goals of the war would be.

Central Banks Should Be Accountable

The fifth guiding principle, that policymakers should be accountable, indicates that the central bank should be subject to government and public scrutiny. One way of ensuring accountability is to make the independence of the central bank subject to legislative change by allowing the act that created the central bank to be modified by legislation at any time. Another way is to mandate periodic reporting requirements to the government. For example, as was done in the Humphrey-Hawkins legislation which requires the Chairman of the Federal Reserve to testify to Congress twice a year.

The need for central banks to be accountable provides an additional reason why central banks should have an explicit nominal anchor. If there is no explicit nominal anchor, it is far less clear upon what criterion the central bank should be judged, and thus it is harder to hold it accountable. On the other hand, with an explicit nominal anchor, like a target for inflation or the exchange rate, the public and the politicians have a clear cut benchmark to assess the performance of the central bank. Thus, an explicit nominal anchor enhances the accountability of the central bank. Indeed, with an explicit nominal anchor, accountability can be enforced by making the central bank governor subject to dismissal if he or she breaches the goals set by the government, as is the case in New Zealand.

Central Banks Should Stress Transparency and Communication

Increased transparency of monetary policymaking is another important way to increase central bank accountability in line with the fifth guiding principle. Central banks need to communicate clearly their monetary policy strategy in order to explain their objectives and how they plan to achieve them. Each time they change their policy instruments, such as the interbank interest rate, they also need to clearly state the decision and then explain the rationale for it. Transparency can be further increased by publication of the central bank's forecast and the minutes of the discussion of monetary policy.

In addition, central banks need to pursue many outreach vehicles to communicate with the public. These include the continual making of speeches to all elements of society, more openness with the press and media, and the development of brochures and reports that are accessible to the public. Particularly noteworthy in this regard are the "Inflation Report" type documents initially developed by the Bank of England and now emulated by many other central banks. These documents depart from the usual dull-looking, formal reports of central banks to take on the best elements of textbook writing (fancy graphics, use of boxes) in order to better communicate with the public.

Increasing transparency and accountability not only helps to align central banks with democratic principles, and is thus worthy of its own right, but it also has benefits for the ability of central banks to conduct monetary policy successfully. Transparency reduces the uncertainty about monetary policy, interest rates, and inflation, thus making private-sector planning easier. Transparency and communication also promote a better public understanding of what central banks can do—promote price stability which, as suggested by the first guiding principle, has the potential to enhance economic growth in the long run—and what central banks cannot do—create permanent increases in output and employment through expansionary policy. Better public understanding of what central banks can and cannot do is then likely to help generate more public support for monetary policy, which is focused on price stability, becoming the long-run, overriding goal.

Although central bankers find their life to be a more comfortable one when they are not accountable and can avoid intense public scrutiny, increased transparency and accountability have important benefits for central bankers, helping them to adhere to the first five guiding principles outlined in the previous section. Because transparency and accountability can increase the public support for the price stability goal and longer-term thinking on the part of the central bank, they can reduce political pressures on the central bank to pursue inflationary monetary policy and, thus, limit the time-inconsistency problem, while generating more support for forward-looking policy by the central bank. Also, greater transparency and communication can help the central bank convince the public that fiscal policy needs to be aligned with monetary policy.

In addition, transparency and accountability can increase support for independence of the central bank.[6] An instructive example is provided by the granting of instrument independence to the Bank of England in May 1997. Prior to this date, monetary-policy decisions in the United Kingdom were made by the government (the Chancellor of the Exchequer) rather than by the Bank of England. When, on May 6, 1997, the Chancellor of the Exchequer, Gordon Brown, announced the granting of instrument independence to the Bank of England, giving it the power to set the overnight interest rate, he made it particularly clear at the press conference that, in his view, the action had been made possible by the increased transparency and accountability of policy under the recently adopted inflation-targeting regime.

Central Banks Should also Have a Financial Stability Goal

Because central banks should care about output fluctuations (Principle 6) and the most serious economic contractions arise when there is financial instability (Principle 7), central banks also need to focus on preventing financial instability. The primary way that central banks prevent financial instability is by acting as a lender of last resort, that is, by supplying liquidity to the financial system to keep a financial crisis from spinning out of control. Because acting as a lender of last resort, in effect, provides a safety net for financial institutions to whom the funds will be channeled, it creates a moral hazard problem in which these institutions who are potential borrowers have incentives to take on excessive risk, which can make financial instability more likely. Thus, central banks need to consider the tradeoff between the moral hazard cost of the role as lender of last resort and the benefit of preventing financial crises. Keeping moral hazard from getting out of hand indicates that central banks should not perform the role of lender of last resort unless it is absolutely necessary; and, therefore, this role should occur very infrequently.

Because lender-of-last-resort lending should be directed at providing funds to solvent, but illiquid, financial institutions and not to insolvent institutions, in order to reduce incentives to take on too much risk by these institutions, the central bank needs to have information regarding to whom it might have to extend loans when it performs this role. One way for the central bank to get this information is for it to have a supervisory role over these institutions. This is an argument for giving central banks a role in prudential supervision (see, e.g., Mishkin, 1992, and Bernanke, 2000). In addition, a supervisory role for the central bank can help it obtain information about whether a situation really is likely to lead to a financial crisis and, thus, requires a lender-of-last-resort intervention. Without this information, the central bank may either intervene too frequently or fail to do so when it is really needed, thus making financial instability more likely. It is possible that central banks can acquire the information they need from supervisory agencies which are separate from the central bank, but some central bank officials doubt this (see Peek, Rosengren, and Tootell, 2000). Thus, there is an argument for the central bank to have a role in prudential supervision, but it is by no means clear cut. Furthermore, there are arguments against central bank involvement in prudential supervision because it may cause a central bank to lose its focus on the price-stability objective.

A Federal Reserve Scorecard

Now that we have outlined what the role of a central bank should be, we can assess how the institutional features of the Federal Reserve measure up. We provide an assessment of whether the way the Fed is set up to conduct its operations is consistent with each of the seven criteria discussed in the previous section.

Price Stability Should Be the Overriding, Long-Run Goal of Monetary Policy

Through their testimony and speeches, high officials in the Federal Reserve System, and especially Alan Greenspan, have made it quite clear that the overriding long-run goal for Fed monetary policy is price stability. However, there is no clear mandate from the U.S. government that price stability should be a long-run, overriding goal. The Humphrey-Hawkins Act passed in 1978, with the revealing title, "Full Employment and Balanced Growth Act," stipulates that monetary policy should have goals of full employment and economic growth, as well as price stability. It is true that the Humphrey-Hawkins Act could be interpreted as allowing for price stability to be the overriding, long-run goal because, as was indicated previously, price stability is a means of promoting high economic growth and full employment in the long-run. However, it is even easier to interpret the legislation as supporting an emphasis on pursuit of full employment and economic growth in the short-run, which is inconsistent with the pursuit of price stability. The lack of a clear mandate for price stability can lead to the time-inconsistency problem in which political pressure is put on the Fed to engage in expansionary policy to pursue short-run goals.

In contrast to the United States, many other countries now have legislation which mandates price stability as the overriding, long-run goal of monetary policy, and this is a growing trend. For example, a mandate for price stability as the overriding, long-run goal for monetary policy was a requirement for entry into the European Monetary Union, and the Maastricht Treaty gives this mandate to the central banking system for the European Monetary Union, which most accurately referred to as the Eurosystem.[7] This trend also has been evident even in emerging market countries, where many central banks have had their mandate revised to focus on price stability.

On the first criterion of the need for an institutional commitment to price stability, as the overriding long-run goal, the United States does not score well.

An Explicit Nominal Anchor Should Be Adopted

Not only has the U.S. government not committed to price stability as the overriding, long-run goal, but also neither it nor the Fed has adopted an explicit nominal anchor. The actions and rhetoric of the Greenspan Fed have made it clear that it will fight to keep inflation from rising from the current level of around 2 percent, and it is fair to characterize the Fed as having an implicit nominal anchor. Nonetheless, the Federal Reserve has not come out and articulated an explicit goal for inflation and has, instead, stated its commitment to price stability. This has been loosely defined by Alan Greenspan as a situation in which changes in the price level are not a major consideration for businesses and households. At the present time, the public (and maybe even members of the FOMC) have no idea of whether the Fed's goal for inflation is 1 percent, 2 percent, or possibly higher. I think it is fair to say that right now the nominal anchor in the United States is Alan Greenspan. The problem is that this leaves some ambiguity as to what the Fed's target is. Even more importantly, the existence of this implicit nominal anchor depends on personalities. Alan Greenspan, despite his recent reappointment, will not be around forever. When he steps down, will the public believe that there is sufficient commitment to a nominal anchor to keep inflation from appearing again?

On the criterion of having an explicit nominal anchor, the institutional set up of the Fed also does not score well.

Central Banks Should Be Instrument Independent

The Federal Reserve has been set up to be far more independent than other government agencies in the United States. Members of the Board of Governors are appointed by the government by 14-year terms, insulating them from political pressure, while Reserve Bank presidents, who also sit on the FOMC, are appointed by the boards of directors at each Reserve Bank and are not subject to Congressional review. Even more important is that the Federal Reserve generates substantial profits, on the order of $20 billion per year, most of which it returns to the U.S. Treasury, so that it has its own revenue base and is not dependent on funds from the government. Indeed, by law the Federal Reserve is exempt from General Accounting Office (GAO) audits of deliberations, decisions, or actions on monetary policy matters.

Given its insulation from the political process and its financial independence, it should be no surprise that the Fed has complete control over setting its monetary policy instruments. This has the benefits of enabling the Fed to resist political pressure to engage in time-inconsistent expansionary policy and to be forward-looking in the setting of its policy instruments.

On the criteria of instrument independence the Fed scores well.

Central Banks Should Be Goal Dependent

We have already seen that independence can go too far. Instrument independence is desirable but goal independence is problematic. The independence of the Fed—described above—and the lack of a clear mandate from the government allows the Fed to make the decisions on what the goals of its policies should be. Thus the Fed has a high degree of goal independence. In some ways goal independence makes the Fed's job easier because it insulates it from political pressure, but it does have a downside. The substantial goal independence of the Federal reserve creates a fair amount of tension in a democratic society because it allows an elite group to set the goals of monetary policy. Indeed, recent criticism of the Federal Reserve may have been prompted by the impression that the Federal Reserve, and particularly its Chairman, has become too powerful.

The goal independence of the Federal Reserve should not be seen as total, however. Politicians do have the ability to influence the goals of the Fed because the Congress can modify the Federal Reserve Act at any time. Also, the Fed has a great interest in other legislation that affects its operations. A case in point is the recent Gramm-Bliley-Leach Financial Services Modernization Act, passed in 1999, which had major implications for whether the Federal Reserve would continue to have supervisory responsibilities over large banking organizations (which it continued to keep). Furthermore, Congress can criticize the budget of the Fed for items that are unrelated to monetary policy or foreign-exchange operations. As an example, in 1996 Senators Dorgan and Reid called for Congress to exercise budgetary authority over the nonmonetary activities of the Federal Reserve because they were concerned that the Fed was too focused on fighting inflation and not enough on reducing unemployment.

As a comparison, the Eurosystem should be seen in some ways as more goal independent than the Federal Reserve System and in other ways less. The Maastricht Treaty specifies that the overriding, long-run goal of the ECB is price stability, so that the goal for the Eurosystem is more clearly specified than it is for the Federal Reserve System. However, Maastricht did not specify exactly what this price stability means so the Eurosystem has defined the quantitative goal for monetary policy, an inflation rate between 0 and 2 percent. From this perspective, the Federal Reserve System is slightly less goal dependent than the Eurosystem. On the other hand, the Eurosystem's statutes cannot be changed by legislation, but only by alterations to the Maastricht Treaty. From this perspective, the Eurosystem is much less goal dependent than the Federal Reserve System because its statutes are specified in a treaty and thus are far harder to change than statutes that are embedded in legislation.

As the examples above indicate, the Federal Reserve is not goal dependent, but we should not take this view too far. Thus, on the goal dependence criteria, the Fed's score is mixed.

Central Banks Should Be Accountable

Closely related to goal dependence is the accountability of the central bank to meet its goals. There are formal accountability mechanisms for the Fed. For example, the Chairman of the Board of Governors has been required to testify twice a year to Congress about the conduct of monetary policy under the Humphrey-Hawkins legislation. Also, as we have seen, the Fed is subject to punitive actions by the Congress if it so chooses, either by amending the Federal Reserve Act or through passage of other legislation that affects the Fed.

On these grounds the Federal Reserve System is more accountable than the Eurosystem. As we have seen, the Eurosystem's statutes cannot be modified by legislation but, rather, requires amendment to a treaty, a far more difficult process. Moreover, although the President of the European Central Bank is required to testify once a year to the European Parliament, this requirement may not guarantee sufficient oversight of the Eurosystem's policies. Since the European Parliament is currently significantly less powerful than the national parliaments of the countries that make up the Monetary Union, scrutiny by that organization would not influence the Eurosystem's behavior as strongly as would oversight by a more powerful body, such as a consortium of national parliaments or the individual parliaments themselves. It is not clear to whom the Eurosystem would be accountable.

However, the absence of an explicit nominal anchor means that there is no benchmark against which the public or Congress can measure the performance of the Federal Reserve System. In contrast, the Eurosystem has outlined its price-stability goal of inflation between 0 and 2 percent, so there is a predetermined criterion to judge its performance. Thus, despite the requirement that the Fed testify to Congress, the accountability of the Fed is not very strong. The Federal Reserve is able to obscure what its strategy and goals are and has indeed done this in the past. This leaves open the possibility that there could be a political backlash against a "high-handed" Federal Reserve that could have adverse consequences on its independence and ability to successfully conduct monetary policy in the future.

On the accountability criteria, the Fed also does not score very well.

Central Banks Should Stress Transparency and Communication

In recent years, the Fed has come a long way on the transparency and communication front. In the past, the Fed had a reputation for not only being unclear about its goals and strategy, but for keeping markets in the dark about its setting of policy instruments. This has changed dramatically in recent years. Starting in 1994, the Fed began to announce its policy actions after every FOMC meeting. It then moved in 1999 to announcing the bias in the direction of future moves in the federal funds rate, which caused some confusion, and so replaced this announcement at the beginning of this year with one that indicates the balance of risks for the future—whether toward higher inflation or toward a weaker economy. Fed officials also have been more active in articulating the strategy of monetary policy, its need to be preemptive, and the importance of the pursuit of price stability.

Despite improved transparency and communication, the lack of explicit goals has meant that Fed transparency is still much less than at many other central banks. In contrast to central banks that have adopted inflation targeting, the Fed produces nothing like an "Inflation Report" in which it clearly lays out in plain English the strategy for monetary policy and how well the central bank has been doing. One consequence of the weakness of Fed transparency and communication is that the public debate on monetary policy in the United States still has a tendency to focus on short-run considerations, as reflected in politicians' focus on "jobs, jobs, jobs" when discussing monetary policy. This focus on short-run considerations is substantially less in countries where central banks use communication vehicles such as "Inflation Reports" to refocus the public debate on longer-run considerations such as price stability.

It is interesting to contrast the way public debate is conducted with what has occurred in Canada, which has adopted an inflation-targeting regime with high transparency and accountability. In 1996, the president of the Canadian Economic Association made a speech criticizing the Bank of Canada for pursuing monetary policy that (he claimed) was too contractionary. His speech sparked off a widespread public debate. Instead of degenerating into calls for the immediate expansion of monetary policy with little reference to the long-run consequences of such a policy change, the debate was channeled into a substantive discussion over what should be the appropriate target for inflation, with both the Bank and its critics obliged to make explicit their assumptions and estimates of the costs and benefits of different levels of inflation. Indeed, the debate and the Bank of Canada's record and responsiveness led to increased support for the Bank of Canada, with the result that criticism of the Bank and its conduct of monetary policy was not a major issue in the 1997 elections as it had been during the 1993 elections.

On the transparency and communication criteria, the Fed's score is mixed, although it has been improving over time.

Central Banks Should also Have a Financial Stability Goal

Here the Fed's performance has been very strong. The Greenspan Fed has made it very clear that it will act decisively to prevent financial crises and has done so not only with words but with actions. The Fed's actions immediately after the October 19, 1987, stock market crash are a textbook case of how a lender-of-last-resort role can be performed brilliantly.[8] The Fed's action was immediate, with Greenspan announcing right before the market opened on October 20 of the Federal Reserve System's "readiness to serve as a source of liquidity to support the economic and financial system," which operated to decrease uncertainty in the marketplace. Reserves were injected into the system, but once the crisis was over, they were withdrawn. Not only was a crisis averted so that the business cycle expansion continued, but also the inflationary consequences of this exercise of the lender-of-last-resort role were small. The 75 basis point decrease in the federal funds rate in the Fall of 1998 immediately after the Russian financial crisis and the near-failure of Long-Term Capital Management, which roiled U.S. capital markets, also illustrated the Fed's commitment to act decisively to prevent financial instability. The aftermath was an economy that continued to expand, with inflation staying at the 2 percent level.

On the criteria of the commitment to the financial stability goal, the Fed's score is excellent.

Conclusion: What Should The Fed Do?

Our scorecard for the Fed indicates that although the institutional set up of the Fed scores well on some criteria, there is room for improvement in others. But, is there a need for the Fed as an institution to change? The Fed's performance in recent years has been extraordinary. It has been able to bring down inflation in the United States to the 2 percent level, which can reasonably be characterized as being consistent with price stability, while the economy has been experiencing the longest business cycle expansion in U.S. history, with very high rates of economic growth. As my son likes to say, "It don't get no better than this." The natural question then arises: If it ain't broke, why fix it?

However, our Fed scorecard suggests that we do need to consider institutional improvements in the way the central bank operates. The absence of an institutional commitment to price stability, along with weak Fed transparency, which stems from the absence of an explicit nominal anchor, leaves the Fed open to political pressure to pursue short-run objectives (i.e., job cre-

ation). This might lead to time-inconsistent expansionary policy and would produce inflation. In the past, after a successful period of low inflation, the Federal Reserve has "fallen off the wagon" and reverted to inflationary monetary policy—the 1970s are one example—and, without an explicit nominal anchor, this could certainly happen again in the future.

Indeed, the most serious problem with the Fed's institutional framework and the way it currently operates is the strong dependence on the preferences, skills, and trustworthiness of the individuals in charge of the central bank. Yes, the Fed under Alan Greenspan has been doing a great job, and so the Fed's prestige and creditability with the public have risen accordingly. But the Fed's leadership will eventually change, and there is no guarantee that the new leadership will be committed to the same approach. Nor is there any guarantee that the relatively good working relationship that now exists between the Fed and the executive branch will continue. In a different economic or political environment—and considering the possibility for a backlash against the Fed's lack of accountability—the Fed might face far stronger attacks on its independence and increased pressure to engage in over-expansionary policies, further raising the possibility that inflation will shoot up again.

So what should the Fed do? The answer is that the Fed should continue in the direction that it has already begun to increase its transparency and accountability. First, it should advocate a change in its mandate to put price stability as the overriding, long-run goal of monetary policy. Second, it should advocate that the price-stability goal should be made explicit, with a numerical long-run inflation goal. Government involvement in setting this explicit goal would be highly desirable, making the Fed goal independent, which should help retain public support for the Fed's instrument independence. Third, the Fed should produce an "Inflation Report" type of document that clearly explains its strategy for monetary policy and how well it has been doing in achieving its announced inflation goal.

The outcome of these changes is that the Fed would be moving to an inflation-targeting regime of the type described in our book, which has been recently published by the Princeton University Press (Bernanke, Laubach, Mishkin, and Posen, 1999). Clearly, the U.S. Congress and executive branch need to play an important role in encouraging the Fed to move toward inflation targeting. A detailed outline of a proposal for how this might be done can be found in our book. I leave you to read it on your own. Otherwise, you will be subjected to another full lecture.

References

Alesina, Alberto, and Lawrence H. Summers. "Central Bank Independence and Macroeconomic Performance: Some comparative Evidence," *Journal of Money, Credit, and Banking* (May 1993), pp. 151–62.

Andersen, Palle, and David Gruen. "Macroeconomic Policies and Growth," in *Productivity and Growth*, Palle Andersen, Jacqueline Dwyer, and David Gruen, eds., Reserve Bank of Australia, 1995, pp. 279–319.

Barro, Robert J., and David Gordon. "A Positive Theory of Monetary Policy in a Natural Rate Model," *Journal of Political Economy* (August 1983), pp. 589–610.

Bernanke, Ben S. "Non-Monetary Effects of the Financial Crisis in the Propagation of the Great Depression," *American Economic Review* (March 1983), pp. 257–76.

_____. "Comment on 'The Synergies Between Bank Supervision and Monetary Policy: Implications for the Design of Bank Regulatory Structure'," in *Prudential Supervision: What Works and What Doesn't*, Frederick S. Mishkin, ed., University of Chicago Press, forthcoming.

_____. Thomas Laubach, Frederic S. Mishkin, and Adam S. Posen. *Inflation Targeting: Lessons from the International Experience*, Princeton University Press, 1999.

Blinder, Alan S. *Central Banking in Theory and Practice*, MIT Press, 1998.

Briault, Clive. "The Costs of Inflation," *Bank of England Quarterly Bulletin* (February 1995), pp. 33–45.

Calvo, Guillermo. "On the Time Consistency of Optimal Policy in the Monetary Economy," *Econometrica* (November 1978), pp. 1411–28.

Corsetti, Giorgio, Paolo Pesenti, and Noriel Roubini. "What Caused the Asian Currency and Financial Crisis? Part I and II," NBER Working Papers, nos. 6833 and 6834, 1998.

Cukierman, Alex. *Central Bank Strategy, Credibility, and Independence: Theory and Evidence*, MIT Press, 1992.

Debelle, Guy, and Stanley Fischer. "How Independent Should a Central Bank Be?" in *Goals, Guidelines, and Constraints Facing Monetary Policymakers*, Jeffrey C. Fuhrer, ed., Federal Reserve Bank of Boston, 1994, pp. 195–221.

English, William B. "Inflation and Financial Sector Size," Finance and Economics Discussion Series No. 96-16, Board of Governors of the Federal Reserve System, April 1996.

Feldstein, Martin. "Capital Income Taxes and the Benefits of Price Stabilization," NBER Working Paper 6200, September 1997.

Fischer, Stanley. "Modern Central Banking," in *The Future of Central Banking*, Forrest Capie, Charles A. E. Goodhart, Stanley Fischer, and Norbert Schnadt, eds., Cambridge University Press, 1994, pp. 262–308.

Friedman, Milton, and Anna J. Schwartz. *A Monetary History of the United States, 1867–1960*, Princeton University Press, 1963.

King, Mervyn, "Changes in UK Monetary Policy: Rules and Discretion in Practice," *Journal of Monetary Economics*, (June 1997), pp. 81–97.

Kydland, Finn, and Edward Prescott. "Rules Rather than Discretion: The Inconsistency of Optimal Plans," *Journal of Political Economy* (June 1977), pp. 473–91.

McCallum, Bennett T. "Inflation: Theory and Evidence," in *Handbook of Monetary Economics*, Ben M. Friedman and Frank H. Hahn, eds., Elsevier Press, 1990, pp. 963–1012.

_____. "Two Fallacies Concerning Central-Bank Independence," *American Economic Review* (May 1995), pp. 207–11.

Mishkin, Frederic S. "Asymmetric Information and Financial Crises: A Historical Perspective," in *Financial Markets and Financial Crises*, R. Glenn Hubbard, ed., University of Chicago Press, 1991, pp. 69–108.

_____. "An evaluation of the Treasury Plan for Banking Reform," *Journal of Economic Perspectives* (Winter 1992), pp. 133–53.

_____. "Understanding Financial Crises: A Developing Country Perspective," in *Annual World Bank Conference on Development Economics*, 1996, pp. 29–62.

_____. *The Economics of Money, Banking, and Financial Markets*, 5th ed., Addison-Wesley Publishing Co., 1998.

_____. "Lessons from the Asian Crisis," *Journal of International Money and Finance* (August 1999a), pp. 709–23.

_____. "International Experiences with Different Monetary Policy Regimes," *Journal of Monetary Economics* (June 1999b), pp. 579–605.

_____, and Adam S. Posen. "Inflation Targeting: Lessons from Four Countries," *Economic Policy Review*. Federal Reserve Bank of New York (August 1997), pp. 9–110.

Peek, Joe, Eric Rosengren, and Geoffrey Tootell, "The Synergies Between Bank Supervision and Monetary Policy: Implications for the Design of Bank Regulatory Structure," in *Prudential Supervision: What Works and What Doesn't*, Frederic S. Mishkin, ed., University of Chicago Press, forthcoming.

Posen, Adam S. "Declarations Are Not Enough: Financial Sector Sources of Central Bank Independence," in *NBER Macroeconomics Annual*, Ben S. Bernanke and Julio J. Rotemberg, eds., MIT Press, 1995, pp. 253–74.

Rogoff, Kenneth. "The Optimal Degree of Commitment to an Intermediate Monetary Target," *Quarterly Journal of Economics* (November 1985), pp. 1169–89.

Sargent, Thomas, and Neil Wallace. "Some Unpleasant Monetarist Arithmetic," *Quarterly Review*, Federal Reserve Bank of Minneapolis (Fall 1981), pp. 1–17.

Svensson, Lars. "Inflation Targeting as Monetary Policy Rule," *Journal of Monetary Economics* (June 1999), pp. 607–54.

Taylor, John, ed. *Monetary Policy Rules*, University of Chicago Press, Chicago, 1999.

Woodford, Michael. "Monetary Policy and Price Level Determinacy in a Cash-in-Advance Economy," *Economic Theory*, vol. 4, no. 3 (1994), pp. 345–80.

_____. "Price-Level Determinacy with Control of a Monetary Aggregate." *Carnegie-Rochester Conference Series on Public Policy* (December 1995), pp. 1–46.

Notes

1. E.g., see English (1996).
2. E.g., see Briault (1995).
3. E. G., see Fischer (1994) and Feldstein (1997).
4. See the survey in Andersen and Gruen (1995).
5. For further discussion of who should set an inflation target in the United States, see Bernanke, Laubach, Mishkin, and Posen (1999).
6. Blinder (1998) also makes a strong case for increased transparency and accountability of central banks.
7. The Eurosystem currently is made up of the eleven national central banks of the countries that have joined EMU, with the European Central Bank (ECB) at the center having a role similar to that of the Board of Governors in the Federal Reserve System.
8. Indeed, this example appears in my textbook (Mishkin, 1998).

How Does Monetary Policy Affect the U.S. Economy?

This is the third of four consecutive issues devoted to our updated and expanded Q&A on monetary policy: (1) "How is the Federal Reserve structured?" and "What are the tools of U.S. monetary policy?" (2) "What are the goals of U.S. monetary policy?" (3) "How does monetary policy affect the U.S. economy?" and (4) "How does the Fed decide the appropriate setting for the policy instrument?" The revised text will appear in a pamphlet soon.

The point of implementing policy through raising or lowering interest rates is to affect people's and firms' demand for goods and services. This section discusses how policy actions affect real interest rates, which in turn affect demand and ultimately output, employment, and inflation.

What are real interest rates and why do they matter?

For the most part, the demand for goods and services is not related to the market interest rates quoted in the financial pages of newspapers, known as nominal rates. Instead, it is related to *real* interest rates—that is, nominal interest rates minus the expected rate of inflation.

For example, a borrower is likely to feel a lot happier about a car loan at 8% when the inflation rate is close to 10% (as it was in the late 1970s) than when the inflation rate is close to 2% (as it was in the late 1990s). In the first case, the real (or inflation-adjusted) value of the money that the borrower would pay back would actually be lower than the real value of the money when it was borrowed. Borrowers, of course, would love this situation, while lenders would be disinclined to make any loans.

So why doesn't the Fed just set the real interest rate on loans?

Remember, the Fed operates only in the market for bank reserves. Because it is the sole supplier of reserves, it can set the nominal funds rate. The Fed can't set real interest rates directly because it can't set inflation expectations directly, even though expected inflation is closely tied to what the Fed is expected to do in the future. Also, in general, the Fed has stayed out of the business of setting nominal rates for longer-term instruments and instead allows financial markets to determine longer-term interest rates.

How can the Fed influence long-term rates then?

Long-term interest rates reflect, in part, what people in financial markets expect the Fed to do in the future. For instance, if they think the Fed isn't focused on containing inflation, they'll be concerned that inflation might move up over the next few years. So they'll add a risk premium to long-term rates, which will make them higher. In other words, the markets' expectations about monetary policy tomorrow have a substantial impact on long-term interest rates today. Researchers have pointed out that the Fed could inform markets about future values of the funds rate in a number of ways. For example, the Fed could follow a policy of moving gradually once it starts changing interest rates. Or, the Fed could issue statements about what kinds of developments the FOMC is likely to focus on in the foreseeable future; the Fed even could make more explicit statements about the future stance of policy.

How do these policy-induced changes in real interest rates affect the economy?

Changes in real interest rates affect the public's demand for goods and services mainly by altering borrowing costs, the availability of bank loans, the wealth of households, and foreign exchange rates.

For example, a decrease in real interest rates lowers the cost of borrowing; that leads businesses to increase investment spending, and it leads households to buy durable goods, such as autos and new homes.

In addition, lower real rates and a healthy economy may increase banks' willingness to lend to businesses and households. This may increase spending, especially by smaller borrowers who have few sources of credit other than banks.

Lower real rates also make common stocks and other such investments more attractive than bonds and other debt instruments; as a result, common stock prices tend to rise. Households with stocks in their portfolios find that the value of their holdings is higher, and this increase in wealth makes them willing to spend more. Higher stock prices also make it more attractive for businesses to invest in plant and equipment by issuing stock.

In the short run, lower real interest rates in the U.S. also tend to reduce the foreign exchange value of the dollar, which lowers the prices of the U.S.-produced goods we sell abroad and raises the prices we pay for foreign-produced goods. This leads to higher aggregate spending on goods and services produced in the U.S.

The increase in aggregate demand for the economy's output through these different channels leads firms to raise production and employment, which in turn increases business spending on capital goods even further by making greater demands on existing factory capacity. It also boosts consumption further because of the income gains that result from the higher level of economic output.

How does monetary policy affect inflation?

Wages and prices will begin to rise at faster rates if monetary policy stimulates aggregate demand enough to push labor and capital markets beyond their long-run capacities. In fact, a monetary policy that persistently attempts to keep short-term real rates low will lead eventually to higher inflation and higher nominal interest rates, with no permanent increases in the growth of output or decreases in unemployment. As noted earlier, in the long run, output and employment cannot be set by monetary policy. In other words, while there is a trade-off between higher inflation and lower unemployment in the short run, the trade-off disappears in the long run.

Policy also affects inflation directly through people's expectations about future inflation. For example, suppose the Fed eases monetary policy. If consumers and businesspeople figure that will mean higher inflation in the future, they'll ask for bigger increases in wages and prices. That in itself will raise inflation without big changes in employment and output.

Doesn't U.S. inflation depend on worldwide capacity, not just U.S. capacity?

In this era of intense global competition, it might seem parochial to focus on U.S. capacity as a determinant of U.S. inflation, rather than on world capacity. For example, some argue that even if unemployment in the U.S. drops to very low levels, U.S. workers wouldn't be able to push for higher wages because they're competing for jobs with workers abroad, who are willing to accept much lower wages. The implication is that inflation is unlikely to rise even if the Fed adopts an easier monetary policy.

This reasoning doesn't hold up too well, however, for a couple of reasons. First, a large proportion of what we consume in the U.S. isn't affected very much by foreign trade. One example is health care, which isn't traded internationally and which amounts to nearly 15% of U.S. GDP.

More important, perhaps, is the fact that such arguments ignore the role of flexible exchange rates. If the Fed were to adopt an easier policy, it would tend to increase the supply of U.S. dollars in the market. Ultimately, this would tend to drive down the value of the dollar relative to other countries, as U.S. consumers and firms used some of this increased money supply to buy foreign goods and foreigners got rid of the additional U.S. currency they did not want. Thus, the price of foreign goods in terms of U.S. dollars would go up—even though they would not in terms of the foreign currency. The higher prices of imported goods would, in turn, tend to raise the prices of U.S. goods.

How long does it take a policy action to affect the economy and inflation?

It can take a fairly long time for a monetary policy action to affect the economy and inflation. And the lags can vary a lot, too. For example, the major effects on output can take anywhere from three months to two years. And the effects on inflation tend to involve even longer lags, perhaps one to three years, or more.

Why are the lags so hard to predict?

So far, we've described a complex chain of events that links a change in the funds rate with subsequent changes in output and inflation. Developments anywhere along this chain can alter how much a policy action will affect the economy and when.

For example, one link in the chain is long-term interest rates, and they can respond differently to a policy action, depending on the market's expectations about future Fed policy. If markets expect a change in the funds rate to be the beginning of a series of moves in the same direction, they'll factor in those future changes right away, and long-term rates will react by more than if markets had expected the Fed to take no further action. In contrast, if markets had anticipated the policy action, long-term rates may not move much at all because they would have factored it into the rates already. As a result, the same policy move can appear to have different effects on financial markets and, through them, on output and inflation.

Similarly, the effect of a policy action on the economy also depends on what people and firms outside the financial sector think the Fed action means for inflation in the future. If people believe that a tightening of policy means the Fed is determined to keep inflation under control, they'll immediately expect low inflation in the future, so they're likely to ask for smaller wage and price increases, and this will help achieve low inflation. But if people aren't convinced that the Fed is going to contain inflation, they're likely to ask for bigger wage and price increases, and that means that inflation is likely to rise. In this case, the only way to bring inflation down is to tighten so much and for so long that there are significant losses in employment and output.

What problems do lags cause?

The Fed's job would be much easier if monetary policy had swift and sure effects. Policymakers could set policy, see its effects, and then adjust the settings until they eliminated any discrepancy between economic developments and the goals.

But with the long lags associated with monetary policy actions, the Fed must try to anticipate the effects of its policy actions into the distant future.

To see why, suppose the Fed waits to shift its policy stance until it actually sees an increase in inflation. That would mean that inflationary momentum already had developed, so the task of reducing inflation would be that much harder and more costly in terms of job losses. Not surprisingly, anticipating policy effects in the future is one of the more difficult parts of conducting monetary policy, and it's a key issue in the next and final *Economic Letter* in this series, "How does the Fed decide the appropriate setting for the policy instrument?"

Suggested Reading

For further discussion of the topics in this article, see the following issues of the *FRBSF Economic Letter*.

93–38 "Real Interest Rates," by Bharat Trehan. http://www.frbsf.org/publications/economics/letter/1993/el93-38.pdf

95–35 "What Are the Lags in Monetary Policy?" by Glenn Rudebusch. http://www.frbsf.org/publications/economics/letter/1995/el1995-05.pdf

95–23 "Federal Reserve Policy and the Predictability of Interest Rates," by Glenn Rudebusch. http://www.frbsf.org/publications/economics/letter/1995/el1995-23.pdf

97–18 "Interest Rates and Monetary Policy," by Glenn Rudebusch http://www.frbsf.org/econrsrch/wklyltr/el97-18.html

2002–30 "Setting the Interest Rates," by Milton Marquis. http://www.frbsf.org/publications/economics/letter/2002/el2002-30.pdf

It's His Economy Now—and Yours

There are big issues facing us as Ben Bernanke takes over for the great Greenspan. The trouble is, there's not a whole lot he can do about them.

JUSTIN FOX

What kind of economy will Ben Bernanke inherit when he takes over from Alan Greenspan as Federal Reserve chairman in February? (We're assuming he'll breeze through his Senate confirmation, possibly before you read this.)

The answers flowing from the nation's ranks of Fed watchers mostly have to do with whether a Bernanke-led Fed will keep raising short-term interest rates. The majority opinion is that, by the new chairman's first meeting in charge of the rate-setting Federal Open Market Committee, scheduled for March 28, the combination of almost two years of rate hikes, high energy prices, and a deflating housing bubble will have cooled down the economy enough that Bernanke will lay off. A minority argues that growth is currently so robust that a slowdown won't come next year. A few even speculate that, whatever's happening in March, Bernanke will push for at least one last rate hike just to show he's not an inflation wimp.

That's what the Fed watchers talk about, and if you buy or sell bonds for a living, it makes sense to listen. It's less evident, though, why the rest of us pay attention. There are far bigger economic issues these days than the question of whether Ben Bernanke will raise interest rates a quarter-point in March: things like housing prices, job insecurity, stagnant pay, the looming crisis in public and private pensions, the dysfunctional health-care system. With the possible and partial exception of housing prices, they are all matters that Ben Bernanke won't be able to do anything about as Fed chairman. But during the Greenspan era Americans became so accustomed to looking to the Fed to solve economic problems that we don't seem to realize how many of today's biggest economic decisions are in our own hands and those of the people we elect—not the appointees and bureaucrats at the Fed's temple on Constitution Avenue.

We have learned over the past two decades to think of the economy on the Fed's terms. Given that the Fed's view of the economy is significantly more informed and rational than any other that we're likely to hear on a daily basis, that isn't all bad. But the Federal Reserve is a single-minded operation with a single significant economic tool at its disposal. To wield a crude analogy: The

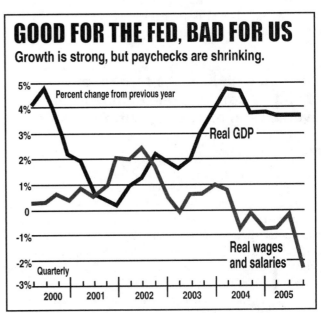

GOOD FOR THE FED, BAD FOR US
Growth is strong, but paychecks are shrinking.

SOURCES: BUREAU OF ECONOMIC ANALYSIS; BUREAU OF LABOR STATISTICS

economy is a plane, and the Federal Open Market Committee—headed by the Fed chairman and consisting of the Fed governors in Washington, D.C., the president of the New York Fed, and a rotating cast of other regional Federal Reserve Bank presidents—controls the throttle. But that's all it controls. Repairs, refueling, route, choice of plane, allocation of seats between first class and economy—not to mention in-flight dining and entertainment—are the responsibility of others. The hand at the throttle can keep the engine from overheating or the plane from stalling out, but that's about it.

Stalling out and overheating were of course big problems for the U.S. economy in the 20th century—with the Great Depression of the 1930s being the most significant stall and the Great Inflation of the 1970s and early 1980s the worst overheating. The realization that the Fed could actually stop inflation in its tracks dawned on Americans in the mid-1980s, after chairman Paul Volcker led a brutal but successful campaign to do just that. His successor, Greenspan, demonstrated in his reaction to the 1987 stock market crash that the Fed could prevent stalls, then showed in the "soft landing" of 1995 that it could halt inflation without throwing everybody out of work. With that, the myth of the all-powerful chairman was born.

As Greenspan himself has been trying to explain in speeches lately, it wasn't all his doing. Many things outside the Fed's control have changed to make its job—and that of central banks around the world—a lot easier. Increasing integration of the global economy, the decline of labor unions, deregulation, new communication and production technologies, and perhaps most of all the rising power and diversity of financial markets have combined both to keep inflation under control and to render the economy far less susceptible to shocks like sudden increases in energy prices. Academic observers—including Fed chairman—elect Bernanke, in a 2004 speech—have taken to calling this change the "Great Moderation." Instead of the sharp swings in economic activity that characterized the U.S. before the 1980s, we now have economic boomlets and bustlets happening all the time, in different industries and different regions.

The Fed's hand at the throttle of the economy can keep the engine from overheating or stalling out. But that's about it.

That's been swell news for central bankers. For the rest of us it's been a mixed blessing. "If you look at the economy today, it's meta-stable. Lots of people can fail, and the system can remain quite strong," says Eamonn Kelly, the CEO of Global Business Network, the consulting and forecasting firm that evolved out of Royal Dutch/Shell's famed scenario-planning operation. "You're not dependent on single lines of connection anymore. Anything that goes wrong in the system, you can route around it pretty quickly." Partly as a result, the U.S. hasn't had a year of negative GDP growth since 1991 (vs. four from 1974 to 1982). Pity those, however, who get routed around: "It's not like it's meta-stable for every actor," says Kelly. "For individuals it's less secure than it used to be."

That is the perversity at work when we speak in Fed-speak: Some of the very changes that have made the Fed's job easier over the past quarter-century have made our lives harder. Jobs are less secure, and benefits like health care and pensions are less certain, than in the decades following World War II. That makes it far harder for workers to force pay raises and far easier for a central bank to keep inflation in check. The Fed view of the world is not quite as worker-unfriendly as it was in the mid-1990s, when the stock market rose whenever the unemployment rate went up because that meant the Fed wouldn't have to raise rates. But there's still something strange about worrying along with Alan Greenspan whether the employment cost index is rising too quickly when the employment cost index is what we get paid. The fact that most of the rise in employment costs in the past three years has come in the form of increased spending on health care and pensions makes it even worse: The Fed feels the

need to crack down because employment costs are rising, but after adjusting for inflation, wages and salaries have actually been declining for the past two years (see chart at the beginning of this article). The point is not that the Fed should ease up: Focusing on stable prices as the sole criterion of success has worked well for the world's central banks over the past two decades. The point is that while it's great that the Fed has gotten the business cycle (somewhat) under control, the business cycle isn't the only thing that matters to our economic lives.

The most important economic measure of all is the standard of living. It increased dramatically and across the board in the U.S. in the 1950s and 1960s. Since then it's been a mixed bag. The most dramatic downer is that the average hourly wage, adjusted for inflation, is lower now than it was in 1973. But overall household wealth is up, per capita consumer spending is up, and the number of really rich people is way up. The great news of the past decade is that labor productivity has been rising at a much faster pace than in the 1970s and 1980s. But while those productivity gains made their way into paychecks in the late 1990s, that has since stopped. The main culprits appear to be competition from the rising economic powers of China, India, and the Internet; skyrocketing health-care costs; pension-funding shortfalls; and unceasing pressure to keep costs down from those global financial markets the Fed likes so much.

This is not a problem that necessarily calls for a massive government solution. It is the sheer free-market vibrancy of the U.S. economy that will probably be its greatest strength in the decades to come. But in a more competitive world, there will be far less room for error in economic policymaking. To thrive, the U.S. needs to churn out better-prepared high school graduates; it needs to lower health-care costs or at least allocate them more rationally; it needs to find a way to pay for the baby-boomers' retirement that doesn't bankrupt all our old-line corporations or result in huge tax hikes; and it needs to find a way to stop borrowing so much money from foreigners. Sure, it will help if the Fed does a competent job with monetary policy, but that's not what's going to determine the economic possibilities for our grandchildren.

Stagnant pay. The pension crisis. The health-care mess. Those are matters that Ben Bernanke won't be able to do anything about.

Yet we seem to have gotten so used to leaving economic policy in the hands of the Fed that those who should be addressing the issues outlined above have been able to get away with going AWOL. Greenspan may deserve the flak he gets from Democrats for reawakening the deficit monster by giving tacit support to President Bush's 2001 tax cuts. But it wasn't the Fed chairman who voted for the cuts and signed them into law, and it certainly wasn't he who launched the federal government on a spending binge that has now surpassed Lyndon Johnson's. (It should also be noted that most of the Bush tax cuts make economic sense, if they are eventually accompanied by spending cuts or hikes in other taxes.) The White House and Congress also have so far shown no interest in making hard decisions about health care, and while corporation pension legislation may pass this year or next, it will probably be just a Band-Aid. As for Social Security, the President did talk about shoring it up but backed down after running into a wall of resistance on Capitol Hill. Congress and the White House have responded to economic competition from overseas mainly with saber rattling and protection for that industry of the future, textile manufacturing.

Why are we letting them get away with this? Mainly because American voters don't like hard decisions any more than politicians do. But it is also because certain segments of informed America and official Washington suffer from the delusion that the truly critical decisions about our economic future will soon be in the hands of the scholarly, bearded, former Princeton economics-department chairman about to take charge of the temple on Constitution Avenue. Sorry, folks, it's time to get over our collective Greenspan-era dream. The really big choices are in the hands of the politicized rabble of the White House and Capitol Hill. Yeah, those guys. The ones we elected.

Banking Consolidation

U ntil this year, Citigroup was the only $1 trillion banking organization in the U.S. Now, there are two more—Bank of America has merged with FleetBoston, and J.P. Morgan Chase is about to complete its merger with Bank One. These megamergers are notable not only for their size but also for the geographic scope that the new institutions will serve. Indeed, they may signal the beginning of a process for building a truly national banking franchise.As mergers continue to shape the structure of the banking industry in the U.S., this *Economic Letter* looks at the economic drivers behind them and highlights some important policy implications.

Background on Recent Consolidation

The Riegle-Neal Act allowed interstate branch banking beginning in 1997, and, since then, the number of large bank mergers has increased significantly. Figure 1 plots this trend along with another noteworthy trend, namely, that most of the large bank mergers in recent years involved institutions headquartered in different states; the latter point suggests that these are market-expansion mergers, where the acquirer and the target have few overlapping operations in their respective banking markets. Although the markets they serve are much bigger, so far none of these three megabanks has come close to having a banking franchise that spans all 50 states, which is now legally possible.

Another noteworthy fact about the recently announced megamergers is that the target banking companies are healthy institutions that are likely to survive as independent organizations. This is in stark contrast both to the late 1980s and early 1990s in the U.S., when many bank mergers involved relatively weak banking companies being acquired by somewhat stronger organizations, as well as to some large bank mergers abroad, most notably in Japan. Today the U.S. banking sector is in good shape, with record profits and relatively low volumes of problem loans. For example, the return on average assets in 2003 for the two merger targets, Bank One and FleetBoston, were 1.27% and 1.34%, respectively, while the top 50 bank holding companies averaged 1.28%.This suggests that the recent megamergers are not motivated by economic weakness but rather by other economic forces.

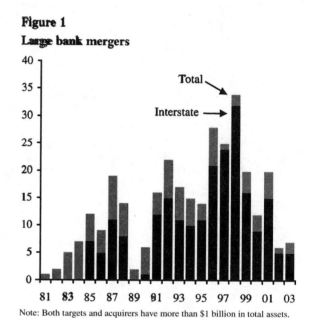

Figure 1
Large bank mergers

Note: Both targets and acquirers have more than $1 billion in total assets.

Economic Forces Driving Megamergers

We can identify four economic forces that may be driving large bank mergers. First is economies of scale—the relationship between the average production cost per unit of output and production volume. A firm that produces a higher volume of output can see its unit cost of production decline because the costs of some of the inputs are fixed, such as administrative and overhead expenses. However, diseconomies of scale also are possible. The average production cost may start to rise when output exceeds a certain volume because it may be more costly to manage a very large firm; these costs may stem from corporate governance issues, difficulties in coordination and execution, and diminished flexibility in responding quickly to changing markets.

While banking researchers generally agree that economies of scale do exist in the industry at low levels of output, there is less agreement about whether diseconomies of scale emerge at high levels of output. Earlier studies found evidence that diseconomies of scale did occur when total banking assets exceeded roughly $10 billion; however, those results were based on banking data prior to the passage of the Riegle-Neal Act, when banking companies operating in multiple states had to maintain separately capitalized, individually chartered bank subsidiaries in those states. The passage of Riegle-Neal allows these banking organizations to consolidate the individual state charters into a single charter, thus greatly streamlining management and operations. On the cost side, it is apparent that the cost structure of running a network of bank branches across multiple states should be more efficient than running a group of individually capitalized bank subsidiaries. On the revenue side, research on megamergers suggests that merged banks experienced higher profit efficiency from increased revenues than did a group of individual banks, because they provided customers with higher value-added products and services (Akhavein, Berger, and Humphrey 1997). Moreover, a banking organization of a certain scale may even earn a "too-big-to-fail" subsidy due to the market's perception of de facto government backing of a megabank in times of crisis. While the combination of all these factors could raise the optimal scale of large banking organizations today, it remains to be seen whether a $1 trillion bank is the "right" size.

The second economic force is economies of scope— a situation where the joint costs of producing two complementary outputs are less than the combined costs of producing the two outputs separately. This may arise when the production processes of both outputs share some common inputs, including both capital (such as the actual building the bank occupies) and labor (such as bank management).The passage of the Gramm-Leach-Bliley Act (GLB) in 1999 changed the scope of permissible financial activities for banking organizations. In the past, banking organizations were not allowed to engage in securities activities except on a limited, case-by-case basis through their so-called Section 20 subsidiaries. Also, general insurance activities were not permitted for banking firms, except in very small towns with fewer than 5,000 residents. GLB allows banking organizations to expand into securities and insurance activities in a much more straightforward way (see Furlong 2000 for more details). Although the two recently announced megamergers mainly involve combining banking activities, the potential of scope economies among banking, securities, and insurance could further increase the optimal size of a large banking organization today compared to pre-GLB days.

The third economic force is the potential for risk diversification. Research suggests that geographic expansion would provide diversification benefits to a banking organization not only by reducing its portfolio risk on the asset side, but also by lowering its funding risk on the liability side, as it spreads funding activities over a larger geographic area (Hughes, Lang, Mester, and Moon 1999). Furthermore, research suggests that product expansion could yield diversification benefits, most notably between banking and securities activities, while less so between banking and insurance (see the survey article by Kwan and Laderman 1999). Thus, a bigger bank is expected to be less vulnerable to economic shocks, and that alone could reduce its cost of capital, further compounding the benefits of scale and scope economies that come only from the production process.

The fourth economic force involves the bank managements' personal incentives. These may include the desire to run a larger firm and the desire to maximize their own personal welfare. Empirical research has shown that managerial compensation and perquisite consumption tend to rise with firm size. Research on stock market reactions to megamerger announcements in the 1990s suggests that, on average, the market did not view mergers of publicly owned banking companies as providing a significant gain to total shareholders' wealth of the combined company (Kwan and Eisenbeis 1999). The muted market response to merger announcements raises questions about the true magnitude of the net economic benefits underlying large bank mergers.

Policy Implications

First and foremost, bank mergers have the potential to raise antitrust concerns, which must be resolved satisfactorily before being approved. Because bank mergers can alter banking market structure and because market structure influences banking competition and hence the price of banking services to customers, all bank merger applications are scrutinized by banking regulators. In addition, the Department of Justice has the authority to challenge any mergers that are deemed harmful to competition. Research suggests that the markets for many banking products and services remain local in nature, despite the advances in information technology and electronic commerce (Rhoades 2000). In fact, the recent market-expansion megamergers themselves are testimony to the importance these large banking organizations attach to maintaining a local market presence. Thus, the current regulatory practices of defining banking markets locally in evaluating the effects of proposed mergers on competition seem justified. When a proposed merger is found to result in an unacceptably high level of concentration in local banking markets, divestitures in those markets are often required as a condition for regulatory approval in order to preserve meaningful competition. Looking at western states, Laderman (2003) found that changes in concentration of local banking markets were quite modest despite the large degree of consolidation in banking over the past 20 years.

In addition to concerns about banking concentration effects on local market competition, existing banking legislation also limits banking concentration at the national level. Perhaps motivated by the fear of concentration of banking power, the Riegle-Neal Act prohibits any merger or acquisition that results in a combined banking organization controlling more than 10% of the total amount of deposits of insured depository institutions in the U.S. A banking organization could exceed the deposit cap through internal growth, but it would not be allowed to engage in any more mergers or acquisitions. While the combined Bank of America and FleetBoston organization would control about 9.9% of the national deposit share, it is still not yet close to being a truly national bank. Thus, the drive toward building a truly nationwide franchise could be severely constrained by current law. As banking organizations get closer to the cap, policymakers will face growing pressure to reconsider both the merits of the deposit cap and the best way to accomplish the associated public policy goals.

The creation of megabanks also heightens concerns about systemic risk. When banking activities are concentrated in a few very large banking companies, shocks to these individual companies could have repercussions to the financial system and the real economy. The desire to limit systemic risk may lead policymakers to maintain some kind of cap on banking concentration at the national level.

The increased potential of systemic risk created by megabanks also intensifies concerns about these banks being considered "too-big-to-fail" (TBTF). In the early 1990s, the FDIC Improvement Act (FDICIA) included measures to limit the extension of TBTF to failing banks. Specifically, it mandated that the FDIC use the least cost resolution method to handle bank failures, thus greatly raising uninsured bank creditors' exposure to default risk. It appears to have led market participants to revise their views towards TBTF. This, in conjunction with the National Depositor Preference law (1993), which put depositors ahead of subordinated debt holders, may explain the research findings showing a significant increase in the sensitivity of the default risk premium of bank subordinated debt to banking organizations' underlying risks after FDICIA. However, there is still an exception in FDICIA—which can be invoked only in extraordinary circumstances—that permits the FDIC to pay off a failing bank's uninsured creditors if the use of least cost resolution would have serious adverse effects on economic conditions or financial stability. Megamergers create more such potentially systemically important banks and put a higher premium on credible policies for the orderly resolution of troubled large banking organizations—policies that limit the potential for moral hazard while containing their adverse impacts on financial markets.

Conclusions

There are a number of possible economic drivers for megamergers, from economic efficiency to the self-interest of bank management. Due to the profound changes in banking laws in the 1990s, earlier research on bank mergers may not be applicable to today's environment; therefore, it remains to be seen whether the current bank megamergers result in any measurable efficiency gains. Nevertheless, the ever-growing scale of bank mergers raises challenging policy questions, including banking concentration at the national level and systemic risk concerns, that must be addressed by policymakers in the course of promoting economic efficiency while safeguarding the nation's financial system.

References

Akhavein, J.D., A.N. Berger, and D.B. Humphrey. 1997. "The Effects of Megamergers on Efficiency and Prices: Evidence from a Bank Profit Function." *Review of Industrial Organization* 12, pp. 95-139.

Furlong, F. 2000. "The Gramm-Leach-Bliley Act and Financial Integration." *FRBSF Economic Letter* 2000-10.

Hughes, J.P., W. Lang, L.J. Mester, and C.G. Moon. 1999. "The Dollars and Sense of Bank Consolidation." *Journal of Banking and Finance* 23, pp. 291-324.

Kwan, S.H., and R.A. Eisenbeis. 1999. "Mergers of Publicly Traded Banking Organizations Revisited." Federal Reserve Bank of Atlanta *Economic Review* 84(4), pp. 26-37.

Kwan, S.H., and E. Laderman. 1999. "On the Portfolio Effects of Financial Convergence: A Review of the Literature." FRBSF *Economic Review* 2, pp. 18-31.

Laderman, E. 2003. "Good News on Twelfth District Banking Market Concentration." *FRBSF Economic Letter* 2003-31.

Rhoades, S.A. 2000. "Bank Mergers and Banking Structure in the United States, 1980-98." Federal Reserve Staff Study 174.

SIMON KWAN, Vice President, Financial Research

Bank ATMs and ATM Surcharges

The automated teller machine (ATM) has become a part of everyday life. According to Dove Consulting (2004), there are approximately 371,000 ATMs in the United States that process 30 million transactions per day. Concurrent with the growing deployment of ATMs has been significant variation in the price of ATM services. In particular, the surcharge fee paid by consumers using an ATM that does not belong to their bank increased from zero in 1996 to an average of roughly $1.50 in 2003. These price increases have been met with opposition from community groups who argue that the price increases fall heaviest on disadvantaged segments of the population. Over the past several years, many municipalities have considered either capping surcharges or banning them altogether.

The proliferation of ATMs and the pricing schemes that accompany them also have attracted a great deal of attention from research economists, because they shed light on how banks compete against each other in the current environment. By studying the pattern of entry of ATMs in certain markets we can gain insight into the potential welfare consequences of the lifting of artificial price controls. This *Economic Letter* reports on recent research on bank ATMs and ATM surcharges.

Industry Structure

The ATM industry infrastructure consists of card-issuing banks, ATM machines, and a telecommunications network to process transactions (see Hayashi, Sullivan, and Weiner 2003). In the early stages of their deployment, ATM machines generally were owned and operated by banks, and the machines were physically located on the bank premises. By the 1990s, much of the growth in ATM deployment shifted to nonblank locations, such as convenience stores and grocery stores. Today, the majority of ATMs are located at sites other than banks. Moreover, many of these ATMs are operated or owned by independent, nonblank operators. In terms of how customers use ATMs, more than 75% of all ATM transactions are cash withdrawals, and the remainder are deposits and balance inquiries.

ATM cardholding customers, ATMs, and card-issuing banks are all linked by shared networks. These networks were typically formed (originally) as joint partnerships among participating banks. In 2002, there were about 40 networks, the largest being the national networks of Cirrus and Plus, which are owned by MasterCard and Visa, respectively.

A transaction involving a customer from Bank A using an ATM owned by Bank B generates a number of fees. Bank A must pay the network a *switch fee* for routing the transaction;

these fees range from 3 cents to 8 cents per transaction. Bank A, the card-issuing bank, must pay the ATM owner, Bank B, an *interchange fee*. These fees range from 30 cents to 40 cents for a withdrawal and are determined by the ATM network. When an ATM and a customer's bank both are linked via multiple networks, the actual interchange fee will vary based upon the agreements between the ATM owner and the different networks. Bank A may charge its cardholding customer a *foreign fee* for using Bank B's machine, and Bank B may charge the customer from Bank A a *surcharge fee* for using its ATM machine. As of 2002, 87% of all ATM deployers levied such surcharges, which accounted for about one-third of all transactions; the average amount of the surcharge across all operators was about $1.50. According to Dove Consulting (2004), the average monthly operating costs for an ATM in 2003 was $1,314, consisting mostly of fixed items such as depreciation, maintenance, telecommunications, and cash replenishment.

The Economics of ATM Deployment

Like many other goods and services, the reasons for deploying ATMs have changed over time. The first ATMs in the United States were deployed primarily to enhance customer service and reduce costs. ATMs were "open" 24 hours a day and tended to have shorter lines than bank tellers did. From the banks' point of view, ATMs promised significant cost advantages over tellers for providing routine services like cash withdrawals and account balance statements.

Of course, deployment decisions can hinge on motives other than customer service and cost. In this *Letter* we consider two such motives. First, banks have considerable scope to use ATM surcharges to compete against each other not only for consumers of ATM services, but also for the larger set of banking services (see Hannan et al. 2003). In particular, the surcharges banks impose on users who are from other banks not only generate extra revenue, but also drive up the costs of the bank's competitors by injecting a degree of incompatibility into the ATM network.

Ishii (2004), and Knittel and Stango (2004) examine this issue and find that the size of the ATM network has a significant impact on the demand for bank deposits. That is, potential bank customers take the size of a bank's ATM network into account when deciding where to bank. Ultimately, this tendency is likely to favor larger banks over smaller banks, as the larger banks typically have more ATMs with which to lure customers. Indeed, one of the messages of these papers is that banks over-invest in machines relative to the social optimum in their attempt to win deposits.

The questions posed in these papers, and a host of others, would have been difficult to address were it not for a regime change in the ATM industry. Up to 1996 the major networks prohibited the levying of surcharges. Once the ban was lifted, deployment increased substantially, tripling between 1996 and 2001. Of course, it is possible that other developments during this time period may have altered the demand for ATM services. But the regime change provided a kind of "before and after" experiment commonly used to examine the predictions of economic models.

Gowrisankaran and Krainer (2005) take a different approach to identifying the effects of ATM surcharging. Rather than using variation over time in the surcharge regime, the authors look at a crosssection of ATM market structures in two states with very different regimes. In Minnesota, as in most of the country, ATM operators raised surcharge prices once the networks permitted it. In nearby Iowa, however, the state legislature upheld the surcharge ban until 2003. Since the counties on either side of the Iowa-Minnesota border are quite similar in terms of population density, industry mix, and income per capita, the authors argued that the relationship between entry and surcharging could be inferred from the entry patterns on either side of the Iowa-Minnesota border in 2002, just before Iowa lifted the ban. This approach is attractive because it sidesteps the question of whether some other factor or factors might have contributed to the surge in ATM deployment since 1996. Whatever such factors may be and whatever their quantitative importance, they should have had the same effect on both the Iowa and the Minnesota markets.

The Gowrisankaran and Krainer study is well-suited to exploring a second motive for ATM deployment: the straightforward profitability of a stand-alone ATM. The study builds on the observation that much of the new ATM deployment has occurred in nonbank locations, such as highway convenience stores, grocery stores, casinos, and bars. Many of these sites tend to be remote from banks, residential areas, or downtown shopping districts, which renders them unattractive for an ATM if the sole source of revenue comes from the interchange fee. However, entry into these locations becomes possible once banks (or more generally, ATM operators) are permitted to charge sufficiently high surcharges to offset the relatively low amount of transaction volume. Not surprisingly, the authors found that Minnesota, which permitted surcharging, had more ATMs per person than neighboring Iowa, where surcharging was banned. Given a set of potential entry points, such as a convenience store or grocery store, the probability of entry was significantly higher in Minnesota than in Iowa.

Gowrisankaran and Krainer went on to estimate a formal entry model where consumer demand functions were allowed to depend on proximity to an ATM and on its price, and where the owners of potential ATM entry points make profit-maximizing decisions about whether to deploy an ATM on a site. With estimates of consumer demands and ATM entry probabilities in hand, the authors conduct experiments to assess the welfare implications of different surcharging regimes. For example, do consumers attach greater value to a market structure with more proximate ATMs that are also more expensive to use? Or would consumers prefer fewer ATMs that are free? If regulators vary the surcharge price, how are the effects of these price changes shared by consumers and ATM operators?

In answer to these questions, Gowrisankaran and Krainer found that consumers are sensitive to the distance they must travel to use an ATM; they are willing to pay an estimated 8 cents to 10 cents to reduce the distance to an ATM by one kilometer. Consumers were found to be surprisingly sensitive to surcharge fees. If the probability of a consumer using a given ATM is 50%, then raising the surcharge by just 10 cents would result in the same consumer using the ATM with 46% probability. The deployment of ATMs was also found to be sensitive to the pricing regime. The Iowa surcharge ban is estimated to have reduced ATM entry by about 12% on average in the counties along the Minnesota border. Correspondingly, experiments that varied the surcharge regime did not reveal big differences in aggregate welfare across regimes. However, different surcharge regimes did imply differences in the sharing of costs across the economy. At one extreme, an outright surcharge ban raises consumer welfare by about 35%, while ATM operator welfare declines by about 20%.

Conclusions

There has been a large amount of research interest on the connection between the recent proliferation of ATMs and the pricing of ATM services. Gowrisankaran and Krainer found that an outright surcharge ban did not deter the deployment of ATMs in a major way in a sample of rural markets. This evidence suggests that the huge increase in deployment in the last several years may be due to factors other than the simple lifting of the surcharge ban. Finally, all of the studies cited corroborated a high degree of consumer sensitivity to ATM fees. It seems likely, then, that ATM deployment and pricing strategy will continue to be an important component of how banks compete against each other in local markets.

References

[URLs accessed December 2005.]

Dove Consulting. 2004."New ATM Study Details a Paradoxical Industry." http://www.doveconsulting.com/PR-2004-05-21CPPS.htm

Gowrisankaran, G., and J. Krainer. 2005."The Welfare Consequences of ATM Surcharges: Evidence from a Structural Entry Model." http://www.frbsf.org/publications/economics/papers/2005/wp05-01bk.pdf

Hannan, T., E. Kiser, R. Prager, and J. McAndrews. 2003. "To Surcharge or Not to Surcharge: An Empirical Investigation of ATM Pricing." *Review of Economics and Statistics* 85, pp. 990–1002.

Hayashi, F., R. Sullivan, and S. Weiner. 2003."A Guide to the ATM and Debit Card Industry." FRB Kansas City. http://www.kc.frb.org/FRFS/ATMpaper.pdf

Ishii, J. 2004. "Interconnection Pricing and Compatibility in Network Industries: ATM Networks in the Banking Industry." Harvard University working paper.

Knittel, C., and V. Stango. 2004. "Compatibility and Pricing with Indirect Network Effects: Evidence from ATMs." NBER working paper 10774. http://papers.nber.org/papers/w10774.pdf

GAUTAM GOWRISANKARAN Visiting Scholar, Washington University in St. Louis and NBER.

JOHN KRAINER Economist.

Reprinted with permission from the Federal Reserve Bank of San Francisco *FRBSF Economic Letter,* No. 2005-36, December 16, 2005, pp. 1–3, by Gautam Gowrisankaran and John Krainer. The opinions expressed in this article do not necessarily reflect the views of the management of the Federal Reserve Bank of San Francisco, or of the Board of Governors of the Federal Reserve System.

Toward a Cashless Society

Hundreds of lives and more than a trillion dollars can be saved each year in a society without cash. Investor David R. Warwick proposes a secure government-operated electronic currency that replaces cash while delivering enormous social and economic benefits. But such an initiative faces current obsessions with privacy and irrational fears of governmental prying.

DAVID R. WARWICK

As far back as 1888, novelist Edward Bellamy envisioned a cashless society by 2000, but it still hasn't come. A major step toward cashlessness came with the advent of electronic funds transfer (EFT) technology, which ushered in the era of credit-card transactions in the mid-twentieth century. As the use of "plastic"—which subsequently included debit cards—gained momentum, the world seemed bound for complete cashlessness as the end of the century neared.

But the march toward cashlessness stalled due to wariness about invasions of privacy. Scholars and public leaders alike are reluctant to consider the idea of replacing cash with an electronic currency system, particularly one operated by government, lest they be seen as willing to compromise privacy. These concerns have also hindered discussion of significant social and economic benefits that could result from ending the use of cash, including major reductions in taxes, vastly improved public services, and the total eradication of many of the most serious and violent crimes.

True cashlessness will come about only if a government undertakes the project since only government can put an end to the production and circulation of cash, and only government can realistically administer an electronic replacement for cash. The payment industry (including VISA, MasterCard, and Citibank) cannot replace cash completely, despite smart cards, cybercash, and other innovations.

Though the public enjoys the conveniences of "plastic," it still loves money. Virtually everyone carries some currency and coin, and the amount of cash in circulation continues to rise. The very idea of abolishing cash in favor of a government-operated electronic currency strikes many citizens as peculiar and questionable. A typical reaction is, "I use very little cash nowadays anyway, because I use a credit (or debit) card for most of my purchases. Cash will probably fade away of its own accord someday." And, "We're getting along fine, so why put everyone to the bother of learning and adopting some new money system?"

The world is hardly "getting along fine" with cash. Most crimes are either committed to steal cash or use cash as a method of payment. Drug trafficking is conducted *exclusively* in cash. The bulk of tax evasion is hidden in cash transactions. Cash carried in purses and wallets continues to make everyone a potential robbery victim. Throughout history, cash, in coin or paper notes, was a problematic necessity for which there was no practical alternative. With the advent of EFT, however, the relative detriments of cash can be targeted, if not eliminated.

Ending the use of tangible cash would greatly boost the quality of life by reducing crime. The most direct and noticeable effect of ending tangible cash would be the disappearance of bank robberies, cash-register robberies, and muggings. Other illicit activities reliant on cash, such as receiving stolen property and bribery, would nosedive as well, because with anonymous cash gone, any alternative payment medium would leave a trail that would serve to detect and prove, and hence deter, those criminal acts.

Crippling underground illicit activities would also generate billions of dollars in previously unreported tax revenues. Ending cash would also save industry the billions of dollars required to handle currency and coin. Overall, the social and economic potential in converting tangible cash to an electronic system is staggering.

Reducing Cash-Related Crime

I have proposed that government replace currency and coin with an electronic equivalent that I label FEDEC, or federal electronic currency, which would emulate tangible cash as closely as possible except for its physical form as paper or coinage. The national government would operate the system and guarantee the new electronic money. FEDEC would not replace credit card and other private-sector EFT systems and networks, nor would it replace bank-checking systems. It would operate as a separate system in which every person and legal entity would have an account. Funds would transfer within the system only from one account to another, and there would be no direct interchange with private-sector payment systems.

Under my proposed system, funds would be completely traceable. It would be completely traceable. It would be foolish for culprits to somehow electronically "steal" FEDEC funds by moving someone else's funds to their own account. All transactions through FEDEC could be tracked, making it simple for authorities to identify and prosecute theieves. Furthermore, if any hacker-type thefts are perpetrated through this system, they would occur without the violence and terror that marks much of today's cash crime. This would be indeed a monumental gain, reducing the number of serious injuries in hospital rooms and on the street and providing a measure of security for users everywhere. The federal government would supply further security by insuring against losses from any theft that happened to slip through the system or any other threat to a FEDEC user's funds.

This type of security would be impossible if the new cash could be used anonymously. A key difference between tangible cash and almost any other form of money lies in traceability. cash itself bears no indicia of ownership, and transactions in cash are not recorded. Whoever possesses it, owns it—no questions asked. Clearly, it is the ideal payment medium for theft and secret dealings. On the other hand, electronic transactions, at least in a non-anonymous system, are recorded. In such a system, transaction dates, sums transferred, and account numbers—as well as the identities of the transacting parties—would leave a paper or electronic trail and would be technically available to legal authorities. Even today, authorities in legally prescribed circumstances often access credit- and debit-card records in criminal investigations, since non-cash payments are recorded and may serve as evidence. FEDEC would operate similarly: In drug investigations or other criminal proceedings, all transaction data and facts could be retrieved and the gathered evidence could be used against criminals in court. Abolishing cash in favor of a recorded medium of exchange has the potential to deter, it not render impossible, the bulk of crimes.

Each year, nearly 3 million Americans are victims of crimes in which criminals target cash, according to extrapolated statistics from the U.S. Bureau of Justice Statistics. All over the world, cab drivers, convenience-store clerks, bank tellers, and others who deal almost exclusively in cash are accosted daily and often murdered, simply because they possess currency, and the impact of these crimes resonates throughout society. A quarter of a million people sustan injuries as a result of crimes perpetrated to obtain cash each year. the 3 million annual burglaries in the United States clearly diminish the security of homes, neighborhoods, and businesses. the use of tangible currency restrains retail business, controls where people shop and travel, and influences the use of guns and other measures citizens take to prevent themselves from becoming crime victims.

Making cash electronic has the potential of making workplaces and crime-ridden neighborhoods safer, reducing prison populations, and freeing up emergency rooms. It could bring down insurance rates, cut public outlays for law enforcement and courts, and much more. If drug crimes and tax evasion, both of which are conducted almost exclusively in cash, are included

in the calculations, the fiscal relief could run as high as a trillion or more dollars each year.

For point-of-sale usage at retail establishments, the new electronic cash would likely employ equipment and procedures similar to that of credit- and debit-card systes. Current products for mobile payments are somewhat bulky and specialized, though wireless terminals exist for use in taxis and delivery vehicles and at temporary sales booths. Non-retail, person-to-person electronic payments, though they would account for less than 1% of "cash" payments, do not have a counterpart currently. That need could be met by the use of personal termials: Each account holder would own and carry a terminal device, perhaps the size of a wallet or a cell phone (and perhaps a combination thereof). If Bob wants to borrow $5 from Alice, all he would have to do is swipe a card in her terminal. She would indicate the amount, and the data would transmit to a processing center. An instant later, Bob would be able to use $5, and the system would know that he owes Alice.

No matter the exact format that a new electronic currency might take, it is difficult to imagine any other single innovation that has the potential of generating such profound social and economic benefits. Hundreds of lives could be saved each year, tens of thousands of debilitating injuries prevented, billions of dollars could be saved in public services, and hundreds of billions of dollars in wrongfully withheld taxes could be raised—enough to finance universal health coverage for the entire United States, for example, or to subsidize other worthy purposes. Why then, one wonders, would anyone resist the idea?

Privacy Issues

The greatest obstacle to a federally operated electronic money system lies in people's suspicion that conversion from anonymous cash transactions might expose private monetary data to official scrutiny, which many regard as a threat to privacy or even as a step toward oppressive governance.

The welcome efficiences of computers, electronic data transmission, and the Internet have, unfortunately, also ushered in abuses, ranging from misuse of medical data to identity theft, spam, and a variety of unwelcome and irritating marketing schemes. The creeping invasion privacy has engendered widespread wariness, if not a negative bias, against any suggestion to create new electronic databanks and to collect personal data. Privacy, which until recent years had been anebulous term, has risen from relative obscurity to a postion of equality with other major rights. But the pendulum can swing too far.

Those who focus their efforts exclusively against invasions of privacy too often are oblivious to greater and more harmful social enemies. In the matter of electronic currency, they stand fixed to defend privacy while ignoring the robbers, murderers, thieves, kidnappers, drug dealers, and tax evaders who attack individuals, wreak widespread misery, and, collectively, compromise the pursuit of happiness.

It is *inconceivable* that an electronic currency system would be enacted without the inclusion of privacy-securing safeguards. As I envision an electronic currency system, no one would be au-

Scenario for Going Cashless

Federal electronic currency, or FEDEC, would have to be implemented in stages. I estimate that it would take about 10 years, coexisting with FEDEC. Following initial trials and a pilot program, the FEDEC system would first be offered to retailers. The cost of FEDEC terminals (or the cost of programming FEDEC into existing universal card terminals) would be borne by industry. I believe the overwhelming majority of retailers will gladly make the switch to the new system, because it will insure against lost sales and reduce the far greater cost, bother, and security risks associated with cash. As an inducement, I foresee the federal government providing transaction cards for free to individuals.

At some point, retailers would be legally allowed to refuse tender of tangible cash. This would further prompt individuals to apply for FEDEC accounts. At about the same time, individuals would be offered various models of federally approved personal terminals for purchase to facilitate interpersonal transactions that don't involve a business, like giving your kids an allowance.

At a later stage, before government withdraws currency from circulation altogether, it would have to address the needs of the poor. Conceivably, government might deploy terminals for everyone's interpersonal use in post poffices and other public places or build the system into public telephones. Perhaps personal terminals might be provided to the poor for free. Any implementation plan has many possible variations.

Clearly, designing, building, and deploying FEDEC would require major governmental outlays and impose significant costs on industry. The mere processing of several hundred million FEDEC account applications alone, each of which would have to be verified, would run in the hundreds of millions of dollars, if not more. Yet, the tradeoff of cost against the benefits to be gained is an absolute lopsided bargain.

FEDEC Monetary Benefits

Handling and processing of tangible cash costs more than $60 billion a year, according to an in-depth study by the Food Marketing Institute. This amount includes the 550 billion annual cash transactions; costs incurred by the U.S. Treasury Department, the U.S. Federal Reserve System, and banks; and the estimated $10 billion stolen from individuals each year. These costs would disappear under FEDEC.

Furthermore, ending cash will likely generate over $30 billion in previously unrealized federal income taxes, $4 billion in unrealized state sales taxes, and $10 billion in state income taxes across the nation. Conversion to FEDEC would also produce savings of $25 billion in criminal justice outlays and $17 billion in reduced outlays and $17 billion in reduced government fraud. The total savings to the nation as a result of converting from cash to FEDEC approaches $150 billion a year.

—David R. Warwick

---

thorized to access private data without legal grounds and a court order or warrant.

In actual operation, tens of millions of daily transactions would be processed automatically, efficiently, safely, and virtually anonymously to all but the transacting parties. Only a minuscule number of transactions would ever come under the eyes of administrators or officials, and then only after due process of law. Cashlessness and privacy are not incompatible concepts.

Who's Afraid of Big Brother?

A number of individuals fiercely oppose the idea of federal electronic cash. Some equate the anonymity of cash with liberty. Such critics are motivated by many factors, perhaps the greatest being the threat of "Big Brother" and all that implies.

Mere mention of the concept to some triggers a reaction that assumes that any government-operated electronic money system could be used by dissolute law-enforcement officials and bureaucrats to carry out authoritarian schemes. They envision such data being collected in government-held dossiers and worry that recording cash-transaction data would afford government a means of absolute control over citizens. One privacy advocate refers to "some [unspecified] people who are just drooling" to acquire the means to invade privacy. Another critic of the proposal for federal electronic currency says it should "terrify anyone with the slightest concern for liberty and freedom."

But concerns must yield to the real terror suffered by convenience-store clerks, cab drivers, and bank tellers. Each month, about 100 Americans are murdered and 3,500 more are seriously injured in crimes involving cash. It is patently wrongheaded to ignore these facts, particularly on the implausible expectation that electronically collected data might somehow facilitate creation of a totalitarian regime.

Despite more than 50 years of unfulfilled prophecy, George Orwell's novel *Nineteen Eighty-Four,* with its Big Brother, two-way television, and Newspeak, still exerts a powerful influence on many people. Orwell warned of how surveillance technology might enable governments to carry out authoritarian schemes to the extreme. As history has unfolded, however, the England and the United States alluded to in his book have hardly become totalitarian states. To the contrary, the technologies Orwell so feared would be used against citizens have been used to protect citizens, as with ubiquitous public cameras in Britain, for example, and screening devices increasingly used in airports worldwide.

The most cynical of Orwell's diciples envision the government employing invasive surveillance and computerized intelligence to control its citizens. Electronic currency, they suspect, would grant cunning politicians a means for totalitarian rule.

But government officials do not need additional technology in order to acquire prohibited personal financial data; they already have ample means at their disposal. For example, they could easily tap into the voluminous checking-account data processed by banks in the U.S. Federal Reserve System and search through private financial data.

Only adherence to law, and not the lack of means, prevents government from intruding on privacy. In the United States, federal officals have an increasingly good record of respecting laws that protect individual privacy, and no valid reason exists to predict that they would flout laws after electronic cash came into being. Indeed, data in a federal electronic currency would serve to deter bribery and other covert and illegal activities that might otherwise be carried out by officials themselves.

Abolishing cash would necessarily entail some loss of privacy because one could no longer transact monetary business without the possibility of recording payment data and thus having it exposed. But this loss would be limited to data from illicit acts and would result only from the fact that cash transactions, as a matter of feasibility, are usually beyond the observance of authorities or others entitled to it. That should not be regarded as a legitimate loss of privacy.

America loses more valuable resources from the side effects of tangible currency than it does from wars, terrorism, and even natural disasters. That makes electronic currency, whether recorded or anonymous, is simply too advantageous a step to pass up.

DAVID R. WARWICK is a real-estate developer, investor, and former attorney. He is author of *Ending Cash: The Public Benefits of Federal Electronic Currency* (Quorum Books, 1998) and many articles in various publications.

Originally published in the July/August 2004 issue of *The Futurist*, pp. 38–42. Copyright © 2004 by World Future Society, 7910 Woodmont Avenue, Suite 450, Bethesda, MD 20814. Telephone: 301/656-8274; Fax: 301/951-0394; http://www.wfs.org. Used with permission from the World Future Society.

UNIT 5

The Changing Global Economy

Unit Selections

34. **Update on the State of the Future**, Jerome C. Glenn and Theodore J. Gordon
35. **As Job Exports Rise, Some Economists Rethink the Mathematics of Free Trade**, Jeff Madrick
36. **Is the Current Account Deficit Sustainable?**, *The NBER Digest*
37. **The High-Tech Threat from China**, Jeffrey E. Garten
38. **Building Blocks**, Christian Caryl
39. **Where the Money Went**, James S. Henry
40. **Asymmetric Globalization: Global Markets Require Good Global Politics**, Nancy Birdsall
41. **Will the World Run Dry? Global Water and Food Security**, Mark W. Rosegrant, Ximing Cai, and Sarah A. Cline
42. **Do Global Attitudes and Behaviors Support Sustainable Development?**, Anthony A. Leiserowitz, Robert W. Kates, and Thomas M. Parris
43. **Eliminating Child Labor**, Miriam Wasserman

Key Points to Consider

• How should the United States respond to the challenges of the global economy?

• Should we be concerned about the large U.S. current account deficit? How does outsourcing affect the demand for U.S. workers?

• Will efforts at economic integration such as the European Union, NAFTA, and ASEAN succeed?

Student Web Site

www.mhcls.com/online

Internet References

Further information regarding these Web sites may be found in this book's preface or online.

The European Union in the U.S.
http://www.eurunion.org

Institute for International Economics
http://www.iie.com

Inter-American Development Bank (IDB)
http://www.iadb.org

North American Free Trade Association (NAFTA)
http://www.nafta-sec-alena.org

Organization for Economic Co-operation and Development (OECD)
http://www.oecd.org

Sustainable Development.Org
http://www.sustainabledevelopment.org

United Nations Development Programme (UNDP)
http://www.undp.org

World Resources Institute
http://www.wri.org

The world economy is in a period of rapid change. Over the last decade we have witnessed a series of unforeseen events; increased international tensions following the events of the September 11, 2001, terrorist attacks; ambitious market reforms in what were formerly centrally planned economies; an acceleration of the process of economic integration in the Americas, Western Europe, and Southeast Asia; and the impoverishment of many small, less-developed countries burdened by staggering international obligations. Simultaneously with these developments has come the "globalization" of trade, reflecting America's increasing economic interdependence with the rest of the world.

The U.S. economic system is extraordinarily resilient. Historically, it has consistently demonstrated an ability to adjust to change, adapt to new technologies, and create new jobs. In absolute terms, the United States is presently the world's most important international trader: total U.S. exports and imports each exceed $1 trillion annually. In addition, the United States has for many years been able to enjoy the advantages of remaining relatively self-sufficient.

Whereas Canada and most Western European countries derive roughly a quarter of their national income from trade, the United States obtains only about 10 percent of all income from this source.

This unit begins with an article that deals with the continuing trend toward the globalization of the world economy. Jerome C. Glenn and Theodore J. Gordon assert that global prospects for improving the overall health, wealth, and sustainability of humanity are increasing, but slowly. Globalization presents humanity with both challenges and opportunities as increased connectivity highlights the strengths and shortcomings as a global community.

Jeff Madrick discusses the possible relationship between "free trade" and outsourcing. He takes issue with the position of many economists that the benefit of lower prices gained from free trade exceeds the cost of lost jobs. The article that follows this—a study by the National Bureau of Economic Research—argues that the risks of a high and rising current account deficit may be more serious than just a few years ago.

The unit continues with three articles that offer perspectives on individual countries and regions. Jeffrey E. Garten focuses on recent news from China—its rising trade surpluses, ballooning currency reserves, relentless search for oil, and tensions with the United States. He cautions that one development has been seriously unreported—the possibility that China may become a technological superstate.

Next, Christian Caryl reports that the Association of Southeast Asian Countries (ASEAN) is considering broadening its membership to include China, Japan, and South Korea. What might this mean for the future of global trade? Finally, James Henry asks: How did the world's developing countries wind up owing $2.5 trillion? He says that Western institutions haven't exactly been innocent bystanders.

This unit concludes with pieces that deal with issues of global economic sustainability. Questions raised in these articles include: Can we avert an impending worldwide water crisis? Do global attitudes support the idea of sustainability? What can the developing world learn from U.S. experience about the elimination of the use of child labor?

Update on the State of the Future

Jerome C. Glenn and Theodore J. Gordon

I s the future getting better or worse? According to the latest edition of State of the Future, global prospects for improving the overall health, wealth, and sustainability of humanity are improving, but slowly.

The picture painted by the report gives much cause for hope. The world has grown to 6.5 billion people, 1 billion of whom are connected by the Internet, and the annual economy is approaching $60 trillion. However, there is also much cause for concern. The great paradox of our age is that, while more and more people enjoy the benefits of technological and economic growth, increasing numbers of people are poor, unhealthy, and lack access to education. In the years ahead, globalization will present humanity with both challenges and opportunities as increased connectivity highlights our strengths and our shortcomings as a global community.

A race is under way between the increasing proliferation of threats and our growing ability to improve humanity's condition. Understanding the nature of this race entails looking at the contradictory forces at work in our world. Here is a brief assessment of those forces, along with possible strategies for positive resolution.

World Trade: Engine of Opportunity and Disparity

Explosive economic growth over the previous decades has led to dramatic increases in life expectancy, literacy, and access to safe drinking water and sanitation, as well as to decreases in infant mortality for the vast majority of the world. At the same time, the ratio of the total income of people in the top 5% to those in the bottom 5% has grown from 6 to 1 in 1980 to more than 200 to 1 now. That ratio is not sustainable.

Unfortunately, economic disparities could grow unless a global partnership emerges between the rich and the poor, using the strength of free markets with rules based on global ethics. That, in turn, could trigger increased migration of the poor to rich areas and result in a range of complex conflicts and humanitarian disasters.

With their high technology and low wages, China and India will become giants of world trade. This should force the developing world to rethink its trade-led economic growth strategies. China alone could produce 25% of all manufactured goods in the world by 2025.

Environmental Sustainability

The Millennium Ecosystem Assessment found that 60% of our life-support systems are gone or in danger of collapse. A collaboration of 1,360 experts from 95 countries produced a global inventory of the state of the Earth's ecosystems. According to their assessment, degradation could grow worse by 2050 as another 2.6 billion people are added to the Earth. Current absorption capacity of carbon by oceans and forests is about 3 to 3.5 billion tons per year. Yet, 7 billion tons are added to the atmosphere annually, which could increase to 14 billion tons per year if current trends continue—eventually leading to greenhouse effects beyond the ability of humans to control. Events like the 2004 Asian tsunami and the Millennium Ecosystem Assessment's pronouncement are helping the world to realize that environmental security deserves greater attention.

At the same time, economic growth (often achieved at the expense of environmental security) is also sorely needed. A measure of the degree to which developing nations need growth can be seen in the increase in development aid from wealthier nations to economically struggling ones over recent years. Official development assistance to cash-strapped nations increased to $78.6 billion in 2004, the highest level ever.

Until Africa shifts from being primarily an exporter of raw materials to a more scientifically oriented culture, it has no chance of closing its economic gap with the developed world.

Organizations like the World Bank and the United Nations Development Program (UNDP) have long relied on economic development indicators, but integrated sustainable development indicators (to measure world progress toward sustainability) are recent inventions. Our ability to measure sustainable economic development has improved. As part of the multilateral Environment and Security Initiative, international organizations such as UNDP and NATO have begun to offer expertise and resources to promote environmental security in addition to economic security.

The Central European Node of the Millennium Project has created a Sustainable Development Index composed of seven major subject areas, 14 indicators (two for each major area), and 64 variables (various numbers of variables for individual indicators). This index was calculated for 179 countries to express their state of development and progress toward sustainable development. It allows a mapping of sustainable development as well as comparison among different countries.

The countries rated as most sustainable were Sweden, Finland, and Switzerland, while those rated as least sustainable were Afghanistan, Somalia, and Burundi. Other sustainable development indicators include the Environmental Sustainability Index, the Dashboard of Sustainability, the Ecological Footprint Calculator, the Living Planet Index, and the Well-Being Index.

The concepts of environmental diplomacy and human security are gaining recognition in both military and diplomatic circles. Our research showed a noticeable increase in the number of articles, formal studies, and conferences related to environmental security during the past year. The environment is becoming recognized as being on a par with cultural and ethnic issues in security analysis. Advances in satellites, sensors, and the Internet are making it possible to monitor environmental situations more effectively.

Development Goals: Moving Ahead or Lagging Behind?

It seems that the UN Millennium Development Goal of cutting poverty in half between 2000 and 2015 may well be met on a global basis—but not in Africa and some parts of Asia. The dynamics of urbanization have facilitated many important improvements to the human condition. In other words, urbanization, once thought a problem, is now seen as part of the solution to poverty, ignorance, disease, and malnutrition.

Hunger and water scarcity will worsen unless more serious and intelligent investments are made. Water supply has to be increased, not simply redistributed. Despite improved access to safe drinking water and better sanitation during the last decade, 1.1 billion people still do not have access to safe drinking water and 2.6 billion people—half the population in developing countries—lack adequate sanitation.

Global Information Culture

Nearly 15% of the world is connected to the Internet, and the majority of the world's population may be connected within 15 years, making cyberspace an unprecedented medium for civilization. This new distribution of the means of production in the knowledge economy is cutting through old hierarchical controls in politics, economics, and finance. It is becoming a self-organizing mechanism that could lead to dramatic increases in humanity's ability to invent its future. Millions share ideas and feelings with strangers around the world, increasing global understanding. Google and other search engines have made the world's knowledge available to previously isolated populations. This will provide a more even playing field for the future knowledge economy.

The advent of the "24-7 always on" globalized world of ubiquitous computing implies that we will be making many more decisions per day and constantly changing our own and others' schedules and priorities. Information overload will make it increasingly difficult to separate the noise from the signal of what is important to know in order to make good decisions. Civilization is also becoming increasingly vulnerable to cyberterrorism, power outages, information pollution (misinformation, pornography, junk e-mail, and media violence), and virus attacks.

As the integration of cell phones, video, and the Internet grows, prices for this technology will fall. This will accelerate globalization and allow swarms of people to quickly form and disband, coordinate actions, and share information ranging from stock market tips to bold new contagious ideas (meme epidemics).

In a sad and ironic twist, despite the expansion of communications technology and, as a result, the power of individuals to speak freely, in 2004 only 17% of the world's people lived in countries that enjoyed a free press.

Medicine Is Becoming Cheaper as Some Illnesses Spread

Many of the world's most devastating illnesses will become less expensive to treat. However, increasing threats from new and reemerging diseases and from drug-resistant microorganisms have attracted the concern of the World Health Organization. Malaria, tuberculosis, and AIDS were expected to kill more than 6 million people in 2005. There were 4.9 million new HIV/AIDS cases in 2004, while more than 3.1 million people died of AIDS—200,000 more than the previous year. The current spread of HIV in eastern Europe and Asia implies that the number of AIDS patients in these areas may eventually dwarf the AIDS population in Africa. As human encroachment on the natural environment continues, increased interspecies contacts could lead to the spread to humans of infectious diseases known previously only in wild animals.

Peace and Security

The United Nations has defined terrorism as "actions already proscribed by existing conventions; any action constitutes terrorism if it is intended to cause death or serious bodily harm to civilians or noncombatants with the purpose of intimidating a population or compelling a government or an international organization to do or abstain from doing any act." This agreement should lead to greater international cooperation.

While prospects for security in places like Kashmir have improved, the horrors in Sudan, the Congo, Iraq, and Israeli-Palestinian areas continue, as do nuclear uncertainties with Iran and North Korea. The world has yet to agree about when it is right to use force to intervene in the affairs of a country that is significantly endangering its own or other peoples. Conventional military force has little effect in combating the asymmetrical and intrastate warfare as the boundaries between war, civil unrest, terrorism, and crime become increasingly blurred. Although Yasser Arafat's death has restarted the Middle East peace process, internal Islamist political reforms have been evolving quietly for the past several years that could lead either to new negotiations or negotiation setbacks as ideological hardliners insert themselves into the negotiation process.

Because weapons of mass destruction may be available to individuals over the next generation, the welfare of anyone should be the concern of everyone. Such platitudes are not new, but the consequences of their failure will be quite different in the future when one person can be massively destructive.

Technology Is Accelerating, Along with Demand for Energy

Most people still do not appreciate how fast science and technology will change over the next 25 years and would be surprised to learn about recent breakthroughs. For example, several years ago light was stopped by a yttrium-silica crystal and then released; it has also been slowed in gas and then accelerated. Adult stem cells have been regressed to embryo-like flexibility to grow replacement tissue. In experiments, humans with small computer chips implanted in their brains have been able to perform limited computer functions via thought. To help the world cope with the acceleration of change, it may be necessary to create an international science and technology organization to arrange the world's science and technology knowledge as well as to examine the potential consequences of various technological breakthroughs.

The factors that caused the acceleration of science and technology innovation are themselves accelerating, hence, the acceleration of scientific and technological accomplishments over the past 25 years will appear slow compared with the rate of change in the next 25. Since technology is growing so rapidly along several fronts, the possibility of it growing beyond human control must now be taken seriously.

In contrast, running this technology will require energy. World energy demand is forecast to increase by 60% from 2002 to 2030 and to require about $568 billion in new investments every year to meet that demand. Oil production is declining among the majority of producers. Meanwhile, in 2003 the Texas Transportation Institute found that U.S. traffic jams alone wasted 2.3 billion gallons of gasoline, adding greenhouse gases and hastening the day when the oil wells run dry.

Technology has the power to resolve this issue if governments and people develop the will to use it toward that end. The time has come for an Apollolike program to increase the world's supply of nonpolluting energy.

Nanotechnology: Growing Possibility and Peril

Nanotechnology will provide an extraordinary range of benefits for humanity, but as with any advance, it is wise to forecast problems in order to avoid them. Little is known about the environmental and health risks of manufactured nanomaterials. For example, artificial blood cells (respirocytes) that dramatically enhance human performance could cause overheating of the body and bio-breakdowns. Disposal of highly efficient batteries that use nanomaterials could affect ecosystem and human health.

Since the military is a major force in nanotechnology research and development, it can play a key role in understanding and managing nanotechnology risks. As a result, the Millen-

nium Project put together an expert Delphi panel to identify and rate important forms of nanotechnology-related environmental pollution, to look at health hazards that could result from any military and/or terrorist activities, and to suggest military research that might reduce these problems.

Other Key Issue Areas

Military expenditures in 2005 were expected to reach $1 trillion. At the same time, annual income for organized crime has passed $2 trillion. It is time for an international campaign to develop a global consensus for action against transnational organized crime, which is increasingly interfering with governments' ability to act. Weapons of mass destruction are still stockpiled and form a threat that has yet to be addressed realistically.

The global population is expanding, retracting and aging. The world population has grown by 4 billion people since 1950 and may grow another 2.6 billion by 2050 before it begins to fall. According to the UN's lower forecasts (which have proven to be more accurate), world population could fall to 5.5 billion by 2100—an astonishing 1 billion fewer people than are alive today. This assumes that there will be no major life extension breakthroughs by then. In any case, civilization will have to adapt to a world in which older people form the majority.

The world is slowly beginning to realize that improving the political and economic status of women is one of the most cost-effective ways to address various global challenges. Despite this, women, on average, are still paid 18% less than are men. Male violence toward women results in more casualties than does war.

The Challenge for Tomorrow's Leaders and Managers

The combination of economic growth and technological innovation has made it possible for 3 to 4 billion people to have relatively good health and living conditions. However, unless our financial, economic, environmental, and social behavior are improved along with our industrial technologies, that could change very quickly.

Few leaders have been trained in the theory and practice of decision making, and few know how advanced decision-support software could help them. We know the world is increasingly complex and that the most serious challenges are global in nature, yet we are unpracticed at improving and deploying Internet-based management tools and concepts. Formalized training in ethics and decision making for policy makers could result in a significant improvement in the quality of global decisions.

The heartening news is that global ethical standards are emerging from a variety of sources, such as the International Organization for Standardization (ISO), corporate ethics indexes, interreligious dialogues, UN treaties, the Olympic Committee, the International Criminal Court, various NGOs, Internet blogs, and the international news media. Ethical decision making in a global context should be informed by an understanding of the key challenges facing our world, as well as of their interconnectedness. The establishment of the eight UN Millennium Development Goals was a giant step in this direction.

The next should be the creation of global transinstitutions for water, energy, AIDS, education, and so on. Current institutional structures are not getting the job done. In addition to the moral imperative and social benefits of addressing these goals and challenges, there is also great wealth to be made resolving these issues on behalf of grateful populations. However, making this a reality will require future-oriented politicians, which in turn will require a better educated public to elect more future-minded leaders globally.

Meeting the Future's Challenges

Although many people criticize globalization's potential cultural impacts, it is increasingly clear that cultural change is necessary to address global challenges. Simply put, the development of genuine democracy requires cultural change, as does preventing AIDS, promoting sustainable development, ending violence against women, ending ethnic violence, etc. The tools of globalization, such as the Internet and global trade, should be used to help cultures adapt in a way that preserves their unique contributions to humanity while improving the human condition. These tools can help policy makers, leaders, and educators who fight against hopeless despair, blind confidence, and ignorant indifference—attitudes that too often have blocked efforts to improve the prospects for humanity.

Future synergies among nanotechnology, biotechnology, information technology, and cognitive science could dramatically increase the availability of food, energy, and water. Connecting people and information will increase collective intelligence and create value and efficiency while lowering costs. Yet a previous and troubling finding from the Millennium Project remains unresolved. It is increasingly clear that humanity has the resources to address global challenges, but how much wisdom, goodwill, and intelligence humanity will focus on these challenges is anyone's guess.

Just as it would be difficult for the human body to work if the neurons, muscles, bones, and so on were not properly connected, so, too, is it difficult for the world to work if people, ideas, resources, and challenges are not seen in a single context. The initial global infrastructure to manage globalization is being built through such mechanisms as the ISO, the World Trade Organization's rules of trade, and Internet protocols.

The moment-by-moment connectivity among ideas, people, resources, and challenges in order to create optimal solutions, however, is yet to be developed. A worldwide race to connect everything not yet connected is just beginning. Wise institutions and organizations will make great wealth by completing the links among systems by which civilizations function and flourish.

JEROME C. GLENN has been the executive director of the American Council for the United Nations University (AC/UNU) since 1988. E-mail jglenn@igc.org.

THEODORE J. GORDON has served as a space scientist in the Apollo program. He is the founder of The Futures Group and was a cofounder of the Institute for the Future. E-mail Tedjgordon@att.net.

Glenn and Gordon have been codirectors of the Millennium Project of the AC/UNU since 1996. This article draws from *2005 State of the Future* (AC/UNU, 2005) which is available from the Futurist Bookshelf, www.wfs.org/bkshelf.htm. The Millennium Project's address is The Millennium Project, American Council for the United Nations University, 4421 Garrison St., N.W., Washington, D.C. 20016. Fax 202-686-5170; Web site www.stateofthefuture.org.

As Job Exports Rise, Some Economists Rethink the Mathematics of Free Trade

JEFF MADRICK

Free trade theory has a growing number of detractors, and one of their traditional concerns has understandably moved to center stage in this presidential election year. How much has the exporting of jobs to foreign nations contributed to the lack of jobs and the absence of wage growth in the current expansion at home?

The standard tenets of free trade theory strongly support the case for outsourcing. Generally, as business finds cheaper ways to make products, it reduces prices to consumers. And some businesses may not survive unless they can reduce labor costs.

In general, most economists believe that the "consumer surplus" that results from lower prices far outweighs the cost of lost jobs or lower wages. In other words, there are many more winners than losers. But recent research suggests that the magnitude of this advantage has been exaggerated. Also, the plight of the losers has clearly been sorely neglected in the economic literature.

And if sending jobs abroad turns from its current relative trickle to a fast-flowing stream, as it well might, the costs of job dislocation will be still higher.

It is more than a little interesting how frequently past research understated the costs of jobs lost to free trade. A literature search published in a 2003 monograph by the economists Michael W. Klein, Scott Schuh and Robert K. Triest, called "Job Creation, Job Destruction and International Competition" (Upjohn Institute), provides a useful summary of this work.

A 1972 study by Stephen P. Magee, for example, toted up the welfare benefits of trade and set them against the costs of unemployment. The study purportedly showed that the benefits of hypothetically eliminating all trade restrictions outweighed the costs of unemployment induced by international competition by a ratio of 100 to 1.

It is hard to argue with such a lopsided benefit. But Mr. Klein, Mr. Schuh and Mr. Triest note that Mr. Magee neglected crucial costs of job dislocation, like the likelihood of displaced workers being paid a lower wage when they got new jobs. A 1980 study took into account more job dislocation costs, but found that benefits from a 50 percent cut in global tariffs still exceeded dislocation costs 20 to 1.

Such results understandably led economists to neglect the costs of job dislocation.

The 1980 adjustments were still not nearly enough, however, Mr. Klein, Mr. Schuh and Mr. Triest argue. The main reason is that such early studies assumed that net changes in jobs—the difference between those destroyed and those created—were a good proxy for those who suffered from job dislocations. But in fact, many more jobs are destroyed and created in the United States than is immediately apparent.

For example, the authors find that in a large sample of manufacturers, 1.3 jobs per 100 were lost on balance each year from 1973 to 1993. But 10.2 jobs per 100 were destroyed, while 8.8 were created. (The discrepancy is a result of rounding.)

Such a high rate of job destruction carries serious costs for workers, even when they eventually find new jobs. There are long periods of unemployment, retraining costs and costs of searching for a job. And the new jobs usually pay less than the old ones. In the meantime, skills are lost as well.

The authors estimate that if some of these costs of job dislocation were taken into account, the benefits of trade would outweigh the costs by a far smaller margin. For example, the ratio in the 1980 study would be reduced from 20 to 1 to only 2 to 1.

The authors remain advocates of free trade; a benefit of 2 to 1 is still hefty. But the findings suggest at the very least that a sizable number of workers are inevitably hurt by free trade.

Are protective tariffs an answer? One valuable contribution of Mr. Klein, Mr. Schuh and Mr. Triest is to show that job losses are rarely if ever uniform in an industry. As a consequence, tariffs may often be too broad a policy tool because they will protect companies that would not fire workers anyway.

Moreover, trade and the exporting of jobs are not the only sources of dislocation. Technological changes that may rapidly make existing products obsolete have the same consequences. Mr. Klein, a professor at Tufts University, says a better policy is to make unemployment insurance more generous. He adds that portability of corporate benefits like pensions and health insurance would also more directly address some costs of job dislocation.

Other economists are beginning to think about policies that efficiently compensate those who lose jobs for the costs of dislocation. Carl Davidson and Steven J. Matusz, in a monograph called "International Trade and Labor Markets" (Upjohn Institute), also argue that such policies must not sweep across industries and the labor force. They favor wage and employment subsidies over broader measures.

Such an analysis by no means tells us everything we have to know about free trade and outsourcing. On the one hand, the benefits of free trade are not necessarily limited to the consumer surplus. For example, to the extent that free trade expands markets, as even Adam Smith might have argued, it stimulates productivity growth because it makes possible enormous economies of scale in manufacturing, services and marketing, and enhances competition.

On the other hand, keeping domestic wages high adds to the demand that can generate productivity gains. Moreover, the basic tenets of free trade assume that the economy is operating at full employment—in other words, almost everyone who wants a job can find one. Not enough research has been done on the trade effects in an economy with persistent unemployment, which has characterized most of the last 30 years.

What is entirely clear, however, is that the losers from free trade require more of the nation's attention. And their numbers are growing as trade and job migration expand.

JEFF MADRICK is the editor of *Challenge Magazine*, and he teaches at Cooper Union and New School University. His new book is "Why Economies Grow," from Basic Books and the Century Foundation. E-mail: challenge@mesharpe.com

Is the Current Account Deficit Sustainable?

Should policymakers be worried that the U.S. current account deficit is on track to set an all-time record in 2004, reaching a level near 6 percent of GDP? Though some believe that the issue is a relatively minor one, NBER Research Associates **Maurice Obstfeld** and **Kenneth Rogoff** argue that the risks may be even more serious today than they were a few years ago. With the United States today absorbing roughly 70 percent of the current account surpluses of China, Japan, Germany, and of all the world's other surplus countries, the increasingly popular view that the current situation is sustainable seems unlikely. This is all the more true when one considers that government deficits rather than high investment now account for the lion's share of the U.S. current account deficit.

In **The Unsustainable U.S. Current Account Position Revisited** (NBER Working Paper No. 10869), Obstfeld and Rogoff update their earlier work and extend it in a number of dimensions, including allowing for global transmission effects. These refinements, together with today's higher deficit (5.5 percent in 2004 versus 4.4 percent in 2000) lead them to conclude that a very gradual re-equilibration of global current account imbalances would imply a depreciation of 15-20 percent in the real trade-weighted dollar. A sudden rebalancing would involve overshooting, with a doubling or more of the dollar's long-term movement. The fact that dollar depreciation tends to favor the U.S. net asset position—because the bulk of U.S. liabilities are effectively indexed to the dollar whereas only roughly half of assets are—turns out to be relatively unimportant to this calibration.

Taking into account the fact that equilibration of the U.S. current account will affect global demand everywhere—not just in the United States—does, however, make a big difference. Just as the United States must absorb considerably more non-traded goods and services relative to traded goods (these include both goods where the United States is a net exporter and goods where it is a net importer) when its current account deficit closes up, foreigners consumers must be induced to start consuming more of the global supply of tradable goods now that U.S. demand is shrinking.

Thus, the bulk of the short-run pressure for dollar depreciation is driven by the need to get U.S. residents to consume fewer tradable goods of all types and for foreigners to consumer more of them, with the opposite true for production. With traded goods comprising only 25 percent of GDP in most OECD countries, a shift in net imports of 5 or 6 percent of GDP (that is, a closing of the U.S. current account deficit by that amount) implies a massive change in the relative price of non-traded versus traded goods, with non-traded goods becoming relatively cheaper in the United States and more expensive abroad. It is true that the price of the goods the United States exports must also decline, and that U.S. import prices must rise. However, contrary to much analysis in the press, this effect is quantitatively much less important, and plays only a secondary role.

> **"A shift in net imports of 5 or 6 percent of GDP ... implies a massive change in the relative price of non-traded versus traded goods, with non-traded goods becoming relatively cheaper in the United States and more expensive abroad."**

The requisite depreciation, of course, depends on the empirical parameters of the economy as well as on the nature of the shock leading to equilibration (a rise in productivity in the foreign non-traded goods sector will reduce global imbalances with somewhat smaller exchange rate effects than would be caused by a rise in U.S. savings). Obstfeld and Rogoff show that an exchange rate change alone (say, caused by appreciation of the Asian currencies) will have only a relatively limited impact on the current account, absent shifts in underlying savings behavior and productivity.

While the analysis does not give a definite timetable, it does point out a number of factors that suggest rebalancing will happen within the next few years. These include the open-ended security costs of the United States, high energy prices, the still expansionary stance of monetary and fiscal policy, and rising old-age pension costs. The authors note that global rebalancing could turn out to be relatively benign, as it was in the late 1980s. Then, despite a 40 percent drop in the trade-weighted dollar, the global economy was able to absorb the shock reasonably well. But post-9/11, the Iraq war, and a succession of tax cuts, the situation appears more nearly parallel to the early 1970s, when the results were far less satisfactory.

Obstfeld and Rogoff consider a number of possible economic developments that might lead to rebalancing, including changes in savings and productivity. Higher foreign productivity helps in the short run if it is focused in the non-traded sector of the economy (where the bulk of output lies). But if foreign productivity increases are disproportionately concentrated in the traded goods sector, the imbalances will get worse before they get better.

The overall conclusion here is that the global economy is more vulnerable today than it seemed four years ago, when it already looked worrisome. If the current account closes up under relatively benign circumstances, then the effects may not be too traumatic, even though there will still likely be a spectacular short-run depreciation of the dollar, 20-40 percent on a trade-weighted basis. But if it occurs concurrently with another major shock, say to security or energy prices, or to consumer confidence, then the global output ramifications could be considerable, with interest rates rising, vulnerabilities in Europe and Asia due to appreciation of their currencies, and risks of financial crises.

From *NBER Digest*, December 2004, pp. 1–2. Copyright © 2004 by National Bureau of Economic Research. Reprinted by permission.

Article 37

The High-Tech Threat from China

America Inc. Is Rushing Beijing Ahead by Sharing R&D Treasures

JEFFREY E. GARTEN

The news is full of headlines about China—its rising trade surplus, ballooning currency reserves, relentless search for oil, and its tensions with the U.S. over textiles and intellectual property rights. But one development has been seriously underreported: China's emergence as a technological superstate. Could Beijing pose a threat in the one area where the U.S. has assumed it would always retain supremacy?

Since 1985, China has repeatedly declared its resolve to reach technological parity with the West. Between 1992 and 2002, the latest period for which figures are available, Beijing has more than doubled the proportion of gross domestic product it spent on research and development, while the level stagnated in America. China boosted its output of PhDs in science and engineering by 14% a year, while the number of U.S. grads fell. Its technology-intensive exports grew by 22% annually, while exports of U.S. high-tech goods have declined. Today, moreover, while American universities award 25% of all their PhDs in science and engineering to Chinese citizens, Beijing is sparing no effort to lure many back. Among China's R&D priorities are superscale integrated circuits, computer software, and information security systems.

WESTERN COMPANIES ARE SPEEDING up China's advancement by establishing huge R&D facilities there. General Electric Co. has 27 labs in China working on projects from composite-materials design to molecular modeling. Microsoft Corp. has nearly 200 researchers in the country. Cisco, DaimlerChrysler, IBM, Intel, and many others are following suit.

Experts are split on the implications of the globalization of R&D. In a forthcoming report, for example, Nicholas Lardy of the Institute for International Economics downplays China's technological position by pointing to the relatively low sophistication of even its high-tech exports, its heavy dependence on imported technology, and the benefits that accrue to U.S. companies investing there. On the other hand, in an upcoming book, Ernest Preeg of the Manufacturers Alliance/MAPI is sounding alarms because of China's steep upward technological trajectory. In a recent study, Kathleen Walsh of the Henry L. Stimson Center calls for Washington to wake up to the economic and national security implications of China's growing R&D capabilities. And the National Science Foundation is upset by the decline in research funding and scientific education in America.

I fear that the U.S. hasn't come to grips with the implications of corporations doing so much R&D in China. U.S. companies are understandably seeking the best talent and lowest cost of operations anywhere. But in the process they are sharing America's intellectual treasures with a foreign rival in unprecedented ways. They are training foreign scientists and engineers and giving them and the omnipresent Chinese government access to their proprietary research programs.

To keep its undisputed technology lead, the U.S. must go beyond larger government-sponsored research budgets, better K-12 education, and closer government-business cooperation, all prescriptions made in the 1980s, when the U.S. last had a competitiveness debate. Now Washington must also figure out how to deepen basic R&D in America when so much is dispersed abroad. And it must adapt to the reality that U.S. multinationals' goals may no longer dovetail with national interests. I've not seen a way to achieve all the goals at the same time.

Intel Corp. is illustrative. CEO Craig Barrett advocates more federally funded research, which would eventually benefit the country and the company. But Congress and the public have to wonder whether Intel should receive, in effect, subsidies if it then shares its knowhow with Chinese partners. At the very least, a quid pro quo should be established. Intel's sharing of technology could enrich its shareholders, China's economy, and to some extent the U.S. But unlike in the past, its goals no longer center on creating industries and jobs in the U.S., which is what American taxpayers deservedly expect.

In the 1960s, Americans were galvanized by Sputnik, and in the 1980s they were spurred on by Japan Inc. As the challenge of remaining technologically superior becomes more complex, the U.S. needs another shot of adrenaline. The perceived threat of China could supply it, but I worry that it won't be strong enough or soon enough.

JEFFREY E. GARTEN is dean of the Yale School of Management (jeffrey.garten@yale.edu).

Building Blocks

At next week's East Asia Summit, there will be talk of creating a regional common market and, eventually, a single currency. Are those plausible ideas or a pipe dream?

CHRISTIAN CARYL

Just imagine: it's a sunny winter's day in 2045, and you're arriving in Bangkok airport on the 1:15 from Shanghai. The flight is considered internal, so there's no customs check; you can keep that dark red Asian Union passport in your pocket. No need to pick up any cash, either—you've still got plenty of yuen (the single Asian currency) left over from your previous stops, including Tokyo and Seoul. After your business meetings you head over to the magnificent glass-and-aluminum building that houses the Asian Parliament. You dodge the cheerful, prosperous-looking tour groups from Laos and Burma and find your way to an exhibition commemorating the 40th anniversary of the founding of the East Asian Community, back in the momentous year of 2005. "It was," reads a sign, "the first sign of light after the long dark years when no one thought that Asians had much of a chance of emulating the European Union."

On Dec. 12, when leaders from 16 Asian countries gather for three days in the Malaysian city of Kuala Lumpur, their deliberations may well determine whether the scenario described above remains a teasing exercise in science fiction—or a genuine vision for the future of the region. The East Asia Summit (EAS) is set to bring together representatives from the ASEAN+3 countries—that's the 10 Southeast Asian nations plus China, Japan and South Korea—and their counterparts from Australia, New Zealand and India. The idea has been percolating for years, but this is the first time that key players in the region have come together for the explicit purpose of deepening integration, not just economically but also politically. The agenda remains vague, but participants will probably talk not only about reducing tariffs and other trade barriers but also about how to intensify cooperation on other fronts, such as energy, avian flu and counterterrorism.

The Asian Development Bank recently revealed that it has started monitoring exchange rates—a move that lays the groundwork for a future Asian currency unit. In a speech in October, ADB president Haruhiko Kuroda discounted the view that the most East Asia can aim for is a NAFTA-type free-trade area. Instead, he argued, "our long-run objective should be the creation of an Asian monetary union with a single currency." He went on to cite the area's deepening intraregional trade as a reason for harmonizing exchange rates (since currency turbulence can have terrible knock-on effects). The benefits could be huge. ASEAN+3 alone encompasses one third of the world's population, one quarter of its GDP and half its foreign-exchange reserves. Some of its members boast the world's highest growth rates. A bloc capable of pooling that entrepreneurial energy and potential resources would represent a potent international force.

Skepticism is clearly warranted. East Asia, critics point out, is hardly comparable to Europe, where the EU members all adhere to a set of shared political values—namely, parliamentary democracy combined with free markets and advanced social-welfare systems. By contrast, the Kuala Lumpur participants include robust democracies (Australia, Japan), communist-capitalist hybrids (China, Vietnam), countries engaged in messy democratization (Cambodia, Indonesia) and one backward military dictatorship (Burma). Territorial disputes abound, and the threat of military conflict hovers fitfully over parts of the region. If anything scuttles the EAS, it could be the continuing tensions between Japan and its neighbors over Prime Minister Junichiro Koizumi's visits to the controversial Yasukuni Shrine war memorial. Last week China and South Korea hinted that, at Kuala Lumpur, the three nations won't be getting together in a summit parallel to the one held by ASEAN nations.

And then there are the vast differentials in national income. The richest countries in the EU are about 10 times more prosperous than the poorest ones (based on purchasing power parity), while in East Asia today the ratio is more like 100 to 1. It's hard to imagine how such diverse economies could manage to establish a true common market any time soon. Given that vast inequality, it's no surprise that one of the hottest topics is labor mobility; at least one Japanese newspaper has already voiced the opinion that the summit is just a clever gambit by Beijing to open up Japan to waves of Chinese immigrants. Most analysts are keeping their expectations modest. Simon Tay, chairman of the Singapore Institute of International Affairs, argues that the best analogy for the EAS at this stage is the G8, the club of major industrial nations that gets together periodically to air common concerns. Notes Tay: "The G8 meets, we all pay attention to it, but what does it actually achieve straightaway?"

True enough. And yet the meeting in Kuala Lumpur may also end up serving as a salutary snapshot of just how much has already been done. Denis Hew, a fellow at the Institute of Southeast Asian Studies in Singapore, says that over the last 20 years East Asian integration has had two main engines: "There has been a lot of foreign direct investment from Japan to the region, and production networks have been formed. China has now become a new member in this configuration, where you see a lot of parts manufactured here being exported to China and then re-exported to Western economies. Both are driving closer integration." Stephen Leong, assistant director-general of the Institute of Strategic and International Studies in Kuala Lumpur, adds: "Now in the region, we have a very basic institution-alization taking place. Our Finance ministers meet, our foreign ministers meet; we are building a structure. We can already see an East Asian community in the works. It is an inevitability."

Eisuke Sakakibara, a former senior Finance Ministry official in Japan, notes that trade among the countries of East Asia has "increased dramatically" over the course of the past decade or so—to an extent that outsiders may not have recognized. According to the ADB, intraregional trade in East Asia in 2003 accounted for 54 percent of total trade—approaching the level of the EU (64 percent) and higher than that of NAFTA (46 percent). The ADB points out that the 54 percent figure is about the same as that in the EU countries when the Maastricht Treaty was signed in 1992. "Economically," asserts Sakakibara, "we've already reached the stage of Europe." In terms of political integration, he concedes, Asia is still far behind, but that's because the process in Asia has been driven by markets rather than by political elites.

That's exactly the opposite of the situation in post-1945 Europe, where national leaders made a conscious decision to draw their region more tightly together as a way of avoiding future wars. East Asia, by contrast, is strikingly lacking in visionaries like the Frenchman Jean Monnet, who dreamed of European political convergence at a time when the idea looked like utter lunacy. (If anyone, the closest Asian equivalent would probably be former South Korean president Kim Dae Jung, who back in 1998 provided the impetus for the current summit.) The flurry of free-trade agreements sweeping the region shows that national leaders have finally started to follow where businesses long since began to tread. Japan, China and South Korea have all signed ASEAN's Treaty of Amity and Cooperation, which calls for the settlement of disputes by peaceful means and non-interference in the internal affairs of other countries. And the ASEAN Regional Forum has been used by ASEAN and China as a "confidence building" mechanism to smooth out security problems in the South China Sea.

If you thought the alphabet soup in Europe was bad, get ready for the East Asian version. EAVG, NEAT, ARF, AMM+3: they're but a few of the regional mechanisms that are already bringing bureaucrats, businessmen and scholars together to puzzle out shared concerns. ASEAN+3, now in its ninth year, has 48 ongoing projects promoting community building and economic integration. The so-called Chiang Mai Initiative brings together central banks from the ASEAN+3 countries in a forum aimed at preventing a recurrence of the financial crisis that shook the region in 1997. Then there's the Asian Bond Fund, inaugurated by the ADB, which has been quietly trying to enhance the liquidity and stability of regional bond markets. Masahiro Kawai, head of the ADB office of regional economic integration and special adviser to the ADB president, tells NEWSWEEK that while the idea of a common currency "has a long way to go," it "will help increase trade, investments and cross-border economic transactions, because of the stable exchange rate."

While those are priorities for Southeast Asian nations—trade between ASEAN and China has been surging by 20 percent annually in recent years—they're also concerned with reining in a newly powerful China. The Japanese voice similar concerns. When Japan learned that the United States hadn't been invited to the summit, Tokyo lobbied vigorously for including Australia and India as counterweights to China. Although irked by America's perceived failure to help out after the 1997 financial crisis, many leaders in the region are not eager to replace U.S. leadership with Chinese hegemony.

Still, when the dust settles in Kuala Lumpur, the summit will probably be judged less on the basis of grand strategic calculations than on the nuts-and-bolts issues that promise to deliver economic growth. One of those invited to the EAS is Tony Fernandes, CEO of AirAsia, a no-frills airline that's arguably the only ASEAN regional brand. He credits ASEAN with helping to keep the peace, but sees plenty of room for measures that would promote his business—tax incentives for cross-border investment, greater labor mobility, industry deregulation. His airline still doesn't have full landing rights in Singapore, so many of his planes are landing at a nearby airport in Malaysia. One of his biggest headaches, says Fernandes, is getting approval for a bus that can bring passengers across the border between the two countries. In short, before any grand dream can be realized, lots of little problems must be solved.

With Joe Cochrane in Bangkok, Marites D. Vitug in Manila, Sonia Kolesnikov-Jessop in Singapore and Lorien Holland in Kuala Lumpur.

Editor's Note: The original version of this report incorrectly stated that South Korea, China and Japan had announced that the three nations would not be holding a tripartite summit parallel to the one held by ASEAN nations. In fact, the three countries had not made any formal statement to this effect at the time this piece was written.

Where the Money Went

**How did developing countries wind up owing $2.5 trillion?
Hint: Western institutions haven't exactly been innocent bystanders.**

JAMES S. HENRY

By the dawn of the 21st century, after 30 years of development strategies that were designed in Washington, New York, London, Frankfurt, Paris, and Tokyo, and trillions of dollars in foreign loans, aid, and investment, more than half of the world's population still finds daily life a struggle, surviving on less than $2 a day—about the same level of real income they had 30 years ago. More than two billion people still lack access to basic amenities like electricity, clean water, sanitation, land titles, police and fire protection, and paved roads, let alone their own phones, bank accounts, or medical care.

And despite years of rhetoric about debt relief and dozens of structural adjustment plans, the real value of Third World debt has continued to grow, to more than $2.5 trillion. The cost of servicing that debt now exceeds $375 billion a year—more than all Third World spending on health or education, almost 20 times what developing countries receive each year in foreign aid, and more than twice as much as they have recently received annually in foreign direct investment.

How did 30 years of greatly expanded international lending, investment, aid, and development efforts end up producing such a fiasco? Where did all that money actually go? And what can we do, if anything, to undo all the damage that has been done?

There is no shortage of armchair analyses of the so-called Third World debt crisis, or even of the globalization crisis that succeeded it and continues to this day. The 1980s debt crisis became visible as early as August 1982, when Mexico, Argentina, and 26 other countries suddenly rescheduled their debts at once. Our disappointments with globalization have been a popular subject for economists and development policy-makers at least since the Mexico crunch of January 1995, as amplified by the East Asian and Russian crises in 1997–98, and in Turkey, Ecuador, Bolivia, Argentina, Venezuela, and other countries since then.

But there has been no detailed account of the *structural roots* of this prolonged development crisis. Among orthodox economists, the conventional wisdom is that the crisis originated in a combination of unpredictable shocks and Third World policies that were either stupid or corrupt, on top of factors like bad geo-graphic luck. In other words, we have a slightly more sophisticated version of the same blame-the-victim ideology that ruling elites have used for centuries to explain poverty and wealth: It is either "tough luck" or "their own damn fault."

For example, the conventional view of the 1980s debt crisis is that, in response to the 1973 oil-price rise, Western banks recycled oil deposits from the Middle East back to the Third World, lending to finance oil imports and development projects. Independently, a huge tidal wave of capital flight sprang up alongside all this lending. Then an unfortunate combination of events—rising interest rates, recession, and the 1982 Falklands conflict—supposedly took everyone by surprise. In this version of the crisis, no one was responsible for it. There were no villains or victims—just innocent bystanders.

Conventional portraits of the global development crisis are fairy tales.

Similarly, in the case of more recent debacles in submerging markets like Indonesia and Thailand, the official story is that these resulted almost entirely from Third World mistakes and market imperfections; poorly designed bank regulations, faulty accounting, inexplicable failures to privatize and liberalize fast enough, or indigenous "corruption, cronyism, and collusion." The notion that there might be serious oversimplifications in the development paradigms themselves, that Western banks, investors, policy-makers, and the structure of international capital markets might have aggravated such problems—or that they might have conspired with local elites and even taught them a thing or two about "clever chicanery"—has received much less attention. And while numerous globalization critics have recently emerged, including some prominent economists and international investors as well as a rising tide of mass protesters, much of this criticism has dealt in generalities, lacking the gory investigative details needed to drive the points home and do justice to the problem's global scale.

Behind the Official Story

The fact is that conventional portraits of the global development crisis are economists' fairy tales. They leave out the blood and guts of what really happened—all the payoffs for privatizations, fraudulent loans, intentionally wasteful projects, black market "round-trip" transfers, arms deals, insider deals, and the behind-the-scenes operation of the global-haven banking network that has facilitated all this and more. They ignore the fact that in the mid-1970s, and again in the mid-1990s, repeated warnings of deep trouble were ignored: Irresponsible overlending, poorly conceived projects and privatizations, phony back-to-back loans, outright looting of central-bank reserves, and massive capital flight continued right under the noses of Western bankers and government officials who were in a position to do something about the problems but chose not to.

This begs the question of why some developing countries and banks got into so much more trouble than others, and why certain bankers, investors, and officials got rich. Standard analyses focus on uncontrollable shocks to the system, skate far too quickly over the structure of that system itself, and ignore the systematic role of specific global interests in shaping this structure.

Most importantly, the official story of shocks, surprises, and indigenous corruption ignores the pivotal role that was often played by sophisticated banks and multinationals. They were aided by their governments and the local elites in pressing countries first to overborrow, then to overservice their debts—to honor their overpriced privatization contracts—and then to liberalize and privatize far too quickly. Many of these players were also aggressively recruiting flight capital and investment deals from these very same countries and teaching their clients the basics of how to launder, plunder, and conceal.

The conventional fairy tales gloss over many key questions. What really became of all the loans and investments? Why did foreign banks lend so much money to these governments, even while their private banking arms knew full well that they were financing a massive capital-flight exodus? Who ended up owning all the juicy assets? How much did the IMF and the World Bank know about all these shenanigans, and why didn't they do more to stop them?

It is not easy to give precise answers to such questions. Studying the global underground economy is an exercise in night vision, not double-entry accounting or armchair analysis. One actually has to get up out of the armchair and do some investigative reporting. And the patterns that become visible turn out to be full of villains and victims.

Unfortunately, it has taken years to uncover the truth about such matters, and we've really only begun to scratch the surface. In the last decade, bits and pieces of this story have become more accessible. The demise of "kleptocracies" like those of Abacha, Andres Perez, Collor, Duvalier, Marcos, Mobuto, Milosevic, Salinas, Suharto, and Stroessner focused attention on the billions that such nefarious regimes managed to steal and stash abroad. The collapse of leading money-laundering banks like BCCI and BNL, and the corrupt regimes of Salinas in Mexico, Menem in Argentina, the ruling cliques in Turkey, and Suharto in Indonesia demonstrated the risks that corrupt banking poses to the entire global financial system.

However, partly because this kind of investigative research is so difficult, there are only a few rather armchairish studies of the global underground economy and the "real-economique" of underdevelopment. And these have also usually treated the subjects of irresponsible lending, wasteful projects, capital flight, corruption, money laundering, and havens separately, In fact, they go hand in hand. The rise of Third World lending in the 1970s and 1980s laid the foundations for the haven network that now shelters the wealth of the world's most venal citizens. And the corruption that this network facilitated was just a special case of a much more general phenomenon—the export of vast quantities of capital and tax-free incomes by the elites of poor countries, even as their countries were incurring vast debts and struggling to service them. Individual kleptocratic regimes and evil dictators come and go, but this sophisticated transnational system is more vibrant than ever.

A Marshall Plan in Reverse

This haven network has matured in the last 30 years, coinciding with the rise of global lending, the liberalization of capital markets, and the development crisis. Of course, "private banking" is hardly new. Except for electronic transfers and airplanes, most of its paraphernalia—secret accounts, shell companies, black-market exchanges, mis-invoicing, back-to-back loans, and backdated transactions—were very important early innovations in the history of capitalism. They helped to bring "mattress money" out into the open so that it could be productively invested.

For decades, these tools were underutilized. Then, from the 1970s through the 1990s, their use expanded tremendously under the impact of the greatest torrent of loose lending in history. This torrent was driven by a coalition of influential interests that included leading Western private banks, equipment vendors, and construction companies—plus their allies among aid donors, export finance agencies, the multilateral banks, and local elites. It drove a hole in developing-country defenses against overborrowing and created a source of fundamental instability in the world's financial system that continues to this day.

It is possible to estimate the volume and composition of the flight capital that was financed by all this lending. Sag Harbor Group estimates rely on a combination of statistical methods and interviews with more than 100 private bankers and their wealthy clients. They show that at least *half* the funds borrowed by the largest "debtor" countries flowed right out the back door, usually the same year or even the same month that the loans arrived. For the developing world as a whole, this amounted to a huge Marshall Plan in reverse.

The corresponding stock of unrecorded foreign wealth owned by Third World elites is even larger than these outflows, since the outflows were typically invested in tax havens where—unlike the earnings of low-income "guest workers"—they accumulate tax-free interest, dividends, and capital gains. By the late 1980s, there was already enough anonymous Third World flight wealth on hand in Europe and the United States that the income it generated would have been able to service the *entire* Third World debt—if only this stock of "anonymous capital" had been subjected to a modest global tax. By the late 1990s, the market value of private wealth accumulated outside developing countries by their resident elites totaled at least $1.5 trillion. As one Federal Reserve official chuckled at the time, "The problem is not that these countries don't have any assets. The problem is, they're in Miami."

Most of the resulting flight wealth—defined simply as foreign capital whose true ownership is concealed—ended up in just a handful of First World havens. Their identity may surprise those who usually associate "tax havens" and money laundering with obscure nameplate banks in sultry tropical paradises. BCCI's exceptional case notwithstanding, shady banks have never been very important in the flight market—most rich people would never trust them. Rather, Third World decapitalization has taken place with the active aid of pre-eminent global financial institutions, including Citigroup, JP Morgan Chase (Chemical MHT), UBS, Barclays, Credit Suisse First Boston, ABN-AMRO Merrill Lynch, ING Bank, the Bank of New York, American Express Bank, and two dozen other leading Swiss, British, Dutch, French, German, and Austrian banks. These august institutions led the way in knowingly facilitating these perverse capital flows. In fact, despite their reputations as lenders, many of these institutions were actually net borrowers from poor countries for most of the last 30 years. International private banking—a large share of which was for Third World elites—thus became one of their most profitable lines of business.

The leading global banks were successful at profiting from Third World grief.

Because their leading global banks were so successful at profiting from Third World grief, the United States, the United Kingdom, and Switzerland were also—despite their reputations as major capital providers and aid donors—net debtors with respect to the Third World throughout the last 30 years. It is really misleading to speak of a "Third World debt" crisis—for developing countries, it has really been an *assets* crisis, while for these key First World countries and their banks, it was an incredibly profitable *global bleed-out*.

The upshot is that ownership of Third Wealth onshore and offshore wealth is even more concentrated than it was before the 1980s debt crisis and the 1990s privatization wave. Depending on the country, the top 1 percent of households now accounts for 70 to 90 percent of all private financial wealth and real estate. We are not talking about millions of diligent middle-class savers. These are the 700 members of the Rio Country Club, the 1,000 top landowners of Argentina, El Salvador's *catorce*, the 50 top families of Caracas, the 300 top families of Mexico City, and so on. These are not people who merely observe the rules of the game. When a minister builds a dam, nationalizes a private company or its debts, privatizes a state enterprise, and floats a currency or manipulates tax provisions, these folks have the inside track. This is not to say that there are no new self-made

Third World elites, or that the top tier is limited to capitalists—there are also quite a few politicians, generals, diplomats, union bosses, and even a bishop or cardinal.

Conventional explanations ignore the international community's responsibility.

But the overall system is beautifully symbiotic. On the one hand, havens provide an ideal way to launder loot. On the other, in the long run, corruption, insider deals, and the inequalities they generate encourage still more disinvestments and emigration. For individuals living in these countries, of course, the incentives for engaging in money laundering were often so powerful that it would have been quixotic not to do so. At the macroeconomic level, however, conventional explanations of capital flight, overborrowing, and mismanaged privatizations, which focus on technical policy errors and the "riskiness" of Third World markets, ignore these systemic factors. They also ignore the international community's collective responsibility for perpetuating a system that encourages noneconomic lending, tax evasion, flight-prone speculative investments, and perverse privatizations.

The Borderline of Existence

Other key ingredients in the "money trail" puzzle, in addition to capital flight, were wasteful projects and arms purchases. Hundreds of billions of Third World loans were devoted to nonproductive projects and the corruption that encouraged them. Many of these debt-financed projects also had harmful long-term consequences. In some cases, there was novel chicanery on a purely local level. But what is most striking are the global patterns—overpricing, rigged bids, endless delays, loans to front companies with close ties to the government, investments in dubious technologies and excessively capital-intensive projects, "public" projects undertaken for private motives, and private debts assumed by the state.

Over and over again, the handiwork of the very same international banks, contractors, equipment vendors, and export credit agencies grew fat while the countries grew poorer. These were not ideological errors—regimes of different ideological hues proved equally vulnerable. Nor were they due to random policy mistakes or indigenous corruption. A sophisticated *transnational system* of influential institutions contrived to produce similar mistakes over and over again, in every region of the world. Corruption has always existed, but without this global system, the abuses simply could not have been generalized on such a massive scale.

Recently, some of the leading players in the global haven industry, Citigroup and JP Morgan Chase, had also applied their "haveneering" skills to help Enron, WorldCom, and Global Crossing, using Panama and Cayman Islands shell companies to conceal billions in off-balance-sheet loans from their stockholders. When this scandal surfaced in 2001-02, the resulting bankruptcies cost investors several hundred billion dollars. Analysts who had not followed the history of these banks in the Third World were shocked ... shocked! Those who knew them better were just reminded that "character is destiny" and that "what goes around comes around." As a wise, rather ethical business colleague of mine once said, "The problem with a rat race is that, even if you win, you are still a rat."

The emphasis on these darker details is not meant to imply that every banker was a briber, or every public official a crook. But dirty money, bad banking, money laundering, and self-seeking chicanery were not incidental to the development crisis. As a governor of the Bank of International Settlements admitted privately in the late 1980s, "If Latin America's corrupt politicians simply gave back all the money they've stolen from their own countries, the debt problem could be solved. And most of that thievery simply could not have occurred without the active assistance of leading First World banks, contractors, vendors, multilateral lenders, advisors, and governments. This was not a natural catastrophe but a *manmade* one. For the developing world to overcome it, it is not only the developing world that will have to be reformed."

Today, despite decades of official development efforts and trillions in foreign loans, bonds, and investments, the vast majority of the world's residents are living on the borderline of existence. Yet the "developing countries" they inhabit are not really poor at all, in terms of natural resources, technical know-how, and raw human talent.

Some have searched for the explanation among the natural disadvantages of climate, pestilence, and topography that many of these countries experience. Some have pointed toward cultural deficiencies—for example, a purported lack of trust outside the family in some countries, or an unusual propensity for corruption at all levels of society in others. Some have invoked the *deus ex machina* of "policy errors" like overvalued exchange rates, excessive borrowing, and weak security laws, as if these were uncaused causes and as if policy was made in a disinterested vacuum, where ministers don't own bank accounts and everything would have worked out fine if only they'd been Ivy-educated. Still others have emphasized the ill winds of misfortune to which developing countries are subject—the HIV/AIDS epidemic in Africa, China, India, and Russia; Indonesia's bad luck in having Thailand as a neighbor when its currency plummeted in July 1997, Brazil's bad luck in having Russia's 1998 crisis compound Indonesia's, Argentina's in having Brazil as a neighbor, and so on.

These explanations are all the profound contribution that First World countries and their global agents have made, not only in the last 30 years but for much longer, in tolerating, contributing to, and profiting from the immiseration around them.

If one really looks objectively at why countries like the Philippines, Guatemala, Indonesia, the Congo, South Africa, Argentina, Venezuela, Brazil, Mexico, Haiti, and India have ended up as they have in the world economy, one cannot ignore the negative influence of First World corporations, governments, and financial institutions. As a rule, the closer and more unequal those relationships have been, the worse things have turned out for developing countries.

Today, the developing world is in its deepest crisis in a half-century. The First World, now so concerned about security, needs to place these security concerns and the "war on terrorism" in the context of an even more global war—underdevelopment. The world is simply getting too rickety, too interdependent, for us to ignore this other war any longer. Forest fires in the Amazon or Kalimantan set by poor people clearing land because they can't find jobs threaten the whole world's air supply. Epidemics left untreated in Africa or Russia threaten to create drug-resistant diseases that could sweep the planet. And the hatred bred by the real "weapons of mass destruction"—outrageous poverty and inequality—are only a plane or boat ride away in Port-au-Prince, Jakarta, Cairo, Kabul, and Karachi.

The first step is understanding. First Worlders, in particular, are living in a bubble—only about 20 percent of Americans have passports, just 21 percent of non-Hispanic Americans speak a second language, less than a fifth of adults have traveled abroad, and a poll taken in late 2002 showed that only 13 percent of 18-to-24-year-olds in the United States could even find Iraq on a map, 14 percent could find Israel, 31 percent could find the United Kingdom, and 42 percent could find Japan, and only two-thirds could even find the Pacific Ocean. This kind of ignorance is not just unfortunate. It is dangerous. It is especially menacing to the citizens of the Third World, because the First World now has more political, economic, and military hegemony than ever before. It is also a menace to ourselves, because if this power is not used wisely, a growing portion of the Third World will simply disappear into "the Fourth World," a vast, impoverished, hostile labor camp without visitors or investments. And that, in turn, will only heighten our insecurities, raise the drawbridge even higher, and increase hostilities.

Those who wish to alter these current trends toward immiseration and anti-development may choose to put their faith in the global economy, free trade, investment, technology, and entrepreneurship. But these market-based nostrums have not been sufficient. To go beyond them, people will need to invest in their own globalization, their own practical education about how the world really works.

Today, the developing world is in its deepest crisis in a half-century.

This kind of education is not available in university economics courses. People need to understand why political parties, the police, the military, the media, the courts, and the church are often so unresponsive to popular demands, even in nominal "democracies"; why senior officials, banks, corporations, and the elite continue to prefer monster projects to schools and clinics; why courts rarely enforce laws against people of means, let alone global companies like Freeport McMoran or Citigroup; why the radical liberalization of global capital markets and trade has taken precedence over the enforcement of tax codes, labor laws, health codes, security regulation, environmental laws, education rights, pension reform, and property rights for ordinary people; and why the poor are subject to unavoidable excise taxes while the elite are encouraged to invest, tax-free, at home and abroad.

They also need to ask why developed and developing countries alike, after 50 years of malpractice, still permit First World bankers, corporations, and investors to engage in business practices in the Third World that are grossly illegal; why the anti-foreign bribery statutes of the United States and the OECD countries are so underenforced; why undocumented capital is recruited so aggressively from developing countries while undocumented labor is increasingly harassed; and why the huge proportion of the Third World's $2.5 trillion debt that was con-tracted illegally and spent on failed projects and elite bank accounts deserve to be serviced at all.

But first, they may want to start with the question of where the money went.

JAMES S. HENRY is founder and managing director of the Sag Harbor Group, a strategy consulting firm, former chief economist for McKinsey & Co., and former vice president of strategy for IBM/Lotus. From *The Blood Bankers: Tales From the Underground Global Economy* (Four Walls Eight Windows). © 2003

Asymmetric Globalization

Global Markets Require Good Global Politics

NANCY BIRDSALL

The globalization of markets can benefit—and has benefited—rich and poor alike. But the integration of the global economy is outpacing the development of a healthy global polity. To realize the values and rules critical to a secure and just world—and to make the full benefits of a global market available to all—will require a better global politics.

The debate about the implications of market-led globalization for the poor has taken on new urgency in the past several years. On one side are most mainstream economists, international institutions such as the United Nations and the World Bank, most finance ministers and central bank governors in poor and rich nations alike, and most professional students of development. They argue that globalization is not to blame for any increase in world poverty and inequality—and point out that the world's poorest people, those living in rural Africa and South Asia, are those least touched by globalization. On the other side of the debate are most social activists, members of nonprofit civil society groups who work on environmental issues, human rights, and relief programs, most of the popular press, and many sensible, well-educated observers. To them, the issue seems self-evident. Globalization may be good for the rich countries and the rich within countries, but it is bad news for the poorest countries and especially for the poor in those countries.

One central issue is whether the current distribution of economic and political power in the world is just or fair—whether it provides for equal opportunities to those who are poor and, in global affairs, relatively powerless. On this score, I believe it is time for the first group to internalize the arguments of the second and recognize the need for an improved global politics, in which more democratic and legitimate representation of the poor and the disenfranchised in managing the global economy mediates the downside of more integrated and productive global markets.

Globalization, Poverty, Inequality

Most developing countries began to be tied into the world economy only in the 1980s. Before that, although they participated in some multilateral trade agreements, special preferences permitted them to protect their own markets. In the 1980s, however, and increasingly in the 1990s, most developing countries took steps to open and liberalize their markets. In addition to reducing and eliminating tariffs and nontariff barriers, they made fiscal and monetary reforms, privatized and deregulated their economies, eliminated interest rate ceilings, and, in the 1990s, opened capital markets—a package that came to be known as the Washington Consensus. These market reforms and accompanying, often socially painful, structural changes were encouraged and supported by the International Monetary Fund, the World Bank, and the U.S. Treasury with large loans typically conditioned on countries' adopting and implementing agreed policies. The increasing reliance on markets in the developing world and, in the 1990s, in the countries of the former Soviet empire is with good reason seen as part and parcel of globalization. And because of the conditioned loans, many opponents of globalization today see the turn to the market—and thus to global capitalism—as imposed on the developing countries. (Ironically, the loans often were disbursed even when agreed conditions were not implemented.)

With the growing influence of markets in the past two decades have come changes in global inequality and world poverty. Over the past century, global inequality by most measures has been growing. At the end of the 19th century, the ratio of the average income of the richest to the poorest country in the world was 9 to 1. Today the average family in the United States is 60 times richer than the average family in Ethiopia or Bangladesh (in terms of purchasing power). The increase in inequality is the result of a simple reality. Today's rich countries, already richer 100 years ago (thanks to the Industrial Revolution), have been blessed with economic growth and have gotten a whole lot richer. Poorer countries, poor to start with, have grown little if at all.

In the past two decades, the picture has changed a bit. Some developing countries, including China and more recently India, have grown faster than the already rich countries. Incomes in China and India will not soon equal those in rich countries—it would take them almost a century of faster growth even to reach current U.S. levels. Still, some developing countries have done some dramatic catching up.

And the rapid growth in India and China has caused world poverty to decline. Between 1987 and 1998, the share of the world's population that is poor (using World Bank figures and the Bank's poverty line of $1 a day in 1985 dollars) fell from about 25 percent to 21 percent; the absolute number fell from an estimated 1.2 billion to 1.1 billion. The decline was concentrated in India and China; elsewhere in the developing world, numbers rose.

Measured in yet another way—by a "world" distribution of income that ranks all individuals or households around the world according to income, giving each person (or household) the same weight in the distribution—world inequality is extremely high but is leveling off. Although today the richest fifth of world households is about 25 times richer than the poorest fifth, in the past 20 years the rapid growth of India and China has slowed increases in world inequality. (The world distribution of course gives much greater weight to these high-population countries.)

At the world level, then, it is fair to say that poverty is declining and inequality is not increasing. Today's global inequality is mostly a matter of differences between rich and poor countries in past rates of growth. That brings us back to the main argument of globalization's proponents: countries that have successfully entered the global market and participated in globalization have grown most. Historically, that included Japan, beginning in the Meiji era between 1868 and 1912, the poorer countries of Western Europe during the 19th century and then again after World War II, and the so-called miracle economies of East Asia between about 1970 and 1998. More recently, it has included China and India, as well as Bangladesh, Brazil, Malaysia, Mexico, Mozambique, the Philippines, Thailand, Uganda, and Vietnam. Poverty remains highest in the countries, including many in Africa and some in South Asia, and among people, especially in the rural areas of China, India, and Latin America, that are marginal to global markets. To the extent that globalization has "caused" increasing inequality, it is not because some have benefited a lot—a good thing—but because others have been left out altogether.

Globalization Is Not the Solution

But if globalization is not the cause, neither is it the solution to the world's continuing poverty and haunting inequality. Consider the plight of many of the world's poorest countries. Highly dependent on primary commodity and natural resource exports in the early 1980s, they have been "open" for at least two decades, as measured by their ratio of imports and exports to GDP. But unable to diversify into manufacturing (despite reducing their own import tariffs), they have seen the relative world prices of their commodity exports fall—and have been left behind. Despite rising exports, tariff reductions, and market-oriented reforms including greater fiscal and monetary discipline and the divestiture of unproductive state enterprises, they have been unable to increase their export income, failed to attract foreign investment, and grown little if at all.

Many of these countries in sub-Saharan Africa, as well as Haiti, Nepal, and Nicaragua, seem trapped in a vicious circle of low or unstable export revenue, weak and sometimes predatory government, terrible disease burdens (the HIV/AIDS pandemic

being only one recent example), and failure to deliver to their children education and the other services that are critical to sustainable growth. For these countries, despite efforts by their governments to enter global markets, globalization has not worked. Success in global markets might come with success in growth and development itself, but it is not likely to come on its own.

For better-off emerging market economies, globalization has failed to work in a second way. For them global trade has been generally a boom, but global financial markets pretty much a bust. In the past decade, Mexico, Korea, Thailand, Indonesia, Russia, Brazil, Ecuador, and Turkey, and this year Argentina, were all hit by financial crises triggered or made worse by their exposure to global financial markets. Weak local financial markets and wary local and foreign creditors made these countries highly vulnerable to the panicked withdrawal of capital typical of bank runs. And the resulting financial instability was especially costly for the working poor and the emerging middle class. In Turkey, Argentina, and Mexico, hit repeatedly by inflation and currency devaluations in the past two decades, wealthy citizens move substantial financial assets abroad, often simultaneously acquiring bank and corporate debt that is then socialized and paid by taxpayers, worsening inequality—and certainly appearing unfair. In parts of Asia and much of Latin America, inequality had already increased during the mid-1990s boom as portfolio inflows and high bank lending fueled demand for assets, such as land and stocks, owned by the rich.

In both regions the poor and working class gained the least during the boom and then lost the most, certainly relative to their most basic needs, in the post-crisis bust. The high interest rates that the affected countries used to stabilize their currencies also hurt most small capital-starved enterprises and their low-wage employees. The bank bailouts that often follow financial crises create public debt that again implies a transfer from taxpayers to rentiers. China and India, whose capital markets remained relatively closed, survived the financial crises of the late 1990s better than did Mexico, Argentina, and Thailand. More open trade is good for growth and benefits the poor, but the effects of the rapid and near-complete opening of capital markets pushed by the IMF and the U.S. Treasury throughout the 1990s were not so benign. No wonder social activists are suspicious of corporate and financial influence in global markets.

Opportunities in the global economy are not equal.

A third problem with globalization has been that privatizing and liberalizing financial markets in the absence of adequate regulatory institutions and banking standards and supervision invite corruption. Russia is only the most visible example. Open capital markets make it easier for corrupt leaders to burden their own taxpayers with official and private debt while padding their own foreign bank accounts. Unregulated markets make money laundering and tax evasion easier and raise the costs asymmetrically for poor countries to defend their own tax systems. Global capital markets do not cause all these problems, but like an occasion of sin they increase the likelihood that human failings will corrupt the system, usually at a cost to the poor and powerless.

Unequal Opportunities

Not all the suspicions of the activists are necessarily warranted. But the activists are right in one important respect. The opportunities in the global economy are not equal.

In the global market, those without the right training and equipment can easily lose. That is because markets that are bigger and deeper reward more efficiently those countries and those people who already have productive assets. For people the relevant assets include financial, physical, and, perhaps most crucial today, human capital. For countries what matters are healthy and stable country institutions—established political systems, secure property rights, adequate banking supervision, reasonable public services. It is no accident that 80 percent of all foreign investment occurs among the industrialized countries—and that just 0.1 percent of all U.S. foreign investment went to sub-Saharan Africa last year.

At the individual level, the best example of how healthy markets can generate unequal opportunities is the rising returns to higher education throughout the world. In the high-tech global economy, the supply of university-educated people has not been keeping up with ever-increasing demand, leading to wage gains for college graduates and wage losses for those with high school education or less. Just about everywhere in the world (Cuba, China, Kerala state in India, all socialist entities being exceptions), education reinforces initial advantages instead of compensating for initial handicaps.

The global market for skilled and talented people is another illustration of the asymmetrical effect of markets. The highly skilled are highly mobile. Indian engineers can quadruple their earnings by moving from Kerala to Silicon Valley. For the individuals concerned, this "brain drain" is a good thing, and eventually it can generate offsetting remittances and return investments if the institutional and policy setting in India and other poor countries improves. But in the short run, it makes it harder for the poorer countries to build those institutions and improve those policies. The annual loss to India of its brain drain to the United States is estimated at $2 billion. The farmers and workers whose taxes finance education in poor countries are subsidizing the citizens of the rich countries—whose tax revenues are boosted by the immigrants' contributions.

The efficiency gains and increased potential for growth of a global market economy are not to be disdained. Rising wage gaps in open and competitive markets should not surprise or alarm us: they may be the short-term price worth paying for higher long-run sustainable growth. They create the right incentives for more people to acquire more education, in principle eventually reducing inequality. But in modern market economies, a well-defined social contract tempers the excess inequalities of income and opportunity that efficient markets easily

generate. Progressive tax systems provide for some redistribution, with the state financing at least minimal educational opportunities for all and some social and old-age insurance. There is no global analogue.

When the Market Fails

Global market failures also raise new costs for the vulnerable and compound the risks faced by the already weak and disadvantaged. The rich countries that historically have the highest per capita greenhouse gas emissions have not internalized the costs of their pollution but have imposed them on the poor countries, whose citizens have few resources to protect themselves.

Financial contagion across countries, affecting even those emerging market economies with relatively sound domestic policies, can also hit hardest the already vulnerable. Financial contagion has not only brought instability and slower growth to Latin America and East Asia; it has weakened their capacity to develop and sustain institutions and programs to protect their own poor. With global market players doubting the commitment of nonindustrialized countries to fiscal rectitude at the time of any shock, countries are forced to tighten fiscal and monetary policy to reestablish market confidence, rather than stimulate their economies to combat recession. These austerity policies are the opposite of the policies the industrial economies implement—reduced interest rates, unemployment insurance, increased availability of food stamps and public works employment. All these are fundamental ingredients of a modern social contract. And the effects of unemployment and bankruptcy can be permanent for the poor. In Mexico, increases in child labor that cut school enrollment during the 1995 crisis were not reversed: some children did not return to school when growth resumed.

Those concerned with global justice face a daunting problem of global collective action.

Contagious diseases, transnational crime, and potentially beneficial but risky new technologies such as genetically modified foods also entail asymmetric costs and risks for poor countries and poor people. Similarly, poor countries that protect global resources such as tropical forests and biological diversity are paying the full costs but are unable to capture the full benefits of these global goods. Within countries, governments temper market failures through regulations, taxes and subsidies, and fines; and they share the benefits of such public goods as security, military defense, management of natural disasters, and public health through their tax and expenditure decisions. Ideally those decisions are made in a democratic system with fair and legitimate representation of all people, independent of their wealth. In nations, such political systems seldom work perfectly. In the global community, a comparable political system just barely exists.

Economic Power and Global Rules

Unequal opportunities for the poor, and the risk they bear when the market fails, are not the whole story. In the global game, economic power matters. The rich and powerful can influence the design and implementation of global rules to their own advantage. Political constraints in rich and powerful countries dominate, for example, the design of global trade rules. The resulting protection in the United States and Europe of agriculture and textiles—both sectors that could generate jobs for the unskilled—locks many of the world's poorest countries out of potential markets. The U.S. African Growth and Opportunity Act and the European Union's recent initiative to eliminate all barriers to imports from the world's 49 poorest countries are steps in the right direction—but very small steps indeed since the countries that can benefit make up only a minuscule proportion of all world production. And even those initiatives were watered down considerably by domestic political pressures and include complicated rules that create uncertainty and limit big increases in poor-country exports.

Political constraints also affect the way trade rules are implemented. Complicated negotiations and dispute resolution put countries with limited resources at a disadvantage. The use of antidumping actions by U.S. producers, even when they are unlikely to win a dispute on its merits, creates onerous legal and other costs to producers in developing countries and chills new job-creating investment in affected sectors. About half of antidumping actions are directed against developing country producers, who account for 8 percent of all exports.

International migration too is governed by rules stacked against the developing countries, especially their poor and unskilled citizens. Permanent migration has slowed because higher-income countries restrict immigration. In the 25 years before World War I, 10 percent of the world's people changed their permanent country residence; in the past 25 years, that figure has fallen to 2 percent. Yet just as the huge influx of Europeans to the Americas in the 19th century reduced inequality, more migration today would do the same. An auto mechanic in Ghana can quintuple his income just by moving to Italy. During the recent information technology boom, the United States allowed highly skilled workers to enter with temporary visas—a boom, no doubt, for the beneficiaries, but also a drain on the working taxpayers in poorer countries who helped educate them and yet another example of the capacity of the already rich to exploit their power.

Economic power also affects the rules and conduct of the international institutions. The International Monetary Fund is meant to help countries manage macroeconomic imbalances and minimize the risks of financial shocks. But in the 1990s the IMF, heavily influenced by its richer members, was too enthusiastic in urging developing countries to open their capital accounts. Even when the policies supported by the IMF and the World Bank have made sense—and I believe for the most part they have—the policymakers have no real accountability to the people in developing countries most affected by them. Develop-

ing countries are poorly represented in these institutions' voting and other forms of governance.

A New Agenda of Good Global Politics

That poverty is declining worldwide and inequality is leveling off are not signs that all is well in our new globalized economy. Proponents of market-led globalization must recognize that the global economy is not addressing the problems of poverty and inequality and is ridden with asymmetries that add up to unequal opportunities. Social activists must rethink their demands for dismantling the limited institutions for managing globalization's downside. Both groups must join forces to push a new global agenda, aiming for a new global politics to accompany the global economy.

Statements of social and economic rights in the United Nations and relatively minor transfers of financial and technical resources from rich to poor countries are as close as we have come to anything like a global social contract. Anyone arriving from another planet into our highly unequal global economy would have to conclude that rich countries have no interest in doing anything much to help the poor in poor countries—surprising given what could be their enlightened self-interest in a more secure and prosperous global economy. The logic of a global social contract is clear, but it cannot be constructed out of nothing. As is the case within countries, a social contract involves some transfers—for investments in the human capital and the local institutions that can ensure equal opportunities for the poor.

Past mistakes in foreign aid policy—multiple and onerous standards of different donors, conditionality that doesn't work—should not be an excuse for the rich countries' minimal spending on foreign aid. With many poor countries consolidating reforms, their ability to spend resources productively now far exceeds the amount of aid available. In the industrialized economies, domestic social contracts—public transfers for investing in education, health, and housing and for social-safety-net programs such as unemployment and disability insurance and welfare and pension programs—usually amount to more than 10 percent of GDP. Foreign aid for a global social contract is below 0.5 percent of rich countries' combined GDPs.

Most important, the global and regional institutions that are the world's most obvious mechanisms for managing a global social contract must be reformed, not dismantled. It is ironic that the World Bank and the IMF have been the lightning rods for antiglobalization protests. Accused of being too powerful, they may well be too limited in their resources and insufficiently effective to manage a global contract that would bring equal education, health, and other opportunities to the poor in poor countries. Making these institutions more representative and more accountable to those most affected by their programs, and thus more effective, has to be on the agenda of better global politics.

That agenda must also include opening rich-country markets to developing countries and rethinking the rich world's restrictions on immigration of the unskilled. Developing countries should also be more fully and fairly represented in international institutions, especially the financial institutions, whose policies and programs are so central to their development prospects.

Those concerned with global justice, whether economists and finance ministers or activists, face a daunting problem of global collective action. They need to make a common agenda for a global social contract. In practical terms that means working together in the short run to build a more level playing field in global governance. It means insisting that a new global development architecture be based on good global politics and not just expanded global markets.

NANCY BIRDSALL is president of the Center for Global Development. This article is drawn from a speech given at the Carter Center in February 2002.

Will the World Run Dry?

Global Water and Food Security

MARK W. ROSEGRANT, XIMING CAI, AND SARAH A. CLINE

Demand for the world's increasingly scarce water supply is rising rapidly, challenging its availability for food production and putting global food security at risk. Agriculture, upon which a burgeoning population depends for food, is competing with industrial, household, and environmental uses for this scarce water supply. Even as demand for water by all users grows, groundwater is being depleted, other water ecosystems are becoming polluted and degraded, and developing new sources of water is becoming more costly.

These challenges are receiving significant international attention, notably with the third World Water Forum that was convened in Japan from 16 to 23 March 2003. This meeting was the third in a series of meetings held every three years, bringing together water experts, government leaders, representatives from nongovernmental organizations (NGOs), and other interested parties to examine the major dilemmas facing the water sector and to seek solutions to these problems. The third forum hosted more than 24,000 participants from more than 180 countries and held sessions focusing on many of the most crucial water issues facing the world today. Some of the key issues addressed include the need for safe, clean water for all individuals; good governance in water management, including an integrated water resources management approach; capacity building, including education and access to information; financing of water resources infrastructure; and increased participation of all stakeholders, including women and the poor. More than 100 commitments on water were made during the forum, based primarily on the key water issues.

But despite this attention, the challenge of meeting both water and food security remains formidable. Planning of how to meet the increasing needs of various water users depends upon an understanding of the current situation and potential impacts of policy decisions. To this end, a global model of water and food supply and demand was developed to examine long-term prospects for water and food security under alternative policies.

A Thirsty World

Water development underpins food security, people's livelihoods, industrial growth, and environmental sustainability throughout the world. In 1995 the world withdrew 3,906 cubic kilometers (km^3) of water for these purposes. By 2025 water withdrawal for most uses (domestic, industrial, and livestock) is projected to increase by at least 50 percent. This will severely limit irrigation water withdrawal, which will increase by only 4 percent, in turn constraining food production.[1]

About 250 million hectares are irrigated worldwide today, nearly five times more than at the beginning of the twentieth century. Irrigation has helped boost agricultural yields and outputs and stabilize food production and prices. But growth in population and income will only increase the demand for irrigation water to meet food production requirements. Although the achievements of irrigation have been impressive, in many regions poor irrigation management has markedly lowered groundwater tables, damaged soils, and reduced water quality.[2]

Water is also essential for drinking and household uses and for industrial production. Access to safe drinking water and sanitation is critical to maintain health, particularly for children. But more than 1 billion people across the globe lack enough safe water to meet minimum levels of health and income.[3] Although the domestic and industrial sectors use far less water than agriculture, the growth in water consumption in these sectors has been rapid.

Water is integrally linked to the health of the environment. Water is vital to the survival of ecosystems and the plants and animals that live in them, and in turn ecosystems help to regulate the quantity and quality of water. Wetlands retain water during high rainfall, release it during dry periods, and purify it of many contaminants. Forests reduce erosion and sedimentation of rivers and recharge groundwater. The importance of reserving water for environmental purposes has only recently been recognized.

Alternative Futures for Water

The future of water and food is highly uncertain. Some of this uncertainty is due to relatively uncontrollable factors such as weather. But other critical factors can be influenced by the collective choices of the world's people. These factors include income and population growth; investment in water infrastructure; allocation of water to various uses; reform in water management; and technological changes in agriculture. Policy decisions—and the actions of billions of individuals—

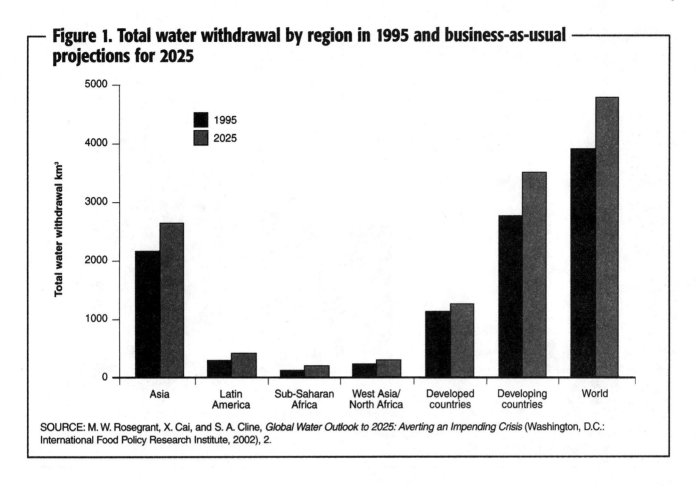

Figure 1. Total water withdrawal by region in 1995 and business-as-usual projections for 2025

SOURCE: M. W. Rosegrant, X. Cai, and S. A. Cline, *Global Water Outlook to 2025: Averting an Impending Crisis* (Washington, D.C.: International Food Policy Research Institute, 2002), 2.

determine these fundamental, long-term drivers of water and food supply and demand. Three alternative futures for global water and food show the very different outcomes that policy choices produce.[4]

Business-as-Usual Scenario

In the business-as-usual scenario, current trends in water and food policy, management, and investment would remain as they are. International donors and national governments, complacent about agriculture and irrigation, would cut their investments in these sectors. Governments and water users would implement institutional and management reforms in a limited and piece-meal fashion. These conditions would leave the world ill-pre-pared to meet major challenges facing the water and food sectors.

Policy decisions—and the actions of billions of individuals—determine fundamental, long-term drivers of water and food supply and demand.

Over the coming decades, the area of land devoted to cultivat-ing food crops would grow slowly in most of the world because of urbanization, soil degradation, and slow growth in irrigation

investment, as well as the fact that of arable land is already culti-vated. Moreover, steady or declining real prices for cereals would make it unprofitable for farmers to expand harvested area. As a result, greater food production would depend primarily on in-creases in yield. Yet growth in crop yields would also diminish because of falling public investment in agricultural research and rural infrastructure. Moreover, many of the actions that produced yield gains in recent decades—such as increasing the density of crop planting, introducing strains that are more responsive to fer-tilizer, and improving management practices—cannot and would not easily be repeated.

In the water sector, the management of river basin and irri-gation water would become more efficient, but slowly. Govern-ments would continue to transfer management of irrigation systems to farmer organizations and water-user associations. Such transfers would increase water efficiency if they are built upon existing patterns of cooperation and backed by a support-ive policy and legal environment. But these conditions are often lacking.

In some regions, farmers would adopt more efficient irriga-tion practices. Economic incentives to induce more efficient water management, however, would still face political opposi-tion from those concerned about the impact of higher water prices on farmers' income and from entrenched interests that benefit from existing systems of allocating water. Water man-agement would also improve slowly in rainfed agriculture as a result of small advances in water harvesting, better on-farm

Figure 2. Water consumption by sector and region in 1995 and business-as-usual projections for 2025

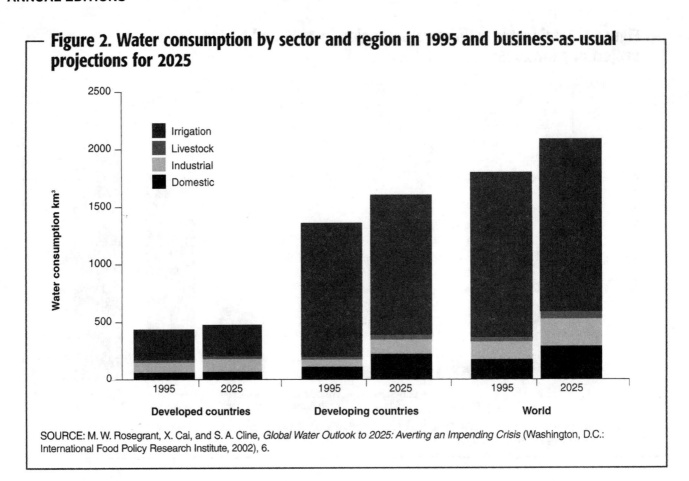

SOURCE: M. W. Rosegrant, X. Cai, and S. A. Cline, *Global Water Outlook to 2025: Averting an Impending Crisis* (Washington, D.C.: International Food Policy Research Institute, 2002), 6.

management techniques, and the development of crop varieties with shorter growing seasons.

In the business-as-usual scenario, public investment in expanding irrigation and reservoir storage would decline as the financial, environmental, and social costs of building new irrigation systems escalate and the prices of cereals and other irrigated crops drop. Nevertheless, where benefits outweigh costs, many governments would construct dams, and reservoir water for irrigation would increase moderately.

With slow growth in irrigation from surface water, farmers would expand pumping from groundwater, which is subject to low prices and little regulation. Regions that currently pump groundwater faster than aquifers can recharge—such as the western United States, northern China, northern and western India, and West Asia and North Africa—would continue to do so.[5]

The cost of supplying water to domestic and industrial users would rise dramatically. Better delivery and more efficient home water use would lead to some increase in the proportion of households connected to piped water. Many households, however, would remain unconnected. Small price increases for industrial water improvements in pollution control regulation and enforcement and new industrial technologies would cut industrial water-use intensity (water demand per $1,000 of gross domestic product). Yet industrial water prices would remain

relatively low and pollution regulations would often be poorly enforced. Thus, significant potential gains would be lost.

Environmental and other interest groups would press to increase the amount of water allocated to preserving wetlands, diluting pollutants, maintaining riparian flora and other aquatic species, and supporting tourism and recreation. Yet because of competition for water for other uses, the share of water devoted to environmental uses would not increase.

Almost all users would place heavy demands on the world's water supply under the business-as-usual scenario. Together, consumption of water for domestic, industrial, and livestock uses—that is, all nonirrigation uses—would increase dramatically, rising by 62 percent from 1995 to 2025. Because of rapid population growth and rising per capita water use, domestic consumption would increase by 71 percent, more than 90 percent of which would be in developing countries. Industrial water use would grow much faster in developing countries than in developed countries. The intensity of industrial water use would decrease worldwide, especially in developing countries (where initial intensity levels are very high), thanks to improvements in water-saving technology and demand policy. Nonetheless, the sheer size of the increase in the world's industrial production would still lead to an increase in total industrial water demand. Direct water consumption by livestock is very small compared with other sectors. But the rapid increase of livestock production, particularly in developing countries, means that livestock water demand is projected to increase 71 percent between 1995 and 2025. Although irrigation is by far the largest user of the world's water, use of irrigation water is projected to rise much more slowly than other sectors.

Water scarcity under the business-as-usual scenario would lead to slower growth of food production and substantial shifts in where the world's food is grown. Farmers would find themselves unable to raise crop yields as quickly as in the past in the face of a decline in relative water supply. Crop-harvested area is expected to grow even more slowly than crop yield in the coming decades, with all of the growth projected to occur in developing countries.

By substituting cereal and other food imports for irrigated agricultural production (so-called imports of virtual water), countries can effectively reduce their agricultural water use.[6] Under the business-as-usual scenario, developing countries would dramatically increase their reliance on food imports by 2025. The water (and land) savings from the projected large increases of food imports by the developing countries are particularly beneficial if they are the result of strong economic growth that generates the necessary foreign exchange to pay for the food imports. But even when rapidly growing food imports are primarily a result of rapid income growth, national policy makers concerned with heavy reliance on world markets often see them as a signal to set trade restrictions that can slow growth and food security in the longer term. More serious food security problems arise when high food imports are the result of slow agricultural and economic development that fails to keep pace with basic food demand driven by population and income growth. Under these conditions, countries may find it impossible to finance the required imports on a continuing basis, causing a further deterioration in the ability to bridge the gap between food consumption and the food required for basic livelihood.

Water Crisis Scenario

A moderate worsening of many of the current trends in water and food policy and in investment could build to a genuine water crisis. In the water crisis scenario, government budget problems would worsen. Governments would further cut their spending on irrigation systems and accelerate the turnover of irrigation systems to farmers and farmer groups but without the necessary reforms in water rights. Attempts to fund operations and maintenance in the main water system, still operated by public agencies, would cause water prices for irrigators to rise. Water users would fight price increases, and conflict would spill over to local management and cost-sharing arrangements. Spending on the operation and maintenance of secondary and tertiary systems would fall dramatically, and deteriorating infrastructure and poor management would lead to falling water-use efficiency. Likewise, attempts to organize river basin organizations to coordinate water management would fail because of inadequate funding and high levels of conflict among water stakeholders within the basin.

In the water crisis scenario, national governments and international donors would reduce their investments in crop breeding for rainfed agriculture in developing countries, especially for staple crops. Private agricultural research would fail to fill the investment gap for these commodities. This loss of research funding would lead to further declines in productivity growth in rainfed crop areas, particularly in more marginal areas. In search of improved incomes, people would turn to slash-and-burn agriculture, thereby deforesting the upper watersheds of many basins. Erosion and sediment loads in rivers would rise, in turn causing faster sedimentation of reservoir storage. People would increasingly encroach on wetlands for both land and water, and the integrity and health of aquatic ecosystems would be compromised. The amount of water reserved for environmental purposes would decline as unregulated and illegal withdrawals increase. The cost of building new dams would soar, discouraging new investment in many proposed dam sites. At other sites, indigenous groups and NGOs would mount opposition over the environmental and human impacts of new dams. These protests and high costs would virtually halt new investment in medium and large dams and storage reservoirs. Net reservoir storage would decline in developing countries and remain constant in developed countries.

A moderate worsening of many of the current trends in water and food policy and in investment could build to a genuine water crisis.

In the attempt to get enough water to grow their crops, farmers would extract increasing amounts of groundwater for several years, driving down water tables. But because of the accelerated pumping, after 2010, key aquifers in northern China, northern and northwestern India, and West Asia and North Africa would begin to fail. With declining water tables, farmers would find the cost of extracting water too high, and a big drop in groundwater extraction from these regions would further reduce water availability for all uses.

As in the business-as-usual scenario, the rapid increase in urban populations would quickly raise demand for domestic water. However, governments would lack the funds to extend piped water and sewage disposal to newcomers. Governments would respond by privatizing urban water and sanitation services in a rushed and poorly planned fashion. The new private water and sanitation firms would be undercapitalized and able to do little to connect additional populations to piped water. An increasing number and percentage of the urban population must rely on high-priced water from vendors or spend many hours fetching often dirty water from standpipes and wells.

Total worldwide water consumption in 2025 under the water crisis scenario would be 13 percent higher than under the business-as-usual scenario, but much of this water would be wasted and of no benefit to anyone. Virtually all of the increase would go to irrigation, mainly because farmers would use water less efficiently and withdraw more water to compensate for water losses. The supply of irrigation water would be less reliable, except in regions where so much water is diverted from environmental uses to irrigation that it balances the lower water-use efficiency.

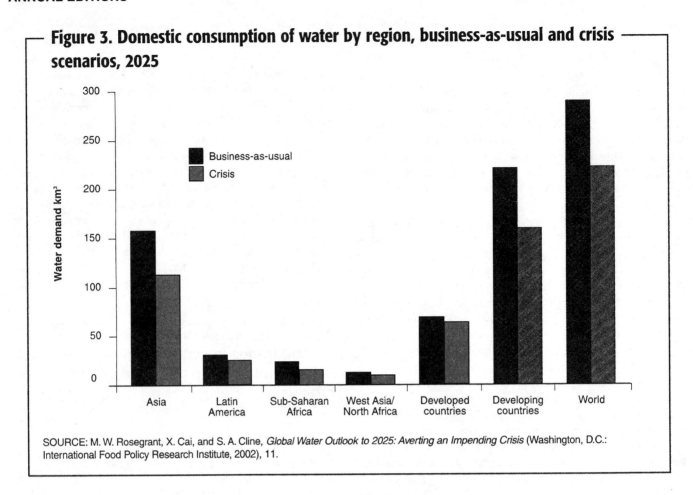

Figure 3. Domestic consumption of water by region, business-as-usual and crisis scenarios, 2025

SOURCE: M. W. Rosegrant, X. Cai, and S. A. Cline, *Global Water Outlook to 2025: Averting an Impending Crisis* (Washington, D.C.: International Food Policy Research Institute, 2002), 11.

For most regions, per capita demand for domestic water would be significantly lower than under the business-as-usual scenario, in both rural and urban areas. The result is that people would not have access to the water they would need for drinking and sanitation. Compared with outcomes under the business-as-usual scenario, the total domestic demand under the water crisis scenario would be 28 percent less in developing countries, 7 percent less in developed countries, and 23 percent less globally.

The water crisis scenario would also have significant impacts on other water users. Demand for industrial water would increase, owing to failed technological improvements and economic measures. With water diverted to make up for less efficient water use in other sectors, the water crisis scenario would hit environmental uses particularly hard.

The water crisis scenario would have severe consequences for food production. Total cereal production, for example, would be 10 percent less than under the business-as-usual scenario—the result of declines in both cultivated area and yields. This reduction is the equivalent of an annual loss of the entire cereal crop of India, or the combined annual harvest of sub-Saharan Africa and West Asia and North Africa. The decline in food production would help push up food prices sharply under the water crisis scenario. These high prices would in turn dampen food demand.

The ultimate result of this scenario is growing food insecurity, especially in developing countries. Per capita cereal consumption in 2025 in the developing world would be 2 percent lower than 1995 levels. This scenario makes it clear that increasing water scarcity, combined with poor water policies and inadequate investment in water, has the potential to generate sharp increases in cereal food prices over the coming decades. Price increases of this magnitude would take a significant bite out of the real income of poor consumers. Malnutrition would increase substantially, given that the poorest people in low-income developing countries spend more than half their income on food. Sharp price increases could also fuel inflation, place severe pressure on foreign exchange reserves, and have adverse impacts on macroeconomic stability and investment in developing countries.

Sustainable Water Scenario

A sustainable water scenario would dramatically increase the amount of water allocated to environmental uses, connect all urban households to piped water, and achieve higher per capita domestic water consumption while maintaining food production at the levels described in the business-as-usual scenario. It would achieve greater social equity and environmental protection through both careful reform in the water sector and sound government action.

Governments and international donors would increase their investments in crop research, technological change, and reform of water management to boost water productivity and the growth of crop yields in rainfed agriculture. Accumulating evidence shows that even drought-prone and high-temperature rainfed environments have the potential for dramatic increases in yield. Breeding strategies would directly target these rainfed areas. Improved policies and increased investment in rural infrastructure would help link remote farmers to markets and reduce the risks of rainfed farming.

To stimulate water conservation and free up agricultural water for environmental, domestic, and industrial uses, the effective price of water to the agricultural sector would be gradually increased. Agricultural water price increases would be implemented through incentive programs that provide farmers income for the water that they save, such as charge-subsidy schemes that pay farmers for reducing water use, and through the establishment, purchase, and trading of water-use rights. By 2025, agricultural water prices would be twice as high in developed countries and three times as high in developing countries compared with the business-as-usual scenario. The government would simultaneously transfer water rights and the responsibility for operation and management of irrigation systems to communities and water user associations in many countries and regions. The transfer of rights and systems would be facilitated with an improved legal and institutional environment for preventing and eliminating conflict and with technical and organizational training and support. As a result, farmers would increase their on-farm investments in irrigation and water management technology, and the efficiency of irrigation systems and basin water use would improve significantly.

River basin organizations would be established in many water-scarce basins to allocate water among stakeholder interests. Higher funding and reduced conflict over water, thanks to better water management, would facilitate effective stakeholder participation in these organizations.

Farmers would be able to make more effective use of rainfall in crop production, thanks to breakthroughs in water harvesting systems and the adoption of advanced farming techniques, like precision agriculture, contour plowing, precision land leveling, and minimum-till and no-till technologies. These technologies would increase the share of rainfall that goes to infiltration and evapotranspiration.

Spurred by the rapidly escalating costs of building new dams and the increasingly apparent environmental and human resettlement costs, developing and developed countries would reassess their reservoir construction plans, with comprehensive analysis of the costs and benefits, including environmental and social effects, of proposed projects. As a result, many planned storage projects would be canceled, but others would proceed with support from civil society groups. Yet new storage capacity would be less necessary because rapid growth in rainfed crop yields would help reduce rates of reservoir sedimentation from erosion due to slash-and-burn cultivation.

Policy toward groundwater extraction would change significantly. Market-based approaches would assign rights to groundwater based on annual withdrawals as well as the renewable stock of groundwater. This step would be combined with stricter regulations and better enforcement of such tighter controls. Groundwater overdrafts would be phased out in countries and regions that previously pumped groundwater unsustainably.

Domestic and industrial water use would also be subject to reforms in pricing and regulation. Water prices for connected households would double, with targeted subsidies for low-income households. Revenues from price increases would be invested to reduce water losses in existing systems and to extend piped water to previously unconnected households. By 2025, all households would be connected. Industries would respond to higher prices, particularly in developing countries, by increasing in-plant recycling of water, which reduces water consumption.

With strong societal pressure for improved environmental quality, allocations for environmental uses of water would increase. Moreover, the reforms in agricultural and nonagricultural water sectors would reduce pressure on wetlands and other environmental uses of water. Greater investments and better water management would improve the efficiency of water use, leaving more water instream for environmental purposes. All reductions in domestic and urban water use, due to higher water prices, would be allocated to instream environmental uses.

In the sustainable water scenario, the world consumes less water but reaps greater benefits than under the business-as-usual scenario, especially in developing countries. In 2025, total worldwide water consumption would be 20 percent lower under the sustainable scenario than under the business-as-usual scenario. This reduction in consumption would free up water for environmental uses. Higher water prices and higher water-use efficiency would reduce consumption of irrigation water by 296 km^3 compared with the business-as-usual scenario. The reliability of irrigation water supply would be reduced slightly in the sustainable scenario—as compared with the business-as-usual scenario—because of a higher priority on environmental flows. Over time, however, more efficient water use in this scenario would counterbalance the transfer of water to the environment and would result in an improvement in the reliability of supply of irrigation water by 2025.

This scenario would improve the domestic water supply through universal access to piped water for rural and urban households. Other water sectors would also be affected under the sustainable water scenario. Industrial water demand would be reduced under the sustainable water scenario through technological improvements and effective economic incentives. The environment would be a major beneficiary of the sustainable water scenario, with large increases in the amount of water reserved for wetlands, instream flows, and other environmental purposes.

The sustainable water scenario can raise food production slightly over the business-as-usual scenario, while achieving much greater gains for domestic water use and the environment. The total harvested area under the sustainable water scenario in 2025 would be slightly lower than under the business-as-usual scenario, owing to less water for irrigation and slightly lower crop prices. With faster growth in rainfed yields making up for slower growth in harvested area and irrigated

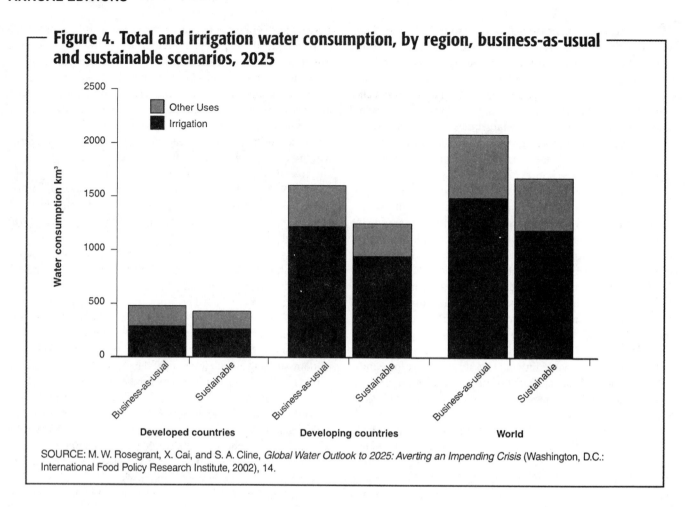

Figure 4. Total and irrigation water consumption, by region, business-as-usual and sustainable scenarios, 2025

SOURCE: M. W. Rosegrant, X. Cai, and S. A. Cline, *Global Water Outlook to 2025: Averting an Impending Crisis* (Washington, D.C.: International Food Policy Research Institute, 2002), 14.

yields, total cereal production in 2025 would be 19 million tons more (a 1 percent difference) under the sustainable water scenario than under the business-as-usual scenario.

The sustainable scenario shows that with improved water policies, investments, and rainfed cereal crop management and technology, growth in food production can be maintained while universal access to piped water is achieved, and environmental flows are increased dramatically. Compared with the water crisis scenario, the increase in environmental flows under the sustainable water scenario would be about 1,490 km^3, equivalent to 5 times the annual flow of the Mississippi River, 20 times the annual flow of the Yellow River, and 4 times the annual flow of the Ganges River.

Implications for the Future

Water scarcity will get much worse if policy and investment commitments from national governments, international donors, and development banks weaken further. The water crisis scenario—predicated on the worsening of a number of already evident trends—would lead to a breakdown in domestic water service for hundreds of millions of people, a devastating loss of wetlands, serious reductions in food production, and skyrocketing food prices that would force declining per capita food consumption in much of the world. Failure to adopt water-saving

technology improvements and policy reforms could make demand for nonirrigation water grow even faster than projected, further worsening water scarcity.

In the sustainable water scenario, the world consumes less water but reaps greater benefits, especially in developing countries.

Water scarcity can lead to declining food demand and increasing food prices. As shown in the water crisis scenario, major cereal crop prices may be more than double the projections under the business-as-usual scenario, and at the same time food demand may be significantly reduced, especially in developing countries. Moreover, price increases can have an even larger impact on low-income consumers.

Water scarcity will get much worse if policy and investment commitments from national governments, international donors, and development banks weaken further.

Excessive diversion of water flows and overdraft of groundwater have already caused environmental problems in many regions around the world. The analysis shows that the problems, from a local to a worldwide scale, will likely be even more serious in the future. If current investment plans and recent trends in the water and food sectors continue, expanding the environmental uses of water would require reducing the consumption of irrigation water or domestic and municipal water or both. Thus, in the absence of policy and investment reform, competition over water between households and industries and between farmers and environmental uses will increase in many parts of the world.

With water becoming increasingly scarce, continued high flow diversions would become self-defeating. Excess extraction speeds the recession of ecological systems and lowers water quality, finally reducing the qualified water supply for human uses. This has already occurred in the Aral Sea Basin in Central Asia. Groundwater overdraft can likewise lead to the loss of an important water source for human uses, as is already happening in many regions.

However, the analysis also reveals cause for hope. The scenarios explored here point to three broad strategies that can address the challenge posed by water scarcity for food production:

- investment in infrastructure to increase the supply of water for irrigation, domestic, and industrial purposes;
- conservation of water and improvements in the efficiency of water use in existing systems, through reforms in water management and policy, including stronger incentives for water conservation; and
- improvements in crop productivity per unit of water and land through integrated water management and agricultural research and policy efforts, including crop breeding and water management for rainfed agriculture.

Although the financial, environmental, and social costs of new water supply projects are high, in some regions, especially in developing countries, it is still crucial to selectively expand water supply, storage, and withdrawal capacities. Storage and water distribution systems (such as water lift projects and canals) are particularly needed for sub-Saharan Africa, some countries in South and Southeast Asia (such as Bangladesh, India, and Vietnam), and some countries in Latin America. These countries must consider not only the full social, economic, and environmental costs of development but also the costs of failure to develop new water sources. Projects must be designed to account for full costs and benefits, including not only irrigation benefits but also health, household water use, and catchment improvement benefits. It is also essential to improve compensation programs for those who are displaced or negatively affected by water projects.

Expanding water supplies can help alleviate water scarcity, but the results show that the most promising avenue is likely to be water management reforms, incentive policies, and investments in infrastructure and technology to enhance efficiency in existing uses. Feasible improvements in the efficiency of basin-scale irrigation water use can, on a global scale, compensate for irrigation reduction resulting from the phasing out of groundwater overdraft worldwide, increased committed environmental flows, higher prices for agricultural water use (which themselves encourage investments in improved efficiency), and low irrigated area development. In addition, improving irrigation water-use efficiency is an effective way to increase water productivity.

In severely water-scarce basins, however, relatively little room exists for improving water-use efficiency, and food production and farm incomes could fall significantly if water for irrigation is transferred to other uses. In these basins, governments will need to seek alternative means to compensate for the negative impact of growing water scarcity on agriculture, such as investing in agriculture to obtain more rapid growth in crop yields, promoting the diversification of farming into less water-intensive crops, and diversifying the economy to reduce the economic role of agriculture over time.

Making big improvements in river-basin efficiency in specific river basins will require site-specific analysis and implementation. Basin efficiency depends on improvements both in water-saving technologies and in the institutions governing water allocation, water rights, and water quality. Industrial water recycling, such as recirculation of cooling water, can be a major source of water savings in many countries. Much potential also exists for improving the efficiency of domestic water use. Steps may include anything from detecting and repairing leaks in municipal systems to installing low-flow showerheads and low-water or waterless toilets. Treated wastewater can be used for a variety of nonpotable purposes including landscape and recreational irrigation, maintenance of urban stream flows and wetlands, wastewater-fed aquaculture, and toilet flushing. To encourage water-saving innovation, domestic and industrial water prices should be increased. Generalized subsidies should be replaced with subsidies targeted to the poor. Water providers should charge low prices for a basic entitlement of water, with increasing prices for greater amounts of water.

Improvements in the irrigation sector can be made at the technical, managerial, and institutional levels. Technical improvements include advanced irrigation systems, such as drip irrigation; sprinklers; conjunctive use of surface and groundwater; and precision agriculture, including computer monitoring of crop water demand. Managerial improvements include the adoption of demand-based irrigation scheduling systems and improved equipment maintenance. Institutional improvements involve the establishment of effective water user associations and water rights, the creation of a better legal environment for water allocation, and the introduction of higher water prices. Great care must be taken in designing a water pricing system for agriculture. Direct water price increases are likely to be punitive to farmers because water plays such a large role in their cost of production. Better alternatives would be pricing schemes that pay farmers for reducing water use, and water rights and water trading arrangements that provide farmers or water user associations with incentives to reduce wasteful water use.

Rainfed agriculture is a key to sustainable development of water and food. Rainfed agriculture still produces about 60 percent of total cereals, and its role remains very important in both the business-as-usual and the sustainable water scenarios. Improved water management and crop productivity in rainfed areas would relieve considerable pressure on irrigated agriculture and on water resources. Exploiting the full potential of rainfed agriculture, however, will require investing in water-harvesting technologies, crop breeding targeted to rainfed environments, agricultural extension services, and access to markets, credit, and input supplies in rainfed areas.

A large part of the world is facing severe water scarcity, but the impending water crisis can be averted. The precise mix of water policy and management reforms and investments, and the feasible institutional arrangements and policy instruments to be used, must be tailored to specific countries and basins. They will vary based on level of development, agroclimatic conditions, relative water scarcity, level of agricultural intensification, and degree of competition for water, But these solutions are not easy, and they take time, political commitment, and money. Fundamental reform of the water sector must start now.

Notes

1. The source of these data is the 2002 IMPACT-WATER assessments and projections. IMPACT-WATER is a global modelling framework that combines an extension of the International Model for Policy Analysis of Agricultural Commodities and Trade (IMPACT) with a newly developed Water Simulation Model (WSM). For a more detailed description of the integrated model, see M. W. Rosegrant, X. Cai, and S. A. Cline, *World Water and Food to 2025: Dealing with Scarcity* (Washington, D.C.: International Food Policy Research Institute, 2002).

2. Food and Agricultural Organization of the United Nations (FAO), *FAOSTAT Database 2000* (Rome: FAO, 2000), accessible via **http://apps.fao.org/.**

3. World Health Organization (WHO) and United Nations Children's Fund (UNICEF), *Global Water Supply and Sanitation Assessment 2000 Report* (Geneva: UN, 2000).

4. For a more detailed analysis of these and other scenarios and a detailed discussion of methodology, see M. W. Rosegrant. X. Cai, and S. A. Cline, *Global Water Outlook to 2025: Averting an impending Crisis* (Washington, D.C.: International Food Policy Research Institute, 2002); and Rosegrant, Cai, and Cline, note 1 above.

5. West Asia and North Africa is one of the regional groupings used in the IMPACT-WATER model. The region consists of the following countries: Egypt, Turkey, Algeria, Cyprus, Iran, Iraq, Jordan, Kuwait, Lebanon, Libya, Morocco, Saudi Arabia, Syria, Tunisia, United Arab Emirates, and Yemen.

6. J. A. Allan, "Water Security Policies and Global Systems for Water Scarce Regions," in *Sustainability of Irrigated Agriculture—Transactions*. Vol. 1 E, special session: "The Future of Irrigation under Increased Demand from Competitive Uses of Water and Greater Needs for Food Supply—R.7" in the symposium on Management Information Systems in Irrigation and Drainage, Sixteenth Congress on Irrigation and Drainage, Cairn (New Delhi: International Commission on Irrigation and Drainage, 1996). 117–32.

MARK W. ROSEGRANT is senior research fellow at the international Food Policy Research Institute (IFPRI) and principal researcher at the International Water Management Institute (IWMI). Rosegrant has extensive experience in research and policy analysis in agriculture and economic development, with an emphasis on critical water issues as they impact world food security, rural livelihoods, and environmental sustainability. He alto developed IFPRI's International Model for Policy Analysis of Agricultural Commodities and Trade (IMPACT) and the IMPACT-WATER models. He continues to lead the team that maintains the models, which have been used to examine key policy options concerning food prices, food security, livestock and fisheries demand, agricultural research allocation, water resources, environment, and trade. He also currently coordinates a joint modeling team between IFPRI and IWMI, developing integrated global water and food models, and has written and edited numerous publications on agricultural economics, water resources, and food policy analysis. He can be reached via e-mail at m.rosegrant@cgiar.org. **XIMING CAI** is a research fellow at IFPRI and a researcher with IWMI, Cai's current research interests include water resource planning and management, operations research and their application to integrated water resources, and agricultural and economic systems. He can be reached via e-mail at x.cai@cgiar.org. **SARAH A. CLINE** is a research analyst with IFPRI. Cline's work at IFPRI focuses on water resources policy and management, as well as global food supply, demand, and trade issues. She can be reached via e-mail at s.cline@cgiar.org. The authors retain copyright.

From *Environment,* September 2003, pp. 26–36. Copyright © 2003 by Mark W. Rosegrant, Ximing Cai, and Sarah A. Cline. Reprinted by permission of the authors at the International Food Policy Research Institute. www.ifpri.org

Do Global Attitudes and Behaviors Support Sustainable Development?

ANTHONY A. LEISEROWITZ, ROBERT W. KATES, AND THOMAS M. PARRIS

Many advocates of sustainable development recognize that a transition to global sustainability—meeting human needs and reducing hunger and poverty while maintaining the life-support systems of the planet—will require changes in human values, attitudes, and behaviors.[1] A previous article in *Environment* described some of the values used to define or support sustainable development as well as key goals, indicators, and practices.[2] Drawing on the few multinational and quasi-global-scale surveys that have been conducted,[3] this article synthesizes and reviews what is currently known about global attitudes and behavior that will either support or discourage a global sustainability transition.[4] (Table 1 provides details about these surveys.)

None of these surveys measured public attitudes toward "sustainable development" as a holistic concept. There is, however, a diverse range of empirical data related to many of the subcomponents of sustainable development: development and environment; the driving forces of population, affluence/poverty/consumerism, technology, and entitlement programs; and the gap between attitudes and behavior.

Development

Concerns for environment and development merged in the early concept of sustainable development, but the meaning of these terms has evolved over time. For example, global economic development is widely viewed as a central priority of sustainable development, but development has come to mean human and social development as well.

Economic Development

The desire for economic development is often assumed to be universal, transcending all cultural and national contexts. Although the surveys in Table 1 have no global-scale data on public attitudes toward economic development per se, this assumption appears to be supported by 91 percent of respondents from 35 developing countries, the United States, and Germany, who said that it is very important (75 percent) or somewhat important (16 percent) to live in a country where there is economic prosperity[5] What level of affluence is desired, how that economic prosperity is to be achieved, and how economic wealth should ideally be distributed within and between nations, however, are much more contentious questions. Unfortunately, there does not appear to be any global-scale survey research that has tried to identify public attitudes or preferences for particular levels or end-states of economic development (for example, infinite growth versus steady-state economies) and only limited or tangential data on the ideal distribution of wealth (see the section on affluence below).

Data from the World Values Survey suggest that economic development leads to greater perceived happiness as countries make the transition from subsistence to advanced industrial economies. But above a certain level of gross national product (GNP) per capita—approximately $14,000—the relationship between income level and subjective well-being disappears (see Figure 1). This implies that infinite economic growth does not lead to greater human happiness. Additionally, many of the unhappiest countries had, at the time of these surveys, recently experienced significant declines in living standards with the collapse of the Soviet Union. Yet GNP per capita remained higher in these ex-Soviet countries than in developing countries like India and Nigeria.[6] This suggests that relative trends in living standards influence happiness more than absolute levels of affluence, but the relationship between economic development and subjective well-being deserves more research attention.

Human Development

Very limited data is available on public attitudes toward issues of human development, although it can be assumed that there is near-universal support for increased child survival rates, adult life expectancies, and educational opportunities. However, despite the remarkable increases in these indicators of human well-being since World War II,[7] there appears to be a globally pervasive sense that human well-being has been deteriorating in recent years. In 2002, large majorities worldwide said that a variety of conditions had worsened over the previous five years, including the availability of well-paying jobs (58 percent); working conditions (59 percent); the spread of diseases (66 percent); the affordability of health care (60 percent); and the ability of old people to care for themselves in old age (59 percent). Likewise, thinking of their own countries, large majorities worldwide were concerned about the living conditions of the elderly (61 percent) and the sick and disabled (56 percent), while a plurality was concerned about the living conditions of the unemployed (42 percent).[8]

Development Assistance

One important way to promote development is to extend help to poorer countries and people, either through national governments or nongovernmental organizations and charities. There is strong popular support but less official support for development assistance to poor countries. In 1970, the United Nations General Assembly resolved that each economically advanced country would dedicate 0.7 percent of its gross national income (GNI) to official development assistance (ODA) by the middle of the 1970s—a target that has been reaffirmed in many subsequent international agreements.[9] As of 2004, only five countries had achieved this goal (Denmark, Norway, the Netherlands, Luxembourg, and Sweden). Portugal was close to the target at 0.63, yet all other countries ranged from a high of 0.42 percent (France) to lows of 0.16 and 0.15 percent (the United States and Italy respectively). Overall, the average ODA/GNI among the industrialized countries was only 0.25 percent—far below the UN target.[10]

By contrast, in 2002, more than 70 percent of respondents from 21 developed and developing countries said they would support paying 1 percent more in taxes to help the world's poor.[11] Likewise, surveys in the 13 countries of the Organisation for Economic Co-operation and Development's Development Assistance Committee (OECD-DAC) have found that public support for the principle of giving aid to developing countries (81 percent in 2003) has remained high and stable for more than 20 years.[12] Further, 45 percent said that their government's current (1999–2001) level of expenditure on foreign aid was too low, while only 10 percent said foreign aid was too high.[13] There is also little evidence that the public in OECD countries has developed "donor fatigue." Although surveys have found increasing public concerns about corruption, aid diversion, and inefficiency, these surveys also continue to show very high levels of public support for aid.

Public support for development aid is belied, however, by several factors. First, large majorities demonstrate little understanding of development aid, with most unable to identify their national aid agencies and greatly overestimating the percentage of their national budget devoted to development aid. For example, recent polls have found that Americans believed their government spent 24 percent (mean estimate) of the national budget on foreign assistance, while Europeans often estimated their governments spent 5 to 10 percent.[14] In reality, in 2004 the United States spent approximately 0.81 percent and the European Union member countries an average of approximately 0.75 percent of their national budgets on official development assistance, ranging from a low of 0.30 percent (Italy) to a high of 1.66 percent (Luxembourg).[15] Second, development aid is almost always ranked low on lists of national priorities, well below more salient concerns about (for example) unemployment, education, and health care. Third, "the overwhelming support for

Table 1. Multinational surveys

One-time Surveys		
Name	Year(s)	Number of Countries
Pew Global Attitudes Project	2002	43
Eurobarometer	2002	15
International Social Science Program	2000	25
Health of the Planet	1992	24
Repeated Surveys		
GlobeScan International Environmental Monitor	1997–2003	34
World Values Survey	1981–2002	79
Demographic and Health Surveys	1986–2002	17
Organisation for Economic Co-operation and Development	1990–2002	22

NOTE: Before November 2003, GlobeScan, Inc. was known as Environics International. Surveys before this time bear the older name.
SOURCE: For more detail about these surveys and the countries sampled, see Appendix A in A. Leiserowitz, R. W. Kates, and T. M. Parris, *Sustainability Values, Attitudes and Behaviors: A Review of Multi-national and Global Trends*, CID Working Paper No. 113 (Cambridge, MA: Science, Environment and Development Group, Center for International Development, Harvard University, 2004), http://www.cid.harvard.edu/cidwp/113.htm.

foreign aid is based upon the perception that it will be spent on remedying humanitarian crises," not used for other development-related issues like Third World debt, trade barriers, or increasing inequality between rich and poor countries—or for geopolitical reasons (for example, U.S. aid to Israel and Egypt).[16] Support for development assistance has thus been characterized as "a mile wide, but an inch deep" with large majorities supporting aid (in principle) and increasing budget allocations but few understanding what development aid encompasses or giving it a high priority.[17]

Environment

Compared to the very limited or nonexistent data on attitudes toward economic and human development and the overall concept of sustainable development, research on global environmental attitudes is somewhat more substantial. Several surveys have measured attitudes regarding the intrinsic value of nature, global environmental concerns, the trade-offs between environmental protection and economic growth, government policies, and individual and household behaviors.

Human-Nature Relationship

Most research has focused on anthropocentric concerns about environmental quality and natural resource use, with less attention to ecocentric concerns about the intrinsic value of nature. In 1967, the historian Lynn White Jr. published a now-famous and controversial article arguing that a Judeo-Christian ethic and attitude of domination, derived from Genesis, was an underlying historical and cultural cause of the modern environmental crisis.[18] Subsequent ecocentric, ecofeminist, and social ecology theorists have also argued that a domination ethic toward people, women, and nature runs deep in Western, patriar-

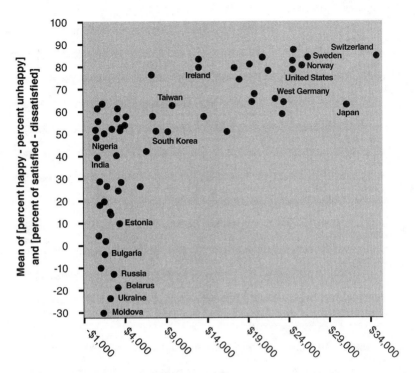

NOTE: The subjective well-being index reflects the average of the percentage in each country who describe themselves as "very happy" or "happy" minus the percentage who describe themselves as "not very happy" or "unhappy"; and the percentage placing themselves in the 7–10 range, minus the percentage placing themselves in the 1–4 range, on a 10-point scale on which 1 indicates that one is strongly dissatisfied with one's life as a whole, and 10 indicates that one is highly satisfied with one's life as a whole.

SOURCE: R. Inglehart, "Globalization and Postmodern Values," *Washington Quarterly* 23, no. 1 (1999): 215–228. Subjective well-being data from the 1990 and 1996 World Values Surveys. GNP per capita for 1993 data from *World Bank, World Development Report, 1995* (New York: Oxford University Press, 1995).

Figure 1 Subjective well-being by level of economic development

chal, and capitalist culture.[19] The 2000 World Values Survey, however, found that 76 percent of respondents across 27 countries said that human beings should "coexist with nature," while only 19 percent said they should "master nature" (see Figure 2). Overwhelming majorities of Europeans, Japanese, and North Americans said that human beings should coexist with nature, ranging from 85 percent in the United States to 96 percent in Japan, By contrast, only in Jordan, Vietnam, Tanzania, and the Philippines did more than 40 percent say that human beings should master nature.[20] In 2002, a national survey of the United States explored environmental values in more depth and found that Americans strongly agreed that nature has intrinsic value and that humans have moral duties and obligations to animals, plants, and non-living nature (such as rocks, water, and air). The survey found that Americans strongly disagreed that "humans have the right to alter nature to satisfy wants and desires" and that "humans are not part of nature" (see Figure 3).[20] This very limited data suggests that large majorities in the United States and worldwide now reject a domination ethic as the basis of the human-nature relationship, at least at an abstract level. This question, however, deserves much more cross-cultural empirical research.

Environmental Concern

In 2000, a survey of 11 developed and 23 developing countries found that 83 percent of all respondents were concerned a fair amount (41 percent) to a great deal (42 percent) about environmental problems. Interestingly, more respondents from developing countries (47 percent) were "a great deal concerned" about the environment than from developed countries (33 percent), ranging from more than 60 percent in Peru, the Philippines, Nigeria, and India to less than 30 percent in the Netherlands, Germany, Japan, and Spain.[22] This survey also asked respondents to rate the seriousness of several environmental problems (see Figure 4). Large majorities worldwide selected the strongest response possible ("very serious") for seven of the eight problems measured. Overall, these results demonstrate very high levels of public concern about a wide range of environmental issues, from local problems like water and air pollution to global problems like ozone depletion and climate

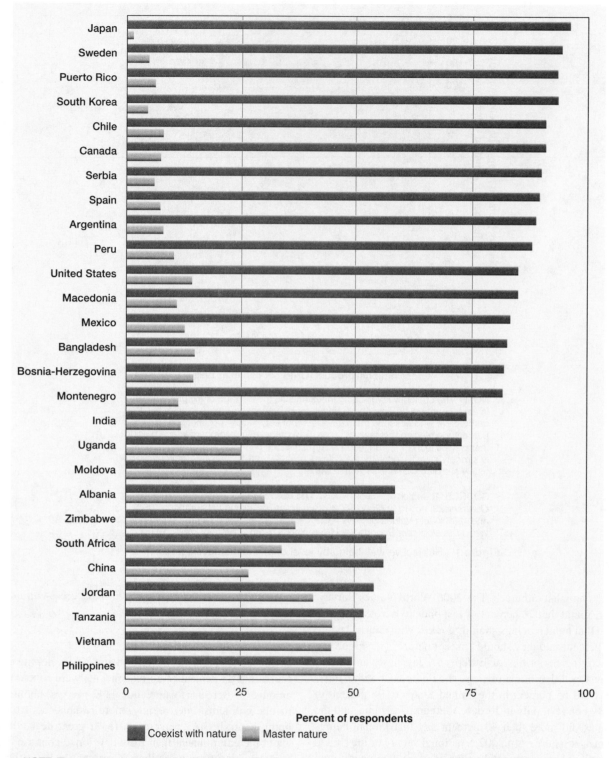

Percent of respondents

Coexist with nature   Master nature

NOTE: The question asked, "Which statement comes closest to your own views: human beings should master nature or humans should coexist with nature?"

SOURCE: A. Leiserowitz, 2005. Data from World Values Survey, *The 1999–2002 Values Surveys Integrated Data File 1.0, CD-ROM in R. Inglehart, M. Basanez, J. Diez-Medrano, L. Halman, and R. Luijkx, eds., Human Beliefs and Values: A Cross-Cultural Sourcebook Based on the 1999–2002 Values Surveys, first edition* (Mexico City: Siglo XXI, 2004).

Figure 2   Human-nature relationship

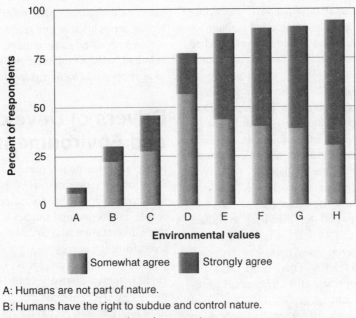

Somewhat agree   Strongly agree

A: Humans are not part of nature.

B: Humans have the right to subdue and control nature.

C: Humankind was created to rule over nature.

D: Humans should adapt to nature rather than modify it to suit them.

E: Humans have moral duties and obligations to non-living nature.

F: Humans have moral duties and obligations to plants and trees.

G: Humans have moral duties and obligations to other animal species.

H: Nature has value within itself regardless of any value humans place on it.

SOURCE: A. Leiserowitz, 2005.

Figure 3   American (U.S.) environmental values

change.[23] Further, 52 percent of the global public said that if no action is taken, "species loss will seriously affect the planet's ability to sustain life" just 20 years from now.[24]

Environmental Protection versus Economic Growth

In two recent studies, 52 percent of respondents worldwide agreed that "protecting the environment should be given priority" over "economic growth and creating jobs," while 74 percent of respondents in the G7 countries prioritized environmental protection over economic growth, even if some jobs were lost.[25] Unfortunately, this now-standard survey question pits the environment against economic growth as an either/or dilemma. Rarely do surveys allow respondents to choose an alternative answer, that environmental protection can generate economic growth and create jobs (for example, in new energy system development, tourism, and manufacturing).

Attitudes toward Environmental Policies

In 1995, a large majority (62 percent) worldwide said they "would agree to an increase in taxes if the extra money were used to prevent environmental damage," while 33 percent said they would oppose them.[26] In 2000, there was widespread global support for stronger environmental protection laws and regulations, with 69 percent saying that, at the time of the survey, their national laws and regulations did not go at all far enough.[27] The

1992 Health of the Planet survey found that a very large majority (78 percent) favored the idea of their own national government "contributing money to an international agency to work on solving global environmental problems." Attitudes toward international agreements in this survey, however, were less favorable. In 1992, 47 percent worldwide agreed that "our nation's environmental problems can be solved without any international agreements," with respondents from low-income countries more likely to strongly agree (23 percent) than individuals from middle-income (17 percent) or high-income (12 percent) countries.[28] In 2001, however, 79 percent of respondents from the G8 countries said that international negotiations and progress on climate change was either "not good enough" (39 percent) or "not acceptable" (40 percent) and needed faster action. Surprisingly, this latter 40 percent supported giving the United Nations "the power to impose legally-binding actions on national governments to protect the Earth's climate."[29]

Environmental Behavior

Material consumption is one of the primary means by which environmental values and attitudes get translated into behavior. (For attitudes toward consumption per se, see the section on affluence, poverty, and consumerism below.)

In 2002, Environics International (GlobeScan) found that 36 percent of respondents from 20 developed and developing countries stated that they had avoided a product or brand for environmental reasons, while 27 percent had refused packaging, and 25 percent had gathered environmental information.[30] Recycling was highly popular, with 6 in 10 people setting aside garbage for reuse, recycling, or safe disposal. These rates, however, reached 91 percent in North America versus only 36–38 percent in Latin America, Eastern Europe, and Central Asia,[31] which may be the result of structural barriers in these societies (for example, inadequate infrastructures, regulations, or markets). There is less survey data regarding international attitudes toward energy consumption, but among Europeans, large majorities said they had reduced or intended to reduce their use of heating, air conditioning, lighting, and domestic electrical appliances.[32]

In 1995, 46 percent of respondents worldwide reported having chosen products thought to be better for the environment, 50 percent of respondents said they had tried to reduce their own water consumption, and 48 percent reported that in the 12 months prior to the survey, they reused or recycled something rather than throwing it away. There was a clear distinction between richer and poorer societies: 67 percent of respondents from high-income countries reported that they had chosen "green" products, while only 30 percent had done so in low-income countries. Likewise, 75 percent of respondents from high-income countries said that they had reused or recycled something, while only 27 percent in low-income countries said this.[33] However, the latter results contradict the observations of researchers who have noted that many people in developing countries reuse things as part of everyday life (for example, converting oil barrels into water containers) and that millions eke out an existence by reusing and recycling items from landfills and garbage dumps.[34] This disparity could be the result of inadequate survey representation of the very poor, who are the most likely to reuse and recycle as part of survival, or, alternatively, different cultural interpretations of the concepts "reuse" and "recycle."

In 2002, 44 percent of respondents in high-income countries were very willing to pay 10 percent more for an environmentally friendly car, compared to 41 percent from low-income countries and 29 percent from middle-income countries.[35] These findings clearly mark the emergence of a global market for more energy-efficient and less-polluting automobiles. However, while many people appear willing to spend more to buy an environmentally friendly car, most do not appear willing to pay more for gasoline to reduce air pollution. The same 2002 survey found that among high-income countries, only 28 percent of respondents were very willing to pay 10 percent more for gasoline if the money was used to reduce air pollution, compared to 23 percent in medium-income countries and 36 percent in low-income countries.[36] People appear to generally oppose higher gasoline prices, although public attitudes are probably affected, at least in part, by the prices extant at the time of a given survey, the rationale given for the tax, and how the income from the tax will be spent.

Despite the generally pro-environment attitudes and behaviors outlined above, the worldwide public is much less likely to engage in political action for the environment. In 1995, only 13 percent of worldwide respondents reported having donated to an environmental organization, attended a meeting, or signed a petition for the environment in the prior 12 months, with more doing so in high-income countries than in low-income countries.[37] Finally, in 2000, only 10 percent worldwide reported having written a letter or made a telephone call to express their concern about an environmental issue in the past year, 18 percent had based a vote on green issues, and 11 percent belonged to or supported an environmental group.[38]

Drivers of Development and Environment

Many analyses of the human impact on life-support systems focus on three driving forces: population, affluence or income, and technology—the so-called I=PAT identity.[39] In other words, environmental impact is considered a function of these three drivers. In a similar example, carbon dioxide (CO_2) emissions from the energy sector are often considered a function of population, affluence (gross domestic product (GDP) per capita), energy intensity (units of energy per GDP), and technology (CO_2 emissions per unit of energy).[40] While useful, most analysts also recognize that these variables are not fundamental driving forces in and of themselves and are not independent from one another.[41] A similar approach has also been applied to human development (D=PAE), in which development is considered a function of population, affluence, and entitlements and equity.[42] What follows is a review of empirical trends in attitudes and behavior related to population, affluence, technology, and equity and entitlements.

Population

Global population continues to grow, but the rate of growth continues to decline almost everywhere. Recurrent Demographic and Health Surveys (DHS) have found that the ideal number of children desired is declining worldwide. Globally, attitudes toward family planning and contraception are very positive, with 67 percent worldwide and large majorities in 38 out of 40 countries agreeing that birth control and family planning have been a change for the better.[43] Worldwide, these positive attitudes toward family planning are reflected in the behavior of more than 62 percent of married women of reproductive age who are currently using contraception. Within the developing world, the United Nations reports that from 1990 to 2000, contraceptive use among married women in Asia increased from 52 percent to 66 percent, in Latin American and the Caribbean from 57 percent to 69 percent, but in Africa from only 15 percent to 25 percent.[44] Notwithstanding these positive attitudes toward contraception, in 1997, approximately 20 percent to 25 percent of births in the developing world were unwanted, indicating that access to or the use of contraceptives remains limited in some areas.[45]

DHS surveys have found that ideal family size remains significantly larger in western and middle Africa (5.2) than elsewhere in the developing world (2.9).[46] They also found that support for family planning is much lower in sub-Saharan Africa (44 percent) than in the rest of the developing world (74 percent).[47] Consistent with these attitudes, sub-Saharan Africa

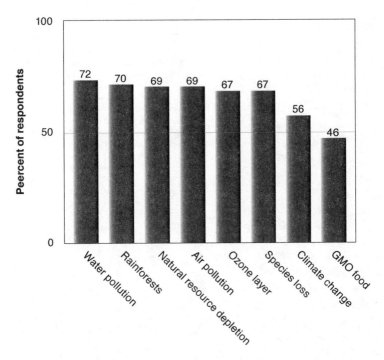

SOURCE: A. Leiserowitz, 2005. Data from Environics International (Globe Scan), *Environics International Environmental Monitor Survey Dataset* (Kingston, Canada: Environics International, 2000), http://jeff-lab.queensu.ca/poadata/info/iem/iemlist.shtml (accessed 5 October 2004).

Figure 4 Percent of global public calling environmental issues a "very serious problem"

exhibits lower percentages of married women using birth control as well as lower rates of growth in contraceptive use than the rest of the developing world.[48]

Affluence, Poverty, and Consumerism

Aggregate affluence and related consumption have risen dramatically worldwide with GDP per capita (purchasing-power parity, constant 1995 international dollars) more than doubling between 1975 and 2002.[49] However, the rising tide has not lifted all boats. Worldwide in 2001, more than 1.1 billion people lived on less than $1 per day, and 2.7 billion people lived on less than $2 per day—with little overall change from 1990. However, the World Bank projects these numbers to decline dramatically by 2015—to 622 million living on less than $1 per day and 1.9 billion living on less than $2 per day. There are also large regional differences, with sub-Saharan Africa the most notable exception: There, the number of people living on less than $1 per day rose from an estimated 227 million in 1990 to 313 million in 2001 and is projected to increase to 340 million by 2015.[50]

Poverty

Poverty reduction is an essential objective of sustainable development.[51] In 1995, 65 percent of respondents worldwide said that more people were living in poverty than had been 10 years

prior. Regarding the root causes of poverty, 63 percent blamed unfair treatment by society, while 26 percent blamed the laziness of the poor themselves. Majorities blamed poverty on the laziness and lack of willpower of the poor only in the United States (61 percent), Puerto Rico (72 percent), Japan (57 percent), China (59 percent), Taiwan (69 percent), and the Philippines (63 percent) (see Figure 5).[52] Worldwide, 68 percent said their own government was doing too little to help people in poverty within their own country, while only 4 percent said their government was doing too much. At the national level, only in the United States (33 percent) and the Philippines (21 percent) did significant proportions say their own government was doing too much to help people in poverty.[53]

Consumerism

Different surveys paint a complicated and contradictory picture of attitudes toward consumption. On the one hand, majorities around the world agree that, at the societal level, material and status-related consumption are threats to human cultures and the environment. Worldwide, 54 percent thought "less emphasis on money and material possessions" would be a good thing, while only 21 percent thought this would be a bad thing.[54] Further, large majorities agreed that gaining more time for leisure activities or family life is their biggest goal in life.[55]

More broadly, in 2002 a global study sponsored by the Pew Research Center for the People & the Press found that 45 percent worldwide saw consumerism and commercialism as a threat to their own culture. Interestingly, more respondents

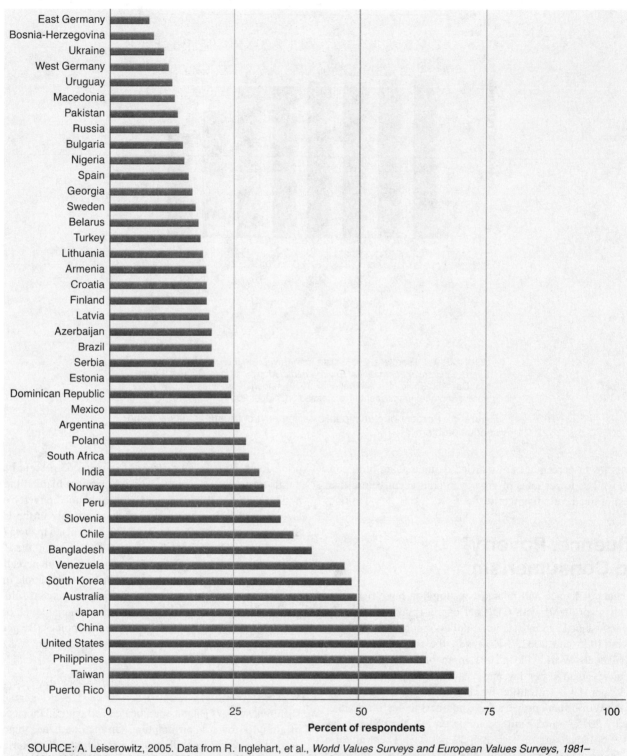

SOURCE: A. Leiserowitz, 2005. Data from R. Inglehart, et al., *World Values Surveys and European Values Surveys, 1981–1984, 1990–1993, and 1995–1997* [computer file], Inter-university Consortium for Political and Social Research (ICPSR) version (Ann Arbor, MI: Institute for Social Research [producer], 2000; Ann Arbor, MI: ICPSR [distributor], 2000).

Figure 5 Percent blaming poverty on the laziness and lack of willpower of the poor.

from high-income and upper middle-income countries (approximately 51 percent) perceived consumerism as a threat than low-middle- and low-income countries (approximately 43 percent).[56] Unfortunately, the Pew study did not ask respondents whether they believed consumerism and commercialism were a threat to the environment. In 1992, however, 41 percent said

that consumption of the world's resources by industrialized countries contributed "a great deal" to environmental problems in developing countries."[57]

On the other hand, 65 percent of respondents said that spending money on themselves and their families represents one of life's greatest pleasures. Respondents from low-GDP countries

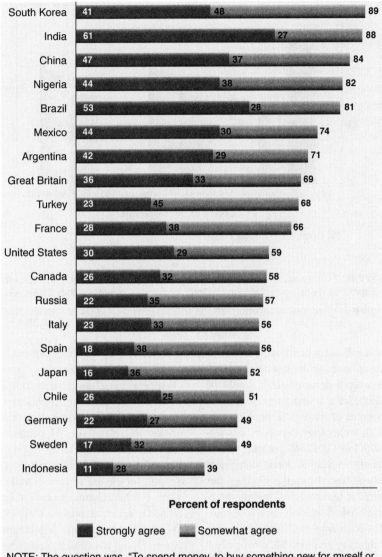

	Strongly agree	Somewhat agree	Total
South Korea	41	48	89
India	61	27	88
China	47	37	84
Nigeria	44	38	82
Brazil	53	28	81
Mexico	44	30	74
Argentina	42	29	71
Great Britain	36	33	69
Turkey	23	45	68
France	28	38	66
United States	30	29	59
Canada	26	32	58
Russia	22	35	57
Italy	23	33	56
Spain	18	38	56
Japan	16	36	52
Chile	26	25	51
Germany	22	27	49
Sweden	17	32	49
Indonesia	11	28	39

Percent of respondents

■ Strongly agree   ■ Somewhat agree

NOTE: The question was, "To spend money, to buy something new for myself or my family, is one of the greatest pleasures in my life."

SOURCE: Environics International (GlobeScan), *Consumerism: A Special Report* (Toronto: Environics International, 2002), 6.

Figure 6 Purchasing for self and family gives greatest pleasure ("strongly" and "somewhat" agree)

were much more likely to agree (74 percent) than those from high-GDP countries (58 percent), which reflects differences in material needs (see Figure 6).[58]

Likewise, there may be large regional differences in attitudes toward status consumerism. Large majorities of Europeans and North Americans' disagreed (78 percent and 76 percent respectively) that other people's admiration for one's possessions is important, while 54 to 59 percent of Latin American, Asian, and Eurasian respondents, and only 19 percent of Africans (Nigeria only), disagreed.[59] There are strong cultural norms against appearing materialistic in many Western societies, despite the high levels of material consumption in these countries relative to the rest of the world. At the same time, status or conspicuous consumption has long been posited as a significant driving force in at least some consumer behavior, especially in affluent societies.[60]

While these studies are a useful start, much more research is needed to unpack and explain the roles of values and attitudes in material consumption in different socioeconomic circumstances.

Science and Technology

Successful deployment of new and more efficient technologies is an important component of most sustainability strategies, even though it is often difficult to assess all the environmental, social, and public health consequences of these technologies in advance. Overall, the global public has very positive attitudes toward science and technology. The 1995 World Values Survey asked respondents, "In the long run, do you think the scientific advances we are making will help or harm mankind?" Worldwide, 56 percent of respondents thought science will help man-

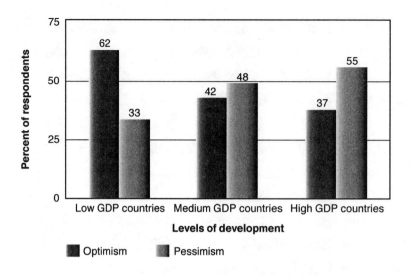

SOURCE: A. Leiserowitz, 2005. Data from Environics International (GlobeScan), *International Environmental Monitor* (Toronto: Environics International, 2002), 135.

Figure 7 Technological optimism regarding environmental problems

kind, while 26 percent thought it will harm mankind. Further, 67 percent said an increased emphasis on technological development would be a good thing, while only 9 percent said it would be bad.[61] Likewise, in 2002, GlobeScan found large majorities worldwide believed that the benefits of modern technology outweigh the risks.[62] The support for technology, however, was significantly higher in countries with low GDPs (69 percent) than in high-GDP countries (56 percent), indicating more skepticism among people in technologically advanced societies. Further, this survey found dramatic differences in technological optimism between richer and poorer countries. Asked whether "new technologies will resolve most of our environmental challenges, requiring only minor changes in human thinking and individual behavior," 62 percent of respondents from low-GDP countries agreed, while 55 percent from high-GDP countries disagreed (see Figure 7).

But what about specific technologies with sustainability implications? Do these also enjoy strong public support? What follows is a summary of global-scale data on attitudes toward renewable energy, nuclear power, the agricultural use of chemical pesticides, and biotechnology.

Europeans strongly preferred several renewable energy technologies (solar, wind, and biomass) over all other energy sources, including solid fuels (such as coal and peat), oil, natural gas, nuclear fission, nuclear fusion, and hydroelectric power. Also, Europeans believed that by the year 2050, these energy sources will be best for the environment (67 percent), be the least expensive (40 percent), and will provide the greatest amount of useful energy (27 percent).[63] Further, 37 percent of Europeans and approximately 33 percent of respondents in 16 developed and developing countries were willing to pay 10 percent more for electricity derived from renewable energy sources.[64]

Nuclear power, however, remains highly stigmatized throughout much of the developed world.[65] Among respondents from 18 countries (mostly developed), 62 percent considered nuclear power stations "very dangerous" to "extremely

dangerous" for the environment.[66] Whatever its merits or demerits as an alternative energy source, public attitudes about nuclear power continue to constrain its political feasibility.

Regarding the use of chemical pesticides on food crops, a majority of people in poorer countries believed that the benefits are greater than the risks (54 percent), while respondents in high-GDP countries were more suspicious, with only 32 percent believing the benefits outweigh the risks.[67] Since 1998, however, support for the use of agricultural chemicals has dropped worldwide. Further, chemical pesticides are now one of the top food-related concerns expressed by respondents around the world.[68]

Additionally, the use of biotechnology in agriculture remains controversial worldwide, and views on the issue are divided between rich and poor countries. Across the G7 countries, 70 percent of respondents were opposed to scientifically altered fruits and vegetables because of health and environmental concerns,[69] while 62 percent of Europeans and 45 percent of Americans opposed the use of biotechnology in agriculture.[70] While majorities in poorer countries (65 percent) believed the benefits of using biotechnology on food crops are greater than the risks, majorities in high-GDP countries (51 percent) believed the risks outweigh the benefits.[71]

More broadly, public understanding of biotechnology is still limited, and slight variations in question wordings or framings can have significant impacts on support or opposition. For example, 56 percent worldwide thought that biotechnology will be good for society in the long term, yet 57 percent also agreed that "any attempt to modify the genes of plants or animals is ethically and morally wrong."[72] Particular applications of biotechnology also garnered widely different degrees of support. While 78 percent worldwide favored the use of biotechnology to develop new medicines, only 34 percent supported its use in the development of genetically modified food. Yet, when asked whether they supported the use of biotechnology to produce more nutritious crops, 61 percent agreed.[73]

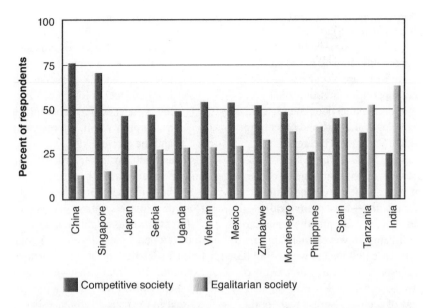

Competitive society   Egalitarian society

SOURCE: A. Leiserowitz, 2005. Data from World Values Survey, *The 1999–2002 Values Surveys Integrated Data File 1.0*, CD-ROM in R. Inglehart, M. Basanez, J. Diez-Medrano, L. Halman, and R. Luijkx, eds., *Human Beliefs and Values: A Cross-Cultural Sourcebook Based on the 1999–2002 Values Surveys*, first edition (Mexico City: Siglo XXI, 2004).

Figure 8   Multinational preferences for a competitive versus egalitarian society.

Income Equity and Entitlements

Equity and entitlements strongly determine the degree to which rising population and affluence affect human development, particularly for the poor. For example, as global population and affluence have grown, income inequality between rich and poor countries has also increased over time, with the notable exceptions of East and Southeast Asia—where incomes are on the rise on a par with (or even faster than) the wealthier nations of the world.[74] Inequality within countries has also grown in many rich and poor countries. Similarly, access to entitlements—the bundle of income, natural resources, familial and social connections, and societal assistance that are key determinants of hunger and poverty[75]—has recently declined with the emergence of market-oriented economies in Eastern and Central Europe, Russia, and China; the rising costs of entitlement programs in the industrialized countries, including access to and quality of health care, education, housing, and employment; and structural adjustment programs in developing countries that were recommended by the International Monetary Fund. Critically, it appears there is no comparative data on global attitudes toward specific entitlements; however, there is much concern that living conditions for the elderly, unemployed, and the sick and injured are deteriorating, as cited above in the discussion on human development.

In 2002, large majorities said that the gap between rich and poor in their country had gotten wider over the previous 5 years. This was true across geographic regions and levels of economic development, with majorities ranging from 66 percent in Asia, 72 percent in North America, and 88 percent in Eastern Europe (excepting Ukraine) stating that the gap had gotten worse.[76]

Nonetheless, 48 percent of respondents from 13 countries preferred a "competitive society, where wealth is distributed according to one's achievement," while 34 percent preferred an "egalitarian society, where the gap between rich and poor is small, regardless of achievement" (see Figure 8).[77]

More broadly, 47 percent of respondents from 72 countries preferred "larger income differences as incentives for individual effort," while 33 percent preferred that "incomes should be made more equal."[78] These results suggest that despite public perceptions of growing economic inequality, many accept it as an important incentive in a more individualistic and competitive economic system. These global results, however, are limited to just a few variables and gloss over many countries that strongly prefer more egalitarian distributions of wealth (such as India). Much more research is needed to understand how important the principles of income equality and equal economic opportunity are considered globally, either as global goals or as means to achieve other sustainability goals.

Does the Global Public Support Sustainable Development?

Surprisingly, the question of public support for sustainable development has never been asked directly, at least not globally. But two important themes emerge from the multinational data and analysis above. First, in general, the global public supports the main tenets of sustainable development. Second, however, there are many contradictions, including critical gaps between what people say and do—both as individuals and in aggregate. From these themes emerge a third finding: Diverse barriers stand between sustainability attitudes and action.

- *Large majorities worldwide appear to support environmental protection and economic and human development—the three pillars of sustainable development.* They express attitudes and have taken modest actions consonant with support for sustainable development, including support for environmental protection; economic growth; smaller populations; reduced poverty; improved technology; and care and concern for the poor, the marginal, the young, and the aged.

- *Amid the positive attitudes, however, are many contradictions.* Worldwide, all the components of the Human Development Index—life expectancy, adult literacy, and per capita income—have dramatically improved since World War II.[79] Despite the remarkable increases in human well-being, however, there appears to be a globally pervasive sense that human well-being has more recently been deteriorating. Meanwhile, levels of development assistance are consistently overestimated by lay publics, and the use of such aid is misunderstood, albeit strongly supported. Overall, there are very positive attitudes toward science and technology, but the most technologically sophisticated peoples are also the most pessimistic about the ability of technology to solve global problems. Likewise, attitudes toward biotechnology vary widely, depending on how the question is asked.

Further, there are serious gaps between what people believe and what people do, both as individuals and as polities. Worldwide, the public strongly supports significantly larger levels of development assistance for poor countries, but national governments have yet to translate these attitudes into proportional action. Most people value the environment—for anthropocentric as well as ecocentric reasons—yet many ecological systems around the world continue to degrade, fragment, and lose resilience. Most favor Smaller families, family planning, and contraception, but one-fifth to one-quarter of children born are not desired. Majorities are concerned with poverty and think more should be done to alleviate it, but important regions of the world think the poor themselves are to blame, and a majority worldwide accepts large gaps between rich and poor. Most people think that less emphasis on material possessions would be a good thing and that more time for leisure and family should be primary goals, but spending money often provides one of life's greatest pleasures. While many would pay more for fuel-efficient cars, fuel economy has either stagnated or even declined in many countries. Despite widespread public support for renewable energy, it still accounts for only a tiny proportion of global energy production.

- *There are diverse barriers standing between pro-sustainability attitudes and individual and collective behaviors.*[80] These include at least three types of barriers. First are the direction, strength, and priority of particular attitudes. Some sustainability attitudes may be widespread but not strongly or consistently enough relative to other, contradictory attitudes. A second type of barrier between attitudes and behavior relates to

individual capabilities. Individuals often lack the time, money, access, literacy, knowledge, skills, power, or perceived efficacy to translate attitudes into action. Finally, a third type of barrier is structural and includes laws; regulations; perverse subsidies; infrastructure; available technology; social norms and expectations; and the broader social, economic, and political context (such as the price of oil, interest rates, special interest groups, and the election cycle).

Thus, each particular sustainability behavior may confront a unique set of barriers between attitudes and behaviors. Further, even the same behavior (such as contraceptive use) may confront different barriers across society, space, and scale—with different attitudes or individual and structural barriers operating in developed versus developing countries, in secular versus religious societies, or at different levels of decisionmaking (for example, individuals versus legislatures). Explaining unsustainable behavior is therefore "dauntingly complex, both in its variety and in the causal influences on it."[81] Yet bridging the gaps between what people believe and what people do will be an essential part of the transition to sustainability.

Promoting Sustainable Behavior

Our limited knowledge about global sustainability values, attitudes, and behaviors does suggest, however, that there are short and long-term strategies to promote sustainable behavior. We know that socially pervasive values and attitudes are often highly resistant to change. Thus, in the short term, leveraging the values and attitudes already dominant in particular cultures may be more practical than asking people to adopt new value orientations.[82] For example, economic values clearly influence and motivate many human behaviors, especially in the market and cash economies of the developed countries. Incorporating environmental and social "externalities" into prices or accounting for the monetary value of ecosystem services can thus encourage both individual and collective sustainable behavior.[83] Likewise, anthropocentric concerns about the impacts of environmental degradation and exploitative labor conditions on human health and social well-being remain strong motivators for action in both the developed and developing worlds.[84] Additionally, religious values are vital sources of meaning, motivation, and direction for much of the world, and many religions are actively re-evaluating and reinterpreting their traditions in support of sustainability.[85]

In the long term, however, more fundamental changes may be required, such as extending and accelerating the shift from materialist to post-materialist values, from anthropocentric to ecological worldviews, and a redefinition of "the good life."[86] These long term changes may be driven in part by impersonal forces, like changing economics (globalization) or technologies (for example, mass media and computer networks) or by broadly based social movements, like those that continue to challenge social attitudes about racism, environmental degradation, and human rights. Finally, sustainability science will play a critical role, at multiple scales and using multiple methodologies, as it works to identify and explain the key relationships between sustainability values, attitudes, and behaviors—and to apply this knowledge in support of sustainable development.

Notes

1. For example, see U. S. National Research Council, Policy Division, Board on Sustainable Development, *Our Common Journey: A Transition toward Sustainability* (Washington, DC: National Academy Press, 1999); and P. Raskin et al., *Great Transition: The Promise and Lure of the Times Ahead* (Boston: Stockholm Environment Institute, 2002).

2. R. W. Kates, T. M. Parris, and A. Leiserowitz, "What Is Sustainable Development? Goals, Indicators, Values, and Practice," *Environment,* April 2005, 8–21.

3. For simplicity, the words "global" and "worldwide" are used throughout this article to refer to survey results. Please note, however, that there has never been a truly representative global survey with either representative samples from every country in the world or in which all human beings worldwide had an equal probability of being selected. Additionally, some developing country results are taken from predominantly urban samples and are thus not fully representative.

4. For more detail about these surveys and the countries sampled, see Appendix A in A. Leiserowitz, R. W. Kates, and T. M. Parris, *Sustainability Values, Attitudes and Behaviors: A Review of Multi-national and Global Trends* (No. CID Working Paper No. 113) (Cambridge, MA: Science, Environment and Development Group, Center for International Development, Harvard University, 2004), **http://www.cid.harvard.edu/cidwp/113.htm.**

5. Pew Research Center for the People & the Press, *Views of a Changing World* (Washington, DC: The Pew Research Center for the People & the Press, 2003), T72.

6. See R. Inglehart, "Globalization and Postmodern Values," *Washington Quarterly* 23, no. 1 (1999): 215–28.

7. Leiserowitz, Kates, and Parris, note 4 above, page 8.

8. Pew Research Center for the People & the Press, *The Pew Global Attitudes Project Dataset* (Washington, DC: The Pew Research Center for the People & the Press, 2004).

9. Gross national income (GNI) is "[t]he total market value of goods and services produced during a given period by labor and capital supplied by residents of a country, regardless of where the labor and capital are located. [GNI] differs from GDP primarily by including the capital income that residents earn from investments abroad and excluding the capital income that nonresidents earn from domestic investment." Official development assistance (ODA) is defined as "[t]hose flows to developing countries and multilateral institutions provided by official agencies, including state and local governments, or by their executive agencies, each transaction of which meets the following tests: (a) it is administered with the promotion of the economic development and welfare of developing countries as its main objective; and (b) it is concessional in character and conveys a grant element of at least 25 per cent." UN Millennium Project, *The O. 7% Target: An In-Depth Look,* **http://www.unmillenniumproject.org/involved/ action07.htm** (accessed 24 August 2005). Official development assistance (ODA) does not include aid flows from private voluntary organizations (such as churches, universities, or foundations). For example, it is estimated that in 2000, the United States provided more than $4 billion in private grants for development assistance, versus nearly $10 billion in ODA. U.S. Agency for In-

ternational Development (USAID), *Foreign Aid in the National Interest* (Washington. DC, 2002), 134.

10. Organisation for Economic Co-operation and Development (OECD), *Official Development Assistance Increases Further—But 2006 Targets Still a Challenge* (Paris: OECD, 2005), **http:// www.oecd.org/document/ 3/0,2340,en_2649_34447_34700611_ 1_1_1_1,00.html** (accessed 30 July 2005).

11. Environics International (GlobeScan), *The World Economic Forum Poll: Global Public Opinion on Globalization* (Toronto: Environics International, 2002), **http://www.globescan.com/brochures/ WEF_Poll_Brief.pdf** (accessed 5 October 2004), 3. Note that Environics International changed its name to GlobeScan Incorporated in November 2003.

12. OECD, *Public Opinion and the Fight Against Poverty* (Paris: OECD Development Centre, 2003), 17.

13. Ibid, page 19.

14. Program on International Policy Attitudes (PIPA), *Americans on Foreign Aid and World Hunger: A Study of U.S. Public Attitudes* (Washington, DC: PIPA, 2001), **http://www.pipa.org/ OnlineReports/BFW** (accessed 17 November 2004); and OECD, note 12 above, page 22.

15. See OECD Development Co-operation Directorate, *OECD-DAC Secretariat Simulation of DAC Members' Net ODA Volumes in 2006 and 2010,* **http://www.oecd.org/dataoecd/57/30/35320618.pdf;** and Central Intelligence Agency, The World Factbook, **http:// www.cia.gov/cia/publications/factbook/.**

16. OECD, note 12 above, page 20.

17. I. Smillie and H. Helmich, eds., *Stakeholders: Government-NGO Partnerships for International Development* (London: Earthscan, 1999).

18. L. White Jr., "The Historical Roots of Our Ecologic Crisis," *Science,* l0 March 1967, 1203–07.

19. See C. Merchant, *The Death of Nature: Women, Ecology, and the Scientific Revolution* (1st ed.) (San Francisco: Harper & Row 1980); C. Merchant, *Radical Ecology: The Search for a Livable Worm* (New York: Routledge, 1992); and G. Sessions, *Deep Ecology for the Twenty-First Century* (1st ed.) (New York: Shambhala Press 1995).

20. World Values Survey, *The 1999–2002 Values Surveys Integrated Data File 1.0,* CD-ROM in R. Inglehart, M. Basanez, J. Diez-Medrano, L. Halman, and R. Luijkx, eds., *Human Beliefs and Values: A Cross-Cultural Sourcebook Based on the 1999–2002 Values Surveys,* first edition (Mexico City: Siglo XXI, 2004).

21. These results come from a representative national survey of American Climate change risk perceptions, policy preferences, and behaviors and broader environmental and cultural values. From November 2002 to February 2003, 673 adults (18 and older) completed a mail-out, mail-back questionnaire, for a response rate of 55 percent. The results are weighted to bring them in line with actual population proportions. See A. Leiserowitz, "American Risk Perceptions: Is Climate Change Dangerous?" *Risk Analysis,* in press; and A. Leiserowitz, "Climate Change Risk Perception and Policy Preferences: The Role of Affect, Imagery, and Values," *Climatic Change,* in press.

22. These results support the argument that concerns about the environment are not "a luxury affordable only by those who have enough economic security to pursue quality-of-life goals." See R. E. Dunlap, G. H. Gallup Jr., and A. M. Gallup, "Of Global Concern: Results of the Health of the Planet Survey," *Environment,* November 1993, 7–15, 33-39 (quote at 37); R. E. Dunlap, A. G. Mertig, "Global Concern for the Environment: Is Affluence a Prerequisite?" *Journal of Social Issues* 511, no. 4 (1995): 121–

37; S. R. Brechin and W. Kempton, "Global Environmentalism: A Challenge to the Postmaterialism Thesis?" *Social Science Quarterly* 75, no. 2 (1994): 245–69.

23. Environics International (GlobeScan), *Environics International Environmental Monitor Survey Data-set* (Kingston, Canada: Environics International, 2000), **http://jeff-lab.queensu.ca/poadata/info/iem/iemlist.shtml** (accessed 5 October 2004). These multinational levels of concern and perceived seriousness of environmental problems remained roughly equivalent from 1992 to 2000, averaged across the countries sampled by the 1992 Health of the Planet and the Environics surveys, although some countries saw significant increases in perceived seriousness of environmental problems (India, the Netherlands, the Philippines, and South Korea), while others saw significant decreases (Turkey and Uruguay). See R. E. Dunlap, G. H. Gallup Jr., and A. M. Gallup, *Health of the Planet: Results of a 1992 International Environmental Opinion Survey of Citizens in 24 Nations* (Princeton, N J: The George H. Gallup International Institute, 1993); and R. E. Dunlap, G. H. Gallup Jr., and A. M. Gallup, "Of Global Concern: Results of the Health of the Planet Survey," *Environment*, November 1993, 7–15, 33–39.

24. GlobeScan, *Results of First-Ever Global Poll on Humanity's Relationship with Nature* (Toronto: GlobeScan Incorporated, 2004), **http://www.globescan.com/news_archives/IUCN_PR.html** (accessed 30 July 2005).

25. World Values Survey, note 20 above; and Pew Research Center for the People & the Press, *What the World Thinks in 2002* (Washington, DC: The Pew Research Center for the People & the Press, 2002), T-9. The G7 includes Canada, France, Germany, Great Britain, Italy, Japan and the United States. It expanded to the G8 with the addition of Russia in 1998.

26. R. Inglehart, et al., *World Values Surveys and European Values Surveys, 1981–1984, 1990–1993, and 1995–1997* [computer file], Inter-university Consortium for Political and Social Research (ICPSR) version (Ann Arbor, MI: Institute for Social Research [producer], 2000; Ann Arbor, MI: ICPSR [distributor], 2000).

27. Environics International (GlobeScan), note 23 above.

28. Dunlap, Gallup Jr., and Gallup, *Health of the Planet: Results of a 1992 International Environmental Opinion Survey of Citizens in 24 Nations*, note 23 above.

29. Environics International (GlobeScan), *New Poll Shows G8 Citizens Want Legally-Binding Climate Accord* (Toronto: Environics International, 2001), **http://www.globescan.com/news_archives/IEM_climatechange.pdf** (accessed 30 July 2005).

30. Environics International (GlobeScan), *International Environmental Monitor* (Toronto: Environics International, 2002), 44.

31. Ibid., page 49.

32. The European Opinion Research Group, *Eurobarometer: Energy: Issues, Options and Technologies, Science and Society,* EUR 20624 (Brussels: European Commission, 2002), 96–99.

33. Inglehart, note 26 above.

34. C. M. Rogerson, "The Waste Sector and Informal Entrepreneurship in Developing World Cities," *Urban Forum* 12, no. 2 (2001): 247–59.

35. Environics International (GlobeScan), note 30 above, page 63. These results are based on the sub-smple of those who own or have regular use of a car.

36. Environics International (GlobeScan), note 30 above, page 65.

37. Inglehart, note 26 above.

38. Environics International (GlobeScan), note 23 above.

39. P. A. Ehrlich and J. P. Holdren, review of *The Closing Circle,* by Barry Commoner, *Environment*, April 1972, 24, 26–39.

40. Y. Kaya, "Impact of Carbon Dioxide Emission Control on GNP Growth: Interpretation of Proposed Scenarios," paper presented at the Intergovernmental Panel on Climate Change (IPCC) Energy and Industry Subgroup, Response Strategies Working Group, Paris, France, 1990; and R. York, E. Rosa, and T. Dietz, "STIRPAT, IPAT and ImPACT: Analytic Tools for Unpacking he Driving Forces of Environmental Impacts," *Ecological Economics* 46, no. 3 (2003): 351.

41. IPCC, *Emissions Scenarios* (Cambridge: Cambridge University Press, 2000); and E. F. Lambin, et al., "The Causes of Land-Use and Land-Cover Change: Moving Beyond the Myths," *Global Environmental Change: Human and Policy Dimensions* 11, no. 4 (2001):

42. T. M. Parris and R. W. Kates, "Characterizing a Sustainability Transition: Goals, Targets, Trends, and Driving Forces," *Proceedings of the National Academy of Sciences of the United States of* America 100, no. 14 (2003): 6.

43. Pew Research Center for the People & the Press, note 8 above, page T17.

44. United Nations, *Majority of World's Couples Are Using Contraception* (New York: United Nations Population Division, 2001).

45. J. Bongaarts, "Trends in Unwanted Childbearing in the Developing World," *Studies in Family Planning* 28, no. 4 (1997): 267–77.

46. Demographic and Health Surveys (DHS), *STATCompiler* (Calverton, MD: Measure DHS, 2004), **http://www.measuredhs.com/** (accessed 5 October, 2004).

47. Ibid.

48. U.S. Bureau of the Census, *World Population Profile: 1998,* WP/98 (Washington, DC, 1999), 45.

49. World Bank, *World Development Indicators CD-ROM 2004* [computer file] (Washington, DC: International Bank for Reconstruction and Development (IBRD) [producer], 2004).

50. World Bank, *Global Economic Prospects 2005: Trade, Regionalism, and Development* [computer file] (Washington, DC: IBRD [producer] 2005).

51. For more information on poverty reduction strategies, see T. Banuri, review of *Investing in Development: A Practical Plan to Achieve the Millennium Goals,* by UN Millennium Project, *Environment*, November 2005 (this issue), 37.

52. Inglehart, note 26 above.

53. Inglehart, note 26 above.

54. Inglehart, note 26 above.

55. Environics International (GlobeScan), *Consumerism: A Special Report* (Toronto: Environics International, 2002), 6.

56. Pew Research Center for the People & the Press, note 25 above.

57. Dunlap, Gallup Jr., and Gallup, *Health of the Planet: Results of a 1992 International Environmental Opinion Survey of Citizens in 24 Nations,* note 23 above, page 57.

58. Environics international (GlobeScan), note 55 above, pages 3–4.

59. Environics International (GlobeScan), note 55 above, pages 3–4.

60. T. Veblen, *The Theory of the Leisure Class: An Economic Study of Institutions* (New York: Macmillan 1899).

61. Inglehart, note 26 above.

62. Environics International (GlobeScan), note 30 above, page 133.

63. The European Opinion Research Group, note 32 above, page 70.

64. Environics International (GlobeScan), note 23 above.

65. For example, see J. Flynn, P. Slovic, and H. Kunreuther, *Risk, Media and Stigma: Understanding Public Challenges to Modern Science and Technology* (London: Earthscan, 2001).

66. International Social Science Program, *Environment II,* (No. 3440) (Cologne: Zentralarchiv für Empirische Sozialforschung, Universitaet zu Koeln (Central Archive for Empirical Social Research, University of cologne), 2000), 114.

67. Environics International (GlobeScan), note 30 above, page 139.

68. Environics International (GlobeScan), note 30 above, page 141.

69. Pew Research Center for the People & the Press, note 25 above, page T20.

70. Chicago Council on Foreign Relations (CCFR), *Worldviews 2002* (Chicago: CCFR, 2002), 26.

71. Environics International (GlobeScan), note 30 above, page 163.

72. Environics International (GlobeScan), note 30 above, page 156–57.

73. Environics International (GlobeScan), note 30 above, page 57.

74. W. J. Baumol, R. R. Nelson, and E. N. Wolff, *Convergence of Productivity: Cross-National Studies and Historical Evidence* (New York: Oxford University Press, 1994).

75. A. K. Sen, *Poverty and Famines: An Essay on Entitlement and Deprivation* (Oxford: Oxford University Press, 1981).

76. Pew Research Center for the People & the Press, note 5 above, page 37.

77. World Values Survey, note 20 above.

78. World Values Survey, note 20 above.

79. The human development index (HDI) measures a country's average achievements in three basic aspects of human development: longevity, knowledge, and a decent standard of living. Longevity is measured by life expectancy at birth; knowledge is measured with the adult literacy rate and the combined primary, secondary, and tertiary gross enrollment ratio; and standard of living is measured by gross domestic product per capita (purchase-power parity US$). The UN Development Programme (UNDP) has used the HDI for its annual reports since 1993. UNDP, *Questions About the Human Development Index (HDI)*, **http://www.undp.org/hdr2003/faq.html#21** (accessed 25 August 2005).

80. See, for example, J. Blake, "Overcoming the 'Value-Action Gap' in Environmental Policy: Tensions Between National Policy and Local Experience," *Local Environment* 4, no. 3 (1999): 257–78; A. Kollmuss and J. Agyeman, "Mind the Gap: Why Do People Act Environmentally and What Are the Barriers to Pro-Environmental Behavior?" *Environmental Education Research* 8, no. 3 (2002): 239–60; and E C. Stem, "Toward a Coherent Theory of Environmentally Significant Behavior," *Journal of Social Issues* 56, no. 3 (2000): 407–24.

81. Stern, ibid., page 421.

82. See, for example, P. W. Schultz and L. Zelezny, "Reframing Environmental Messages to Be Congruent with American Values," *Human Ecology Review* 10, no. 2 (2003): 126–36.

83. Millennium Ecosystem Assessment, *Ecosystems and Human Well-Being: Synthesis* (Washington, DC: Island Press, 2005).

84. Dunlap, Gallup Jr., and Gallup, *Health of the Planet: Results of a 1992 International Environmental Opinion Survey of Citizens in 24 Nations,* note 23 above, page 36.

85. See *The Harvard Forum on Religion and Ecology,* **http://environment.harvard.edu/religion/main.html;** R. S. Gottlieb, *This Sacred Earth: Religion, Nature, Environment* (New York: Routledge, 1996); and G. Gardner, *Worldwatch Paper # 164: Invoking the Spirit: Religion, and Spirituality in the Quest for a Sustainable World* (Washington, DC: Worldwatch Institute, 2002).

86. R. Inglehart, *Modernization and Postmodernization: Cultural, Economic and Political Change in 43 Societies* (Princeton: Princeton University Press, 1997); T. O'Riordan, "Frameworks for Choice: Core Beliefs and the Environment," *Environment*, October 1995, 4–9, 25–29; and E Raskin and Global Scenario Group, *Great Transition: The Promise and Lure of the Times Ahead* (Boston: Stockholm Environment Institute, 2002).

ANTHONY A. LEISEROWITZ is a research scientist at Decision Research and an adjunct professor of environmental studies at the University of Oregon, Eugene. He is also a principal investigator at the Center for Research on Environmental Decisions at Columbia University. Leiserowitz may be reached at (541) 485-2400 or by email at ecotone@uoregon.edu. **ROBERT W. KATES** is an independent scholar based in Trenton, Maine, and a professor emeritus at Brown University, where he served as director of the Feinstein World Hunger Program. He is also a former vice-chair of the Board of Sustainable Development of the U.S National Academy's National Research Council. In 1991, Kates was awarded the National Medal of Science for his work on hunger, environment, and natural hazards. He is an executive editor of *Environment* and may be contacted at rkates@acadia.net. **THOMAS M. PARRIS** is a research scientist at and director of the New England office of ISCIENCES, LLC. He is a contributing editor of *Environment*. Parris may be reached at parris@isciences.com. The authors retain copyright.

From *Environment*, Vol. 47, no. 9, November 2005, pp. 23–38. Published by Heldref Publications, Washington, DC. Copyright © 2005 by Anthony A. Leiserowitz, Robert W. Kates, and Thomas M. Parris. Reprinted by permission of the authors.

Eliminating Child Labor

Today's debates on child labor and international trade echo arguments heard in the United States less than a century ago

MIRIAM WASSERMAN

I n 1995, when news broke in the United States that the soccer balls used in kids' games were routinely made by children in other countries, many were horrified. It was not the first time such a scandal had hit the spotlight. Reports were frequent in the 1990s of children working in garment factories, shoe shops, and mines producing goods that would ultimately make their way to U.S. markets. Although child labor is not a new problem, increased trade and more widespread information have brought us closer to practices, problems, and institutions that can conflict with our own beliefs. The intensity of the feelings on the issue was highlighted last December during the World Trade Organization's (WTO) ministerial conference in Seattle. Thousands of protesters clamored for tighter rules on labor in international trade. President Clinton chose the setting to sign an international treaty to eliminate the worst forms of child labor and urged other countries to follow his lead. The United States also called on the WTO to make child labor and other labor rights issues part of the agenda. But the measure faced stringent opposition from developing nations. Countries such as Thailand, Brazil, and India feared that mandating higher labor standards could rob them of their comparative advantage in cheap labor, price them out of the market, and block their prospects for greater growth and economic development. They argued, in effect, that the industrialized-country focus on child labor used in exports would not only lead to the loss of jobs, but also end up hurting the very children it was intended to help.

Such arguments echoed the heated debates heard in this country less than a century ago. At the beginning of the twentieth century, pressure for federal legislation covering child labor was growing nationally, but especially in the North. It was greeted with resentment in many segments of southern society. They saw it as interference from a richer North which—after having benefited from child labor in its own industrial development—was trying to limit the South's development.

In spite of the controversy, however, the movement to limit child labor prevailed. Today, the number of American children employed full-time has been vastly reduced. But these changes took almost a century and required a host of changes in family income, education policy, production technologies, and cultural norms.

Although the recent scandals have linked child labor to trade, child labor goes well beyond export industries, is widespread, and deeply rooted. Looking at the U.S. experience in reducing child labor can help us get a better understanding of the profound transformation that the elimination of child labor involves.

The Ball Is in Whose Court?

The public outcry in the mid 1990s over child labor used to stitch soccer balls put enormous pressure on soccer ball importers such as Reebok, Nike, and Baden Sports. The changes they and other importers made resulted in one of more successful efforts to eliminate child labor from a specific industry. Consumers can now buy imported soccer balls without feeling as if they are encouraging or benefiting from child labor. But the effect on the children involved is less clear.

The impact was felt most directly in and around the city of Sialkot, Pakistan, a region known for over 80 years for its soccer ball industry. In 1996, 75 percent of the world's soccer balls were made there. The industry was a major source of employment, giving jobs to about 10,000 urban workers and 30,000 rural workers in the surrounding villages. Among them, more than 7.000 children, the vast majority of them between the ages of 10 and 14 (but some as young as five), stitched balls on a full-time basis, according to the U.S. Department of Labor. Other children worked part-time outside of school hours. Middlemen and subcontractors took soccer ball kits to village workshops or households, where workers hand-stitched individual pieces together, glued the bladder to the material, and sewed in the final piece. Once completed, the balls were taken back by the middlemen to the factories for packing and shipment. Children were paid about $0.50 to $0.55 per ball; and depending upon skill and experience, they could be stitching between one and five balls per day.

As a result of the international uproar and bad publicity, Reebok and Nike both contracted with Pakistani manufacturers to make balls in new facilities where all the production was centralized. External monitoring was setup so that no children entered the factory and no soccer ball kits were taken out. The

Working Children Around the Globe

These estimates undercount children whose work in the household is not sold in the market.
They also include children who work part-time.

	NUMBER OF CHILDREN 5-14 WORKING (MILLIONS)	% OF CHILDREN 5-14 WHO WORK			
World	250	24.7			
Africa	80	41.4			
Asia[1]	152.5	21.5			
Latin America & Caribbean	17.5	16.5			
Oceania[2]	0.5	29.3			
SAMPLE COUNTRIES	(THOUSANDS)		GNP PER CAPITA (US$)	% OF POPULATION UNDER POVERTY	% OF CHILDREN ATTENDING PRIMARY SCHOOL	% OF PRIMARY SCHOOL CHILDREN REACHING 5TH GRADE
Bangladesh	6,584	19.1	350	36	76	61
Nepal	2,596	41.7	210	42	70	52
Pakistan	3,313	8.0	480	34	66	48
Philippines	1,863	10.6	1,050	41	89	70
Turkey	1,495	12.6	3,160	NA	73	89

1. EXCLUDES JAPAN. 2. EXCLUDES AUSTRALIA AND NEW ZEALAND. SOURCES: ILO, WORLD BANK, AND UNICEF
NOTE: SAMPLE COUNTRIES WERE CHOSEN BECAUSE THEY HAD AVAILABLE CHILD LABOR ESTIMATES BASED ON THE SAME ILO METHODOLOGY

German firm Baden Sports Inc. moved its manufacturing operations to China.

Although well intentioned, these changes were not wholly beneficial to the former child workers and their families. "While Baden Sports can quite credibly claim that their soccer balls are not sewn by children, the relocation of their production facility undoubtedly did nothing for their former child workers and their families," write economists Drusilla Brown, Alan Deardorif, and Robert Stern. Although Nike, Reebok, and the other firms who switched to centralized stitching centers did not displace work from the region, they reduced the income opportunities for women who formerly stitched soccer balls from home in between other household tasks.

About one-quarter of the world's children work; almost half of them, 120 million, do so full-time

Brown notes that although the children worked long hours (between eight and nine hours a day), the working conditions were better than in other industries. Most of the children could read, and were not exposed to toxic chemicals or hazardous tools. Moreover, there was no evidence of the practice of intergenerational debt bondage—one of the most blatant forms of exploitation, in which children are given to their parents' "creditor" so that they repay the family's debt through work. In a region that specializes in handmade soccer balls, says Brown, "perhaps learning a trade was the most appropriate use of their time."

What Is the Alternative?

As the soccer ball example illustrates, if the goal is to improve the welfare of the children, removing them from work is only part of the issue. The larger question is how to provide them with better alternatives.

"Stopping child labor without doing anything else could leave children worse off," says former Secretary of Labor Robert Reich. "If they are working out of necessity, as most are, stopping them could force them into prostitution or other employment with greater personal dangers. The most important thing is that they be in school and receive the education to help them leave poverty," he adds.

That children and their families need alternatives was clearly demonstrated in Bangladesh in 1993. Garment employers, fearing the passage of a law in the United States to ban imports made with child labor, summarily fired an estimated 50,000 children from their factories. The Child Labor Deterrence Act

Domestic Restrictions on Child Labor

The evolution of laws regulating child labor in the United States was a slow and uneven process. The industrial Northeastern states started restricting the employment of children much before the more agrarian and poorer states. And opposition was fierce when it came to passing a federal law on child labor. All in all, more than a century went by between the passage of the first state law limiting the employment of youth and the adoption of an effective national standard on child labor.

The first law in the country to place limitations on the employment of children was enacted by Massachusetts in 1836. The driving concern was not the age of working children, the hours they worked, or the danger involved in their occupations. Rather, state legislators were worried about work's impact on children's education. The Massachusetts law stipulated that no children under age 15 could be employed unless they had attended school for at least three months in the preceding year. Education was later made compulsory in Massachusetts in 1852. Compulsory schooling laws were enacted in most of the states outside the South during the last half of the nineteenth century, according to William M. Landes and Lewis C. Solomon.

Massachusetts was also first to limit children's workdays, banning children under 12 from working more than 10 hours in 1842. Pennsylvania established the first minimum age in 1848: 12 years for work in cotton, woolen, and silk mills. The first night-work provision was enacted in 1888, when Massachusetts prohibited children under 14 from working between 7 p.m. and 6 a.m. A few, mostly Northeastern states, followed these legal examples, setting minimum age and other requirements according to their local needs and preferences.

Enforcement of these laws was scant. No proof of age was required for employment, and it wasn't until 1867 that Massachusetts instituted the nation's first factory inspection. Even so, the wording of the laws gave ample space for loopholes. For instance, "in Massachusetts, New Jersey, and Rhode Island, the only punishable violations of child labor were those committed 'knowingly,'" according to historian Walter Trattner.

In 1879, only seven states restricted the age of children in manufacturing, with an average minimum age of 11. The uneven formulation of state laws led reformers to push for a national standard. But this turned out to be a drawn-out fight. Two federal laws, the Keating-Owen Bill of 1916 and the Pomerene's Tax Bill of 1919 were declared unconstitutional in 1918 and 1922, respectively, by the U.S. supreme court, which considered them in violation of states' rights. Beginning in 1922, anti-child-labor reformers pushed for a constitutional amendment intended to grant Congress specific authority to legislate protections for working children.

Most of the opposing votes in Congress came from southern textile states, and it was the Southern Cotton Manufacturers, an industry group, which contested the constitutionality of the laws. Southern states had a larger agricultural base and, particularly after the Civil War, were afflicted with widespread poverty—both factors associated with a greater incidence of child labor. Also, the textile industry, which relied heavily on children, spread and grew dramatically in the South during the second half of the nineteenth century, particularly in Georgia, Alabama, and the Carolinas.

With the Great Depression, the national mood on federal child labor legislation changed. It seemed to many that adult workers were being replaced by young children at lower wages, and this helped shore up the support for restricting child labor.

In 1938, with the passage of the Fair Labor Standards Act, a national standard on the employment of children was finally set. The FLSA prohibited interstate commerce in goods made by children under 16 years of age and by children under 18 years in particularly hazardous occupations. Exceptions could be made for 14- and 15-year-olds in occupations other than manufacturing and mining, if the work did not interfere with their schooling, health, or well-being. Still, the law did not cover children employed in agriculture during their school vacations or migratory child workers.

did not make it into the law books, but the threat of a boycott was serious enough that garment manufacturers began firing children. Some of the displaced children tried to replace the lost income by engaging in stone crushing, street hustling, and prostitution. In response, international agencies and nongovernmental organizations urged the industry to stop firing underage workers until a safety net was in place. After extended negotiations, the Bangladesh Garment Manufacturers and Exporters Association, the International Labor Organization (ILO) and UNICEF agreed to jointly sponsor schools. They also provided monthly stipends to children to help their families replace lost income. By 1997, over three hundred schools were established that served a total of 9,710 children.

Where Do Children Work?

The U.S. Dept. of Labor estimates that less than 5 percent of working children produce manufacturing and mining goods for export

	PERCENT OF TOTAL
Agriculture, hunting, forestry, and fishing	70.4
Mining and quarrying	0.9
Manufacturing	8.3
Electricity, gas, and water	0
Construction	1.9
Wholesale and retail trade, restaurants, and hotels	8.3
Transport, storage, and communication	3.8
Financing, insurance, real estate, and business services	0
Community, social, and personal services	6.5

SOURCE: ILO Bureau of Statistics.

Just banning exports made with child labor can push children into more harmful occupations

This incident set an example that is now being followed in Sialkot, attempts are being made to provide the displaced children with some form of social protection. An agreement modeled after the one drafted in Bangladesh was reached between the Sialkot Chamber of Commerce and Industry, UNICEF, and the ILO to provide children and their families with informal education for the children and help for the adults in finding other opportunities to earn income. As of August 1999, 5,795 children were attending classes at the 176 centers sponsored.

Still, replacing work with education can be a difficult task. In many developing countries, particularly in remote rural areas, schools are often not available or not affordable for the poorest families. Countries where child labor is prevalent have very limited resources, and, in some cases, governments have not invested sufficiently to have adequate schools in place. In both Pakistan and Bangladesh, special schools needed to be created for the children leaving the soccer and garment industries. In Pakistan, according to the latest figures from UNICEF, only 66 percent of children attended primary school and fewer than half of them reached fifth grade. Bangladesh fared somewhat better with 76 percent of children attending primary school and 61 percent of them reaching fifth grade.

And getting the children to attend schools presents its own challenges, since education is not always seen as something that will be useful. In Sialkot, where the children were offered no stipends, it has required considerable mobilization and awareness raising with the children and their families, particularly if the children had significant earnings.

A Global Picture

Children working in the Pakistani soccer ball industry and in the garment sector of Bangladesh received much attention because they were working in industries that produced goods destined for export to the United States. But children in export manufacturing industries represent only a tiny share of all child labor.

About 120 million children 5 to 14 years of age work full-time in the developing world. If part-time work is included, the number of children working grows to 250 million. Even this figure is probably an underestimate because it excludes unpaid work that does not make its way into the market, such as the work of children—particularly girls—who stay home to do household chores or watch over younger siblings. Probably less than 5 percent of all child workers are employed in export industries in manufacturing and mining, according to the U.S. Department of Labor. The vast majority of children who work—over 70 percent—do so in agriculture.

The best predictor of the incidence of child labor is poverty. Child labor declines steeply as one moves from low-income to high-income countries, notes Princeton economist Alan Krueger. Asia, the most densely populated region of the world, has the largest number of child workers, but it is in poverty-stricken Africa where the highest proportion of children work. About 20 percent of African children aged 5 to 14 work full-time—a little under 40 million children. Eighty million children work if part-time work is in-

Photography for Change

Lewis Hine's camera was one of the most powerful weapons mustered by the child labor reformers in the early twentieth century. Employed full-time by the National Child Labor Committee (NCLC) between 1908 and 1918, Hine investigated and photographed the working conditions of children in industries in most states east of the Mississippi River and in Missouri, Colorado, Texas, and California. He was among the first to use photography to promote social change, and his images left a lasting impression.

The match between the NCLC and Hine was rather fortuitous. Hine was born in Oshkosh, Wisconsin, in 1874. He started out his professional career as an educator and began using photography as an educational tool, through his acquaintance with Frank A. Manny, a professor of education and psychology, at the Ethical Culture School in New York City. Both men were interested in studying the immigrant tide flowing through Ellis Island at the turn of the century, and Manny assisted Hine in taking some of his first successful pictures.

In the meantime, Edgar Gardner Murphy, an Episcopal clergyman in Montgomery, Alabama, and the founder of the Alabama Child Labor Committee, had pioneered the use of photography in the anti-child-labor campaign. Around 1901, Murphy had smuggled a camera into some of Alabama's textile mills and produced a powerful pamphlet called *Pictures from the Mills*. When the child labor committees in Alabama and New York joined forces and founded the NCLC in 1904, Murphy was one of the movement's most influential figures. In 1906, Hine began photographing children at work for the NCLC on a freelance basis, and by 1908 his passion for photography replaced his teaching career.

The images Hine captured for the NCLC left a deep impression not just because of the emotional topic, but also thanks to Hine's aesthetic sensibilities. In order to obtain the photographs, Hine defied difficult circumstances. His photographic equipment—a modified box-type 5" x 7" camera—weighed up to 50 pounds and the explosive magnesium flash-powder used in interior settings could be quite dangerous. (Apparently, Jacob Riis, a famous contemporary social reform photographer, twice set the places he was photographing on fire.)

Hine's entry was not welcomed at the mills, mines, or factories. He often had to pass as a fire inspector, an insurance salesman, a Bible salesman, or an industrial photographer. To document the specific cases of child labor, he surreptitiously wrote notes in the notebook he kept in his pocket, and he used the buttons on his jacket to measure the children's height. He directed his attention to the particular industries or trades that the NCLC targeted: coal mines, glass factories, Southern and Northern textile mills, seafood canneries, street trades (newsboys and messengers), and agriculture. All in all, he took over 5,000 photographs for the NCLC.

By 1918, the NCLC decided to focus more on the investigative work than on photography, and Hine moved on to other projects. He photographed the Red Cross's efforts at the end of World War I, created a series on men at work, participated in photography projects during the New Deal, and documented the construction of the Empire State building. But commissions for his work declined in the last decade of his life, and he died in poverty in 1940.

cluded. In countries where 1990 income per capita exceeded $5,000, the employment of children was negligible, says Krueger.

The relationship between poverty and child labor is also true within countries. A range of studies in settings as varied as contemporary Côte d'Ivoire and nineteenth century Philadelphia have found that the incidence of child labor decreases as family income rises. Because of this, many believe that economic growth—if evenly distributed—is a key factor in reducing child labor.

Yet, the issue is not just poverty. Cultural factors also play an important role. In many instances, whether a child works or not depends on such factors as gender, religion, or social caste. In his work on child labor in India, MIT political scientist Myron Weiner pointed out that India's incidence of child labor was higher than that of some countries with lower income per capita. He speculated that religious beliefs and India's hierarchical caste system have prevented education from playing an equalizing role in society. "Those who control the education system are remarkably indifferent to the low enrollment and high dropout rate among the lowest social classes," he writes. "The result is one of the highest child labor rates in the world."

In terms of work hazards, children are more susceptible to injuries or work-related illnesses than adults doing the same type of work. The greatest number of illnesses and injuries occur in agriculture, not surprisingly, given the number of children working in that sector. But the likelihood of injury is by far the greatest for children who work in construction and mining, sectors that employ about 3 percent of working children.

Children also tend to work very long hours, leaving little time for school even when it is available. In surveys of 20 countries, the ILO found that in some countries more than half of the children who worked were doing so for nine or more hours per day and up to four-fifths of them did it seven days a week. But evidence on the relationship between school and work is mixed. In a study of child labor in Côte d'Ivoire, World Bank economist Christian Grootaeert found that working actually allowed many children to attend (afford) school.

Learning from the United States

The plight of working children in the developing world today is not very different, and in some cases even less harsh, than that prevalent in countries such as the United States and England during the nineteenth and early twentieth centuries. As recently as 1900, the U.S. Census estimated that 1.75 million children between the ages of 10 and 15 were employed—about 18 percent of the population that age. The majority of these children worked in agriculture. But young children also worked long hours in factories and textile mills, in the anthracite coal mines of Pennsylvania, and in many other industries.

Yet, the contrast between then and now is dramatic. Today, we take for granted that full-time work for children is bad; but in the early eighteenth century, work was believed to be beneficial for a child's character and moral upbringing. The work of children was integral to the agricultural and handicraft economy. Children and not wives were the most common source of family income aside from what fathers earned. They not only worked on the family farm, but also were often hired out to other farmers.

By the early 1800s, with the beginning of the Industrial Revolution, children went into the factory. New machines raised their productivity and also generated a growing demand for their labor. Economists Claudia Goldin and Kenneth Sokoloff estimate that boys and girls under 15 years of age accounted for 23 percent of all workers in manufacturing in the Northeast in 1820. The work of minors was so important to rising industry that Goldin and Sokoloff have speculated that the availability of relatively cheaper labor from women and children gave the Northeast a comparative advantage over the South, and was one of the factors that facilitated for the region's greater industrial development. (Women in the preindustrial South earned considerably higher wages than their counterparts in the North, according to Goldin and Sokoloff, because they were more productive in southern crops, such as cotton and tobacco, than in the hay, grains, and dairy products produced in the North.)

Child labor laws have been more effective when combined with compulsory education

But as children started working in the mills, the nature of their work changed dramatically. No longer were children working on family farms or in small workshops, but rather on factory floors in repetitive motions, for extremely long hours, with dangerous machinery and often abusive supervisors. Public acceptance of children in work began to change. At the same time, the social view of children was shifting and people began to believe that child's play and leisure were not vices but important aspects to healthy development. Also, as infant mortality rates diminished, parents moved from having many children to having fewer, but investing more in their success.

By the end of the nineteenth century, child labor was clearly on the decline. Social opposition to child labor became organized and very active in demanding legislation to limit the employment of minors. The National Child Labor Committee, founded in 1904, pioneered techniques of mass political action. It hired photographer Lewis Hine to capture the poor conditions of children at work and widely distributed his influential photographs.

Major legislative change took place between 1880 and 1910, during which time 36 states set legal limits on the minimum age of workers in manufacturing—14 years, on average. Finally, a federal law setting a national minimum standard of employment for children was passed in 1938 (see sidebar).

The relative contribution of laws, economic development, and cultural change in reducing child labor is a matter of debate. Between 1880 and 1900, there was a perception that the proportion of children in manufacturing was increasing and this helped fuel the movement for reform. But even though child labor might have increased in the cotton mills of the South and in industries that employed the growing flow of impoverished European immigrants, economists today believe that the fraction of the industrial labor force composed of youth had actually been declining throughout the latter part of the nineteenth century. They attribute this in part to rising incomes, which had made it possible for families to depend less on the income earned by their children. Additionally, new technologies requiring more highly skilled workers led to a decrease in the demand for the unskilled labor of children and to an increase in the returns to education.

Thus, Ohio State University economist Carolyn Moehling believes today that minimum age limits had relatively little effect on the employment of children at the turn of the century. In this view, increasing wealth and changing technology were more directly responsible for the reduction in child labor. Laws helped to cap a process that was already under way. Indeed, the passage of laws banning child labor was possible because there no longer was fervent opposition from parents and industry groups.

But, regardless of whether laws or economic progress led the change, there is widespread agreement that legislation was more effective in bringing about a decline in child labor when combined with compulsory education. Vanderbilt economists Robert Margo and T. Aldrich Finnegan found that, in turn-of-the century America, compulsory education laws had a significant impact in increasing school attendance only in states that also had child labor laws for children of the same age. They speculate that child labor laws reduced the incentive to seek paid employment and in many cases required children to satisfy educational requirements before starting to work. At the same time, it is easier to monitor and enforce school attendance than to oversee the absence of children from each individual workplace.

The importance of each factor contributing to the decline—laws, rising incomes, and changing production technology—likely varied from region to region and from industry to industry. For example, economists Martin Brown, Jens Christiansen, and Peter Philips found that economic factors played a more significant role than legislation in eliminating child labor in the canning industry in urban areas, but laws had a greater impact in rural ones.

As canneries became more mechanized, they required more steady, reliable labor to maximize the use of the equipment, and children became less desirable as workers. Because of this, child labor declined substantially in urban canneries, which made high investments in capital equipment and whose profitability depended on running the machines continuously and working on a variety of crops year-round. In contrast, rural canneries were smaller-scale and specialized in canning the local crop. They had access to a more limited labor pool and had a much more seasonal schedule of production. Both factors made them highly dependent on child labor during peak production times. Thus, in rural areas more exemptions and qualifications to the laws were passed. But ultimately, the legal restrictions weighed more heavily in reducing child labor there than in urban canneries, where the economics of more capital-intensive production had already diminished its use.

One Size Does Not Fit All

Just as the importance of different forces varied across individual industries and regions of the United States, there is a consensus in the field that no one solution to the child labor problem can be applied to all countries. What can be done to eliminate child labor will vary, depending on the level and distribution of income, the availability of education, and the cultural factors that influence child labor.

For the poorest of countries, it maybe impossible to really eliminate child labor without income growth or some form of international aid. But for countries with relatively more resources, a range of policy alternatives can help bring about change. "Government can intervene in the market to create a variety of incentives, such as providing better and more schools, giving school meals, and improving conditions in the adult labor market, which result in a reduction of child labor," says Cornell economist Kaushik Basu.

What is to be done depends on the educational infrastructure in place. The American example clearly showed that education played a key role. Better educated workers in the United States were more productive and thus were better able to provide for their own children, reducing the need for child labor. And, taking children out of the labor force may help them only if you provide them with a better alternative.

Export goods are only the tip of the iceberg when it comes to child labor. Perhaps international pressure will help bring about a change in the perception of child labor in countries where it is accepted as an integral part of life. But, for the permanent elimination of child labor, a cultural change ultimately has to come from within developing countries.

Looking to the past gives hope for the future. Child labor, once endemic in countries like the United States and Great Britain, has been greatly reduced there. The process was long, and involved sustained change on many different fronts. But the payoff was worth the effort, for it is hard to build a strong future with such small hands.

From *Regional Review*, Second Quarter 2000, pp. 8–17. © 2000 by the Federal Reserve Bank of Boston. Reprinted by permission.

Index

2001 tax cuts, 120–121
2004 Economic Report of the President, flaws regarding health insurance in. 72
9/11, regulatory counter-terrorism and, 10–11

A

adverse selection, private health insurance and, 68, 69
Agricultural Revolution, 39
Agriculture: biotechnology and, 174; rainfed, 164
air travel: demand for, 22; innovation in, 23
airlines: cost structure of, 21; deregulation and, 22; low-cost, 23; ownership rules, 21, 22; performance of, 21; recent financial regulatory barriers, 21, 22; safety, 3, 4, 22; security, 22
Alabama Child Labor Committee, 184
"anonymous capital," 148
antitrust policy: flexible interpretation and enforcement of, 25; four general objectives of, 24; inadequacy of price-based theory of, 26; intellectual property rights and, 25–26; network economy and, 26
Aral Sea, diminished water supply and, 163
ASEA+3, 144
ASEAN Treaty of Amity and Cooperation, 145
Asian Development Bank, 144
Asian Union, 144; analogy to G8, 144–145
ATM surcharging: customer attraction and, 126; deployment implications, 126; pre- and post-1996, 126
ATMs. 125–127; industry structure of, 125; Cirrus and Plus, 125; deployment rationales, 125–126

B

Baden Sports, Inc., 181
balanced growth, 53–54
bank bailouts in developing countries: impact on poor and, 153; public debt in developing countries and, 152
bank mergers, post-1997: anti-trust concerns and, 123; four forces driving, 122–123; market expansion and, 122; policy concerns regarding, 123–124
banks: scope of services, post-Gramm-Leach-Bliley Act, 123; economies and diseconomies of scale and, 122–123; diversification of risk and, 123; economies of scope, and,123; managements' personal incentives and, 123
Bernanke, Ben, 119
Bork, Robert H., 25, 27
Bush, George W., 64; health care costs and, 67

C

Can We Say No? (Aaron and Schwartz), 74
capital flight from developing countries, 152
capital substitution, federally mandated, 10

Carlton, Dennis W., 26–27
cash, disadvantages of, 128
cashless society: functioning of, 128–129; privacy issues and, 128, 129–130; reduction in crime attributable to, 129; scenario for going, 130; thwarting illicit activity and, 128; traceability and, 129
Castro, Fidel, 81
central banks: accountability and, 110, 111; financial stability goal, 110; goal dependency and, 109; guiding principles of, 106; instrument independence and, 110; transparency, 110–111
Chavez, Hugo, 81, 82
chemical industry, counter-terrorism and "free riders," 10
Child Labor Deterrence Act, The, 181–182
child labor: poverty and, 183–184; eliminating in Bangladesh, 182; evolution of U.S. law on, 182; impact of eliminating, 181–182; by industry, 183; soccer ball manufacturing and, 180–181; trends in U.S. and, 180; World Trade Organization and, 180
child-care, 53
China: foreign investment in R&D in, 143; implications of buying U.S. debt and, 81; higher technology, and, 143; predictions on future of, 85
cigarette taxes, increases and impacts, 14–15
Clayton Act of 1914, 25
Clinton, Bill, health care and, 67, 74–75
command-and-control mandates, 10–11
consumer behavior, environmental considerations and, 169–170
"consumer-directed" approach to health care reform, 71–72
consumerism, attitudes toward, 172–173
consumption-based tax, 95: arguments for and against, 100; two types of, 100
Contemporary U.S. Tax Policy (Steuerle), 104
corruption, globalization and, 152–153
Corzine, Jon, 10
Coughlin, Tom, 19
counter-terrorism spending, 10
"creative destruction," 7
current account deficit, 141–142

D

Demographic and Health Surveys (DHS), 170–171
developing countries: education and, 153; export barriers and, 154; impact of global market failures and, 153; unequal opportunities for, 153
development assistance: public support for, 166; public understanding of, 167
digital "set-top" box, 16
digital economy, five needed advances of, 50
digital piracy, 16, 17
digital television, three factions seeking control of, 16–17

diminishing utilities, law of, 6
disease, interspecies contacts and, 136
disincentives to work, 95
Disposable American: Layoffs and Their Consequences, The, (Uchitelle), 60
dollar, hypothetical devaluation of, 80–82; impact of, 82–86
domination ethic, 166–167
"donor fatigue," 166

E

earned income tax credit (EITC), 95
East Asia Summit, 144
East Asia: intraregional trade and, 144, 145; political integration in, 145; regional mechanisms in, 145
eco-economy: compared with market economy, 36; declining industries in, 37; energy and, 36–37; expanding industries in, 37, 38; new jobs in, 39, 40
economic development, global, 165; attitudes toward, 165, 166; subjective well-being by level of, 167
economic growth: government social spending correlation and, 93–96; as religion, 91–92; eco-philosophy, 91
education, U.S. investment in, 143
electronic funds transfer (EFT) technology, 128
Eli Lilly, 52
emergency communication, digital TV and, 17
emissions credits, 11
employer-based health insurance, 67, 69; rising costs undermining, 69; under strain, 69
employment cost index, 120
Employment Policy Foundation, 53
environmental concern, global, 167–169
environmental policies, attitudes toward, 169
Environmental Protection Agency (EPA), counter-terrorism regulations and, 10–11
environmental protection versus economic growth, global attitudes toward, 169
Environmental Revolution, 39–41
ethical standards, global, 137–138
ex ante standards-setting, 26
"excess cost growth," of health care, 70–71; ramifications of, 71

F

family planning, 170
"family service credit," 64
FDIC Improvement Act (FDICIA), 124
Federal Communications Commission, 16
Federal deficit: longevity and, 81; prescription-drug coverage to Medicare and, 73, 81; Republicans and, 79; tax cuts of 2001 and, 80–81
federal electronic currency (FEDEC), 128–129
Federal funding for research, 143
Federal government solvency, health care and, 67

Index

Federal Reserve, scorecard for, 111–114
Federal Trade Commission (FTC), 25
financial crises and global financial markets, 152
financial instability, economic downturns and, 108
financial stability, central banks and, 111
fiscal and monetary policy, central banks and, 106–107
Fischer, Thorsten, 33
flat tax, 99, 101
flexible exchange rates, U. S. inflation and, 117
flight wealth, 147–148
"free rider" problem, 10
free trade theory, 139

G

gas stations, pricing and, 31
gasoline: externalized costs of, 29–30; pollution-related costs of, 29–30; protection subsidies and, 29; retail pricing of, 31; social costs related to, 30; subsidies and, 29; tax breaks and, 29
globalization, failures of, 151–152; prescription for overcoming, 154–155
Gramm-Leach-Bliley Act (GLB), 123
Great Depression, 108, 119
Great Inflation, 119
Great Moderation, 120
Greenspan, Alan, 119–120
Gross Domestic Product (GDP), 90; accounting for intangibles and, 90; impact of social spending on, 93–96

H

haven network, 147
health care: as portion of GDP, 117; rising costs of , 85, 120
Health Care Mess (Richmond and Fein), 69
health care rationing, 74
health care, U.S.: inefficiencies in, 72; international comparisons, 72; three crises of, 67; fragmentation of, 67
health savings accounts, tax-advantaged, 71; objections to, 71–72
Healthy, Wealthy, and Wise (Cogan, Hubbard, and Kessler), 71
high-performance work organization, 51
Hine, Lewis, 184
HIV/AIDS, 136, 138, 149, 152

I

I=PAT identity, 170
income distribution: global disparity, 135; global inequities in, 151–152; hypothetical projections of, 85; shift in, 55
income equity, attitudes toward, 175
income tax simplification, Federal, 99
Industrial Revolution, 40
innovation system, outsourcing and, 8
interest rates, real: defined, 116; how changes in affect demand, 116–117
International Labor Organization, child labor and, 182, 183, 184
international migration, 154
International Monetary Fund, 154
international private banking, 148

Internet, as self-organizing mechanism for civilization, 136; vulnerabilities of, 136
irrigation: current scale of, 156; possible improvements in, 163; projections by region, 157, 158

J

jobs lost to free trade, 139; tariffs and, 139

K

Keynes, John Maynard, 50
"kleptocracies," 147

L

layoffs: impact on employers, 60; impact on workers and families, 60; reemployment realities and, 60
life, saved, value of, 3–5; table of regulations and, 4;

M

manufactured goods, China, India and, 135
market economy: ecological costs and, 34–35
Marx, Karl, 91, 92
means-tested welfare system, 95
Medicaid, 67: creation of, 68–69; efficiency compared to private insurance, 73; growth in coverage, 69; rising costs of, 69, 70; strains on, 69
Medicare, 96; costs, compared to employer-based health insurance plans, 67–68
Mill, John Stuart, 100
Millenum Ecosystem Assessment, 135
minimum wage, state, 61–62
monetary policy: forward looking, 107; inflation and, 117; lags in impact of changes in, 117–118
Moynihan, Daniel Patrick, 85
Murphy, Edgar Gardner, 184

N

nanotechnology, pollution and, 137
National Child Labor Committee (NCLC), 184
national sales tax, 101–102
network economy, antitrust policy and, 26
Nike, 180–181
non-destructive sales, 8

O

Obsfeld, Maurice, 141
ODA/GNI (official development assistance/gross national income), 166
oil companies, U.S.: exploration and, 33; protection subsidies for, 29; refining capacity and, 33; subsidies to, 29; tax breaks to, 29
oil depletion, 32–33
oil prices, hedge funds and, 31–32; government intervention and, 33
Organization for Economic Cooperation and Development, 105
organized crime, 137
Orwell, George, 130

output, ,6; fluctuations, monetary policy and, 107
outsourcing jobs: domestic jobs dynamics and, 57–58; how U.S. benefits from, 56–57; rationale for, 56;; in service industries, 58
outsourcing, 7–8

P

Painful Prescription: Rationing Hospital Care (Aaron and Schwartz), 74
parental leave, 95–96
payment industry, 128
peak oil theory, 32–33
pension-fund shortfalls, 120
policymakers, accountability of, 107, 110
pollution credits, 11
population growth, global projections of, 137; global rates of, 170
poverty, attitudes toward, 171, 172
Powell, Michael, 17
prescription-drug coverage to Medicare, flaws of, 73–74, 81
price stability, 106, 108; explicit nominal anchor for, 108–109
principles of private pricing, 43–44
private health insurance: costs of avoiding adverse selection, 73; paperwork costs and, 73
"prosumers," 50
public day care, 95–96
public pricing, principles of, 44–45; political considerations of, 45–46; submarkets of public goods and, 46
Putnam, Robert, 52

R

R&D, GDP and, 90
real wages, decline in, 119, 120
Reebok, 180–181
refining capacity, 33
Reid, Harry, 10
Republicans, federal deficit and, 79, 80
Riegle-Neal Act, 122, 123
risk analysis, 3
risk-risk calculations, 4
river-basin efficiency, 163
Rogoff, Kenneth, 141

S

sales tax, national, 98–99
savings rate, personal, in U.S., 81
savings-exempt income tax, 101
Schumpeter, Joseph, 7
scientific advances, attitudes toward, 173–174
security analysis, environmental assessments and, 136
Sensenbrenner, F. James, Jr., 24
Sherman Act of 1890, 25
Simmons, Matt, 32
Simon, William E., 104
Slemrod, Joel, 98, 104
"smog markets," 11
Social Security: African Americans and, 64, 65; benefits designed for women and, 63; Bush proposal for, 64
social spending, economic growth and, 94

South Carolina, proposed changes to Medicaid by, 70
standards-setting, antitrust policy and, 26–27
Stelzer, Irving M., 25
substitution, 7; versus creating new markets, 7
Sun Microsystems, Inc., antitrust policy and, 26
sustainable development: attitudes toward, 175–176; indices, 135–136; promotion of, 176
sustainable economy, 34

T

tax breaks to oil companies, 29
tax compliance, cost of, 97
tax cuts of 2001, Federal deficit and, 80–81
"tax expenditures" list, 104
Tax Reform Act of 1986, 104
tax reform: four approaches to, 100–103
tax subsidy, for employer-based health insurance, 69
tax trade-offs, 97–98
taxation/unemployment correlation, 105
taxes on labor, 95
technology, accelerating rate of development, 137
technology: job displacement and, 58; public policy and, 56, 58–59
terrorism: defined, 136; federal budget shifts and, 10; "productivity shock" and, 10

Third World: capital flight from, 147–148; concentrated wealth in, 148; debt crisis, 146; decapitalization in, 148; financial abuses in, 147, 148; transnational system of exploitation, 148–150
time inconsistency, central banks and, 107
"too-big-to-fail" (TBTF) subsidy, 123
"transient monopolies," 26
treated wastewater, uses for, 163

U

U.S. African Growth And Opportunity Act, 154
U.S. Anti-Trust Modernization Commission: four charges to, 24; intellectual property and, 26
U.S. Department of Justice Antitrust Section, 25
U.S. economy: growth in imports in, 7; long-term needs, 120
U.S.: child labor in, 182, 185–186; education advantage and, 96; growth in per capita GDP, 6; health care disadvantage and, 96
UNICEF, child labor and, 182, 183
USA tax, 101

V

vacation days by law by country, 52
value added tax (VAT), 101–102; welfare states and, 95

Veterans Administration: health care costs and, 73; integrated health care and, 73
Vodafone, 21–22
Volcker, Paul, 119

W

wage disparity, GDP and, 90
Wal-Mart: in California, 19; corporate isolationism and, 18; employee misconduct and, 19 external communications and, 18, 19, 20; public policy issues confronting, 18, 19; unions and, 19
Washington Consensus, 151
water consumption, future: projections, 156; under various scenarios, 157–162
water scarcity for food production, three strategies to address, 163
weapons of mass destruction, access to, 136
Weiner, Myron, 184
welfare state: definitions, 94; value added taxes and, 95
women and Social Security, 63–66; impact of Bush proposal on, 64, 65; parental leave, public day care, earnings and, 95–96
work hours, U.S., 52
workforce participation, U.S., 52
workplace laws, 51, 53
World Values Survey, 165, 167, 173
World Water Forum, 156

Test Your Knowledge Form

We encourage you to photocopy and use this page as a tool to assess how the articles in *Annual Editions* expand on the information in your textbook. By reflecting on the articles you will gain enhanced text information. You can also access this useful form on a product's book support Web site at *http://www.mhcls.com/online/*.

NAME: DATE:

_____

TITLE AND NUMBER OF ARTICLE:

_____

BRIEFLY STATE THE MAIN IDEA OF THIS ARTICLE:

_____

LIST THREE IMPORTANT FACTS THAT THE AUTHOR USES TO SUPPORT THE MAIN IDEA:

_____

WHAT INFORMATION OR IDEAS DISCUSSED IN THIS ARTICLE ARE ALSO DISCUSSED IN YOUR TEXTBOOK OR OTHER READINGS THAT YOU HAVE DONE? LIST THE TEXTBOOK CHAPTERS AND PAGE NUMBERS:

_____

LIST ANY EXAMPLES OF BIAS OR FAULTY REASONING THAT YOU FOUND IN THE ARTICLE:

_____

LIST ANY NEW TERMS/CONCEPTS THAT WERE DISCUSSED IN THE ARTICLE, AND WRITE A SHORT DEFINITION:

We Want Your Advice

ANNUAL EDITIONS revisions depend on two major opinion sources: one is our Advisory Board, listed in the front of this volume, which works with us in scanning the thousands of articles published in the public press each year; the other is you—the person actually using the book. Please help us and the users of the next edition by completing the prepaid article rating form on this page and returning it to us. Thank you for your help!

ANNUAL EDITIONS: Economics 34/e

ARTICLE RATING FORM

Here is an opportunity for you to have direct input into the next revision of this volume.
We would like you to rate each of the articles listed below, using the following scale:

1. **Excellent: should definitely be retained**
2. **Above average: should probably be retained**
3. **Below average: should probably be deleted**
4. **Poor: should definitely be deleted**

Your ratings will play a vital part in the next revision.
Please mail this prepaid form to us as soon as possible.
Thanks for your help!

RATING	ARTICLE	RATING	ARTICLE
	1. How Much for a Life? Try $3 Million to $5 Million		24. Why Are Taxes So Complicated and What Can We Do About It?
	2. More, Bigger, Faster		25. The Tax Reform Revolution
	3. Counter-Terrorism: The Private Cost of More Security		26. Tax Reform R.I.P.
	4. Smoke Signals		27. Link Between Taxation, Unemployment Is Absent
	5. Jousting for Television's Holy Grail		28. What Should Central Banks Do?
	6. Bruised in Bentonville		29. How Does Monetary Policy Affect the U.S. Economy?
	7. Airlines		30. It's His Economy Now—And Yours
	8. Modernizing U.S. Antitrust Law: The Role of Technology and Innovation		31. Banking Consolidation
	9. The Real Price of Gas		32. Bank ATMs and ATM Surcharges
	10. The Truth About Oil		33. Toward a Cashless Society
	11. The Eco-Economic Revolution: Getting the Market in Sync with Nature		34. Update on the State of the Future
	12. Congested Parks—A Pricing Dilemma		35. As Job Exports Rise, Some Economists Rethink the Mathematics of Free Trade
	13. Building a More-Humane Economy		36. Is the Current Account Deficit Sustainable?
	14. The Rich Get (Much) Richer		37. The High-Tech Threat from China
	15. Outsourcing Jobs: The Myths and Realities		38. Building Blocks
	16. Laid Off and Left Out		39. Where the Money Went
	17. Multiple Minimums		40. Asymmetric Globalization: Global Markets Require Good Global Politics
	18. The Gender Gyp		41. Will the World Run Dry? Global Water and Food Security
	19. The Health Care Crisis and What to Do About It		42. Do Global Attitudes and Behaviors Support Sustainable Development?
	20. Countdown to a Meltdown		43. Eliminating Child Labor
	21. Seizing Intangibles for the G.D.P.		
	22. The Elephant in the Room		
	23. Social Spending and Economic Growth, Interview with Peter Lindert		

BUSINESS REPLY MAIL
FIRST CLASS MAIL PERMIT NO. 551 DUBUQUE IA

POSTAGE WILL BE PAID BY ADDRESEE

McGraw-Hill Contemporary Learning Series
2460 KERPER BLVD
DUBUQUE, IA 52001-9902

NO POSTAGE
NECESSARY
IF MAILED
IN THE
UNITED STATES

ABOUT YOU

Name   Date
_____

Are you a teacher? ☐ A student? ☐
Your school's name
_____

Department
_____

Address   City   State   Zip
_____

School telephone #
_____

YOUR COMMENTS ARE IMPORTANT TO US!

Please fill in the following information:
For which course did you use this book?
_____

Did you use a text with this ANNUAL EDITION? ☐ yes ☐ no
What was the title of the text?
_____

What are your general reactions to the *Annual Editions* concept?
_____

Have you read any pertinent articles recently that you think should be included in the next edition? Explain.
_____

Are there any articles that you feel should be replaced in the next edition? Why?
_____

Are there any World Wide Web sites that you feel should be included in the next edition? Please annotate.
_____

May we contact you for editorial input? ☐ yes ☐ no
May we quote your comments? ☐ yes ☐ no